BENTHAM

The Arguments of the Philosophers

EDITOR: TED HONDERICH

Reader in Philosophy, University College, London

The group of books of which this is one will include an essentially analytic and critical account of each of the considerable number of the great and the influential philosophers. The group of books taken together will comprise a contemporary assessment and history of the entire course of philosphical thought.

Already published in the series
Plato   J.C.B. Gosling
Meinong   Reinhardt Grossman
Santayana   Timothy L.S. Sprigge
Wittgenstein   Robert J. Fogelin
Hume   Barry Stroud
Descartes   Margaret Dauler Wilson
Berkeley   George Pitcher
Kant   Ralph C.S. Walker
The Presocratic Philosophers (2 vols)   Jonathan Barnes
Russell   R.M. Sainsbury
Socrates   Gerasimos Xenophon Santas
Sartre   Peter Caws
Karl Popper   Anthony O'Hear
Gottlob Frege   Hans D. Sluga
Schopenhauer   D.W. Hamlyn
Karl Marx   Allen Wood
Nietzsche   Richard Schacht
Kierkegaard   Alastair Hannay

BENTHAM

Ross Harrison

King's College, Cambridge

Routledge & Kegan Paul
London, Boston, Melbourne and Henley

First published in 1983
by Routledge & Kegan Paul plc
39 Store Street, London WC1E 7DD,
9 Park Street, Boston, Mass. 02108, USA,
464 St Kilda Road, Melbourne,
Victoria 3004, Australia, and
Broadway House, Newtown Road,
Henley-on-Thames, Oxon RG9 1EN
Set in Journal 11/12 point
by Columns of Reading
and printed in Great Britain by
The Thetford Press Ltd.,
Thetford, Norfolk

Library of Congress Cataloging in Publication Data

Harrison, Ross.
Bentham.
(The arguments of the philosophers)
Bibliography: p.
Includes index.
1. Bentham, Jeremy, 1748-1832. I. Title. II. Series.
B1574.B34H37   1983   192   83-9543

ISBN 0-7100-9526-0

Contents

	Preface	vii
	A Note on the Texts	ix
	Abbreviations	xxv
I	The End	1
II	The Pestilential Breath of Fiction	24
III	The Clew to the Labyrinth	47
IV	Nonsense upon Stilts	77
V	The Duty and Interest Junction Principle	106
VI	A Clear View of Interest	135
VII	The Greatest Happiness Principle	167
VIII	The People is my Caesar	195
IX	The Benthamite State	225
X	Private Deontology	263
	Bibliography	278
	Index	283

Preface

The series in which this work appears, the *Arguments of the Philosophers*, should, ideally, identify the arguments of a particular philosopher and then subject them to relentless, modern, critical examination. The work which follows diverges from this ideal type in having rather more attention given to the identification than to the criticism of its subject's arguments. Once the arguments are identified, criticism would indeed follow easily and naturally, given that much recent thought has provided, or depended upon, assumptions which are inimical to several of the basic elements of Bentham's thought. However, I have not felt that this was what was primarily needed at present in a book on Bentham. Before being reinterred, it is first necessary that the whole body be exhumed; and outlining the complete shape of Bentham is what I have therefore taken to be my principal task. It seems to me that Bentham is insufficiently well known. Philosophers tend to concentrate on a few elements, indeed on one single chapter, in his works. The greater number of students of other disciplines who read Bentham concentrate on their own particular aspects. Yet it seems to me, and it is a thesis of the work which follows, that the work as a whole exhibits a coherence in which better sense can be made of the parts when seen in the context of a more overall view. The more familiar ethical and political thinking, for example, should be seen in the context of less familiar work on metaphysics and the theory of meaning. Yet, as well as this more abstract thought, it must be remembered that Bentham was a practical thinker; according to the theory, the test of theory was practice. So the theoretical work, whether metaphysical or moral, needs to be seen and understood in the context of particular practical proposals. These proposals, in turn, rest on rigorously developed theory. So in the work which follows I have attempted to uncover and bring out some idea of the thought as a whole, dealing with all those parts which could be called in any sense philosophical, and attempting to display their interrelations. Since this has absorbed the space available, I have left prolonged and extensive criticism as an exercise for the reader. As its title suggests, this book is a book about Bentham, not a work of modern philosophy.

Since there is considerable interest in Bentham outside Departments of Philosophy, I have tried to write it in a way which presupposes no knowledge of philosophy. However, the bias of the work is clearly analytical rather than historical, although I hope that I have managed to convey some sense of the particular, historically rooted, problems on which Bentham worked. It follows from what I have just said about the general thesis that different people will find different parts more familiar or more easy going. However, if it is true that the more familiar parts make better sense in the context of the work as a whole, in particular in terms of the metaphysical core, then I would gently suggest to those students of political thought, more at home in chapters V and VIII, or to those students of ethical theory, more at home in chapter VII, that they should try as well chapters III and IV where this metaphysical core is exhibited. It may seem wilfully paradoxical to save Bentham's best known doctrine, the principle of utility, for chapter VII; yet although wilful, it is not intended as a paradox.

Chapter I is of a different character to the others. It is an overture. Some of the themes are played, but there is no voice, no argument, no one on the stage singing. It is designed to set a mood, a mood that there might be something in Bentham after all, or at least something interestingly puzzling about his thought. It is also designed to give some basic biography and intellectual context. However, those who like to enter when the curtain rises and start with the action are advised to start with chapter II.

Like many others working on Bentham, I am grateful for the help of the members of the Bentham project at University College London and the staff of the manuscript library at the College. I am particularly grateful to Jimmy Burns, John Dinwiddy, and Claire Gobbi. My own ideas on Bentham have benefited greatly from conversations with Gerry Postema and, particularly, David Lieberman.

Ross Harrison
Cambridge

A Note on the Texts

Bentham is textually more difficult to work with than most great philosophers. Normally there is a relatively easily identifiable central work or works, unproblematically written by the man himself. With Bentham, however, there is a straggling mass of material which varies greatly not only in subject matter and intrinsic value but also in its mode of production. Much of the published material upon which any study of Bentham must inevitably be based was not written by Bentham himself in the form in which we now have it. After writing his first books he developed the habit of devoting his main effort to the production of piles of manuscript which were to be made into books by other people. This is how, in fact, his reputation was made. The chief work which he saw through the press for himself, the *Introduction to the Principles of Morals and Legislation*, although now usually regarded as his main work, failed to excite any notice or comment on its first publication. Bentham then shortly after turned over his great mass of manuscript to a French-speaking editor, Etienne Dumont, who thirteen years later produced from it and the *Introduction* a classic which did sell well, and was widely and highly regarded, the *Traités de législation civile et pénale*. Its success, however, was partly due to the fact that Dumont took what would nowadays be regarded as an unacceptably dynamic view of the functions of an editor. It also, of course, appeared in a different language. Dumont produced several successors to the *Traités*, based on other parts of the manuscript, and these were then all subsequently translated or retranslated back into English by other disciples. Together with works produced directly from the manuscript in English by his followers, this material edited by others forms an important part of the corpus of work on which Bentham's fame rests, and which is the basis for study of his thought. Yet there is at least infelicity, and quite possibly downright inaccuracy, in attributing to Bentham remarks which are often at two removes from his pen.

Much of the retranslated Dumont ended up in the collected edition of Bentham's works produced shortly after his death and normally called the Bowring edition. As well as reprinting already printed material, this edition also published for the first time works taken directly from manuscript, and edited to varying standards by varying hands. Starting with Elie Halévy's great work *La jeunesse de Bentham*, it has become a custom to demonstrate by means of parallel texts just how damaging to Bentham's thought the work of his editors has been; and David Baumgardt has given a sample of four parallel texts showing the transmission of Bentham's manuscript, via Dumont to the Bowring edition, and so to J.S. Mill (Baumgardt 1952 pp. 26-7). Werner Stark has produced detailed case studies of Bowring's editorial activities on the economic manuscripts, showing how at times Bowring seems to have shuffled the manuscript as if it were a pack of cards (Stark i 46, 49). More recently, the new edition of the *Deontology* directly from the manuscripts reveals that Bowring was incapable of leaving a single sentence in the form in which Bentham wrote it when he produced his nineteenth-century edition.

In these circumstances, once one leaves the early works which Bentham saw through the press for himself, it might seem that the only appropriate course would be to ignore all work published in the nineteenth century, including the whole of the Bowring collected edition, and work entirely from manuscript and the new collected edition which is at present in the process of production. Yet the former is, I think, impossible — Bentham took a very long life to write manuscripts, and he seems to have written them faster than the normal reader can read them — while the latter would mean, at the best, a very long wait before any general study of Bentham's thought would be possible. However, I do not think myself that the situation is as bad as this, and in the following study I have been prepared to use material published by editors and acolytes in the last century. I think that the material needs to be handled with care, and have accorded it a lower status when used as evidence. When I can, I have relied on more certain material, but when I have needed it, I have been prepared to supplement this with use of the more suspect material. I have also devised a reference system which should allow the reader to keep track of the different streams of material, and so enable him to discount material to a greater or lesser extent according to how suspicious he is. In the rest of this note I explain and attempt to justify my own division of the material, and my use of the more suspicious parts of it.

Since the Bowring edition contains material of highly different status, I have not thought that mere references to this edition are sufficient, but have in all cases tried to name the particular work referred to, so that the reader can check on its status. Since the reader, however, may not remember the provenance of the various works, I have made a very crude division of the material into two, marking with an asterisk (*) all material which has passed by way of a constructive editor like Dumont or Bowring. When there is no asterisk, this means that I think that the text is fairly reliable, even for some work which was published for the first time in the Bowring collected edition, or edited in the nineteenth century. The material which I am considering to be reliable as an expression of Bentham's thought includes the early works he edited himself and all manuscript (I do not mean that there are no problems in the interpretation of manuscript, only that it is a reliable enough indicator of his thought at the moment that he was writing it.) Then there are also, naturally, the volumes in the new collected edition (although, unfortunately, even these have not been produced without an editorial hiccup, and anyone possessing the first produced copy of *Of Laws in General* should apply to the Bentham Committee for a printed brochure of errata). There is Stark's edition of the economic writings. However, fortunately, Bentham's more philosophical writings were relatively carefully edited by contemporary editors. The philosophical works in volume VIII of the Bowring edition, *Logic, Ontology, Language* were edited by Southwood Smith, who seems to have transcribed fairly carefully without addition or deletion. Of course, he did decide what to transcribe, and he did not worry overmuch about the temporal sequence of the material. However, I think that he can be taken as reliable. There is also the massive *Rationale of Judicial Evidence*, over a million words of it, which was edited by the youthful J.S. Mill. Although Mill reorganised the material in the sense that he collated the manuscripts and eliminated redundancy, he was careful to mark editorial additions. Hacking a million words out of a much greater mass of illegible manuscript may have contributed to Mill's nervous breakdown, but at least it means that we possess a fairly reliable text of this important work, and that no one who is not a fanatic or wants a breakdown need look at the manuscript again.

There is, therefore, quite a body of reliable material, including edited manuscript. This leaves the questionable material, that is the work which comes via disciples who engaged in more positive editorial practices, in particular Dumont. Although I have marked this as suspicious, I have also, as I said, been prepared to use it; and this now needs to be defined. My chief reason for accepting the Dumont material is that Bentham himself accepted it as such, and my own sample comparisons with the manuscripts have led me to believe that the material which Dumont provides is nearly all in the manuscripts. With Dumont, it has energy, brevity, polemical value; with Bentham it is ponderous, repetitive, difficult to read. Anyone who would like to test the difference without leaving published material can compare Dumont's *Traité des preuves judiciares* (Paris 1823) with J.S. Mill's careful edition of 1827 (or, without leaving the English language, compare the 1825 London translation of Dumont with Mill). Dumont (or the translation, which seems accurate enough) is more readable and convincing than Mill's edition, while on the other hand, the philosophical details are much more completely and carefully developed in Mill. They both cover the same ground yet Dumont is much shorter. Mill is clearly nearer Bentham, and for philosophical purposes it is certain that Dumont should be bypassed as much as possible. Luckily, where it matters, this can be done, as here with *Evidence*, or with the first part of the *Traités*, where Bentham's own *Introduction to the Principles of Morals and Legislation* covers the same ground more fully.

However, even in these areas, as well as more generally, Dumont succeeds in revealing features of Bentham's thought which are harder to appreciate when looking at the close textured detail of Bentham's prose. The genius or importance of Bentham is not only in the details but in the choice of targets and in the overall approach, and these can come through better when filtered through Dumont. The legendary difficulty of Bentham's late style — leading to Hazlitt's crack that Bentham had been translated into French, he ought to be translated into English — means that Dumont is an important component of the production of that body of thought that made Benthamism something worth bothering about. By making Bentham readable, he made Bentham read.

This readability, however, is only the first of several reasons for allowing some status to the Dumont material. Another is that an attempt to bypass it in areas where there is not a better printed source by direct appeal to the manuscripts has its own problems. The manuscripts in such areas, *Penal Code* and *Civil Code*, for example, are extensive and disorganised. Dumont worked on them for years to produce the *Traités*. They are unfinished, incomplete, disorganised, repetitive; and Bentham himself provides alternative readings and variations. So anyone working on them faces some of the same editorial problems as Dumont. Just before the *Traités* were published, Bentham wrote to Dumont hoping that he would point out that in some of the material used his 'ideas had not been formed; 2. or not fully developed; 3. or this or that paper had not come to your hands' (letter of 17 May 1802, quoted in Ogden 1931 p. xlv). These are problems which anyone faces with the manuscript, even if they managed to avoid Bentham's fourth circumstance '4. you had misconceived my meaning'. Furthermore, when Dumont, or the use of Dumont, is criticised, it is not always realised that Dumont was often (as with *Civil Code* or *Reward*) working on French manuscripts of Bentham. There may be translation of the material in the sense of transposition of its content; but for much of those parts of the *Traités* where I use him, Dumont is not altering the language. Because of the intrinsic importance for Bentham's thought of the axioms of mental pathology, as they appear in the *Civil Code*, I made a close comparison of Dumont's text in the *Traités* with the original manuscript. The manuscript is not easy to read (and indeed one minor conjecture I entertained was that occasionally Dumont left something out because it was illegible; certainly Dumont was only the first of many editors to complain about the difficulty of reading Bentham's hand). However, it seems to me, that at least for this important part of the *Civil Code*, nearly all of what is in Dumont is in Bentham, nearly all in the same words. What Dumont did was to leave a lot out, to correct or improve the French, and to reorder the material so that single sentences or images are sometimes lifted out of context and used elsewhere. Often what at first looks like a Dumont interpolation turns up elsewhere in Bentham's own manuscript. So, although Dumont's text is clearly nothing like Bentham's thought as Bentham wrote it, it is still Bentham's thought; and so it seems that this part at least is sufficiently related to Bentham's own work for it to be appropriate that it should be used in a study of Bentham.

As noticed above, the *Traités* made Bentham's name; hence, unsurprisingly, Bentham did not refuse to accept the *Traités*. The final reason for accepting Dumont's work as an expression of Bentham's thought was that Bentham himself did. Like Picasso signing paintings brought to him, he did not object to the appearance of 'Bentham' on its cover. Like many claims about Bentham's attitudes, the evidence for this is not wholly one-sided, and his attitude at times seems to have been ambiguous. He gave Dumont very little help in the production of the *Traités*, and on its appearance was inclined to say defensively that 'as to Dumont's book, it is not mine' (X 387), or to refer to it as 'Dumont's principles' (X 389). Indeed, much later in his life in a moment of vexation, he said 'he does not understand a word of my meaning' (X 185). On the other hand, and to my mind more convincing, is what Bentham wrote to Dumont when he thanked him for his copy of the *Traités*, when he said that 'with very few exceptions' he was 'not able to distinguish' Dumont's work from his own (X 388). In the same year he tried to get Romilly to translate it into English; scarcely the act of someone disowning his progeny (X 396). Perhaps unsurprisingly, he did not object to Talleyrand pressing it on Napoleon as a work of genius; but he was also prepared in his later work to cite it as evidence of his capacity while trying to recommend himself to various authorities as a codifier of laws. So, it seems to me, Bentham's own description of the *Traités* in a letter of 1810 as 'a selection ... that was made ... from my papers' (X 458) correctly expresses both his own normal attitude and also the actual nature of the material itself.

I now give a list of most of Bentham's works, which forms the primary bibliography for the following work. This shows the edition cited, the methods of citation, the abbreviations used, and also allows a few remarks on editing, status, and provenance. The rough division between works of varying status mentioned above is here given with an asterisk affixed to the more questionable material; it will be remembered that this asterisk is then used in all subsequent references to these works.

It should be stressed that this bibliography is not complete. Anyone wanting something more complete should consult C.W. Everett's in the English translation of Halévy's *The Growth of Philosophic Radicalism* (Halévy 1928 pp. 522-46). I would suggest the following emendations:

p. 530 The Hildreth translation was first published in 1840. The other translation which appeared in America, mentioned in the next line, is by Neal, Boston, 1830.

p. 530 *Panopticon* Everett gives the title page of the English printing; but the Panopticon really did appear separately first in Ireland (Muirhead in the *Library* 1946 gives the evidence; and this is also clear from *Correspondence* IV, e.g. 177. However, most convincingly, actual individual copies with the Dublin imprint alone still exist).

p. 533 *Scotch Reform* The publication date given, is correct, but Bentham had copies printed but not published in 1807, using the same printer (Taylor) but with a differently set title page.

p. 540 *Constitutional Code* Two copies of parts of volume ii have turned up, in the Library of Congress and at Forde Abbey (Chapter one; otherwise known as chapter 10 in the complete work).

p. 542 *Pauper Management Improved* What Everett says is correct; but all that happened in 1812 was that the already printed sections (with the original manuscript emendations) were bound up with a new title page.

Everett also omits some cross references to the Bowring edition and does not, of course, list work published after 1928.

As the emendations to Everett bring out, in Bentham the dates of printing of a work often do not correspond to dates of publication. The most famous example is the major work, the *Introduction to the Principles of Morals and Legislation*, most of which lay printed but unpublished between 1780 and 1789. In this case I use the date of publication, when the complete work as we now have it first appeared. However, in many other cases, where the printed copy was the complete work, I list the date of printing. In some cases, like the *Panopticon*, although printed copies, bound up with title page, circulated, the work was not published at all in Bentham's lifetime.

Outline List of Bentham's Works

Manuscript

The major collection of manuscript is in University College London, although there are also collections in the British Library and at Geneva. All the references in this work are to the University College collection cited in the form (UC 15.26), where the first number refers to the box and the second to the page (in references to Bentham, the first number elsewhere is often in roman numerals).

Collected works

The Bowring Edition. This appeared first between 1838 and 1843, and has been relatively recently reprinted. References are given in the standard form with a roman numeral indicating the volume and an arabic number indicating the page; thus a reference like V 512 is always to the Bowring edition. Except for the *Autobiography*, the particular work referred to is also identified by name. The *Autobiography* is identifiable because it occupies volume X of the Bowring edition, so that a reference like (X 145) is always to the *Autobiography*.

W. Stark (ed.) *Jeremy Bentham's Economic Writings*, 3 volumes,

1952-4. All references to the economic writings are to this edition, cited in the form [Stark i 178].
For the new collected edition, works are listed separately below.

Individual Works.

Date of printing	Short title	Abbreviation	Edition cited, status and editor
1774	The White Bull (Preface by Bentham)		original edn
1776	A Fragment on Government	FG	New Collected works
1778	A View of the Hard Labour Bill		original edn
1787	Defence of Usury		Stark ed. Bentham
1789	An Introduction to the Principles of Morals and Legislation	IPML	New Collected works
1790	Draught of a new plan for the organisation of the Judicial Establishment in France		Bowring IV ed. Bentham
1791	Panopticon and Panopticon Postscripts, parts one and two	PANO	Bowring IV ed. Bentham
1791 (and later)	Essay on Political Tactics		Bowring III ed. Bentham (*and Richard Smith)
1793	Emancipate your Colonies		Bowring IV ed. Bentham
1793	A Protest against Law Taxes (first published, 1795, with Escheat)		Bowring III ed. Bentham

Date of printing	Short title	Abbreviation used	Edition cited, status and editor
1793	*Escheat Vice Taxation*		Stark ed. Bentham
1797	*Preliminary sketches relative to the poor* and	PAUPER	original edn ed. Bentham
1798	*Pauper Management Improved*		
1802	*Traités de législation civile et pénale*	*Traités*	original edn *ed. Dumont
	(the standard translation, which is normally quoted here is Hildreth's		
	Legislation	LEGIS	Ogden 1931)
1802	*Second letter to Pelham Panopticon versus New South Wales*		Bowring IV ed. Bentham
1803	*A Plea for the Constitution*		
	(these are occasional pamphlets devoted to *Panopticon*)		
1807	*Scotch Reform*		Bowring V ed. Bentham
1808	*Summary view of the plan of a judiciary under the name of the Court of Lords Delegates*		Bowring V ed. Bentham
1810(?1809)	*Elements of the Art of Packing*		Bowring V ed. Bentham
1810(?)	*Introductory View of the Rationale of Evidence*		Bowring VI *ed. James Mill
	(this was neither published nor completely finished)		

Date of printing	Short title	Abbreviation used	Edition cited, status and editor
1811	*Théorie des peines et des récompenses*		original edn *ed. Dumont (see below for translation)
1813	*Swear not at all*		Bowring V (?) ed. Bentham
1815	*A Table of the Springs of Action*	SPRINGS	Bowring I (?) ed. Bentham
1816	*Tactique des Assemblées législative suivi d'un traité des sophismes politiques* (for *Anarchical Fallacies*, I have used the better text, newly edited, of Parekh 1973)		(see above, 1791 *Tactics* and below 1824 *Fallacies* and 1840s *Anarchical Fallacies*) ed. Dumont
1815 1816 and later	*Chrestomathia* and *Chrestomathia, Part II*		Bowring VIII ed. Bentham and Southwood Smith
1817	*Church of Englandism* (this spawned several other extracts and editions)		original edn (?) ed. Bentham
1817	*Papers relative to Codification and Public Instruction*		Bowring IV (?) ed. Bentham
1817	*Plan for Parliamentary Reform*		Bowring III (?) ed. Bentham
1819	*Bentham's Radical Reform Bill*		Bowring III (?) ed. Bentham
1821	*On the Liberty of the Press and Public Instruction*		Bowring II *ed. Bowring

Date of printing	Short title	Abbreviation used	Edition cited, status and editor
1822	*Analysis of the influence of Natural Religion on the Temporal Happiness of Mankind*		Original edn *ed. George Grote
1822	*Codification Proposal*		Bowring IV ed. Bentham
1823	*Not Paul, but Jesus*		*original edn ed. Place
1822	*Preface* to second edition FG	FG	*New Collected Works* ed. Bentham (with help from Place)
1823	*Traité des preuves judiciaires*		*original edn ed. Dumont (see 1825 *Evidence*)
1823	*Leading Principles of a Constitutional Code, for any State*		Bowring II (?) ed. Bentham
1823	*Truth versus Ashurst*		Bowring V ed. Bentham (supposed to be unaltered printing of 1792 MS)
1824	*The Book of Fallacies*	FALL	*original edn ed. Mill, Place, and Bingham
1825	*A Treatise on Judicial Evidence*		*original edn (= translation of 1823 *Preuves*)
1825	*The Rationale of Reward*		*original edn ed. R. Smith (in part translation 1811 *Récompenses*)

Date of printing	Short title	Abbreviation used	Edition cited, status and editor
1827	*Rationale of Judicial Evidence* (5 volumes)	RJE	original edn ed. J.S. Mill
1829	*Justice and Codification Petitions*		Bowring V ed. (?) Bentham
1830	*The Rationale of Punishment*		*original edn trans. and ed. R. Smith from 1811 *Peines*
1830	*Houses of Peers and Senates*		Bowring IV ed. (?) Bentham
1830 1843	*Constitutional Code*, Volume I Volumes II and III, and Introductory Material (= Book I in Bowring version)	CODE	all from Bowring IX ed. (?) Bentham (1830) and Richard Doane (1843)
1830	*Official Aptitude Maximised, Expense Minimised* (contains several previously published pamphlets, not here listed separately, most importantly *Defence of the Economy against Burke* (1816))		Bowring V ed. (?) Bentham etc.
1830	*Equity Dispatch Court Proposal*		Bowring III ed.?
1831	*On Death Punishment*		Bowring I ed. (?) Bentham
1831	*Boa Constrictor*		Bowring V ed. (?) Bentham
1832	*Outline plan of a general Register of Real Property*		Bowring V ed. ?

It is convenient to interrupt the list at this point because, although it should be repeated that this is not a complete list, this completes the works listed here which were published in Bentham's lifetime. It is interesting to note that, although it is quite a long list, it does not contain much of central importance in Bentham's work. This was only published posthumously, starting with Bowring's edition, which is here assigned the date 1843, in which the complete, bound, edition appeared (although it had previously appeared in parts after 1838). Even in the above list, much of the material which is really central in Bentham's life and work, such as that on evidence, the constitutional, penal, and civil codes, and reward and punishment is exactly that which has been edited by others. The work produced by Bentham himself after the 1789 *Introduction*, is mainly occasional in nature, with a specific political or polemical purpose.

Date of printing	Short title	Abbreviation used	Edition cited, status and editor
1834	*Deontology* (this edition is highly unreliable, and I have used instead that in the new collected works)		*original edn ed. Bowring
1838	*Observations on the Poor Bill*		Bowring VIII ed. Chadwick
1842	*Auto-Icon*		original edn ? ed. Burton
1843	*A Fragment on Ontology*		Bowring VIII ed. Southwood Smith
1843	*Essay on Logic*		Bowring VIII ed. Southwood Smith
1843	*Nomography*, with appendix, *Logical Arrangements*		Bowring III *ed. R. Smith
1843	*Essay on Language*		Bowring VIII ed. Southwood Smith

Date of printing	Short title	Abbreviation used	Edition cited, status and editor
1843	*Fragments on Universal Grammar*		Bowring VIII *ed. Southwood Smith
1843	*Principles of International Law*		Bowring II *ed. ?
1843	*Principles of Judicial Procedure*		Bowring II *ed. Doane
1843	*Anarchical Fallacies*	ANARCH	PAREKH 1973 ed. Parekh (also Bowring II and Dumont 1816 *Sophismes*)
1843	*Radicalism not Dangerous*		Bowring III *ed. ?
1843	*Pannomial Fragments*	PANN	Bowring III *ed. R. Smith
1843	*(Autobiography)*	X XI	Bowring X; XI ed. Bowring (*except for letters, etc.)
1843	*Essay on the Promulgation of Laws*		Bowring I (*after Dumont, *Traités*)
1843	*Essay on the Influence of Time and Place in Matters of Legislation*		*Bowring II ed. from Dumont *Traités* and MSS
1843	*Principles of the Civil Code*	CIVIL	*Bowring II trans. from Dumont, *Traités*, with additions
1843	*Principles of Penal Law* (in Bowring, this includes 1830 *Punishment*; I cite this part separately)	PENAL	*Bowring II after Dumont

A NOTE ON THE TEXTS

Date of printing	Short title	Abbreviation used	Edition cited, status and editor
1843	*A general view of a complete Code of Laws*		*Bowring III after Dumont, Traités* etc.
1840	*Indirect Legislation*		*Hildreth: Legislation* translated from Dumont *Traités*.
1928	*A Comment on the Commentaries*	COMM	*New Collected Works* ed. Burns and Hart
1952	*Manual of Political Economy*		Stark i ed. Stark
1952	various papers on *Circulating Annuities*		Stark ii ed. Stark
1954	*The True Alarm*		Stark iii ed. Stark
1954	*Defence of a Maximum*		Stark iii ed. Stark
1954	*Institute of Political Economy* (much of this material had come out before Stark in more corrupt forms, but is not here listed separately. The British Library used to have a contemporary printed *Annuities*, now destroyed)		Stark iii ed. Stark
1970	*Of Laws in General* (an earlier version of this is *The Limits of Jurisprudence Defined*, ed. Everett, 1945)	OLG	*New Collected Works* ed. Hart
1968-	*Correspondence*	CORR	*New Collected Works* ed. various hands

There are also important manuscripts first published as appendices in Halévy (1901), Ogden (1932), Baumgardt (1952), Mack (1962), and in Parekh (1973). They are not listed separately here, and reference is to their parent work (or directly to the manuscript when I have reread them in manuscript). There are also extensive quotations from the manuscripts in recent work, in particular in Long (1977).

All secondary material is referred to in the way that I have just referred to Halévy and the others, and is listed in the bibliography at the end.

Abbreviations

For details of Bentham's works, including the particular edition cited, see the Note on the Texts.

AC	*Appeal Cases* [Law Reports]
ANARCH	*Anarchical Fallacies*
CODE	*Constitutional Code*
COMM	*A Comment on the Commentaries*
Co.Rep.	Coke, *Reports* [Law Reports, in ER]
CORR	*The Correspondence of Jeremy Bentham*
ER	*English Reports* [Law Reports]
FALL	*The Book of Fallacies*
FG	*A Fragment on Goverment*
Introduction	*An Introduction to the Principles of Morals and Legislation*
IPML	*An Introduction to the Principles of Morals and Legislation*
LEGIS	*The Theory of Legislation*, translated Richard Hildreth
OLG	*Of Laws in General*
PANN	*Pannomial Fragments*
PANO	*Panopticon*
PAUPER	*Pauper Management Improved*
QB	*Queen's Bench* [Law Reports]
RJE	*Rationale of Judicial Evidence*
SPRINGS	*A Table of the Springs of Action*
Traités	*Traités de législation civile et pénale*
UC	Bentham manuscripts at University College London
X	*Memoirs and Correspondence* (of Bentham), edited John Bowring

I

The End

Jeremy Bentham, citizen of the world, honorary citizen of the French Republic; international figure who invented the word 'international', and whose fame (as Hazlitt observed) grew in direct proportion to the distance from his house in Westminster; born in London 15 February 1748, the son and grandson of a City attorney; died in London 6 June 1832, surrounded by 70,000 sheets of manuscript on the theory of law and all conceivably related subjects. Such, in telegraphic form, are a few details of a man destined by his father to be a supremely successful practitioner of the law but who instead dreamed at an early age that he might be the founder of a sect of people called utilitarians, and who devoted his life to the criticism and reform of the law and other established institutions. Sects need sacred objects, so let us start at the end with Bentham's physical transformation into a relic. Three days after his death, on the evening of 9 June 1832, friends, disciples, the faithful utilitarians, gathered together with medical students and leading doctors in the Webb Street school of anatomy. In the centre of the small circular room, lit only by the skylight, was Bentham in his nightshirt, lying on the dissecting table. Outside, appropriate supernatural commentary, a thunderstorm. The play of lightning flickered on the dead face of the Master, enlivening its expression of placid dignity. Over the corpse the final oration was delivered by Bentham's doctor, Southwood Smith. Southwood Smith was a regular lecturer at the school, but he was also a prominent utilitarian who had participated in the founding of the Benthamite journal, the *Westminster Review*, in which he wrote regularly and in particular on the sanitary question. For him providing the greatest happiness of the greatest number consisted most centrally in providing adequate facilities for the disposal of the sewage of the

1

people of London. Whether this is regarded as mildly absurd or as centrally important, or both, it was representative of the kind of activity in which the proper utilitarian should be engaged. At this time he should also be engaged in editing the works of the Master, converting the piles of illegible manuscript into texts for the sect; and in fact Southwood Smith edited some of Bentham's most philosophical works, the essays on Ontology, Logic, and Language.

Around the table and watching Southwood Smith speak, his face as white as that of the corpse before him, were several who had very recently been engaged in the protracted struggle which led eventually to the passing of the great reform bill, given its Royal assent the day after Bentham died. There was, for example, Brougham, who had been the central presenter of the reform case in the House of Lords. Although not agreeing with all Bentham's political ideas — he was a Whig, not a radical — Brougham endorsed and attempted to promote Bentham's ideas on the reform of the law. Only the year before he had told the Lords that Bentham was 'the father of law reform'. Brougham's own massive six hour speech to the Commons in 1828 on law reform had not won the complete approval of the master — this would have been scarcely possible — but Bentham was, as Brougham put it, 'the reservoir' from which it flowed. The speech led to the setting up of a Royal Commission, which resulted in an important series of reforms of a Benthamite kind. Bentham's own political ideas, in the last two decades of his life, were more closely represented by others around the body such as James Mill and George Grote. In fact the Benthamites were briefly to form a small party of their own in the new, reformed, House of Commons, often called the Philosophic Radicals. This included Grote, who entered the House in this year of 1832 and promoted such Benthamite causes as the secret ballot. These people wanted a much more radical extension of the franchise than the Whigs, but they had naturally co-operated in arranging pressure on the House from without in the recent struggle. Grote and Mill also edited works of Bentham's and co-operated (with Brougham) in such projects as the founding of a University of London.

Other examples of close personal friends of Bentham at his death are Francis Place and Edwin Chadwick. Place, the radical tailor who managed the politics of Westminster and with whom Bentham had walked round the city talking politics interrupted only by Place stopping to measure his clients, had in the latest agitation invented the slogan 'To stop the Duke — Go for gold'. He constantly referred to Bentham as his master. Chadwick was living in Bentham's house at the time he died and nursed him in his final illness. He was later to transverse the whole gamut of committees devoted to worthy legislation: police, factories, sanitary reform. Immediately, he was about to join the Royal Commission whose report led to the infamous Poor Law Amendment Act of 1834. In the house where Chadwick and Bentham lived were piles of manuscript on the poor laws, written forty years before, and some of which Chadwick later published. In this manuscript occurs several times the infamous phrase used by the commissioners, 'lesser eligibility'; the condition of the poor in the workhouses was to be made less eligible than the people outside.

This is only a sample, taken at the moment and place of Bentham's death. It would have been equally possible to assemble a global gallery of Benthamite reformers. It is enough, however, with which to make three, interrelated, points. Firstly, part of the importance of Bentham depends upon his actual influence upon the course of reform in nineteenth-century England. This is a contentious issue which, being purely historical, luckily does not need to be discussed here. Secondly, however much direct influence he had (and people like Chadwick, who was offered by Bentham the job of being the official expositor of his views after his death, must have had some influence), he was thought by the more theoretical political commentators and polemicists to have had an influence. In the analysis and criticism of political ideas throughout the century, Benthamism is conspicuous. Here again the effect is partly due to a direct personal connection. James Mill's more famous son, J.S. Mill, was Bentham's secular godson, and often stayed in Bentham's house when he was young. The younger Mill occupied a dominant position throughout the century; and as a famous, if critical, expositor of the Benthamite doctrine of utilitarianism, was chiefly responsible for this doctrine being taken as one side of debates about political theory and practice in an unbroken tradition which runs up to the present. Although both the general idea and the specific formula of the greatest happiness of the greatest number predate Bentham, it is Bentham who is taken to be the founding father of utilitarianism in these discussions. So, in the theoretical writing of the past hundred and fifty years, Bentham has been taken to be important, and this in itself is enough to make him important. The effect also predates J.S. Mill, because at least by the 1820s (and perhaps in the 1810s, after the *Traités*) Bentham has been identified as the leader of a movement and as a major figure by such independent commentators as Hazlitt or Mackintosh. In the 1820s the activities of the kinds of people who were gathered round the corpse of Bentham

3

on that June evening in 1832 had made the works of Bentham widely available for the first time in English, as well as setting up a quarterly devoted to the exposition of Benthamite views. They were the people who, by first making Bentham discussed, made him important.

The third point to make which arises from considering Bentham's relations with the actively practising writers or politicians who were his disciples is that the centre of gravity of his thought throughout his long life was political or legal reform. His thought, that is, was centrally concerned with the organisation of social, or public, institutions; firstly more specifically with the organisation and content of the law; latterly with developing a blueprint for a complete administrative state. On the way Bentham developed several more limited plans for the organisation of social institutions, for workhouses for the poor, for schools, and above all for the 'mill for grinding rogues honest' (X 226), the panopticon prison. These, however, were all forms of social organisation. Being possessed of a critical, analytical, philosophical mind, Bentham had also been led back from his more particular projects into purely theoretical study of the nature of law, and so of all thought and language, of psychology, and of general metaphysics. That this was so is obviously an important part of the reason for taking him seriously as a philosopher. However, he does not seem to have given so much thought to purely personal ethics (or 'private deontology', in the Benthamite vocabulary). He always recognised that there was such a subject, and he wrote some quite serious manuscript material on it in the 1810s besides the less trustworthy material he dictated to Bowring in the evenings in the 1820s while, as he put it, 'vibrating in my ditch' (that is, walking rapidly along the trench round his elevated desk). However, I think that the way that he divided his time at this period, with the great work of codification undertaken alone, carefully, through the length of the day, while the *Autobiography* and the *Deontology* were dictated after dinner, shows the relative importance which Bentham attached to these projects. And whatever Bentham himself thought, contemporary commentators, such as Mackintosh and J.S. Mill, stressed how much more profound Bentham was as a political or judicial thinker than as a theoretician of private ethics. Since much of the concern with utilitarianism this century has been with it as a system of personal ethics rather than as a justification of a political or legal system, it is important to remember that this is a concern with what Bentham regarded as a relatively peripheral part of his work.

The importance of making this distinction between public and

4

private deontology (to use the Benthamite vocabulary) can be illustrated by one incident in the transmission of the image of Bentham by his early disciples and critics. I have already pointed out how influential J.S. Mill was in this transmission, and Mill occupied both these roles. In his 1838 article in the *Westminster Review* on Bentham, written during a period of relative antipathy, Mill wrote that Bentham 'says, somewhere in his works, that, "quantity of pleasure being equal, push-pin is as good as poetry"' (Mill *Collected Works* X 113). He thus, as he took it, illustrated the partial nature of Bentham's vision, his antipathy to poetry and the arts. He also succeeded in introducing the phrase about pushpin and poetry into general discussion of utilitarianism, for the original source of this now famous remark is exceedingly obscure. It is from the *Rationale of Reward*, one of those works of Bentham which, edited by his disciples, first saw the light in English in the 1820s. If we turn up the original context of the remark, usually only known by way of Mill (*II 253; *REWARD 206), we find that Bentham is concerned with the public encouragement of various activities. That is, the point of the remark is not about the relative value of pushpin and poetry to a private individual, but the relative importance which should be attached by the state in giving reward, or encouragement, to various sorts of activities. That, if it pleases people as much, the state should be as concerned to promote pushpin as poetry, football as opera, is, of course, still a contentious matter; however it is nothing like as contentious as the suggestion that it is an appropriate system of personal values. Yet Mill makes it look as if Bentham is proposing the latter. Remembering that the public, the social, the political, the institutional, is the centre of Bentham's attention may help to counter such mistaken impressions of the point of Bentham's thought, or even of the nature of the man himself (he might have read Milton as a duty; but he was a competent and regular performer on keyboard instruments all his life). It was political problems and institutional change which were the centres of concern to the people gathered round Bentham's body, not personal ethical problems. It was the former rather than the latter about which they took him to speak as a master.

Having considered the nature of the gathered disciples, and the way that they both filtered and revealed Bentham's thought, let us now return to the dead body of Bentham itself and consider part of the physical transformation of Bentham into a relic. For in the end, or demise, of Bentham may be seen the end, or point, of Benthamism. After Southwood Smith gave the oration, he dissected the body; and dissection was a large part of the subject of his lecture. This was why it was held in a school of anatomy. Bentham had in his original will of 1769, renewed shortly before his death, left his body for medical dissection so that mankind 'may reap some small benefit by my disease' (CORR I 136). As such, as Southwood Smith brought out in his lecture, it was an example of the utility principle: utility was to be maximised, and since there was more utility in dissecting a body rather than burying it in the ground, bodies ought to be dissected. Utility, or happiness, depended upon health; health depended upon medical care; which depended upon medical knowledge; which depended upon dissection. Southwood Smith had himself contributed an article to the *Westminster Review* in 1826 entitled 'on the use of the dead to the living' promoting the idea that people should leave their bodies to be dissected. As such, Bentham's act seems perhaps no more than a small, rather humdrum, example of his general principle that utility should be maximised; even perhaps rather absurd like his proposed regulation that the paupers in his workhouses should have the brims of their hats removed ('*necessity* and *use* the standards - not *fashion*' (PAUPER 87)). In fact it was, at the time he died, a highly contentious act, and one which serves as a good illustration of the kind of struggle in which utilitarians were engaged.

The reason for this is that at the time the chief legal source of bodies for dissection for the purposes of medical education was the bodies of convicted and executed murderers. The 1752 Murder Act had declared that it was necessary 'that some further terror and peculiar mark of infamy be added to the punishment' and made the dissection of all murderers compulsory. In an age where there was so much capital punishment, parliament wished to settle on something they thought to be peculiarly nasty for the much worse crime of murder. That it was dissection (by surgeons, for teaching, in a medical school) shows just how dissection was thought of, a mutilation much worse than mere hanging. It was an object of dread or (as the act said) of terror. This was part of the reason Bentham wished his body to be publicly dissected; it was as part of an attempt to allay such terror, or superstitious fears. Earlier Southwood Smith and Bentham had co-operated on a joint article about the teaching of anatomy; now Bentham wished by example to increase the pressure they were exerting for a change in the law; and, indeed, later in that year the Anatomy Act finally repealed the dissection provisions of the 1752 Murder Act and also made it legal for people to leave their bodies for medical dissection. As such Bentham's last act is just another example of the kind of political activity on which I have described his disciples as being engaged. However, it illustrates particularly well the kind of thinking behind such proposed reform. Instead of natural feelings, instead of irrational fears or superstitions, such as the horror of dissection, is to be substituted rational thought and calculation, such as the demonstration that dissection increases utility.

In his 1844 manuscripts Marx wrote that 'the avowedly restless and versatile self-interest of the *enlightenment* [inevitably triumphs] over the parochial, worldly-wise, artless, lazy and deluded self-interest of *superstition*' (Marx, *Early Writings*, ed. Lucio Colletti 340). Whether inevitable or not — no doubt many of the Enlightenment *philosophes* must have wished rather desperately at times that it was — this transition was exactly the one which Bentham was trying in general to effect, and one which is illustrated in the particular case of the disposal of his body. Instead of varying, prejudiced, partial, superstitious attitudes was to be substituted one single, universal, rational, critical standard. Clarity was to be substituted for delusion; people's real self-interests for their supposed ones. In this way Bentham was one of the *philosophes*, an English representative of the international intellectual movement centred in France. He corresponded with Voltaire and d'Alembert; and claimed to be a follower not only of them but also of Beccaria, Priestley, Hume, and, above all, Helvetius. An early, minor, work of his was a translation of Voltaire's *conte*, *The White Bull*, shortly after its original appearance, and to which Bentham added a long, satirical, Voltairean preface 'which may just as well be read afterwards'. With regard to his central project of law reform, he wrote to Voltaire that he took counsel of him oftener than the leading English lawyers, Coke, Hale, or Blackstone (CORR I 367). This work, as he put it to another *philosophe*, Chastellux, was one that he had started at the age of twenty and would finish only with his life (at the time of this prescient forecast, he was already ten years into the job and had fifty more to go); he added that the recompense that he might expect was twofold, firstly the thought of having been useful to humanity, secondly the 'estimation of a small number of people such as you' (CORR II 120). It was this small number, the *philosophes*, which composed the intellectual party to which Bentham belonged. As he wrote to d'Alembert, enclosing a sketch of his system, it could be seen that it was founded on the ideas of Helvetius (CORR II 117). D'Alembert replied that at least if they did not live to see the end of the 'absurdities, indeed even atrocities' of the criminal law, it was at least good that there were 'des philosophes' such as Bentham to prepare the way with their writings (CORR II 135).

7

In thinking of Bentham as a *philosophe* in this way — that is
not just as a latter-day admirer but rather as a fully fledged participant in a contemporary movement — it is important not to be
misled by dates, and to remember the great length of Bentham's
active intellectual life. I said above that Bentham started receiving
general recognition in England as the leader of an important movement of thought for reform in the 1820s when much of his work
first became accessible in English. Yet at that time Bentham was
over seventy, and he was over forty before the start of the French
Revolution. Furthermore, much of this work which first appeared
in the 1820s had been written by Bentham himself thirty to forty-
five years before, that is, at or not long after the time of the correspondence described above with such Enlightenment figures as
Voltaire or d'Alembert. It was written during the Enlightenment,
at a time when Bentham belonged to, and took himself to belong
to, a movement which attempted to reform by direct contact with
an inner establishment, by direct appeal to princes, or by the
mobilisation of a small literary class. It was, however, used,
promoted, and made important by a different group of men who
wished to promote democracy and popular education for all, and
were engaged in the problems of factories, sewers, and other
results of the Industrial Revolution. It is tempting to think of
Benthamism as a technological ethic for a technological age; but
the kind of technological age in which much of it was written is
that of individual gentleman inventors and the beautiful engrav-
ings of machines in the *Encyclopédie*, not the massed housing,
smoke and squalor attending the steam engines at work in factories. To take as an example the work mentioned above, the
Rationale of Reward. This was written in Russia in French in
the 1780s, edited and published by Dumont in 1811, and translated into English and edited by another Benthamite disciple
(Richard Smith) in 1825. It naturally appeared to Mill as a recent
example of the thought of a currently influential thinker. However, not only was the work written forty years before its publication in English, but the reason that Bentham was in Russia and
writing his manuscripts in French was that he was hoping that
Catherine the Great could be persuaded into setting up a complete
code of laws based on utilitarian principles. It was going to be an
example of enlightened thought to guide benevolent dictators,
just as with Voltaire and Frederick the Great.

It is important not to over-emphasise either of these images of
Bentham, the received image transmitted to us by his nineteenth-
century disciples and the image of Bentham as a participant in
the eighteenth-century Enlightenment; nor to think that there is

a very deep divergence between them. The democratic image projected by the Benthamites, appealing not to an inner establishment
but to the people at large, mirrors the views of Bentham himself in
the last twenty years of his life as certainly as his appeal to benevolent despots mirrors his earlier views. Furthermore, this change
of mind is merely a change of idea about the appropriate methods
for getting his reforms accepted. The basic ideas of the reforms
themselves and the final end to which they were devoted, the
maximisation of utility, did not change at all. Nor do the intellectual foundations or attitudes which make such an end seem
appropriate. As in the relatively minor matter of what he did with
his dead body, so in all his written thought Bentham depends
finally upon championing reason against passion or imagination.
Here, at a deeper level, Bentham is consistently an Enlightenment
thinker all his life. Just like Voltaire, he should be seen extirpating
prejudice and superstition. His object, as he puts it at the start of
his main work, *An Introduction to the Principles of Morals and
Legislation*, 'is to rear the fabric of felicity by the hands of reason
and of law' (IPML 11). Felicity is the Helvetian end, law is the
means, but the method is the method of reason. It is well known
that Bentham is a foremost spokesman for the promotion of
felicity (happiness or utility); what should be noticed here is
that the stress is on how this was to be achieved by reason. A man
of the Age of Reason, Bentham again and again stresses reason;
he bases utility on reason or identifies it with reason. For example,
in his first published work, he writes that utility is 'the path of
plain reason' (FG 486); in his main work it is reason rather than
caprice that is declared to be the basis of the principle of utility
(IPML 11); in important central examples of his later work produced from the manuscripts, we find him saying that something
is 'reasonable, i.e. conformable to the principle of utility' (RJE ii
477), or that in some cases judgement is still 'warped by anti-
pathies or prejudices unconnected with the principle of utility,
and therefore irreconcilable to reason' (*Punishment* 69); and so
it continues up until the end when we find in a (typically more
long-winded) pamphlet written and published in this same year
as his death 'I stand pledged to the public never to propose or
advocate — never to oppose and combat — any law or institution
actually established, or proposed to be established, without attaching to it an accompaniment, composed of *reasons* . . .' (*Outline
Plan of a General Register of Real Property*, V 418). These are
just a sample drawn from literally hundreds of examples throughout the work. They illustrate the constant claim that Bentham
makes that his work is based on reason, as opposed to prejudice

or superstition ('superstition' in its turn being occasionally identified by him as 'observances not dictated by the principle of utility' (IPML 64; see also *Punishment 72). As Bentham said, 'thinking men look to consequences' (Law Taxes, II 580).

If utility, felicity, is to be imposed by the hands of reason and of law, then the important thing is to find a power which, uncowed by custom, is strong enough to institute vigorous changes in traditional practices. The change of instrument from benevolent dictator to people at large is not in this context particularly substantial. Throughout, the enemy is the lesser established powers with their historically acquired thicket of abuses, absurdities, and privileges, such as the nobility, church, and law. What was needed was a power which would follow reason instead of precedent and be strong enough to sweep such historically acquired rubbish aside. This could be from on top by use of the monarchy — hence Voltaire's support for the French absolute monarchy — or it could be from below by use of the people outside the privileged positions. The essential thing was that it would follow Bentham's invocation to 'take reason, not custom for your guide' (Logic, VIII 276). There are good, indeed obvious, reasons why if reason was identified with the greatest happiness of the greatest number, then the greatest number itself might be a more efficient means of promoting reason than any dictator, however enlightened. Hence the intellectual rationale for Bentham's change, which will be properly examined at the appropriate time. The concern at the moment is with images rather than arguments: whatever the intellectual merits of Bentham's constant appeal to reason, which also will be considered at the appropriate time, its very existence stamps him as a member of the Age of Reason, one who, as he wrote in an early manuscript work, hoped for people 'enlightened by the prompting of utility' (COMM 315).

This use of 'reason' might be thought to convey little more than a fuzzy sense of approval; 'reason' being a eulogistic word in the same way that Bentham noted that 'superstition' was a dyslogistic word (Springs, I 201; IPML 109). However, if we consider the actual position Bentham intended for reason in his proposed reforms of the law, it becomes much more detailed and precise. For here the important thing is not just that the recommended content and structure of the law should meet the approved canons of rationality, but that the content should be dense with the actual reasons themselves. In the model penal code which he drew up in the 1770s, and tinkered with subsequently, the standard form is statement of offence, statement of punishment, then aggravating and extenuating circumstances, all with explanations ttached; then comes, as the example posthumously printed for illustrative purposes puts it, a 'commentary of reasons upon this law', which is in length equivalent to all the rest of the matter put together (I 166). The Code was part of the work already mentioned for the possible use of an enlightened dictator, but Bentham was still recommending something of the same form to the Presidents of various American States in the next century, in the hope that 'In America thus will *reason* spread her conquests' (IV 506), saying that the proposed code would contain a rationale, and 'by the *rationale* I mean . . . a mass of *reasons*, accompanying, in the shape of *a perpetual commentary*, the whole mass of imperative or regulative matter' (*Papers relative to codification and Public Instruction*, IV 454). It was because Brougham did not propose such a rationale as part of the law that Bentham dissented from his proposals, for example on the Bankruptcy Court Bill (*Boa Constrictor*, V 554). So the idea throughout was not just that the law should be reasonable but that it should contain, as part of itself as promulgated, an explicit display of reasons. As Bentham put it in his 1790 *Draught of a new Plan for the organisation of Judicial Establishment in France*, 'power gives existence to a law for the moment, but it is upon reason that it must depend for its stability' (IV 310). This stability, this necessary factor in good laws which would persuade obedience rather than rely upon brute force, depends again upon Bentham's Enlightenment confidence that the advantage of laws not only being rational but also of their seeming to be rational is that, if they seem to be rational, people will generally wish to be rational and so obey. Again and again he attempts to insert or induce an explicit display of reason, hoping that the display will be sufficient to promote the desired good effects. For example, one part of his enormous mass of material on judicial procedure is the recommendations of a quasi-jury quite simply to force the judge to give grounds or reasons for his decision (*II 146); the assumption is again that if only the judge is forced to give reasons, his judgements will in fact be more reasonable.

The attempt to mould the law in this way, using reason rather than custom as a guide, is alien to the essential spirit of the law with which Bentham grew up and to which he was apprenticed. For not only was the spirit of the common law tradition to follow precedent, history instead of reason, but the relative amounts of law that derived from the judges and from parliament was very different from today. Outside the criminal law, the law was almost entirely a judge-made creation, to be learnt up by new practitioners only after a laborious study of decided cases and sitting watching the established judges at work in Westminster Hall. As a young man, Bentham went through this routine but instead of, or as well as, learning he criticised. Instead of learning how the law was — its history and established practice — Bentham thought also of what the law ought to be. What he found seemed to him to be highly deficient, irrational, inequitable, relying upon fiction and manifestly absurd practices. He therefore sought to see how it could be improved by the use of philosophy. As he wrote in an early manuscript, hitherto philosophy and law had been 'two distinct worlds' with a 'gulph' between; adding 'I have endeavoured to throw a bridge over this gulph' (UC 27.6). Changing the metaphor, he recognised Bacon as one of his few predecessors in the 'trackless waste' between philosophy and practical law (UC 27.12). Bacon, as Bentham here remarks, makes the distinction between law as it is and law as it ought to be. More interesting, however, in the present context of considering the use of reason in the law, is the dispute between James I of England and the common lawyers, whose spokesman was Coke. Here was an earlier example of the king attempting to use his power to declare about the nature of the law, backed up by his Lord Chancellor, Bacon, against the lawyers depending upon custom. The source, the justification, which Bacon and the king wished to use for their criticism, just as Bentham later, was reason. They were met however, by Coke in the debate, by the use of a different sort of reason. He reminded the king that 'causes . . . are not to be decided by natural reason, but by the artificial reason and judgement of the law, which law is an act which requires long study and experience before that a man can attain to the cognizance of it' (12 Coke Reports 65; ER 77 1343). It was in this spirit that Bentham was told that the law was the perfection of human reason; that is a completed mental artefact, needing no further finishing. However, just as for Bacon, by any reason that he could recognise as such, it was clearly deficient. For a start the procedure depended upon uttering straightforward untruths which were not allowed to be questioned in the court. In Bentham's eyes the artificial reason of the law had to be reconstructed in the light of the natural, or real, reason of the philosophers. Bentham's near contemporary, Eldon, did everything that Bentham's father had hoped that he would do: after Oxford and a successful career at the bar he ended up as Lord Chancellor. Eldon said that success at the law could only be achieved by one who would 'live like a hermit and work like a horse': such was the effort needed to master the precedents. Bentham conspicuously lived like a hermit and worked like a horse for all his long life: such was the effort needed to try and change a class of lawyers fed by precedent.

In this assault on the traditional system of arcane lawyer's law, Bentham depended partly upon enlightening, that is on clarifying and informing, in a direct manner. The spirit of the enlightenment worked its way even into his perceptual metaphors. Thus in a pamphlet written in 1792, but first published in 1823, called *Truth versus Ashurst; or, law as it is contrasted with what it is said to be*, Bentham, as the title indicates, was concerned to probe beneath the illusion and show what was really there; that is to clarify the situation. He writes: 'the lies and nonsense that law is stuffed with, form so thick a mist, that a plain man, nay even a man of sense and learning, who is not in the trade, can see neither through nor into it' (V 233). Hence the abiding interest in clarification, which stretches from the earliest manuscripts, in which he is concerned 'to frame a Dictionary of moral terms; a Dictionary in which clear ideas shall stand annexed to each expression' (UC 27.4), through to such later work as that published in the *Logic*, where he lists one use of logic as 'the establishment of clear and determinate ideas' (VIII 221). The earlier interest is explicitly inspired by Helvetius and Locke, Enlightenment figures or idols; but the latter remarks carry on exactly the same idea. The whole rests on the assumption that, as he puts it in other late work, 'until . . . the nomenclature and language of law shall be improved, the great end of good government cannot be fully attained' (*Nomography, III 271). The explicit interest in close and precise analysis and in the exact signification of language marks off Bentham both as a philosopher of a notably modern temper and also as a *philosophe*, who believed that clarification, illumination, revelation of the truth, would help to bring about a better world. It shows the temper of mind of a man which, however practical and particular his specific concerns were, would generate general theoretical enquiry.

So much for some images which can be invoked by the dead body of Bentham surrounded by his disciples in June 1832, and by the desire for freedom from superstition which bound both them and their Enlightenment predecessors. It is time to set such images against a somewhat more orderly account of his biography such as might have been given, and to some extent was given, by Southwood Smith in his funeral oration. However, before doing so, it is interesting to notice how even in these images can be seen problems in Bentham's overall project which make it of philosophical interest and importance. For the practical aims which made Bentham valued sit uneasily with the theoretical interest in clarification. There is a problem of which drives which, truth or utility. For if Bentham's thought is really severely practical, devoted to the single end of advancing utility, then all theory, or all clarification, is simply a means to an end. Yet at times Bentham seems to regard enlightenment, clarification, truth, as ends in themselves. This problem of priority may be soluble, but it is related to another one about the priority of facts and values. Bentham held that facts and values should be distinguished and neither reduced to the other. Yet if the overall aim is to substitute reason for sentiment; that is, the new scientific temper of the Enlightenment for natural feelings; then it seems that observed facts should be substituted for creative emotions, which would seem to imply the reduction of value to fact. However, in that case the elimination of subjectivity, of arbitrary, capricious feelings, would mean the elimination of value, and so the elimination of Bentham's own censorial, critical, independent, stance. These two related problems can be subsumed under a general problem about foundations. Once we get beyond the satisfying sound produced by constant invocation of the word 'reason' we meet the problem of what actually it is that carries the weight of justification in Bentham's philosophy. The values that are invoked in the general project of enlightenment, criticism, and improvement must have some basis if they are to succeed in persuading opinion and changing practice. Yet there is no clear basis for them: observation, intuitive belief, shared opinion, all would seem unable to play the role demanded. Observations would turn values into facts; intuitions would make them too like individual caprice; and shared opinion could not serve as a basis for a project whose aim is to criticise and change established opinion. The followers round the body may have been following him in an attempt to change their world, and Bentham himself may have provided the theory that would substantiate such change. There still remains the problem of how the two are to be connected. This problem alone makes Bentham's thought worth philosophical study; and that there are such problems may be worth bearing in mind as a counterweight to the following short recital of bare biographical facts.

The son and grandson of attorneys in the City of London, Bentham came from a relatively prosperous middle-class background. However, being destined by his father for a high position in the law from an early age, he was educated like a gentleman at Westminster and Oxford. It was the age at which he attended these institutions, in particular Oxford, which in fact distanced himself from his colleagues more than difference in background. Totally unlike his heavy drinking, sporting, fellow students he seems to have embarked early on his life-long habit of solitary study. His fellow students were, after all, pretty well grown up, whereas Bentham entered Oxford at the age of twelve and took his BA (after leaving) at the age of sixteen. On many occasions in his later life he referred to himself as a hermit, and when he could he buried himself in 'colleges, chambers, and cottages' (CORR IV 184). Even when he visited his brother in a fairly remote part of Russia, he went off to live in an even more remote cottage where, secure from all interruption, he could work 'double tides' (CORR III 525) from sunrise until eight each evening. On return to England, both before and after he inherited his father's large, central, house, he buried himself for long periods in a room in a dilapidated farm at Hendon, eight miles from London. Even when he did move into the family house at Queens Square Place, for the last part of his long life, his standard designation of himself was as the hermit of Queens Square Place. This solitary life went with a regularity of work commented on by various people. Southwood Smith, who knew him at the end of his life, merely endorsed the reminiscences of earlier observers when he claimed in his funeral oration that Bentham had spent eight to twelve hours a day in intense study for the previous fifty years.

The chambers which Bentham referred to, when he said that he had lived in colleges, cottages, and chambers, were those of the Inns of Court. Bentham was admitted to Lincoln's Inn in 1763, at the age of fifteen, and started on the conventional training of a law student, which involved constant observation of the actual proceedings in court (law was case law; precedence was crucial; court reports were unreliable). He returned to Oxford to hear some lectures, including Blackstone's unconventional attempt to make 'Jurisprudence to speak the language of the Scholar and the Gentleman' (FG 413); an attempt which was sufficiently successful to draw prolonged criticism from Bentham a decade later. He also moved for three years to another Inn, the Middle Temple (1766-9). However, Lincoln's Inn, of which he in later life became a bencher, was his most constant place of residence until he moved into his father's old house. Conventional place for a prospective lawyer to live, Bentham soon ceased to be a conventional, or even a prospective, lawyer. When he fully came of age in 1769, the same year as he was admitted to the bar, he started to read Beccaria and Helvetius. The previous year he had read Priestley on government (throughout this time Bentham was interested in chemistry, and Priestley would have been a naturally appealing author for him). Exposed to these Enlightenment influences, Bentham seems to have decided that he was temperamentally better suited for an elaborate, precise, and philosophically founded study of law as it ought to be rather than with the everyday, money-making, practice of law as it is. Living on a small allowance, and accepting no briefs, his main work throughout the 1770s was on the criminal law. He analysed offences and studied the foundations of punishment, with a view to the construction of a complete penal code. At the end of the decade, in 1780, was printed the *Introduction* to this code, with the division of offences and discussion of basic principles; however Bentham also wrote much of the actual code, as well as much other discussion of general principles, all of which still only exists in manuscript.

Impressive as this body of work was, it did not just appear as a smooth flow throughout the decade. On the one side, Bentham had to hold off his father, who still wanted him to become Lord Chancellor. On the other, he ran into problems by falling in love with exactly the kind of penniless girl of which his father would disapprove. So, quite apart from the emotional cross-currents, there was an interruption to the general pattern of work in the middle of the 1770s when Bentham, spurred on by his pamphleteering friend Lind, tried to make some money quickly by writing some more easily sellable and immediately profitable work. There were several ideas, such as a digest of the statutes, but the only thing of lasting importance was the idea of writing a critical commentary on the popular work of Blackstone, his published Oxford lectures called *Commentaries on the Laws of England*. This led to Bentham's long unpublished *Comment on the Commentaries*, and the fragment of it which he did see through the press and which did cause a stir, the *Fragment on Government* (1776).

This sense of parts, fragments, uncompleted projects, which is already present in the early Bentham, forms a constant theme throughout his life. However much analysis and thought had been given to a particular area, there was always more that was possible; and Bentham always wished to fill up all the gaps and explore all relevant by-ways. Digressions from a main project took on a life of their own and often in fact (as with the *Fragment*) were the only part completed. The problem which he ran into at the beginning of the 1780s, and which meant that he did not complete or publish the printed *Introduction*, was that of the nature of law, more specifically of what constituted the identity of an individual law and of what constituted the distinction between civil and penal law. This 'metaphysical maze' in which he was 'unexpectedly entangled' (IPML 1) led Bentham to produce profound, original, work in the philosophy of law and

16

deontic logic, all unpublished until this century (as *Of Laws in General*). It also led him to widen his study to include the whole of civil law, and to consider reward as well as punishment. This work, continuing the same, largely solitary, accumulation of manuscript was the main occupation of Bentham throughout the decade of the eighties.

If Bentham's intellectual productions reached on to a wider stage at this period, so also did his social relations. The Earl of Shelburne (later the Marquis of Lansdowne) was a politician loosely attached to the Whig cause and more closely to the elder Pitt. He had a small political patronage of his own, but was briefly Prime Minister in 1782-3, with the younger Pitt as his Chancellor of the Exchequer. He was interested in new ideas; in intellectual, economic, and administrative progress; and he took up leading progressive intellectuals in these areas, such as Priestley and Richard Price. In 1781 he visited Bentham in his chambers in Lincoln's Inn, and pressed him to spend some of the summer at his large country estate at Bowood, Wiltshire. This would give Bentham a chance to let some of the leading Whig lawyers see his newly printed *Introduction*. Although Bentham made great play about not being able to be bought, and was indeed commended by Shelburne to Bentham's father for his highly unusual disinterestedness (X 225), Bentham went and so entered a new political and social circle. The meetings with the lawyers were disappointing, but Bentham kept up fairly close relations with the Shelburne circle for the next twenty years. It also enabled him to pay court, very indirectly and discreetly, to some highly eligible ladies; too eligible for him to have any chance of success.

If Shelburne commended Bentham to his father for disinterest, the one thing his father tried to commend to Bentham was push; '"pushing" was the one thing needful' (X 4). As well as pushing him, or pushing him to push, Bentham's father had remarried shortly after Bentham had become a law student, providing him not only with a stepmother but also with stepbrothers who acted as foils to him by being successful in worldly terms in a way that Bentham was not. However, Bentham found an increasing ally inside the family in his own full brother, Samuel. Nine years younger than Bentham (only the first and last of a family of six survived), Bentham was at first interested in his education, succeeding in getting him apprenticed to a shipwright rather than following him to Oxford. However, by the time he finished his apprenticeship and came of age, he was much more of an equal. Both Benthams, in different ways, wished to reform the world and were sympathetic to each others projects, as well as being

sympathetic in resistance to their father. Not finding sufficient
outlets for his talents in the English Navy, Samuel Bentham moved
to Russia in 1779, and became involved in helping Prince Potemkin
open up the Steppes. Factories and farms were built, and Samuel
had the chance to try out an unceasing stream of ideas from trains
of barges to recoil-less guns (he became involved in the fighting
against the Turks). He urged his admiring elder brother to join
him, and Bentham, who had his own interest in going to Russia,
since he felt that Catherine the Great was the ruling monarch most
likely to adopt his new penal and other codes, at last complied.
He left in 1785 and, travelling by way of France, Italy, and Turkey
reached the Potemkin estates six months later. As described, he
continued to work steadily, writing the *Panopticon* and *Defence
of Usury* as well as the manuscripts on Reward and the Civil Code
later used by Dumont. However, perhaps inevitably, he lacked the
push to meet Catherine, even when she came to visit the estates to
inspect the new improvements. Bentham stayed two years in
Russia, returning via Poland and Germany in 1788. Even if Bentham
is often thought of like a man writing in a study (a chamber or a
cottage), such visits meant that he had experienced widely different forms of life and social organisation (such as Turkish slave
ships), and seen the possibilities of development when the same
people were put into different institutional contexts. 'By coming
here', Bentham writes in the *Panopticon*, meaning Russia, 'I have
learnt what human powers are capable of, when unfettered by the
arbitrary regulations of an unenlightened age' (57; IV 52).

On return to England, Bentham moved back into the Shelburne
(now, after his elevation, known as the Lansdowne House) circle.
The pace of practical activity quickened, inspired by the revolutionary events in France. As Bentham wrote to Lansdowne's son
in March 1789 'for these five or six months past, my head and my
heart have been altogether in France' (CORR IV 33). He embarked
on a stream of pamphlets designed to instruct the French, such as
Political Tactics, and distributed to the revolutionaries by way of
the Lansdowne House connections. The work on the manuscripts
stopped, although as the Revolution turned more nasty, it was
again through Lansdowne House that he met his great editor
Dumont, and Dumont effectively exiled in England by the turn of
the Revolution had time to work on the manuscripts. Instead, the
theme of the whole decade continued to be practical projects.
The *Panopticon*, originally written in Russia to promote one of
Samuel's bright ideas, and then thought of as another scheme
which might be taken up by the French or Irish (correspondence
with officials in both countries led to a French translation and a

Dublin printing, both in 1791), was taken up seriously by Bentham himself as a money-making project by which he was to become the individual manager envisaged in the original plan, working the nation's convicts for a profit. So started a twenty years' struggle in which Bentham tried to persuade the British government to contract with him for the building and management of a panopticon in London. Several times he was within a signature of success: the contract was drafted, cleared by the Treasury, and awaited only the final signature of the Prime Minister, Pitt. Acts of parliament were successfully passed giving the requisite powers, but the thing which always looked as if it might come off in the next few months dragged on through the 1790s without success and then, at a slower tempo, through the 1800s. It was blocked by the landowners who did not want a prison built near their estates, depreciating property values. However good the arguments, they were wrecked by the interests of those who held the power. The chief opponent was Earl Spencer, not only a landowning member of the House of Lords able to amend the enabling acts in his own interests, but also a member of the government with access to Pitt. So instead of writing manuscript, Bentham devoted his main effort to attempting to influence actual people: corresponding with, and meeting landowners; walking endlessly round the Treasury corridors trying to catch officials; encouraging people to come and look at his model of the building. He emerged, not with the panopticon, but with a better, if bitter, perception of the role of interest in government, a perception which informs all the work of the new century.

Bentham's engagement in the panopticon project himself seems to have started with a rather fortuitous set of circumstances. His brother Samuel returned from Russia, full of new inventions, in 1791 and the death of his father in the following year meant that Bentham had at last some capital with which to set the venture up. The idea was that the prisoners were to provide the motive power to turn the machines invented by Samuel, and the projected capital was to obtain its due entrepreneurial reward. In fact, at least until the end, it was a financial disaster as the Benthams anticipated the signing of the contract, arranged for the casting of large amounts of iron in Sheffield for the building, and set up model workshops, employing several people, to test the new inventions. By 1796, having inherited substantial property, they had spent £10,000 on the project and had for some time been trying to stave off creditors, raise loans, and avoid imprisonment for debt. The payoff did not come until the next century when, on the advice of a parliamentary committee of enquiry, Bentham received £23,000 compensation in 1813.

However accidental or otherwise it was that it was the panopticon that absorbed all his energies in the 1790s, there are clear signs that Bentham wished to engage in something more practical, or have more visible signs of success, in this decade. In 1790 he was 42. However resistant to the idea of pushing, and however disinterested he might appear, he had been brought up from an early age with the idea of achieving public success and recognition. Yet nothing had happened after over twenty years of work at reform of the law. All the patrons, or possible patrons, to whom he had appealed, or had in mind, to promote reform in the law, or even to recognise the importance, truth, and genius of his views, had all successively failed him. The great work, the *Introduction*, had been half consumed by rats and disregarded by the general public. The important thought of the manuscripts lay in disorganised piles without hope of an effective outlet. Catherine the Great; the central Whig lawyers met through Lansdowne; the new French Revolutionaries; none of them had seized on and promoted his ideas. The frustration produced by this, and the contrast with his successful stepbrothers in his father's eyes, explain the movement into practical projects. The decade started with an extraordinary exchange of letters with Lansdowne in which Bentham accuses his friend, with whom he had just been in close co-operation producing pamphlets for France, of not being a true patron by failing to get him into parliament. The apparently disinterested philosopher turned and bit the hand he thought had failed to feed him. Lansdowne replied in a dignified, friendly, but justifiably puzzled way. So, shortly after, just when Dumont was starting the work on the manuscripts that was eventually to make Bentham famous and give him his public, Bentham himself engaged with the panopticon. Dumont himself was given no help at all and instead, when the panopticon temporarily waned in activity, Bentham passed on to other practical projects. He tried to use his contacts with the Treasury to sell them other schemes, on taxation, currency, or speaking tubes. The idea of the panopticon was diverted to proposals about the poor laws. There were also private money-making ideas, like the operation of a train of carts between London and Edinburgh, or the deep freezing in large quantities of vegetables, so that fresh peas could be brought to the market at Christmas. While these ideas were not absurd, any more than his idea of building a Panama canal, and were researched with proper Benthamite thoroughness, they marked digressions from the consideration and composition of ideas which, both until then and also later, formed the main thread of Bentham's life.

The return to writing, to the abstract and theoretical, came gra-dually. It seems to have started with economics, where Bentham's more particular, practical, proposals for a form of interest-bearing currency (*Circulating Annuities*) led on to a more abstract con-sideration of economic issues, leading to the development of new theory, and, by way of considering how the legislator should view economics, renewed consideration of the oughts of legislation. However, the take-off really came with his work on evidence, which he started about 1803. By now the first phase of Dumont's work had been completed, and the *Traités* had been published. Given notice in Britain by review in the *Edinburgh Review*, the basis had been laid for an intellectual reputation commensurate with the scale of Bentham's whole project (as opposed to the previously successful incidental works, such as the *Fragment* or *Defence of Usury*). It also gave scope for disciples, particularly Scottish disciples, and Bentham met the most prominent of these, James Mill, for the first time in 1809. From now on the pattern of most of the rest of Bentham's life was established, particularly when he became finally disengaged from the panopticon. Bentham, the hermit, sat at his raised desk in the centre of a web of acolytes. He returned to the solitary writing of manuscript, progressively setting back the time of his dinner hour to give himself a longer and longer day for the great work. Devoted personal secretaries, living in or near the house, Mill, Bowring, Chadwick, ran his affairs. The manuscripts were hacked into shape by others. Com-ing into the 1820s, Benthamite works flowed from the press. A Benthamite quarterly was established to rival the Whig *Edinburgh* and the Tory *Quarterly*. The team of friends and admirers des-cribed at the beginning of this chapter was set up. Political con-tacts were made. Changes, particularly in the law, at last started coming into effect; and so Bentham died, surrounded by the makers of part of Victorian England.

In this later work there are two threads, a more abstract thread and a more practically political thread. Both, however, traverse a much grander stage than the more practical projects of the 1790s or the first years of the new century. The abstract thread marks a return to the early theoretical issues, and Bentham took up again his first ideas on the nature of thought and language and gave his most fully developed account of them. He also took up constitutional law, neglected in his early work, and developed a blueprint for a complete administrative state in the *Constitutional Code*. The political thread was devoted to the attempt to change England into a representative democracy. This was again political activity, the attempt to influence actual people. However, this time the attempt was not by talking with the insiders in the corridors of the Treasury, or in the houses of the established. The appeal was instead to the people without. The control of a single, identified establishment (church, government, and law), of education, juries, and opinion was attacked in a series of polemical works (*Church of Englandism; Fallacies; Packing*). General works were written in favour of parliamentary reform, and Bentham allowed his name to be used in the more particular agitation involved in electing radical members devoted to reform in his own borough of Westminster. So, although the theoretical work flourished again in his seventies, he also stayed engaged. The appearance of reformers and active politicians around his body on that June evening in 1832, two days after the Royal assent had been given to the Great Reform Bill, was absolutely appropriate.

With followers, Bentham had started his own sect, just as he had earlier dreamed that he would. Among his other intellectual activities and practical projects at the end of his life, he spent time considering how he could give his own sect an icon. The result was the work he called the *Auto-Icon*; and the result of the work was the actual auto-icon itself, which now sits in a sort of telephone box in a corridor in University College London. It may be remembered that Southwood Smith's article, in which the ideas behind Bentham's dissection were promoted, was entitled 'on the use of the dead to the living'. Bentham's own subtitle for the *Auto-Icon* was 'further uses of the dead to the living'. Just as in the former case, the ideas behind it were a fully developed and proper consequence of general utilitarian theory. Obviously, or so Bentham thought, people after his death would want some representation of the founder of such an important movement. Yet what could be a more efficient method of achieving a representation of something than the thing itself? Conducting a proper Benthamite cost-benefit analysis reveals that the three-dimensional map on a scale of a mile to a mile is the most efficient way of achieving the benefit. Hence, instead of inefficiently produced and imperfectly representing statues, people should be the representatives of themselves; that is, they should be auto-icons.

And so it came to pass. The sect acquired its relic, and Bentham sits with his walking stick Dapple in his hand representing himself. The situation is shot through with different kinds of absurdities and ironies. There is the irony of such a determinedly secular figure as Bentham, or of such a determinedly secular movement as utilitarianism, needing its sacred relic. Matthew Arnold's gentle mocking, some thirty years later, of the Benthamite 'on a pious pilgrimage, to obtain from Mr Bentham's executors a secret bone of his great, dissected master' hits a target (*Essays in Criticism*, Preface). There is the absurdity of Bentham's work on head shrinking among the Maoris, or his habit of bringing out the glass eyes that were to be used to show his friends. However, the best irony is the failure of the project in its most vital detail. Because the actually preserved head, all research on head shrinkers notwithstanding, looked so horrible and so unlike the alive Bentham, shortly after his death it was replaced by a commissioned wax head. So, in the end, even though the clothes, skeleton, and stick turned out to be adequate representatives of themselves, the head did not. The most central icon in his religion, as in others, was created by an artist; and was not the product of theoretically inspired technology.

Notes

(a) A description of Southwood Smith's oration being given is in Lewes 1898, and the oration itself was published in 1832.

(b) The wording quoted in the main text does not reappear exactly in Bentham's final will, drafted and signed in the week he died. However, the sentiment does, and the will contains precise details about how Southwood Smith, who was bequeathed the body, was to give a lecture over it and eventually put together the skeleton 'in such a manner as that the whole figure may be seated in a chair usually occupied by me' (UC 155.36) and place it in a box. Not only was this carried out, so that box and dressed skeleton still survive at University College London (having for many years adorned the room in which Smith practised), but also Bentham's further suggestion that the auto-icon might be produced at gatherings of Benthamites (ibid.) is still adopted one hundred and fifty years later. The actual transition of Bentham into auto-icon is described in Marmoy (1958).

(c) A more precise account of Helvetius and Beccaria and the project they bequeathed to Bentham is given in Chapter V, together with an account of the intellectual foundations of the panopticon, which was an application of the same general project.

(d) The biography of Bentham in this chapter, like all biography of Bentham, inevitably makes use of the unreliable *Autobiography*. For the earlier period this is usefully supplemented by Everett (1931), and there is a list of the principal events in the life in the years which are covered by each volume of the *Correspondence*.

II

The Pestilential Breath
of Fiction

'What the *hatchet* is to the Russian peasant, *fiction* is to the English lawyer — an instrument of all work' (*Peers and Senates*, IV 447). Commenting on the current state of English law in his first main published work, Bentham says that some improvement has been made in removing the 'mask of mystery from the face of Jurisprudence' by the publication of legal proceedings in English instead of law French. However: 'This was doing much; but it was not doing every thing. Fiction, tautology, technicality, circuity, irregularity, inconsistency, remain. But above all the pestilential breath of Fiction poisons the sense of every instrument it comes near,' and he notes that 'the consequence is, that the Law, and especially that part of it which comes under the topic of Procedure, *still* wants much of being generally intelligible' (FG 410; 411n). Earlier, in his preface to his translation of Voltaire's *White Bull*, he had satirised such procedure, capitalising on the fact that his rival translator had castrated the bull by mistranslation. Bentham describes an imaginary process of law being brought against him, the lawyer arriving with the indictment explaining 'it's our maxim to make things as unintelligible as we can' and then the quoted blackletter indictment containing phrases such as 'Nebuchandnezzer of Babylon in the parish of St Martin's in the Fields' (*Bull, Preface*, 95; 97). Surveying in the 1770s the obscurity, absurdity, and confusion of the law that he was supposed to be studying as the perfection of human reason, Bentham noted above all the prevalent use of legal fiction. Things were blatantly falsely described, straightforward falsehoods were accepted in court and not allowed to be traversed. In this way the proceedings were rendered mysterious to anyone but the initiates of the craft, just as when they had all been described in

24

a language no one spoke but lawyers. Such a procedure Bentham found ripe for satire, obviously absurd, obviously alien to anyone with a natural belief in clarity, truth, and consistency.

In this chapter the operation of such legal and also other more general fictions will be described, and Bentham's criticisms examined. Such criticisms lead to other, more fundamental, problems of justification which will be looked at later. Bentham, in his criticism, is supposing that there is, in principle, a way in which things can be made ideally clear and so described really as they are without any trace of fiction. This metaphysical presupposition of the possibility in principle of an ideal analysis will form the centre of the next chapter. However, even if we assume such clarification is possible, there is still another problem about the foundation or justification of what Bentham is doing in his attempt to eliminate fictions. For if his starting point was truth, the desirability of true belief, then there would be no problem about the point of the elimination of fictions or falsehoods. Yet, if Bentham's starting point in justification is the desirability of the principle of utility, that is with welfare rather than with truth, then the problem of why it is appropriate to eliminate fiction reappears. Perhaps it does not always have good consequences to believe the truth; perhaps fictions have utility. Bentham, in the *Fragment on Government*, criticises his target Blackstone both for his failure to adopt the right critical attitude and for inaccuracy in exposition, thinking that it was 'no wonder' that someone exhibiting the one defect should exhibit the other (404). Yet it is not obvious that someone might not have the right affections and yet cloudy understanding, or clear understanding and disreputable affections. However intimate the connection between an interest in clarity and an interest in welfare, it is at best contingent.

Let us assume for the moment, however, that clarity, truth, and consistency are unproblematically good things, which is certainly Bentham's assumption at the time at which he wrote the early work in which the phrase 'the pestilential breath of fiction' appears, the *Fragment on Government*. Bentham's aim in this work is to show that the highly regarded legal treatise, Blackstone's *Commentaries on the Laws of England*, was susceptible to criticism and insidious in effect, tending to make people more satisfied with the current state of the law than they had any right to be. The rhetorical devices he uses in it, that is, the procedures adopted which are designed to sway and convince its audience, are demonstrations of the unclarity and inconsistency of what Blackstone says. As Bentham says at one point, in mock misery, 'what distresses me is, not with the meeting with any positions, such as, thinking them false, I find a difficulty of proving so: but the not meeting with any positions, true or false, (unless it be here and there a self-evident one,) that I can find a meaning for' (439). He does not rely so much, that is, upon giving Blackstone the lie direct as in showing that it is so unclear what he is saying that it cannot be told whether what he says is true or false. To show this, he assumes, is enough to show Blackstone to be deficient in the eyes of the audience. So let us for the moment, as part of this audience, agree that the path of clarity is the path of virtue, and see what Bentham, in the interests of clarity, makes of fictions and the law.

Let us start with the most obvious case of the use of fiction in the description and justification of the current state of the law, the case of explicitly legal fictions. Later Bentham identified a legal fiction as 'a wilful falsehood, uttered by a judge, for the purpose of giving injustice the colour of justice' (*Scotch Reform*, V 13); the last part of this description is clearly polemical, but the first part is accurate enough on any account of the matter: legal fictions are clearly wilful falsehoods in the sense that everyone professionally engaged in the court in which they are used knows them to be literally false, and asserts and uses them knowing their literal falsity. Yet this is not supposed to count against them in the way that the wilful assertion of falsehoods outside a court of law would. Hence the gentler name of 'fiction'; as Bentham says, 'uttered by men at large, wilful falsehood is termed wilful falsehood: uttered by a judge as such, it is termed fiction: understand judicial *fiction*' (*Justice and Codif. Petitions*, V 452). In these later studies, fiction fits in as part of a whole system of artificial devices, developed in the interests of the class of lawyers; in his earlier work, when Bentham was more likely to see them as the product of 'inattention and prejudice' rather than 'sinister interest and artifice' (*Second edn Preface*, FG 508), these elements, although present, are not picked out in such a systematic or sustained manner. The implied question, however, is the same, whether in the early or the later thought: what could serve to turn an otherwise despised practice into a highly approved form of procedure; how is it that a court of law can make a wilful falsehood respectable. Simply described, as in the preface to the *White Bull*, or once they are no longer used and are matters of mere history, they are liable to seem merely absurd. Babylon is declared to be in London, or, as Bentham wrote in 1795 of persons summoned to court 'sometimes he is told that he is in jail: sometimes that he is lurking up and down the country, in company with a vagabond of the name of Doe; though all the while he is sitting quietly by his fireside: and this my Lord Chief Justice sets his hand to' (*Truth versus Ashurst*, V 234); this also, he might have added, Blackstone defended (Bla *Comm* III 431). These fall under the head of what Bentham called 'jurisdiction stealing' falsehoods (RJE iv 307); a false claim is made which allows a court to try something which would normally lie outside its jurisdiction. The procedure Bentham is describing here was an outstanding contemporary example of this, the writ known as *latitat* ('he lurks'), which enabled the Court of King's Bench to take over the business (and fees) which should on the face of it have gone to the Court of Common Pleas. By falsely claiming that the subject of the writ was imprisoned for, or on the run from, a kind of offence which the Court was empowered to try, any other claim against the person could be brought against the person in the same Court; hence King's Bench heard cases with respect to debt. The procedure was well established and considered to be unproblematical. Bentham's view, by contrast, as expressed in a Commonplace book he kept shortly before writing the *Fragment* was that 'the first judge who had the effrontery to remand a debtor brought before him on pretence of a criminal charge, whereas there was no criminal charge, should have gone to gaol himself, and not the debtor' (X 75).

In his Preface to the second edition of the *Fragment*, Bentham even went so far as to say 'a fiction of law may be defined − a wilful falsehood, having for its object the stealing legislative power' (FG 509). However, not all the central legal fictions were of the jurisdiction stealing form. Also central, and described on another occasion as 'the causes of the greatest importance of any in the civil line' (OLG 186n), was the action of *ejectment*. Here, as Bentham puts it, 'a foolish story is told about somebody called Doe, that was turned out by somebody called Roe; an imaginary man by another, as anybody may see in Blackstone' (RJE iv 282). Again, although he does not add it, if they do, they will also see that Blackstone actually described but also defended what a recent legal historian has referred to as 'a remarkable series of fictions' (Baker 1971, p. 167). What happened here was that people wishing to prove their freehold titles found that they were bound up in a cumbrous and ancient procedure, whereas people leasing land were able to use a much simpler more modern procedure for proof of title. Hence they fictionally claimed to have leased the title to a fictional person (for example, Doe), who was fictionally claimed to have been ejected from the land by the fictional lessee of the person they claimed the title from. This means that the titles of eighteenth-century cases are often an action between two entirely fictional people, and explains one reason why Bentham held that case reports in this area were as good a description of what actually happened as Bede would be as a description of the current war (the American War of Independence) (OLG 186). After his description of it, Blackstone comments that the procedure succeeded 'as being infinitely more convenient for attaining the end of justice: because, the form of the proceeding being intirely fictitious, it is wholly in the power of the court to direct the application of that fiction, so as to prevent fraud and chicane' (*Comm* III 205).

The explicit defence of such procedures by Blackstone shows that Bentham needs to do more than just reveal what is going on in the courts in order for it automatically to be exposed as absurd. Here, for example, is Blackstone commenting on the earlier described writ of *latitat*:

> these fictions of law, although at first they may startle the student, he will find upon further consideration to be highly beneficial and useful: especially as this maxim is ever invariably observed, that no fiction shall extend to work an injury; its proper operation being to prevent a mischief, or remedy an inconvenience, that might result from the general rule of law. So true is it, that *in fictione juris semper subsistit aequitas*. (*Comm* III 43)

As defender of the common law tradition, Blackstone gives a reference to its great master, Coke, in justification of both the maxim and the tag. The normal startled student clearly followed Blackstone's advice, if he worried about it at all. Bentham, an abnormal student, here as elsewhere never forgot the way that he was startled by established practice, and never wished to conform, even to what others would regard as mere form. Here is his later, trenchant, comment: first he notes that 'to the youth of both sexes, when flocking to a ball-room or a theatre, it has never yet been proposed, as a condition precedent to their admission into those seats of social pleasure and innocent delights, that they should, each of them, before the delivery of the ticket, take a roll in the contents of a night-cart, kept in waiting for that purpose', then states that this is what happens in the law where students are 'rolled . . . through the mire of mendacity'. For Bentham it is mendacity, wilful falsehood, lies, 'filth', dung; on his way to his coming out ball as a prospective great lawyer, the delight of his father's eye, he finds that he has to roll in a night cart. For Blackstone a little explanation not only justifies the existence of, but also reveals the positive advantages of, the use of legal fictions.

And behind Blackstone stands the great master, Coke. We must now try to assess who is right.

If truth were the final justification of practice, then Bentham's concern to replace the word 'fiction' by 'lie' (just as the modern supermarket manager's concern to replace the word 'shoplifting' by 'theft'), would be sufficient for him to make his case. However, given that his final justification for practice is utility, then Blackstone's defence should give him more problems. For what Blackstone appeals to is the utility of fictions; they are 'beneficial and useful'. Henry Maine, in *Ancient Law* claimed that Bentham had overlooked the 'peculiar office' of fictions in the historical development of law (27); and clearly the law has often been developed by the use of fiction, as the action of *ejectment* illustrates. The question, though, as Bentham would put it, is not as to what has happened but as to what ought to happen; given that fictions have been used in the development of the law, is there any good reason why they should be so used, or should be used in the future. The utility of fictions comes from their ability to generalise a successful procedure. They are similar to the use of models in science. In science it may be useful, may aid conceptual grip or operational control, to think of some process or structure as being like something which is much better understood or controlled; the unknown is thought of after the model of the known. Similarly in law, when new problems arise, it may be efficient to think of them on the model of ways that have been successfully used elsewhere; or, as in the *ejectment* procedure, to apply a procedure which works well in one area to an area which was formally handled by a different procedure. The fiction consists in treating one thing as if it were a different kind of thing, whereas clearly it is not. Legal personality is another good example. When a nexus of legal relations has been established between real people, it is then possible to insert such items as churches and corporations into this nexus (so that, for example, an individual can have a duty to a corporation, or convey land to a church) by treating them as if they were persons, although literally they are not. This is convenient in that it allows use to be made of well established and relatively easy to understand legal relations in an area which would otherwise be problematical with even the nature of the related entities difficult to grasp. It can also, of course, cause problems; just because they are legal persons and not real persons, they differ from real persons and behave in ways which have not been taken account of when establishing the legal relations between real persons.

Blackstone in his defence links the use of fiction with equity, a connection which goes back at least as far as such medieval commentators on Roman Law as Bartolus. The original idea of equity, as Blackstone implies with his reference to a 'general rule of law', was some machinery of intervention in particular cases where operation of the general rule would bring about unjust results. Yet it would be highly inappropriate to use legal fictions in this way, since they only work beneficially in the way that Blackstone describes if everybody understands that a fiction is being used; and surely this can be so only if the use of fictions in an area is a regular procedure, understood to be so, and predictable by all parties to the dispute. This was certainly the case in the examples cited above, *latitat* and *ejectment*, the use of both of which was the absolutely standard and normal procedure in their respective areas. So the point of the use of fictions, in spite of what Blackstone says, is not so much individual intervention in the harsh rigour of the law but, rather, a mechanism for general improvement; that is, for the replacement of one set of general rules with another which is more just. The point is that fictions will only be tolerated when they lead to the removal of mischiefs, when they lead to a new set of rules which is, as a set of rules, more equitable. The actual reasons for the changes in the rules produced by fiction in the two cited cases were in fact more mundane than the increase of justice or equity. In both cases it was the saving of fees, by permitting use of a cheaper court or a simpler and hence cheaper form of procedure. Yet, even though more mundane, this is not a defence that Bentham could object to, committed as he was to the removal of 'vexation, expence, and delay' from the law. Cheaper and more rapid decisions obviously increased utility, as he understood the term. So what basis could be left to him for objecting to the introduction of fictions which introduced utility in this way?

What purpose, Bentham asks himself in the Commonplace book mentioned earlier, can be served by legal fictions; and answers his own question 'One may conceive two — either that of doing in a roundabout way what they [the judges] might do in a direct way, or that of doing in a roundabout way what they had no right to do in any way at all' (X 75). This persists as his standard answer to the question of whether legal fictions might not have a use. As it appears in the *Book of Fallacies* fifty years later, it comes as a similar alternation: 'had you power to do without the lie? — your lie is a foolish one. Had you no such power? — it is a flagitious one' (*327n); or, similarly and from the same period, 'what you have been doing by the fiction, could you, or could you not, have done it without the fiction? If not, your fiction is a wicked lie: if

30

yes, a foolish one' (RJE iv 300). This seems acceptable with respect to the foolish alternative; since there obviously are costs involved in the use of fictions, such as the confusion of the uninitiated public, the danger of confusion even of the initiates, the creating of a cavalier attitude with respect to truth, and so on. The other alternative is not so clear, however: given that, if a fiction is avoidable, its use is foolish, might not use of a fiction be justifiable when there was no alternative? In the passage referred to by Blackstone on the prevention of mischief, Coke actually said that 'the law will never make any fiction but for necessity' (3 Co. Rep. 30a; ER 76 at 694); and although necessity in the law is not the cast iron rail that it is in logic, might not a fiction be the necessary means of achieving good consequences? Bentham must answer such questions in the negative, and to do so he must rely either on the claim that there always is in fact an alternative means of achieving the beneficial results (so it is not really necessary) or that fictions are so bad that, even if they are the necessary means to a good result, the badness of the means must outweigh the goodness of the result. Unless he relies just on the absolute wrongness of false description, an almost Kantian aversion to any form of lie, he cannot really claim the latter. We are taking truth for the moment as merely *prima facie* a virtue, not something inevitably always justified by the utility principle, and certainly not something which produces so much utility that it always outweighs any other utility. So Bentham must rely on the former claim, that is that there always really is an alternative method of producing the good result.

Whether this case can be made universally is difficult to show, but it is easy enough to show it taking such typical examples as the central eighteenth-century examples described above. If it is desired to provide legal business at less fees, then there are alternative means to making false claims designed to get cases which properly belong to one court tried by another. Fees can be lessened at all courts, the jurisdiction of the courts changed, and so on. Similarly, it is possible to get the benefits of the *ejectment* action without a rigmorole of false names and false claims; this is, after all, just what happened when the fictions were abolished in 1852. It is not necessary to utter literal falsehoods in a court in order to transfer the benefits of a successful, well-established, or well-understood part of law to a new area. It can be done explicitly, or use made of technical terms, or words which were formerly part of common speech given a technical legal meaning. This happens, inevitably, to any term involved in the law to some extent, in that the boundaries of its application have to be more

31

precisely marked. It means, furthermore, that not all cases of generalisation in the law, in which an established concept is applied in a new area, need involve any kind of fiction. When Lord Atkin, in his famous judgment in *Donoghue v. Stevenson* said that, in law, 'the question, who is my neighbour? receives a restricted reply' and then answered that in law it 'seems to be persons who are so closely and directly affected by my act that I ought reasonably to have them in contemplation as being so affected' when contemplating acts or omissions ((1932) AC at 580), he in fact extended the legal meaning of 'neighbour', so that an established body of law could be applied to new areas. However, in that the sense was still restrictive compared with a perfectly normal, biblical, sense of the term, no fiction was involved; it did not mean that persons who were really not neighbours had to be treated in future as if they were. All these cases of extension, or the creation of technical terms, are also quite different from the eighteenth-century examples in that the latter involve straightforward falsehoods with all words being used in the normal sense; when someone alleged in court that he leased his land to John Doe, no special sense of 'lease' was involved.

Hence it looks as if Bentham could defend the claim that fictions, at least those involving straightforward falsehood, are always dispensable. However this just brings us to another layer of difficulty, which is in fact the real heart of the matter. The ways of dispensing with fictions just described, such as changing the form of actions to prove title to property, depend upon explicit legislation. The reason that fictions were used instead results from development of law by the judges. It must be remembered that at the time that Bentham was writing, almost the whole of the law outside the criminal law, such as the law about property, was a judge-made creation. Yet, although perhaps eighteenth-century judges were not as worried as present-day judges about the idea that they were creating the law, the fundamental idea was the same: judges do not make the law but describe how it already is, and apply it. Since the only authority that judges had was authority, it had to look as if cases were being judged in the same kinds of way as they had been by the previous judges, by the authorities. So when they wished to develop the law and apply it in new ways, they had to make it look as if it was the same old law that was being applied. Hence the use of fiction; the law did not change in the use of *latitat* and *ejectment*; instead, wilful falsehoods allowed the same old laws to be applied in new areas. So the real root of Bentham's objection is an objection to judge-made law; and that point is a point about power. The judges are using powers that they ought not to have, the power to legislate. This is what lies behind Bentham's claim that if the fiction is unavoidable, it is flagitious, wicked, or doing something the judges 'had no right to do'.

The point about power is also crucial to the enlargement of Bentham's understanding of the nature of his opponents and the importance of fictions to the judges. He had always, in a rich brew of medical metaphors, diagnosed the 'pestilential breath of fiction' as the chief poison of the law, saying of lawyers, for example, in the larger manuscript from which the *Fragment* is drawn, that 'they can no more speak at ease without a fiction in their mouths, than Demosthenes without pebbles. Such is the power of professional prejudice to deprave the understanding' (COMM 58). This is of a piece with the claim in such a central late work as the *Rationale of Judicial Evidence* that 'as nonsense succeeds to nonsense, absurdity to absurdity, so does lie to lie, from the beginning of the [legal] career to the end of it' (RJE iv 34). However, as noted above, his attitude changed with respect to the causes of these fictions in the law. In the Preface to the second edition of the *Fragment* (1822), in which he dwells at length on fictions and reflects on his earlier thought, he says that when he wrote the *Fragment*, in scarcely any of the imperfections in 'the general frame of the Government' did he 'see the effect of any worse cause than inattention and prejudice: he saw not in them then, what the experience and observations of near fifty years have since taught him to see in them so plainly – the elaborately organised, and anxiously cherished and guarded products of sinister interest and artifice' (FG 508). The word prejudice is a fine word of the period which Bentham could have picked up from Voltaire – he heads an early manuscript 'Préjugés in favour of antiquity' (X 69), that is, using the French form – indicating the state of the people before enlightenment; the judgments made before thinking. Fifty years of attempted enlightenment later, Bentham needed another explanation than inattention or judgments made before thinking. He felt that what before had seemed almost accidental defects were in fact explicit devices by which certain groups kept themselves in power. The lawyers protected their self-interest by propagating myths; fictions were an ideology created by, and designed to uphold the power of the lawyers. The difference in his thought, noticeable first in *Scotch Reform*, is more a difference of tone than content. He was always aware that lawyers had interests. A very early manuscript has a chart listing the 'interests' and 'prejudices' of lawyers as 'obstacles' to legislation. In it he noted that 'fiction has kept off Amateurs . . . law alone has been abandoned as it were by general consent to the narrow industry of its professors' (UC 97.1; 4). This is a constant theme, as in the passage quoted at the beginning from the *Fragment*, lawyers have tried to make the law incomprehensible ('uncognoscible') so that they alone can control it. Yet the consequences are more fully laid out in the later work. In *Scotch Reform* he notes that the use of 'jargon' — 'fiction' is only one of several listed examples — is

> to produce — 1. *on the part of the law*, uncertainty, incognoscibility, matter of sham science; 2. *on the part of the non-lawyer*, conscious ignorance, thence consultation and advice (*opinion-trade*) or misconception, thence misconduct, litigation, lawyer's assistance or vicarious service, with advice at every step; 3. *on the part of the lawyer* . . . propensity to regard reform as hopeless, or undesirable; 4. *for professional lawyer*, monopoly of succession to judicial offices. (V 13)

This comprehensive catalogue illustrates how the interests of the lawyers as a class are involved in the propagation of fictions; that 'in the profit made out of each fabrication, would be seen the final cause of it' (*Second edn Preface*, FG 510). It shows how hard it was to work for the elimination of fictions: if fictions gave the lawyers power, then the lawyers' power preserved fictions.

Even though Bentham had always known that he had to work against established interests, and that, as he put it in the *Fragment*, 'Interest smooths the road to Faith' (FG 442), this revelation of how the power of established interests was based upon, and used to uphold, fiction and fraud posed new problems for him. If what was needed was not intellectual enlightenment, food for the understanding, but rather some method of changing a class holding 'power, by means of *corruption* and *delusion*' (FG 513), then Bentham was faced with the problem of what rival, countervailing, power he could call on. This is a central problem about the practical effectiveness of his later thought: however good his diagnosis, the very accuracy of his description did not seem to leave him space to insert a lever of change. As such, it will be treated later, particularly in connection with the *Book of Fallacies* which came out at much the same time as Bentham was writing the Preface to the Second Edition of the *Fragment*. The central problem of this chapter is the problem of justification, rather than of the practical mechanism of change; we are presupposing for the moment that truth and justification are good things, and enlightenment is a sufficient goal. We have seen that the justification of legal fictions, if any, rests upon the justification of judge-made law. So the question now is whether judge-made law is justified. In Bentham's eyes, it is not:

> the judges make the common law. Do you know how they make it? Just as a man makes laws for his dog. When your dog does anything you want to break him of, you wait till he does it, and then beat him for it. That is the way you make laws for your dog: and this is the way that the judges make law for you and me. They won't tell a man before hand what it is he *should not do*. (*Truth versus Ashurst*, V 235)

The problem about judge-made law, that is, is that it is retrospective legislation; it is not possible for a man to know at the time at which he acts whether what he does is or is not against the law. It offends, just like fictions themselves, against the canons of certainty and clarity in the law. Although Bentham's argument here, as in the cases above, appeals to intermediate principles, such as the badness of lying, falsity, or retrospective legislation, it is important to realise that, in his eyes, all such principles can be justified by the little-mentioned principle of utility: it is not because it is unjust, in Bentham's eyes, that it is wrong to legislate retrospectively, but, because it prevents someone predicting whether he will get into trouble with the law, it prevents him planning his life in a way which maximises his happiness. Unclarity and uncertainty diminish utility.

In the published attack on Blackstone, Bentham was not particularly concerned with the explicitly legal fictions of the kind discussed so far, or with the defects of the common law tradition, in which they occur. He does deal with both, and even in fact singles out Blackstone for a highly unusual moment of praise for criticising one of these judicial fictions, that of *recoveries* (FG 420). The praise, however, if not quite faint enough to damn on its own account, is surrounded with a few damns to make sure of his main work of demolition; in the footnote he thinks that Blackstone 'like an artful partizan' has sacrificed a few fictions in order to save the rest, and in the text he notes that 'one would think some Angel had been sowing wheat among our Author's tares'. However, the main text of the *Fragment* is devoted to consideration of just seven pages of Blackstone's *Commentaries*, dealing with the nature and the rights of established government. As one of the preliminary pages to the exposition of the present nature of English law, which was his central interest, this part of the *Commentaries* was scarcely at the centre of Blackstone's concern. Needing an argument justifying the authority of the state, that is justifying its right to make law at all, he took one made to measure off the peg, and offered the idea of original contract as in Locke. Expressing surprise that this argument needs again to be criticised when Hume has done it all so well before him, Bentham rips into the original contract and its surroundings and subjects Blackstone's seven pages to five chapters of close analysis. What relates this main topic, though, to the legal fictions discussed before, and why it is appropriate for Bentham to discuss them both together in his Preface to the second edition, is that the original contract is another example of a fiction. It is a 'chimera' and, as Bentham put it in the *Fragment*, 'the indestructible prerogatives of mankind have no need to be supported upon the sandy foundation of a fiction' (FG 439-41). As he commented on it fifty years later, 'the existence of that pretended agreement . . . was and is a fable: authors of the fable, the Whig lawyers' (FG 509). The Whigs, of whom Blackstone was one, were particularly concerned to uphold the Revolution Settlement in which James II had been succeeded by William III, and original contract was one possible justification of this; a more obvious fable, though, and one which was explicitly written into the 1689 Bill of Rights, was the claim that James II had 'abdicated the government'; this one Bentham did not pick up until the Preface to the second edition, while contrasting English with Scottish law (FG 541).

The fiction involved in the idea of an original contract differs from the purely legal fictions discussed above in that it is not used in courts of law but, rather, figures in the explanation and justification of what happens in the courts given by jurists and constitutional theorists. It explains or justifies why there is law at all. As such it is example of the class of fictions which Bentham was particularly concerned to attack, both in the *Fragment* and also in the longer *Comment* of which the *Fragment* forms a part. Another good example of this kind of fiction, used by Blackstone and criticised by Bentham, is that of the notoriety of the law (of its being known to the people subject to it). That the law must be notified to the people who are to obey it is held by Blackstone by turns to be a condition for something being law at all, and for it being good law. Noticing this ambiguity, Bentham then proceeds to criticise Blackstone's explanation of why English statute law is so notified, which is that the people are present at its making in the form of their representatives. Just as earlier, it was suggested that the law could be naturally extended by treating one thing as if it was something else, a church as if it were a person for example, so here it seems also that we can usefully extend the idea of presence by use of the notion of a representative; the idea of a representative is that he acts as if he were the person he represents (that is, on behalf of him, and in his interests). Yet whatever may be the usefulness of such extensions in the application of the law, as discussed above, it is clear that it is of little use in justification of the operation of the law as a whole. It is too easy to meet a necessary condition by just supposing that it holds, or treating something else as if it met it. As Bentham puts it, discussing this case of notoriety, 'it is a right claimed by our Author [that is, Blackstone], in common with his fellow dealers in fiction, when they speak of a matter of fact as being necessary to any purpose . . . to suppose it to exist, although it does not, nay even though they own it does not' (COMM 45). Even if a straightforward fiction might be of use in the application of the law it obviously gets nowhere in an attempt to justify why the law is notorious; a justification needs true premises as well as a valid inferential structure. A similar fiction is involved in why the common (non-statute) law was supposed to be known; as Bentham puts it in an alternative draft of this section, people 'are supposed to know the Common Law: it is their own Custom: they make it of themselves. Such is the gibberish with which lawyers blush not to insult the public' (COMM 320). That is, it was supposed that what the judges decided really was knowable before they did so, since they were just finding the law, not making it, and what they were finding was (either established by statute or) common custom. This was all, at least in Bentham's eyes, clearly fictional; judges did not find but made the law, leading to all the problems of retrospective legislation just pointed out. Since the justification, or supposed justification, rests on a fiction, it is again no justification at all. So if notoriety is indeed a desirable property of a law, as Bentham is certain that it is, then the whole battery of devices of codification and promulgation in ordinary language, which he was concerned to promote throughout his life, are required. It cannot be thought, as he continually taunts Blackstone for thinking, that 'everything is as it should be'. Criticism of the justifications of the way that the law operated led to criticism of the operations themselves, and so to proposals for change.

Some of these proposals follow immediately after the last quoted passage. Bentham goes on to claim that for the law to be known 'it must be digested by authority: the Common Law must be digested into Statute. The fictitious must be substantiated into real' (COMM 320). Here we have the appearance of a third kind of fiction, a fiction which arises as a result of Bentham's metaphysical analysis. This also will be used in criticism of the explanation and justification of what goes on in the law. It will also be used to devalue common law by comparison with statute law on quite different grounds to those discussed above. For, as he has just put it, the common law is fictitious; and it is natural to presume that the fictitious is inferior to the real. 'What is the *common law?*' Bentham asks elsewhere in the *Comment*, and replies 'as assemblage of fictitious regulations feigned after the images of these real ones which compose the Statute Law' (COMM 120). The reason why common law is fictional follows directly from his metaphysical analysis of the nature of law. Although this analysis has only been published in full in this century in *Of Laws in General*, the relevant points squeeze themselves into a long footnote in the *Fragment*. A law is a command, an expression of will; since the expression of will in common law is only tacit, it is a 'fictitious command' (FG 429n-430n). Here there is no question of literally false statements made with a special purpose, or of concepts being extended so that one thing is treated as if it was something else; here we have something which seems to be quite literally and straightforwardly what it claims to be, law. Yet once the metaphysical analysis gets to work, it appears that it is not really what it seems; it is really something else being treated as if it were law; it is quasi-law (OLG 194). The mask is lifted from the face of common law by clarification and enlightenment. The only trouble with this, if it is meant to have polemical or evaluative purpose and not just be a piece of mere analysis, as clearly it is in the case of common law, is that the terms which Bentham uses himself in the analyses of which he approves, and which he leaves as his monument to posterity, are terms which he explicitly declares to be fictional. Thus the great project of classification of the law on natural principles in the *Introduction* uses such explicitly declared fictional terms as 'relation' (IPML 235), 'condition' (193), 'reputation' (193), 'right' (206; these references are all to where the much used term is declared to be fictitious). Or the great project of the analysis of the law in *Of Laws in General* uses 'property' (42), 'reputation' (202), 'power' (251), 'right' (251), 'possession' (275) and 'condition' (286), all again explicitly noted to be fictitious. So if something being held to be fictional after analysis means that it is in some way improper or devalued, then Bentham's most important or central analyses are improper or devalued. On the other hand, if discovering something to be fictional on analysis is a mere descriptive device, without any condemnatory overtones, common law can wear its fictional status as happily as statute law its real one, and common lawyers continue in their work as happily as Members of Parliament.

Leaving for the next chapter further consideration of the problems arising from fictions only discovered to be so after metaphysical analysis, let us return to the original contract, which can be seen to be fictional in some way without the aid of a metaphysical ghost in the cellarage. The question is whether it is as unsuccessful as a device of justification as Blackstone's claim that the people as a whole are present at the making of statute law, and so know it. If it is supposed to refer to an historical event, then it clearly is similarly unsuccessful. The general idea is to apply a form of justification recognised elsewhere to the relation between individuals and the state (or government); either the legal justification for obligation provided by contract, or the moral justification for obligation provided by making promises. Just as in the case of notoriety, however valid the form of justification, it is not going to provide the justification required if it depends upon the assumption of false premises. Yet if the existence of a contract or promise is taken to be an historical event, a matter of fact about an actual agreement between actual people which was made at one particular time, then, since in most cases of government there has been no such event, any supposition that there is is merely fictional or fabulous; and justification rests on a false premise. If, however, we look back from Bentham to Blackstone, we see that he is quite explicit in saying that he can't believe that individuals entered into an original contract (*Comm* I 47). To this extent it was misleading to say that Blackstone just took his justification off the peg from Locke — he tore off the odd bit he didn't want — and misleading of Bentham in his retrospective Preface of fifty years later to say that it was an obvious fable. The question is, given that Blackstone vacillates here as elsewhere, whether something can be made of the original contract without presupposing that it makes any historical claims; and here it is clearly relevant that a purely hypothetical contract has been taken to be a legitimate device of justification by such a leading recent thinker as John Rawls. The question can be put, picking up the earlier discussion of legal fictions, whether the form of a contract can be looked at as a model of justification, so that something which is not a contract can usefully be looked at as if it were; or whether, as seemed clear in the case of notoriety, once justification of the law is involved rather than its applications, treating one thing as if it were something else can provide no form of justification at all. This question, in turn, can be expressed as whether the fiction can enter at the level of the form of justification or only at the level of the premises; given that we get nowhere in justification by taking false premises and treating them as if they were true, perhaps it might be possible to start with true premises and extend already existing forms of justification, treating clearly different kinds of cases as if they were of the same kind.

Such is what seems to happen in those contract type of justification for the state's authority which depend upon a notion of tacit consent. Here some agreed fact, such as receipt of benefits from the state, or failure to move from its territories, or voting in its elections, is taken to reveal a tacit consent to the activities of the state; and so justifies the state treating the individual as if there had been an explicit agreement between them. Just as in the examples of legal fictions, that is, it is supposed that the one kind of case can be usefully considered as if it were a case of the other; so either a contract can be implied, or else it can be proceeded with as if there were a contract (as in the law of quasi-contract or restitution). Such would be a natural response, certainly of an eighteenth-century lawyer, who was perhaps readier to imply contracts than his modern equivalent. Here the claim would be that the fiction of considering it as a contract even though there was no explicit agreement still provided justification in that the reason for considering it sufficiently like a real case of contract to treat it in this way was that it contained some feature (such as receipt of benefit, raising of expectations, reliance) which occurred in real cases of contract. If this really works as a justification, however, then the individual's obligation to the state is justified because of this feature which it is agreed is literally present. The fiction is now doing no work at all. Citing of contracts is merely at best pointing out a particular example in which the feature provides justification. It is, at best, to point to an analogous, or comparable case. Nothing is gained by implying a contract; or thinking of this case as being treated as if it were a contract. Here, as Bentham said of the legal fiction case, the fiction is either avoidable or wicked. Furthermore, just being quite like a case which is justified does not make something justified, or even make it nearly justified; affirming the consequent in logic is quite like *modus ponens*, but this does not make it anything other than quite unjustified. So, to return to the particular examples, either receipt of benefits from the state by itself directly justifies obligation to the state without mention of contract; or else the fact that this is also a feature of contracts ('consideration') is just a mere similarity, in itself without any justificatory power.

Another way that the concept of a contract can be used in justification without it being supposed that there was an explicit agreement is by making the claim that the situation was actually such that it would be possible to make such an agreement; or that such an agreement would be justified, or that it would be made if only things were different in certain specified aspects. If it is supposed that individuals act in their own self-interest, then to say that the situation is such that a certain contract could be made is a way of saying that it is in the self-interest of all the individuals concerned. If, were they asked about it, all individuals would voluntarily agree to have a state, or to have the kind of state that we actually have, provides pretty good grounds for thinking that a state, or the state we have, is in everyone's interests. If, furthermore, something which satisfies self-interest is good, then this would justify having a state, or having the state we have. Once we assume that people are justified in getting what they want, then showing that they would freely contract to get something is a way of showing that that thing is justified. By showing that they would freely contract to obey the state, we show that the state is justified, even though there is no actual contract. Of course, various changes need to be made before it is the case that everyone would so contract, such as the supposition used by John Rawls that everyone is ignorant of the exact nature of his self-interest, but only acts to defend his self-interest, whatever it might be. These further fictions need not concern us, since the central point is again that the contract, the hypothetical, fictional contract, is eliminable from the justification. It is merely an expository device; a way of showing that something is in everyone's interests, or would be if certain changes were made. It is this which provides the justification, and the reference to contract can be dropped as irrelevant. Again it is the case that either the fiction is unnecessary or else it is wicked; either all the justification is carried by self-interest, or else the contract is brought in in a vain attempt to provide support for something unjustified (such as, in Rawls, that people are bound by the agreements they would make when ignorant even when they are not ignorant; self-interest could never justify this, and it needs an appeal to the morality of keeping promises, but now it becomes important that there are no actual promises, only hypothetical ones).

Part of what Blackstone actually says is that 'though society had not its formal beginning from any convention of individuals, actuated by their wants and fears; yet it is their sense of weakness and imperfection that *keeps* mankind together, that demonstrates the necessity of this union; and that therefore is the solid and natural foundation, as well as the cement, of society. And this is what we mean by the original contract of society' (*Comm* I 47).

It is unnecessary to subject this long remark to even longer Benthamite dissection; all that needs to be done here is to consider whether this apparently purely descriptive remark could be used to provide some kind of justification for an individual obeying the state or (as Blackstone puts it) for the parts obeying the whole. As the basis of a justification, it seems to be of the same kind as the one just discussed. Even though there was not an historical contract, the same basis actually exists in society which could have led to such a contract, namely the wants and fears, the sense of imperfection and weakness, of individuals. Given, again, that it is a good thing that individuals have their wants satisfied and their fears allayed, then the justification of the parts obeying the whole is that it is a means to this good end. Again, however, the reference to a contract is merely analogical and dispensable. The justification is by means of the satisfaction of the desires of individuals. It is, therefore, a utilitarian kind of justification and, as such, much closer to Bentham's own than might be immediately apparent.

In the tradition of the original contract, it was normally supposed that there were two contracts, one between the individuals with each other in order to set up a political society with some kind of sovereign, and one between the sovereign so set up and the individuals composing it. The former justified the existence of political society, or a state; the latter justified obedience to a particular sovereign and delineated its extent. The former is of the kind just discussed in relation to Blackstone, the latter is of the kind discussed in relation to the various notions of tacit consent. Bentham concentrates most of his energy on the latter kind. He notes in an autobiographical footnote in the *Fragment*, which forms a sort of forerunner to the new Preface of fifty years later, that he was familiar with it from conversing with lawyers who were 'full of the virtues of their Original Contract, as a recipe of sovereign efficacy for reconciling the accidental necessity of resistance with the general duty of submission' (FG 440n). We are back here with the Revolution settlement: James II had broken his contract with the people, George III had not. The lawyers unwisely confessed that the whole thing was a fiction and Bentham (who had earlier noted in the *Comment* that 'lawyers feed upon untruth, as the Turks do upon opium' (59)) found, as was to be expected, that his 'unpractised stomach revolted against their opiate' (FG 440n). Bentham's criticism of Blackstone on the original contract, part of the result of that revolt, is too detailed and extensive to be discussed properly here; the overall point, however, which emerges from the several detailed criticisms, is that utility provides a superior justification to contract. Thus, for example, when concerned with justification of resistance by deciding that the king has broken his contract with the people, Bentham comments that, since the king's part of the contract was to promote the happiness of his people, calculation of the utility of having a particular king was involved even for those who wished to use contract as a basis of justification. Once this calculation was made, it provided a much more direct justification, and the contract was not needed; subjects should obey kings 'so long as the probable mischiefs of obedience are less than the probable mischiefs of resistance' (FG 444). The justification can rest upon utility alone; and again the fiction, the contract, is redundant.

Quite apart from any fictions or fallacies involved in employing justification by contract to this particular area, Bentham also considers in this part of the *Fragment* what the justification is for thinking that contracts provide the basis of an obligation in any area. As long as we are concerned with contracts in a legal sense, then Bentham's mature answer to this question is that it is only from 'government that contracts derive their binding force' and hence 'contracts came from government, not government from contracts' (ANARCH, Parekh 271). It is, however, also possible to regard the obligation of a contract as the obligation of a promise (in the *Fragment* he defines a contract as 'a pair of promises, by two persons reciprocally given, the one promise in consideration of the other' (442n)). The question then becomes, as Bentham puts it in the *Fragment*, 'for what *reason* is it, that men *ought* to keep their promises?' (444). His answer is that the only 'intelligible reason' is that 'it is for the *advantage* of society they should keep them'; that is, the obligation to keep one's promises is justified by advantage or utility, and so, again, there is no independent justification given besides utility. Bentham had noted just before that although men universally assent to the proposition that promises ought to be kept, they cannot say why; and if they made a show of proving them 'for form's sake' would use such phrases as '*Justice, Right Reason* required it, the *Law* of *Nature* commanded it, and so forth' (442). The question is why utility provides any better justification than these, or than just starting with the supposition that it is right to keep promises, particularly if, as Bentham says, this is something which everyone believes. The final answer to this question must wait until the utility principle and its justification are examined later on in the present work. Part of it depends upon explaining Bentham's attack on natural law. Since

Blackstone used and accepted the claims of natural law in the pages immediately before his consideration of original contract, Bentham also considers and criticises natural law at length in the *Comment*. He gives this consideration a retrospective glance in the *Fragment*, noting that the law of nature is 'nothing but a phrase' (FG 483). His attitude can be gleaned from the footnote in which he says that 'before Montesquieu all was unmixed barbarism' in jurisprudence, and compares such leading natural lawyers as 'Grotius and Puffendorf were to Censorial Jurisprudence what the Schoolmen were to Natural Philosophy' (FG 403n). The leading idea, that is, is that they all belong before the enlightened period on which the subject could be put on the sure path of a science. The explanation of it is again that process of enlightenment or complete analysis which, just as it could turn common law into a fiction, could reduce natural law into a mere phrase. It is a 'phantom', a 'formidable non-entity', 'sounds without a meaning' (COMM 17 20; 14). It is another of those fictions which classified above as being of the third kind; and to which we shall shortly turn as an essential part of the examination which leads eventually to the justification of the utility principle.

Just before we start this investigation, however, there is one further puzzle about justification in Bentham which needs to be noticed, and ought at some stage to be explained. In Bowring's edition of the *Fragment* he notes that Bentham inscribed his own copy of the work with the words 'This was the very first publication by which men at large were invited to break loose from the trammels of authority and ancestor-wisdom on the field of law' (I 260). This remark fits in well with Bentham's over-riding concern to criticise the accumulated rubbish of the historically minded common law tradition and subject it to the independent criticism of reason. The puzzle is why, in that case, he did not embrace and use the device of natural law, or 'right reason', as an ally rather than something else which was also to be attacked. The much more common justification of the replacement of James II by William III, both at the time and subsequently, was because of what James was taken to have done to the historically established rights and privileges of the people, as listed, for example, in the 1689 Bill of Rights. The criticism came from the historical tradition, not from the independent standpoint of right reason. Locke was here a conspicuous exception, trying to justify such a revolution from first principles, by use of the original contract. The question then is, why Bentham turned upon this form of justification as found in Locke and as used in some of his legal followers; or, to put it the other way round, how utility, the use of natural reason, can end up as anything other than another part of natural law. If we think of the resources of justification open to someone as being either history or reason, established authority or the natural light, then Bentham seems to attack both the available options. This reinforces the puzzle of what the basis of his own work can be; a puzzle which must be solved sometime in this work.

In this chapter an attempt has been made to illustrate how Bentham found law, both in its practice and justification, enfeebled by the pestilential breath of fiction; and how, although these fictions made it seem to him ripe for criticism and change, they also enfeebled the process of criticism, being an opiate to reason, and made the lawyers unduly self-satisfied with their supposedly perfect law and constitution, so that they developed what Bentham identified in Blackstone as 'the hydrophobia of innovation' (COMM 202). Given his interests in clarity, truth, and certainty, themselves supposedly justified by the utility principle, Bentham was naturally led into criticism of these fictions. Such criticism, however, and in particular the absolute nature of the interest in clarification and complete understanding which fuelled it, led Bentham into considering as fictitious many things which, on the face of it, did not seem to be fictitious at all. It is this thoroughgoing analysis, this deeper criticism, to which we must now turn.

Notes

(a) Maine's critical remark on Bentham forms part of Chapter II of *Ancient Law*, a chapter in which Maine identified the development of law as passing through the three stages of fiction, equity, and legislation. Bentham may have been more open to this idea than Maine suggests since several of his remarks allow for historical development with the possibility that fictions once had a role, e.g. 'with respect to this, and other fictions, there was once a time, perhaps, when they had their use' (FG 441). This picks up the spirit of UC 27.88, a relatively early manuscript. Bentham's main point, as he goes on to say, is that 'the season of *Fiction* is now over' (FG 441).

(b) Bentham held that common law was really *ex post facto* legislation in numerous places, for example COMM 50n; OLG 187n; *Judicial Establishment* (IV 315); RJE iv 209; RJE v 409. Bentham thought that in common law 'security for whatsoever is most dear to man' is 'an empty name' (*Justice petition*, V 538).

(c) 'Préjugés' is a common heading for early manuscript, for example UC 97.4; UC 97.15; UC 97.35; UC 70A.33.

(d) Bentham himself was aware of, and distinguished the two kinds of original contract, associating one with Locke and one with Rousseau, UC 100.105. Dumont condensed this material for part of Chapter 13 of the first part of the *Traités*.

(e) John Rawls's use of a hypothetical original contract, briefly discussed in the text, can be found in Rawls (1971).

III

The Clew to the Labyrinth

Bentham's main concern in the 1770s, from which the criticism of Blackstone in the *Fragment* and *Comment* was a relative digression, was to write a work of critical jurisprudence, explaining and justifying the correct principles of legislation, together with the production of a fully rational and justified criminal code. As well as the raw material, he sketched several projected prefaces for the work throughout the decade. In one written near the end he compares what he saw when he started on his study of the law with what he had been led to expect. He had been taught to believe that the law was 'as near to perfection as any thing can be that is human'; instead he 'saw crimes of the most pernicious nature pass unheeded by the law', delay, confusion, expense, 'light shut out from every question by fantastic and ill consider'd rules of evidence', 'the various rights and duties of the various classes of mankind jumbled together into one immense and unsorted heap: men ruined for not knowing what they are neither enabled nor permitted to learn: and the whole fabric of jurisprudence a labyrinth without a clew' (UC 27.172). The only way that he saw to 'cleanse the Augean stable' was 'to pour in a body of severe and steady criticism and to spread it over the whole extent of the subject in one comprehensive unbroken tide'. Some of this criticism, that of fictions in the operation of the law and in its justification, has been examined in the last chapter; and Bentham had provided, in the Preface to the *Fragment*, an earlier justification of criticism, declaring that the motto of a good citizen was 'To obey punctually; to censure freely' (399). However, anyone who succeeded in finally plucking the mask of mystery from the face of jurisprudence, in finding the thread that led to the centre of its labyrinth, needed to do more than criticise these obvious

47

legal fictions. Something was needed which would clarify the whole area, which would show both what law really was, and also how it really ought to be. It is the concern of this chapter to describe and evaluate the metaphysics which Bentham himself developed for this task; the metaphysics which served as his own 'clew' to thread the labyrinth in which he found himself when starting his own study of the law.

Part of Bentham's projected capital work was printed in 1780, and published with a new preface as *An Introduction to the Principles of Morals and Legislation* in 1789. The metaphysics Bentham uses during this period can be reconstructed from this work and the *Fragment*, and from contemporary manuscripts, particularly those now published as the *Comment* and *Of Laws in General*. This work provides examples of its use, and very brief outline accounts; there is also a fuller outline in the unpublished draft of an account Bentham sent to d'Alembert in 1778. Some thirty years later Bentham returned to this area and wrote in the 1810s his fullest explicit accounts, in a series of manuscripts edited by Southwood Smith and incorporated in volume VIII of the Bowring edition, *Ontology, Logic, Language,* although a little came out at the time in *Chrestomathia.* There is also later material in the manuscripts edited in volume III of the Bowring edition and entitled *Pannomial Fragments* and *Nomography.* This all presents a confusing picture. There are many presentations of the same, or similar, points, not all obviously consistent with one another. Nor can this be explained by postulating a process of development, for the later material is as difficult to render consistent with itself as is the earlier material. None of the work is finished in quite the way that one would like; either it is a fragmentary intrusion in something which is basically about something else, or else it is manuscript draft unrevised by its author. In all, Bentham's metaphysical work provides a labyrinth of its own. It is highly important, both in itself and also in understanding of his thought as a whole. Yet the face it reveals is baffling and confusing. So in this chapter an attempt will be made to thread this labyrinth as well; that is, to provide a 'clew' to what was meant to provide a 'clew' to the mysteries of jurisprudence.

The central point of this metaphysical work is to describe and provide the materials for Bentham's project of criticism by clarification. Bentham wants to show how things really are, and how they are falsely or misleadingly described by others. So what he needs is an account of what it is to clarify something; how it is that understanding is achieved about something; how it is discovered what something really is. Although such a concern might make him feel that he was the first voyager into a 'trackless waste' in the specific area of the law, such a concern was a natural part of a more general tradition of thought, a tradition to which Bentham explicitly thought of himself as belonging. He did not think of himself as without predecessors, and the specific person he most frequently settles on is Locke. For example, he writes in the early 1770s: 'a digest of the Laws is a work that could not have been executed with advantage before Locke and Helvetius had written: the first establishing a test of perspicuity for ideas; the latter establishing a standard of rectitude for actions' or, as he sums it up a bit later, 'from Locke [the law] must receive the ruling principles of its form — from Helvetius of its matter' (X 70; 71). Helvetius is an obvious exemplar of the proper content or matter: he reveals the relation of law to human happiness or welfare, and promotes the utility principle as a test of rectitude. It is Locke, however, whom Bentham takes as providing the principles by which it is to be made clear; by which it can be comprehensibly, and so properly, formed. Locke provides tests for perspicuity. Bentham says several times that he derived the central idea of his theory of fictions, the chief plank in his metaphysical enterprise, from d'Alembert's *Mélanges* (e.g. *Nomography*, III 286). In it he would have found that d'Alembert also singles out Locke for special attention, calling him the creator of metaphysics and describing him as finding in 'abstractions and abuse of signs the principal cause of our errors' (*Mélanges*, i 141). Study of signs, of words, will prevent error: Locke has shown us how to clarify our ideas.

Before Locke, Descartes also had an explicit interest in the clarification of ideas. Rule III of his *Regulae* reads that 'our enquiries should be directed, not to what others have thought, nor to what we ourselves conjecture, but to what we can clearly and perspicuously behold and with certainty deduce; for knowledge is not won in any other way' (H & R I, 5). Much of this is similar to Bentham (and the whole later tradition): the protestant refusal to appeal to an external authority based on the belief that there is a natural light, or internal standard, that allows us each individually to be placed directly in touch with the truth; the way that this natural standard is thought of in a perceptual way with use of perceptual metaphors, so that Descartes talks of 'clarity', the 'light of reason', intuition, an 'unclouded' mind, and so on; and, of course, clarity as the desired goal of enquiry. It is no doubt originally because of Descartes that Bentham talks of 'clear, distinct, determinate' ideas (COMM 5), or of 'clear and determinate ideas' (*Logic*, VIII 221). However, in Descartes a clear and distinct idea was often a proposition rather than a concept; this explains why he thinks he can establish 'as a general rule that all things which we conceive very clearly and very distinctly are true' (H & R I, 158, altered). It also explains the project of winning knowledge as given in the first quotation; for if what we clearly and perspicuously behold are those truths of which we have intuitive knowledge, then these can form a foundation from which other truths may be deduced. Clarity here leads directly to truth. In Locke, however, although he did take over from Descartes this idea of foundations, and the related distinction between intuitive and demonstrative truth, the concern is much more with concepts than with propositions. Clarity shows us what it is that we are really thinking about when we are thinking; it provides us with understanding; it shows us the meaning of our ideas. Without pre-empting any position on the relation between concept and proposition, meaning and truth, sense and reference, this is at least *prima facie* a different concern from that of Descartes; for it is at least *prima facie* possible to understand a concept without knowing whether propositions formed by means of it are true or false, that is, to have Locke's clear understanding of a concept or idea without having Descartes' intuitive knowledge. Here clarity does not lead directly to truth. And, as far as this distinction means anything, Bentham is right to single out Locke rather than Descartes, for his starting position is much more like Locke's.

The crucial central idea which Locke propagated was the distinction between simple and complex ideas. Simple ideas arise in us as the passive recipients of impressions either of sensation or reflection; in particular sensory perception. They can therefore be explained in causal terms, in terms of their origins in perception. These simple ideas then form the basic building blocks which can be assembled by the active powers of the mind in order to form all our other ideas, the complex ones. Sometimes the mind forms them after the pattern of what really exists, sometimes not. In all cases, however, they can be explained in terms of the simple ideas of which they are composed. Thus Locke says that

> we shall find, if we warily observe the Originals of our Notions, that even the *most abstruse* Ideas, however remote soever they may seem from Sense, or from any operations of our own Minds, are yet only such, as the Understanding frames to it self, by repeating and joining together *Ideas*, that it had either from Objects of Sense, or from its own operations about them. (*Essay*, 2.12.8)

50

Hence arises the possibility of clarification, or explication, of the nature of our concepts or notions by tracing them back to, or analysing them in terms of ideas derived from perception or the simple operations of the mind (which Locke calls simple ideas of reflection); the project of clarification is now the project of analysis. So, for example, Locke says, while discussing a particular case: 'I think I need not go any further in the Analysis of that complex *Idea*, we call a *Lye*: what I have said is enough to show, that it is made up of simple *Ideas*' (*Essay*, 2.22.9). The exact details of Locke's account (or varying accounts) do not matter; what does matter is the general idea which he bequeathed to the eighteenth century and which became the automatic, unthinking, assumption of the people Bentham read in both France and England: the idea that ideas are clarified by being decomposed into their elementary parts, which in turn can be explained in terms of their origin, principally in sense perception. So, to take as an example an English work which Bentham read, Hume's *Treatise*, we find Hume not only making the distinction between simple and complex ideas on the second page but saying such things as "Tis impossible to reason justly, without understanding perfectly the idea concerning which we reason: and 'tis impossible perfectly to understand any idea, without tracing it up to its origin, and examining that primary impression, from which it arises' (1.3.2).

This is the context from which Bentham starts and which he, to some extent, presupposes in his own writing. He continues with the idea of explanation by relation to sense perception, the desire to make the abstract concrete, and the belief in analysis. It means, for example, that he can talk quite naturally of something being 'the only way to analyse the expression and clear up the ideas that belong to it' (OLG 283n), or note in the Preface to the *Introduction* that 'in addition to the analysis it contains of the extensive ideas signified by the terms *pleasure, pain, motive,* and *disposition*, it ought to have given a similar analysis' of the ideas annexed to other specified terms (IPML 3). It means, for example, that he can make the following claim:

If it be true that our ideas are derived all of them from our senses and that the only way of rendering any of our ideas clear and determinate is to trace it up to the sensible objects in which it originates, the only method that can be taken for explaining them to the purpose is the method I have just been taking here. (OLG 294)

The conclusion of this remark, and the context, shows that it is not really hypothetical in intention: it is a positive endorsement of the Lockean programme. Slightly before he wrote this manuscript, in the draft account of his work which he wrote for d'Alembert, Bentham explained that his method of attacking the science of jurisprudence was to take the fundamental, abstract, words of the science and relate them by long chains of definitions with simple ideas or known assemblies of simple ideas, commenting that the method of working had come from Locke (UC 169.52). Before this again, he projected writing 'a vocabulary of terms of universal jurisprudence with their definitions: the definitions disposed in uninterrupted chain, [?consisting] of words importing simple ideas' (UC 169.1). Holding as he did that 'a sober and accurate apprehension of the import of these fundamental words is the true key to Jurisprudence' (UC 69.62), Bentham clearly felt that this key could be provided by relating these fundamental words to simple ideas.

The remarks just quoted display in Bentham an interest in definition which is not present in Locke (or present in the same way), in spite of Bentham's frequent invocations of Locke in this context. He starts the *Comment* with an account of definition, explaining how definition by *genus* and *differentia* can make an idea determinate for someone, providing that he is already 'acquainted' with (examples of) the *genus* and *differentia* (3-5). This is the first shot in the long campaign against Blackstone; a campaign in which, as we have seen, Bentham sometimes gets more excited and metaphorical than in this cool start. Here, for example, he is again, against Blackstone: 'To purge the science of the poison introduced into it by him and those who write as he does, I know but of one remedy; and that is by *Definition*, perpetual and regular definition, the grand prescription of those great physicians of the mind, Helvetius and before him Locke' (COMM 346); 'Nothing', he continues a bit later, 'has been, nothing will be, nothing even can be done on the subject of law that deserves the name of Science, till that universal precept of Locke, enforced, exemplified and particularly applied to the moral branch of science by Helvetius, be steadily pursued, "Define your words"' (347). Bentham not only repeated these precepts, he also practised them and composed the elements of such a dictionary of fundamental terms; as he says, he had 'dug deep into the mine of Definition ... without which no materials can be obtained, fit to form the foundation of a science' (UC 27.2). These remarks are all from early, or the earliest, work of Bentham. At the time at which he started on his project of critical jurisprudence, he obviously thought that all that he had to do was to take an instrument already forged by Locke and apply it to this new area, being preceded in the general idea of its application to the moral sciences by Helvetius. As he says, just after the last quoted remark, 'the merit of invention belongs to others' (UC 27.3). This, however, was not how it was to turn out. Bentham found that the Lockean instrument was insufficient for his purposes, and that he had, after all, to innovate. He therefore forged a wholly new instrument to supplement the one which he had inherited.

This new instrument Bentham called the method of paraphrasis. It is best seen as a supplement to the old Lockean project of definition; indeed as an application of the central Lockean principles in a new, wider, manner. The relation between paraphrasis and definition can be seen from the contexts in which Bentham introduces his exposition of the idea. The first is in a long footnote to the *Fragment on Government* (495n). This footnote contains several references to Locke and just before the introduction of paraphrasis, Bentham says that 'to *define* or rather (to speak more generally) to *expound* a word, is to resolve, or to make a progress towards resolving, the idea belonging to it into simple ones' (495n). This sounds appropriately Lockean, but the move from definition to exposition reveals that Bentham now regards both definition and paraphrasis as subdivisions of the more general activity of exposition. This structure is repeated forty years later in the fuller account he gives in the *Logic*. Here his account of paraphrasis forms part of a larger block of material entitled 'Clearness in discourse, how to produce it; and hence of exposition' (VIII 242, repunctuated). Before he deals with paraphrasis he again treats of definition; and he still claims in this late work that 'a great light would be thrown' on the moral sciences (which the hardening arteries of his own processes of exposition have now led him into calling 'pneumatological branches of science') by exactness in definition (VIII 246n). There are changes of emphasis; but the continuity of structure reveals how definition and paraphrasis belong together in Bentham's mind.

This later exposition of exposition contains no mention of 'simple ideas'. In fact, the use of this term is relatively unimportant even in the early work. What is important, early and late, is the basic idea that the import of a term can be explained or clarified by tracing its relation to sensible objects; and this idea is also as important for paraphrasis as it is for definition. In fact the Lockean sounding hypothetical quotation from *Of Laws in General* given above, in which Bentham talked of tracing an idea 'up to the sensible objects in which it originates', is from an account of paraphrasis. On the other hand, Bentham thinks of definition on an Aristotelian model as a process of giving genus and differentia, whether he is discussing it in the early *Comment* or the late *Logic*; and on the face of it this is not very like Locke's analysis of complex ideas into simple ones. What seems to have happened is that Bentham has understood as analysis the process of decomposition of an idea into its parts, has then thought of definition as an example or model of such a process, and proceeded to understand definition in a way with which he was familiar from Aristotelian logic. Yet even on this view of definition, clarification is still given by relating terms to perceptible objects. At the beginning of the *Comment* Bentham had noted that definition would only make an idea determinate for someone already acquainted with examples of the genus, and adds that for us to be acquainted with something 'it must in the first place exist' (COMM 5). If we then assume that the existent is that which can be placed in some sort of relation to perception, then any definition which will serve to clarify will place the object defined in some sort of relation to a perceptible object. It is this relation which is central. Bentham can talk in the earlier work of 'simple ideas', but what he is picking out by this phrase is ideas closely related to perceptible objects which can then be used to explain other ideas; the term does not carry for him any further theoretical weight.

One reason that 'simple ideas' are less important for Bentham than for Locke is that Bentham was relatively unworried about any of the traditional problems of perception, which caused such trouble for Berkeley, Hume, Locke himself, and such related philosophers this century as Russell, Moore, or Ayer. He was quite happy to use the term 'metaphysics', but metaphysics was, for Bentham, 'to explain or to inquire what it is a man means' (RJE iii 386) or 'to know and to be able to make others know what it is we mean' (UC 69.155). Such traditional metaphysical problems as the relation between our sensory perceptions and their supposed physical causes was, by contrast, exactly the kind of question which he thought could be summarily dismissed as being of no practical importance. Thus, in one of the early drafts of his projected major work, he starts with a chapter on 'what things exist'; a basic metaphysical topic which one might think was a natural starting point. Bentham, however, starts off at much greater speed than Descartes or Locke. He immediately supposes that he himself, his pen, and indeed the whole material world exist since 'no bad consequences can possibly arise from supposing it to be true and the worst consequence can not but arise from supposing it to be false' (UC 69.52). A little tincture of utility dissolves these fundamental problems; and this means that Bentham has no problem in thinking of perception in terms of our awareness of the physical world. Hence an analysis which clarifies by relation to the perceptible has done its work, in the way he treats it, once relation to material objects has been established. Hence it is unimportant for him to think of the ideas of these material objects as being some kind of collection or combination of simple ideas, as Locke or Berkeley do. Hence simple ideas themselves, understood in Locke's way as an individual colour or taste, are less important for Bentham.

This is not to say that he was unaware of Locke's use of the term. He knows that a corporeal substance is different from a simple idea; hence his reference in the letter to d'Alembert to both simple ideas and known assemblages of simple ideas. He does not ignore mental states; indeed it is crucial to his whole philosophy that 'the idea belonging to the word *pain* is a simple one' (FG 495n). It is just that the centre of his interest, the place where he felt that the crucial problems of analysis lay, was more towards the abstract end than his predecessors. Whereas Locke might worry about the analysis of a substance in terms of ideas, Bentham was quite happy once he had managed to reach substances. His worry, as he puts it in this same footnote to the *Fragment*, the one in which paraphrasis is introduced, is with what Locke called mixed modes. Locke divided his complex ideas into several kinds, substances, modes, and relations; and divided modes into simple modes and mixed modes (although he calls them mixed, he might as well have called them complex, since 'they are compounded of simple Ideas of several kinds' (*Essay*, 2.12.5)). Locke gives as an example of a mixed mode *obligation*, exactly the kind of term which Bentham was particularly concerned to analyse in his critical jurisprudence (*Essay*, 2.22.1). His project is just as in Locke, the production of an analysis which contains words which are '*simple*, or are more immediately resolvable into simple ones. . . . Such as those expressive of *substances* and *simple modes*, in respect of such *abstract* terms as are expressive of what LOCKE has called *mixed modes*' (FG 495n). Bentham's centre of attention here is clearly with the reduction of the mixed modes. Once he has reached substances or simple modes, even though these are still complex ideas, Bentham will be satisfied. Again he is aware of the distinction, here marked by his reference both to simple ideas and things immediately resolvable into simple ideas; but again this distinction is relatively unimportant for him.

Locke distinguishes mixed modes from substances as being 'not looked upon to be the characteristical Marks of any real Beings that have a steady existence, but scattered and independent *Ideas*, put together by the Mind' (*Essay*, 2.12.1), and the feature which leads Bentham to distinguish between mixed modes (or such things as obligation) on the one side and such things as substances and simple ideas on the other is that terms referring to the latter refer to real entities whereas terms referring to the former do not. He divides entities into those that are real and those that are fictitious. Fictitious entities, the most striking exhibits in Bentham's ontological zoo, will be discussed later. As regards real entities, he thinks they are 'either *perceptible* or *inferential*: perceptible, either *impressions* or *ideas*: inferential, either *material*, i.e. *corporeal* or *immaterial*, i.e. *spiritual*' (*Chrest.*, VIII 126n). We can notice here not only the Humean language but that, like Hume or Locke before him, what we now think of as mental states are regarded as individual objects, or entities. There is a distinction between these perceptible entities and 'inferential' ones; but what is much more important is that they are both real entities. So the project of analysis in a Lockean spirit now becomes the project of analysing all that language whose terms do not refer to real entities into language whose terms do refer to real entities.

We now have enough material to attempt an explanation of Bentham's new instrument of paraphrasis, starting with an explanation of why Bentham so often introduced it in the context of definition and, more specifically, as needed when definition was not possible. For if definition only clarifies if it relates to the really existent, to something with which someone is acquainted, then it is not possible to produce this kind of clarification by definition when we have terms which do not refer to the really existent. Definition by genus and differentia only works if someone understands the genus. Of course, such understanding might be provided by another definition; but eventually another method must be used because we shall come to terms having no superior genus. As long as we are acquainted with examples, we can have understanding of this genus, and this will be the method. If, however, we are not dealing with real entities, then we cannot be acquainted with examples; hence there is no way of achieving or conveying understanding of the superior genus. Hence another method is needed than that of definition, the method of paraphrasis.

Sometimes, as in the draft account for d'Alembert, Bentham seems to suggest that the possibility of classifying or arranging, and hence of defining, fictional entities is not possible. He describes there Linneus' arrangement and says that there never appears a general term which does not refer to real individuals; and that it would be a revolting absurdity to have words referring to fictional beings in such an arrangement (UC 169.58). However, the normal accounts follow the above composite one. It is not that the project of classifying fictional entities is impossible, it is just that it is not going to be finally satisfactory since some generic terms so used will have no superior genus. Thus, in *Chrestomathia* Bentham says 'of these fictitious entities, many will be found, of which, they being, each of them, a *genus generalissimum,* the names are consequently incapable of receiving what is commonly understood by a *definition,* viz. a definition *per genus et differentiam*' (VIII 129); or in the *Fragment* footnote he remarks that 'the common method of defining — the method *per genus et differentiam,* as logicians call it, will, in many cases, not at all answer the purpose. Among abstract terms we soon come to such as have no *superior genus*' (495n). Both these remarks allow that definition of fictitious entities will sometimes be possible. So, when Bentham starts his fullest exposition of paraphrasis with the remark 'Paraphrasis is that mode of exposition which is the only instructive mode, where the thing expressed being the name of a fictitious entity, has not any superior in the scale of logical sub-alternation' (*Logic,* VIII 246), this should be read, I think, as a conjunction, saying that the thing expressed both is the name of a fictitious entity and has no superior (rather than the second is true because the first is). This conjunction is slightly clearer in the particular example of obligation, which he works out more fully a little later. Here he says that 'it being the name not of a real, but only a fictitious entity, and that fictitious entity not having any superior genus, it is considered as not susceptible of a definition in the ordinary shape, *per genus et differentiam,* but only of an exposition in the way of paraphrasis' (*Logic,* VIII 247). It is not that it is incapable of definition just because it is fictitious but, rather, that it is both fictitious and also incapable of definition. A remark Bentham makes in a note to the *Introduction* should also, I think, be read in the same conjunctive spirit. He remarks that 'the great difficulty lies in the nature of the words; which are not, like pain and pleasure, names of homogeneous real entities, but names of various fictitious entities, for which no common genus is to be found' (53n); here again I think that the difficulty arises from the combination of fiction and lack of common genus, not that the lack of common genus arises just because of the fiction.

So it is not that definition is impossible with fictitious entities, it is just that it can never be finally satisfactory. This emerges clearly enough once we think of clarification being for Bentham, just like Locke, achieved by relation to the real and the perceptible. The problem which paraphrasis is therefore introduced to solve is the problem of providing such a clarification when we are dealing with terms which do not refer to items which are real, that is, either directly perceptible or knowable by inference based on perception. Somehow a similar understanding has to be provided for these terms as can be provided for terms referring to the real by means of definitions which eventually refer to classes with the individuals of which we are acquainted. The way in which Bentham solves this problem is by moving from the level of a single term to the level of a combination of terms. Instead of looking at the individual words associated with individual ideas, he looks at whole phrases, and in particular sentences. The device of paraphrasis consists in explaining a sentence by means of another sentence, and is particularly to be employed when it is impossible to explain a word by means of other words. So the word which is found to be problematical is made up into a sentence which contains it, and then the sentence as a whole is translated into, or replaced by, another sentence which is not problematical. Although, that is, the term or its associated idea cannot be analysed individually, by dissolution into its components, it can feature in a whole sentence, or thought, which can be analysed by being replaced by another sentence, or thought, which is clearer. As Bentham puts it in the *Fragment* footnote, using a phrase considered above, 'a word may be said to be expounded by *paraphrasis*, when not that *word* alone is translated into other *words*, but some whole *sentence* of which it forms a part is translated into another *sentence*; the words of which latter are expressive of such ideas as are *simple*, or are more immediately resolvable into simple ones than those of the former' (495n). More ponderously, he says in the *Logic* that 'by the word paraphrasis may be designated that sort of exposition which may be afforded by transmuting into a proposition, having for its subject some real entity, a proposition which has not for its subject any other than a fictitious entity' (VIII 246).

This was the device that Bentham felt that he needed for his work in critical jurisprudence, the key to what, as he told d'Alembert, would otherwise be a labyrinth from which no one would ever emerge. This is because all the terms he wished to explain, 'power, right, prohibition, duty, obligation, burthen, immunity, exemption, privilege, property, security, liberty', he regarded as being 'so many fictitious entities' (OLG 251). Hence, if not immediately, then eventually they needed explanation by para-phrasis. In these cases, in fact, such explanation was required immediately: there could be classification of rights or of duties, but the general idea of a right or of a duty was a genus with no superior; and once this other kind of explanation was provided, it would then also explain such partial classifications. So, for example, both rights and duties are explained in terms of what someone is, in law, liable to be punished for not doing; and punishment is explained in terms of the pain to which someone is liable for non-performance. Hence, since pain is a simple idea, a really existing entity, an analysis is possible which explains the central, fundamental, terms of jurisprudence, rights and duties, in terms of simple ideas or real entities. The analysis takes place, however, at the level of sentences: it is not that duties are com-posed of pains, but that I am under a duty to do something if the failure to do that thing makes it probable that I shall suffer pain from a particular source. Or, as Bentham puts it in his worked example in the *Logic*, that of obligation, 'an obligation (viz. the obligation of conducting himself in a certain manner,) is incum-bent on a man (i.e. is spoken of as incumbent on a man), in so far as, in the event of his failing to conduct himself in that manner, pain, or loss of pleasure, is considered as about to be experienced by him' (VIII 247). Bentham then explains how this analysis is produced: starting with the word to be expounded, *an obligation*, it is first made up 'into a fictitious proposition', *an obligation is incumbent on a man*. This proposition can then in turn be explained by one about real entities. In a similar way all the fundamental, abstract, terms of the law can be explained. Yet (as he puts it in *Of Laws in General*) 'it is to this abstract way of speaking, these fictitious entities alone that the law owes all its obscurity'; so 'avoid them or explain them by the relation they bear to the real ones and the law is clear' (252). The 'clew' has been found to the labyrinth.

The long build-up to the account of paraphrasis in this chapter, and the Lockean context which is provided for it, were intended to explain the nature of the problem as Bentham saw it, and so show why paraphrasis is needed. Yet, viewed from a Lockean perspective, this might well still seem to be problematic. For the complete Lockean account does not seem to leave any gaps which need to be filled by supplementary devices such as paraphrasis. The particular example, *obligation*, which we have just seen being given his new treatment by Bentham, was, it will be remembered, one which Locke himself specifically mentions as an example of a mixed mode. Yet, as such, it is a complex idea, and so should be capable of being explained by resolution into simple ideas, straight-forwardly and without the use of any new additional fancy devices. After all, the whole point of the division of ideas into simple and complex is that it allows for ideas which (as Locke said may hap-pen with mixed modes) are not the marks of any real beings in the world, and yet which can be analysed by decomposition into elements which are real, or which are marks of real beings in the world. So, given the assumption common to both Bentham and Locke that analysis has ultimately to be into real elements with which we are acquainted, it still remains problematic why para-phrasis is needed once we are dealing with fictional entities; since it seems that these fictional entities could be decomposed into real constituents with which we are acquainted. To take an example of a fictional entity used by another writer whom Bentham read reasonably carefully, the example of a golden mountain as con-sidered by Hume (*Enquiries*, 19), the idea of a golden mountain can be held to be a complex idea created by the imagination out of simple elements which are the direct copies of perceptual experiences. Fiction does not require paraphrasis for its expla-nation in the Lockean tradition; and, if it works for golden moun-tains, it seems that it might also work for obligations.

In addition to his different view of the nature of definition and of the importance of simple ideas, discussed above, there are three additional good reasons why Bentham could not be satisfied with the standard analysis of fictional entities, at least when the entities were such things as rights or obligations. There is firstly the obvious enough point that there is no obvious way in which to decompose a right into parts in the way that a golden mountain can be decomposed into parts. If we transmute this question into the question of what properties a right has, by which, for example, it can be distinguished from a duty, then this returns the question to one of classification, and so to a Benthamite view of definition, in which we eventually reach a superior genus which needs to be explained in another way. This has already been discussed. How-ever, it is important to realise that an additional problem is posed by the fact that Bentham thinks that a right is a quite different kind of fictitious entity than a golden mountain or an imaginary person (which he calls 'fabulous' entities — *Chrestomathia*, VIII 126n). The explanation and justification of this distinction must wait until the next chapter. If, however, it can be assumed for the moment, it means that even when Bentham has declared rights to be fictitious, he does not mean that their reality is 'denied, in any sense in which in ordinary language the reality of it is assumed'; these fictions have 'a sort of *verbal* reality', which distinguishes them from imaginary persons (*Chrest.*, VIII 126n) or golden mountains. So even if a golden mountain can be analysed by the composition of the imagination out of simple constituents, it is not obvious that this kind of analysis would be able to capture the kind of reality which is possessed by a legal right. Bentham wants to show what is the case, for example, when someone has the right to enforce a contract. Even though he does not think that there is really anything there in such a situation, in the sense that no one is able to perceive the right by simply looking, it would also be wrong to think that it was a wholly imaginary construct, such as a fictional character in a story. So taking the right as an imaginary composition out of real elements is not good enough to explain the situation; rather, the situation as a whole, as described in one proposition which explicitly refers to the right, has to be explained by the use of another proposition which describes the situation as a whole but does not refer to the right (such as one saying that someone can initiate a process which is liable to lead to pain for someone else). The proposition which gives the analysis is a true proposition; it describes the reality of the situation. Unless there is movement to the propositional level from the level of single terms, there is no way to bring out this reality. Yet the official, Lockean, account has to conduct its analysis at the level of single terms. Hence it has no way of distinguishing between obligations and golden mountains. Hence paraphrasis is needed as a supplement to the Lockean account. Bentham was aware of the mind's power of building out of simple ideas, but, as he noted in an early manuscript, obviously with Hume in mind, there is a 'difference between such factitious ideas as that of a golden mountain, a chimera; and such as that of a disposition, a power, a quality, etc' (UC 69.52). The latter were exactly the kind of fictitious entities which Bentham thought had a sort of verbal reality.

Quite apart from this reason why Bentham would not have been able to use the official Lockean analysis of such entities as obligations, there is quite another reason, and one which does not depend upon Bentham's metaphysical views about different kinds of entities. This is that Bentham thought that the process of analysis was different from the process of describing the origin of an idea. Analysis is meant to give understanding; it is meant to clarify, and explain what is really happening. This is not necessarily achieved by an account of the historical origin of the idea to be explained. At the level of Locke's simple ideas, particularly after Hume's treatment, the two processes could be taken to be coincident. The nature of the simple idea was explained or clarified

by relating it to the perception from which it arose: either someone had experienced redness or the taste of a pineapple, in which
case any further explanation was redundant, or they had not, in
which case explanation was impossible. So explanation really got
going with the complex ideas. However, here it still consisted in
tracing the historical origin of a particular idea; showing how it
was produced by the imagination from its sensory constituents.
Bentham thinks that such an account of origins is insufficient to
explain. The basis in his work for this claim about him is that in
his longest treatment of paraphrasis, in the *Logic*, he gives an
account of a process which he calls archetypation. This is giving
indication of the 'emblematic image', the 'image of some real
action or state of things' which is present to the mind when dealing with fictitious entities (VIII 246). It gives 'the origin of the
psychological, in some physical idea' (VIII 246). Such an account
of ideas in terms of images, and images explained in terms of their
origins is characteristic of Locke or Hume. However, the point
about Bentham is not that he also recognises it, but, rather, that
he thinks that it is a separate process from the one with which he
is principally concerned. This may not be quite explicit in his
discursive expositions, but it becomes clear from his examples,
in that the real entities with which fictitious entities are related
by the process of archetypation are different from the real entities
with which they are associated by the process of paraphrasis. This
is sufficient to show that quite different things are involved in the
two processes, and that what is achieved by the relation to the real
in the two cases is quite different. Yet it is archetypation which is
like Locke or Hume. Hence something quite different is achieved
in paraphrasis, which could not be achieved by use of the Lockean
apparatus. It gives an analysis of the meaning of certain terms
which is quite independent of the historical origin of the associated ideas. And, again it is the case that this new account has
necessarily involved going beyond the level of the single term to
its use in complete propositions. To the term could be related an
image, given an historical explanation in terms of its origin; however, displaying what is going on when the term is used involves
giving an account of the several propositions in which it is used.
Its use is in the context of a proposition, and it might therefore
be quite different in different propositions even though the term
was always related to the same image.

The example Bentham uses to display the process of archetypation is again that of *obligation*. He says that 'the emblematical,
or archetypal image, is that of a man lying down with a heavy
body pressing upon him' (*Logic*, VIII 247). Notice that the real

entities used here (a man, a heavy body) are quite different from
the real entities used in the paraphrastic explanation of obligation
(pains, pleasures). Most of the abstract terms used in law, or other
sciences, no doubt can be traced back to original physical descriptions. An original, concrete, directly perceptual kind of description is first extended metaphorically to the non-concrete or non-
perceptual, and then its physical origin is forgotten. Bentham,
indeed, says that it is a good thing if this relation to the physical
is not noticed otherwise the term can only appear explicitly metaphorical (*Logic*, VIII 246-7). The important point is that this
physical image (such as a man with a weight on him) does not,
whether or not it is readily available, provide an appropriate clarification of the idea of obligation. Much more could be said here
which is familiar from present-day criticism of Locke: that quite
different images, or no images at all, might be associated by different people with the use of the word, yet the word be used quite
correctly and successfully to convey information, give commands,
and so on; that this correct use therefore cannot be explained by
such association with an image; and yet it is the use that is the
primary thing to be explained in explanation of the meaning of
terms. It is sufficient here, while discussing Bentham, to point out
that he was aware that the image associated with a word was not
the thing to be used in explaining or clarifying its meaning. He
was aware that the relation to a real, perceptual, basis which can
be given by production of a physical image for an abstract term
is not the kind of relation to a real, perceptual, basis which is
needed for clarification of that term; and in this he was surely
right. Bentham's brief account is open between whether it is the
common origin in the language of the term or its individual origin
with one particular speaker of the language that is central for
him. However, again his example may bring out better what he
wants than his discursive treatment. For the physical basis of the
idea of obligation in the language is not that of someone being
weighed down but, rather, of someone being tied up. So, although
he doesn't bring out the point, his example is an appropriate one
with which to develop the point that one man's image of obligation is not a good enough basis for explanation of the use of the term
in common language about public situations, as in the language
of the law.

If we consider again the case of a contract, someone engaged
in the Benthamite project of clarification and explanation of what
is really happening in law must be able to explain what it really
is for someone to be under a contractual obligation to someone
else. For this it is no good that he has an image in his mind of the

person being under a heavy load, a heavy load placed on him by the second person involved in the contract. It does not matter that the first person might say that his obligations weigh heavily upon him; it would not even matter that, in his unhappiness, his shoulders hunched and his knees sagged. Even so, understanding of the situation is not given by thinking of it as a situation in which a man is weighed down by a heavy load, only one which is invisible; the knees can really be seen to buckle underneath, only the load on top maintains an invisible, ghostly, fictional, presence. Even though this could be a physical origin of the image, and even though this is not just wholly accidental in that certain things can be explained about the situation by thinking of it as structurally similar to one in which there is a real load, this will not give a proper understanding of the situation. For this we need at least an account of what it is that distinguishes this situation from others in which someone acts, or could act, as if he were weighed down; such as someone depressed, or threatened, or with too much to do. Bentham thinks that he can provide such clarification, in terms of the sanctions to which the man is liable for non-performance of the contract; the situation is to that extent similar to one of threat; and the real physical situation in which one man threatens another man provides a better model with which to understand it than a real physical situation in which one man places weights on another man's back. Again, as before, there is something really the case in the situation which cannot be captured by the purely imaginary supposition that there are weights ('fabulous entities', chimeras) on the man's back; otherwise he could just say to himself that he had nothing to fear but fear itself and renege on the contract. In a legal contract there really is something to fear: the possible operations of the legal authorities as initiated by the other party to the contract. This, again, is a situation which can only be explained at the level of propositions, complete utterances which can be used to describe facts or states of affairs. Analysis of individual terms, analysis by use of images, is insufficient for the job in hand.

Bentham's new device of paraphrasis displays, therefore, the primacy of the sentence or proposition in the analysis of meaning, An analysis such as Locke's which takes the term, or individual word, as primary is found to be inadequate. This is, in itself, a highly important insight; and hence Quine is correct in identifying Bentham as making 'the crucial step forward' in the explanation of terms, in the conceptual side of epistemology; a step which leads on to the projects of Russell and Carnap in the present century (Quine 1969 p. 72). If this is thought to be reading too much into the accounts of paraphrasis itself, a device which can be taken to be a mere supplementation of Locke's programme, the explicit recognition of the proposition as primary can be supported from elsewhere in Bentham's work where he is not specifically saying anything about paraphrasis at all. Criticising Blackstone in the *Comment*, Bentham remarks of '"you shall be hanged if . . ."' that 'this has no meaning: it is nothing: it is no will expressed: there is nothing to observe' (77), as compared with the 'compleat expression of . . [a] . . will' which 'may stand compleat of itself as a logical proposition'. Many years later he remarks in his *Evidence* papers that 'in less compass than that of a proposition, neither truth nor falsehood, wisdom nor folly, sense nor nonsense, can be conveyed' (RJE iv 288). These might just be taken as conventional expressions of the doctrine that the proposition is the smallest unit sufficient to express a complete thought; certainly there is nothing innovatory in the idea that a proposition is needed if we are to have something capable of being true or false. However, it is interesting to note that in these remarks, Bentham not only talks about truth but also about meaning: mere fragments of propositions are nonsense, and this makes it plausible to suppose that he does not think of sense as primarily originating with individual terms. The crucial evidence for his view, however, is to be found in his explicit treatment of propositions and terms in his *Essay on Language*. This is exactly where we should expect the main exposition of his views; and they are uncompromisingly in favour of the primacy of propositions. He declares that 'the primary and only original use' of language is the 'communication of thought' (VIII 320): then that 'every man who speaks, speaks in propositions, the rudest savage, not less than the most polished orator'; hence 'terms taken by themselves are the work of abstraction, the produce of refined analysis' (321). In other words, if we start with the central importance of communication, this means that we start with complete thoughts or propositions; and the meanings of words are to be analysed in terms of their contributions to such thoughts. Hence 'no word is of itself the complete sign of any thought'; or 'it was in the form of entire propositions that when first uttered, discourse was uttered. Of these integers, words were but so many fragments, as afterwards *in written discourse* letters were of words' (322). That the relation of word to proposition is similar to that of letter to word is fairly convincing support for the claim that Bentham believed in the primacy of propositions in the explanation of what it is that someone was saying while discoursing. Although (written) words can be analysed into letters, no one would think of starting an analysis of the meaning of words by analysing the meaning of letters, and then inferring the meaning of the composite entity: Bentham suggests that the relation between propositions and words is the same. He also explicitly criticises Aristotle and Condillac, who follows Locke, for starting with terms (322). So the evidence that Bentham precedes Frege in thinking of the sentence as the primary unit in explanation of sense is substantial.

Precedence is interesting; but much more important is correctness. Anyone can be wrong in a new way. What this chapter attempts to bring out is not just that Bentham had some new ideas but that they were important in that they were quite probably correct. Both because of the nature of the fictions involved, and also because of the imperfections of an analysis of ideas in terms of their origins, Bentham was right in starting his analysis with complete thoughts or propositions. Once the analysis works at this level it is then possible to give an explanation of the use of individual terms without associating them with independent ideas, since they can now be given meaning in the context of whole sentences. Bentham was not, in fact, the first in any case to point out that perfectly significant words could not be associated with separate Lockean ideas; he would have been familiar with this claim from another book which he read and referred to, Hartley's *Theory of the Human Mind* (as it was entitled in Priestley's abridgement, which was the one Bentham used). Yet Hartley only said that there were words without ideas in the case of theoretical terms, which could be defined in terms of words which were associated with ideas (110), and 'particles' such as *the, of, to, for, but* (113). Important as this point is, in partial modification of Locke, it is much less significant either ontologically or semantically than Bentham's claim that perfectly normal substantives, such as *right, obligation, property* and so on were quite different from such substantives as *house, dog, mountain*, and so on, and could only get their meaning in context. Bentham looks like a natural forerunner of Russell, the Russell who talks of 'incomplete symbols', that is, 'things that have absolutely no meaning whatsoever in isolation but merely acquire a meaning in context', things which Russell says that he calls 'logical fictions' (Russell 1956 (1918) p. 253). In both cases we have the idea that substantives used in apparently significant sentences do not refer to anything, and that their significance can only be given in the context of a whole sentence, a whole sentence which furthermore has to be translated into another sentence of an approved type in order to bring out its significance. In both cases this approved type is one in which all the referring terms refer to items with which we are perceptually acquainted (or could be). Both talk of fictions in the case of referring terms which do not meet such conditions. Even some of the examples are the same, such as classes, which are fictions for Bentham (*Chrest.*, VIII 123n) and logical fictions for Russell (Russell 1919 pp. 181-2). Both diagnose and cure problems which they think have arisen because of the superficial grammatical similarities between what are really quite different kinds of case; both attack the idea that because there is an apparently significant substantive, there is necessarily something for it to refer to. Both hold therefore, in Bentham's words, that we should recognise the 'constitution of human language as the source from whence the illusion flows', the illusion that to each distinct word there corresponds a distinct real entity (RJE i 115); the idea that 'whenever there is a word, there is a thing' (XI 73).

The parallel is, however, not complete; and, in so far as there are differences, Bentham can reasonably be thought of not as the crude forerunner of a later, more sophisticated doctrine, but, rather, as being in some ways superior. The examples Bentham and Russell give of fictions vary; a particular table is a fiction for Russell but not for Bentham, redness is a fiction for Bentham but not for Russell. The former case shows that Russell is much more worried about what Bentham called real inferential entities than Bentham was, and this way lies all those problems of knowledge that leave us in the end with nothing to know. The latter case shows that Russell (at least at the period we are discussing) was much more tolerant with respect to universals than Bentham was. For Russell, in 'the cat is black', 'black' refers to blackness much more straightforwardly than 'the cat' does to the cat. For Russell, that is, the meaning of predicates is given by their denotation just as with referring terms; both items can appear in a complete analysis in much the same way as names of items with which we are acquainted ('there are at least two sorts of objects of which we are aware, namely, particulars and universals' (Russell 1963 (1910) p. 155)). Bentham, by contrast, held that predicates were functionally different, that with qualities 'the expression is incomplete; that the idea presented by it is but, as it were, the fragment of an idea' (*Language*, VIII 326). That is, we cannot just give meaning to a quality expression by simple reference to an individual item, a universal, to which it refers; but that (as in Frege) predicate expressions are essentially incomplete in the way that subject expressions were not. This other difference from Russell is, again, a sign of superiority rather than deficiency. It has the consequence of meaning that Bentham did not think of the final, satisfactory, analysis as being a mere string of names organised in a particular pattern in the way that some twentieth-century admirers of the analytic method have; and this in turn means that he is much less interested in analysis promoting 'insight into the structure of the fact' (Wisdom 1953 p. 7) than they have been. Notice that in the most famous of Russell's analyses, that of the present King of France, the whole point is that the grammatical structure of a sentence containing 'the present King of France' does not reveal the real, or logical structure; and so it is structure which the analysis reveals. By contrast, Bentham's own worked example, that of obligation, replaces the sentence to be analysed with another sentence which although it is different in structure (molecular rather than atomic, hypothetical rather than categorical) might just as well be of the same subject-predicate structure as the original for all the importance that this is to the analysis. So although both Russell and Bentham agree that in the proper analysis all substantives should refer to real entities, Bentham is not particularly concerned with his analysis revealing the form of a fact. The fact for him is composed of real constituents with certain properties, not a concatenation of individuals with a particular structure.

The important question about analysis which can be asked about both Bentham and also the various twentieth-century practitioners is the question of how it is possible at all. So far it has been shown that the method of paraphrasis was indeed needed by Bentham to perform a kind of analysis which would be impossible if one were restricted solely to the purely Lockean apparatus. It has not yet been shown that this kind of analysis is possible; for it has not yet been shown how Bentham or anyone else can select and justify the sentence that replaces and analyses the sentence that is found to be problematic. This problem could be put as follows. If paraphrasis (or any similar kind of analysis) is to be successful, then it must simultaneously solve two problems, the problem of why the analysis provided is an improvement on the original, and the problem of why it is an analysis of that original and not another one. Joint solution of these two problems is difficult in that the closer the analysis provided is to the original starting point, the less improvement it seems, whereas the further away it is, the less obvious it is that it is an analysis of that starting point. The question of why the analysis is an improvement on the original has an answer in Bentham, in that it is a sentence which names nothing but real entities, and hence can be used in clarification. Nothing, however, has so far been said to show that he has an answer to the other question, the question of why the analyses he provides are indeed analyses of the original problematical sentences. Something has to be found which indubitably or clearly relates these sentences to be analysed to their analyses. Bentham is like a bridge player with a strong hand in dummy. If only he can play off his analyses in terms of real entities, then he can make all the tricks he desires. He starts, however, in his own hand with sentences in terms of fictitious entities. Somehow he must find an entry to dummy, a way of crossing the board to the place where he holds all the cards. He has to find some method of lining up his sentences about fictitious entities in a one-sided relation with sentences naming real entities. Nor is this his problem alone. Taking Wisdom again as an example of later analysis, Wisdom says that philosophical statements have the form 'the fact located by S has the elements and arrangement revealed by S'' (1953 (1933) p. 3). Again there is the problem of relating a particular S with a particular S'; of showing that the S indeed locates the S' that the analysis produces. This problem will now be solved by consideration of the various possible ways in which this can be done. These possibilities could be exemplified by discussion of the various projects of analysis in the first part of the present century; but to save space there will be no more than an occasional reference, even though all the suggestions considered have their own separate, considerable, histories.

The natural solution to start with is that the link between the two sentences is that they possess the same truth value. Since truth or falsity is the most obvious additional element which is available once one moves from the level of terms to the level of propositions, it might seem that Bentham achieves his paraphrastic analyses by giving truth conditions; that is, by stating in his analysing sentence what has to be the case if the original sentence is to be true. Sentences sharing truth-conditions are then related in the desired way. Yet even though this is an obvious solution, it can't be a straightforward solution given the way that Bentham sees the matter. For in Bentham's eyes sentences about fictitious entities are not true: 'a fictitious entity being, as this its name imports, being, by the very supposition, a mere nothing, cannot of itself have any properties: no proposition by which any property is ascribed to it can, therefore, be in itself, and of itself, a true one, nor, therefore, an instructive one' (*Logic*, VIII 246). Yet the propositions which feature in the analyses are sometimes true; hence it would seem that Bentham holds that the analysing sentence could have a different truth value from the sentence it analyses, and hence that truth value cannot be the method of relating them together. Nor can this long, quite carefully thought out, sentence be ignored; it comes from the central treatment of paraphrasis in the *Logic*. Bentham, however, continues: 'whatsoever of truth is capable of belonging to it cannot belong to it in any other character than that if the representative . . . of some proposition having for its subject some real entity'. So he seems to allow that it might have some sort of derivative truth value; and this is in line with how he was understood above when fictitious entities were distinguished from fabulous entities and allowed a kind of verbal reality. Once the analysis has been established, it can be allowed that it does reveal something true about the situation described in the original sentence: it shows, for example, what is true when it is the case that someone is under an obligation. So Bentham does not have to be forced into the position of saying that the two sentences have different truth value. What does seem to be clearly the case, however, is that the truth value cannot be used as a means of telling which particular sentence is analysed by any particular analysing sentence. For it can only be told what the truth value, or truth conditions, of the original sentence is after the analysis has been successfully completed. It then takes, or is found to have, the truth conditions of its 'representative', the analysing sentence. So, in the bridge metaphor, there is no entry to dummy this way; some other means than truth must be discovered of telling which sentence is the proper analysis of which sentence.

If truth is not the method, then the next natural thing to try is sense, or meaning. The sentences line up in a one-one way because they have the same meaning; we gain entry to dummy by finding the analysing sentence which means the same as the sentence for which we desire an analysis. Yet the use of meaning seems to leave us exactly with the original problem. Since it is a notion closely related to that of understanding (the meaning of a term is what we understand when we understand it), it is difficult to see how something which was unclear and needing analysis could be seen to have the same meaning as something which is clear and analysed. If the original is already understood, then it would not seem to require analysis; while if it is not understood, we are back with the same problem of how it can be known that the provided analysis is an analysis of it rather than something else. Of course, there are ways of treating meaning as being quite independent from understanding which would therefore prevent part of this problem arising. If the meaning is just taken to be the use of the words in a particular language, or if it is just taken to be some entity (a Lockean abstract idea, a Platonic Idea) which the expressions are taken to refer to, then there is room for the supposition that one expression means the same as another one, even though the user, or we ourselves, remain unaware of the fact. (In the second option this is because meaning has now become a purely referential notion, hence one can be surprised and learn here just as elsewhere that two expressions refer to the same thing; *the morning star* and *the evening star*, for example.) Hence analysis could clarify by informing someone of this fact. However, quite apart from the fact that none of these accounts of meaning is like that of Bentham's, even on these accounts the main problem still remains. For this is a problem about knowledge of the meaning, not just about the meaning as such. It is the problem of why, if we know the meaning, we should bother about the analysis, while if we do not, how we could possibly produce it. This is, if analysis is taken as providing something with the same meaning as the sentence with which we start.

Bentham certainly talks of paraphrasis as preserving meaning, as giving us the 'import' of the original expression. As he says in a footnote to the *Chrestomathia*, paraphrasis consists in making up a phrase and 'applying to it another phrase, which, being of the same import' is about real entities (VIII 126n). Bentham also talks several times of 'translation' in this connection, saying, for example, that 'to understand abstract terms, is to know how to translate figurative language into language without figure' (*General View*, III 181; see also OLG 283n), and 'translation' was the word used in his original exposition in the *Fragment on Government* footnote (491n). Of course, 'translation' does not have to be understood as specifically in terms of providing something with the same sense, but only in terms of changing one phrase for another (just as the bishop gets translated to a new see). However, Bentham talks often enough directly of meaning or import to show that he did regard his analyses as giving the meaning of the originals, and so all the problems which arise from considering analysis as giving the same meaning would seem to apply to him. He even goes so far in one place to say that the second, analysing sentence provided in paraphrasis 'by being seen to express the same import, it shall explain and make clear the import of the first' sentence, that is the one being analysed (*Radical Reform Bill*, III 594n). Here we have an example where it does not just have the same import, which can be explained in several ways, but that this can be 'seen'; that is that someone can separately understand the import of both and in doing so will realise that it is the same. Here Bentham really is in the problem of why in such a case analysis is needed at all.

The only way that this problem can be avoided is to treat this last remark, which does after all occur in the footnote to a political pamphlet, as not being a perfect expression of Bentham's views. On no other occasion does Bentham talk of the import as being 'seen' to be the same, and the claim which he certainly does make on several occasions, namely that the import is the same, should be understood in a different manner. This is that, just as was claimed for truth above, what happens is that the analysis gives meaning or import to the original. The sentence to be analysed has the same meaning as its analysing sentence just because it is taken to have whatever meaning the latter has; just as before it was taken to give it whatever truth it had, so here it can be claimed to give it whatever meaning it has. This avoids the problem of the meaning of the sentence being analysed already being perfectly understood and the analysis being therefore redundant. It also fits in with several things which Bentham says. He talks in *Nomography* of paraphrasis as being 'the only form of exposition by which the import attached to them [fictitious entities] is capable of being fixed' (*III 286); here the central idea is not that of starting with an already understood import, but, rather, of 'fixing' it. So Bentham says that, by the analysis, the import is 'laid open' (OLG 252) or that it is 'illustrated' (IMPL 207n); it 'renders' the fictitious entities 'intelligible' (OLG 278). These all convey the strong sense that the analysis does not start with something already understood but, rather, makes it understandable. Bentham presents this even more forcefully at times by giving an option with respect to the acceptance of his analyses: either they are accepted and so the area analysed becomes intelligible, or else, if they are rejected, it remains mere nonsense. For example: 'Of either the word obligation or the word right, if regarded as flowing from any other source, the sound is mere sound, without import or notion' (*Nomography*, III 293); or, as it is put in *Of Laws in General* of the same words 'take away the idea of punishment, and you deprive them of all meaning' (136n). If we 'take away *pleasures* and *pains*', then *duty, obligation*, and so on 'are so many empty sounds' (SPRINGS, I 211). These all convey a strong sense that the analysis gives the meaning or, if that is to put it too strongly, at least that the meaning cannot be found independently of the analysis. The options are either nonsense or taking it to mean what the analysis says; there is no separate way of understanding it. Hence the problem of why the analysis is not redundant is not one which arises for Bentham. There is still, however, the problem of how it is possible.

If this account of Bentham's use of paraphrasis is correct, then it matters little whether we explore the problems of analysis in terms of meaning or in terms of truth. In neither case can an already known truth value or meaning of the sentence being analysed give us an answer to the question of which sentence it is that provides the correct analysis; yet in both cases, once the analysis has been provided, this can be taken as giving, or at least as revealing, what it is that is true about the original or what it is that it means. This, in turn, shows that the two notions of truth and meaning are closer for Bentham than they are for some other philosophers. This is suggested by his constant use of the term 'import' for meaning, the import of something being for him what is the case if it is true, or if it enters into true propositions. The analysis of obligation shows us, he says, how it is 'constituted' (*Nomography*, III 293). 'Would a man', he asks, 'know what it is that the law really does . . .?', a request for the content, the reality or truth of the matter (OLG 251). The answer to the request, the analysis of rights, obligations and so on showing how they are 'constituted' gives us knowledge such that 'knowing thus much, we shall have ideas to our words: not knowing it we shall have none' (OLG 251). So the analysis both gives the original sentences whatever truth they have and also, by so doing, gives them sense, ideas to words, import. Whether we start with truth or meaning the key idea is that of substituting one sentence for another in order to give it such truth or meaning; the fit between the two is looser than would be required if we thought of them as already possessing some precise meaning or truth which had to be captured in the analysis. This still does not provide an answer to the problem of how analysis is possible; but it does mean that we can think of the answer in functional terms, as providing something serviceable which can be used in the place of the original, rather than something which has to be exactly the same as it in some respect.

Bentham, of course, thought that fictitious language had many uses, such as the uses by lawyers of legal fictions examined in the last chapter which were designed to confuse the people and increase the wealth and power of the legal monopoly. Not just any substitution of sentence for sentence fulfilling the same use is relevant to the project of analysis. The important use of such terms as 'rights' and 'obligations', however, is that they purport to be descriptive, and this account of how things are is something which Bentham, who wants to describe what happens in law, has to take over in his analysis. His substitute sentences must also be used descriptively, used to say how the situation is which is described in the originals and be an adequate substitute. Given general acceptance of the Lockean account of reality in terms of relation to sense perception, it can be seen what the answer to the general problem of analysis is for Bentham; that is, his answer to the general problem of which sentences can be used as adequate substitutes for the sentences with which he starts. The answer is that it is those sentences which provide verification, and verification in perceptual terms of the original sentences. The original sentences are in need of analysis, on this general Lockean basis, because they do not refer to real, perceptible, entities. No one can see rights. However, in situations in which people talk about rights, there are things which are perceptible, such as commands, or hypothetical statements made by people about the possibility of pain. These, therefore, can serve as the verification of the original sentences; that is, the way in which one could tell whether a specific sentence about rights or obligations holds in the specific situation. It can, therefore, be used as an acceptable substitute for the original; it fulfils the purposes for which the original was required by making distinctions between the same situations. When there is a right, the analysis will say that someone is liable for punishment for doing something; when there is not a right, it will say that this is not the case. It is, therefore, a substitute for the original. It gives to the original whatever truth or meaning the original possesses. By providing the verification, it shows how to establish that the original is true, or in what respect the original is true. By providing the verification, it shows what it means for the original to be true; it shows what someone has to understand in order to use terms like 'right' or 'obligation' with significance or import; that is how they can be used in true sentences. So the Lockean, perceptual, context not only shows why the analysis is superior to the original, since it is in terms of real entities: it also shows just which sentences are analyses of which sentences. Verification is the looked-for entry into dummy; it shows us how to analyse the sentences which are found to be problematic.

'To give some sort of clue to this labyrinth is all that I can hope to have accomplished here' remarks Bentham after suggesting a few of these analyses (OLG 278). This clue is the substitution, at the level of sentences, of sentences which are clear in that they describe real entities, directly perceivable or directly inferable from perception, for sentences which are not clear in that they do not do this. This is the reason for the analysis; it is a way out of the labyrinth. Its possibility depends upon thinking of the unclear sentences as neither possessing a sense or a truth value which can be understood independently but, rather, as thinking of the analysis as providing an acceptable substitute which then gives the originals whatever truth or meaning they possess. It has just been suggested that the solution to the problem of which sentence to substitute for which sentence is in the same terms as the original problem of why substitution was needed at all; in both cases relation to verification or perception is the answer. Apparent lack of it provides the problem to be solved, and provision of it provides the answer. Or part of the answer. If provision of a substitute clarifying the original is taken to be sufficient to justify Bentham's use of what he explicitly holds to be fictitious entities in his account of the law, it remains to be shown that a similar substitute could not be provided which would justify the lawyer's use of fictions in the law and the constitutional theorist's use of fictions in theorising about the law. There still remains the problem for Bentham of distinguishing between the good use of fictions and the bad use of fictions; and the new analytical tool which he has forged just seems to make the problem worse. It has now been shown how language about fictitious entities can be made legitimate. However, if contract can be saved, then why not original contract; if rights can be saved, why not natural rights. It is this question which is the topic of the next chapter.

Notes

(a) I have kept the Benthamite (or contemporary) spelling of 'clew' because I think that it conveys more clearly the idea of a thread, as in the original story of the labyrinth. Bentham often talks about clues, but normally in conjunction with labyrinths.

(b) In the references to *Nomography* in this chapter, I have added an asterisk to the reference because I am not sure how positive an editor Richard Smith was; however the material reads very like Bentham manuscript, and is probably fairly reliable.

(c) Another strong remark in favour of the proposition being primary is Bentham's claim in *Chrestomathia* that 'in language . . . the *integer* to be looked for is an entire proposition' (VIII 188).

(d) For the way in which Helvetius provided the matter, if Locke provided the form, see Chapter V.

(e) I have found Bentham's own attribution to d'Alembert of the idea of a fictitious being (which he certainly makes) problematic. Bentham says in *Chrestomathia* that, in looking through the *Mélanges* again, he cannot find the expression (VIII 127n); and looking through the *Mélanges* for myself, no more can I. So it might be attractive to suppose that the aged Bentham's memory has misled him, and that he had attributed to d'Alembert, an expression (no doubt suggested by d'Alembert's general thought) which he himself had used in his own letter *to* d'Alembert (where the expression, 'etre fictif' does clearly appear (UC 169.54). However, there is at least one place in the earlier work where he also attributes it to d'Alembert (UC 27.148), so I sup- it is in there somewhere.

75

(f) The point made in the main text about exemplification or archetypation was meant to show that Bentham supposed that there could
be a relation between an image and a word which would neither be
that uncovered in analysis (or exposition) nor be one which occurred
in the etymology of the word. It should be noted, however, that
Bentham knew the image involved in the etymology of 'obligation',
and mentioned it in another discussion of exemplification (*Chrestomathia*, VIII 126n).

(g) The contrast with Russell in the main text was not meant to imply
that Bentham did not also think that paraphrasis could be used, in
a way rather similar to Russell, to uncover the form of a proposition.
He knew that the form of discourse could be misleading (for example,
in distinguishing a positive from a negative act (IPML 76), and held
that paraphrasis might clarify syntax (*Logic*, VIII 242), or be used
to eliminate a particular syntactical form, such as adverbs (*Universal
Grammar* VIII 356). The point being made was not that Bentham
could not do what Russell did, but how much more he could do, and
this is I think what is revealed by comparing their most central examples of analysis.

(h) The attempts to use analysis in the earlier parts of this century are
surveyed and criticised in Urmson (1956). As a sample of some of
the various ideas mentioned might be mentioned Moore (1942 663)
on taking concepts as the objects of analysis (and the paradox of analysis), Quine (1960 258-9) on the sufficiency of a functional substitution. The best overall account of Russell of a project in this spirit is
his 'philosophy of logical atomism' (1918) in Russell (1956); and the
most fully sustained attempt at analysis was Wisdom's *Logical Constructions* (appearing between 1931 and 1933, they were printed
together as Wisdom 1969). Wisdom also wrote an account of Bentham's analytic project at much the same time in which Bentham is
compared with more modern analysis (Wisdom 1931). The idea of
using verification to give an account of meaning, another influential
doctrine of the 1930s, informs much of the spirit of Dummett (1976);
by contrast the idea that substituting sentences of the same truth
value can give much of what those who want an analysis of meaning
really want can be found in Davidson (1967).

IV

Nonsense upon Stilts

'A great multitude of people are continually talking of the Law of Nature', Bentham wrote in the *Introduction* (27n); and it has been seen in Chapter II how Bentham distinguished himself from this multitude by trenchantly expressed disagreement with the idea that the law of nature provided any justificatory force whatsoever. This was because, as has been seen, he regarded it as a mere fiction, a 'phantom', a 'formidable non-entity' (COMM 17, 20) and, as such, 'sounds without meaning' (COMM 14), 'nothing but a phrase' (FG 483). It was therefore to be regarded in the same way as more specific fictions such as that of the original contract; and these in turn were thought to have no more validity than the fictions lawyers invented in order to apply the law to new areas. 'Unlicensed thieves use pick-lock keys: licensed thieves use fictions', as he put it in his *Evidence* (RJE iv 308). Such fictions were all to be condemned and eliminated. They could never be used as a basis of justification for something, since this would serve no more than reasoning from false premises would. However, in spite of the fact that these fictions were held by Bentham to be meaningless, or to provide no justification at all, they were being used as an attempt to support their claims by a great multitude of people. In particular, appeal to the existence of natural rights formed an important and conspicuous basis for political claims throughout the period at which Bentham was writing. Citation of natural rights was taken to be the ultimate justification in the fundamental documents issued to support the American and the French Revolutions. As an opponent of natural law, Bentham was also an opponent of that branch of it which was concerned with natural rights, and so an opponent of all such citations. Just as natural law, natural rights were declared to be nonsense, fictitious entities, sounds without meaning. Commenting on the French declaration of rights he wrote that 'natural rights is simple nonsense: natural and imprescriptible rights, rhetorical nonsense, nonsense upon stilts' (ANARCH, Parekh 269).

Although Bentham changed in his political opinions as his thought and life developed, he maintained a consistent opposition to such talk of natural rights. Their use to justify the American side when the Americans declared their independence from Britain came at the time at which Bentham was writing the criticisms of Blackstone discussed in Chapter II. Bentham was at this time a close friend of another lawyer, John Lind, who was a pamphleteer in the government interest. Lind had provided Bentham with the original idea of writing the *Comment*, and Bentham co-operated with him in two pamphlets Lind wrote in defence of Lord North against such opponents as Americans. In one of these, *An Answer to the Declaration of the American Congress*, Bentham supplied detailed criticism of the American declaration of rights which was inserted verbatim by Lind. He criticises their use of particular supposed natural rights, liberty (a concept on which he worked a lot at this time) and equality (CORR I 341-3). Bentham does not here enter into general criticism of the concept of a natural right, even though he had just completed two extended criticisms of the concept of natural law for use in the *Comment* (10-21; 288-95). Perhaps the pamphlet was an inappropriate vehicle for such a fundamental treatment; however, the same is the case with the few brief comments which he makes about one of the new American state's declaration of rights at the end of the *Introduction*, where again he concentrates on the particular case of liberty (309-11).

Whatever may have been Bentham's political views about Lord North and the Americans at the time of the original *Declaration* in 1776, by 1789 he is careful to say that 'who can help lamenting that so rational a cause should be rested upon reasons, so much fitter to beget objections than remove them' (IPML 311n). That is, he is not against the Americans, whom in fact he had just declared to be perhaps 'the most enlightened, at this day on the globe' (309). What he is against is their reasons. His reminiscences of this period, however inaccurate in other respects, seem to be accurate enough about this. Writing to Bowring in 1827, Bentham says: 'for by the badness of the arguments used on behalf of the Americans ... my judgement ... was ranked on the government side. The whole of the case was founded on the assumption of *natural rights*, claimed without the slightest evidence of their existence' (X 57). When he comes to deal with the French declarations of rights, however, his animus is such that he is clearly not just against the reasons but also the positions which these reasons are being used to support. Here he gives a detailed criticism not just of particular claimed natural rights, but of the general idea of a natural right as such. Bentham's work here, usually called by Dumont's title *Anarchical Fallacies* (since it first appeared in French as part of the second volume of *Tactique*) forms three separate criticisms of three separate declarations of rights. Although originally sympathetic to the French Revolution, which he hoped might be a chance for putting some of his own manifold suggestions for change into effect, by the time he came to write these criticisms Bentham had become hostile to the course which the Revolution was taking. He felt that the French use of fictitious entities like natural rights was an attempt they made to cover their wickedness, just as he continuously felt that the lawyers used fictitious entities as a cover to their wickedness. He even offered one of his manuscripts for publication under the title 'pestilential nonsense unmasked; or an Anatomy of the First French Declaration of Rights' (UC 146, 238), a title which echoes his earlier treatment of the pestilential breath of fiction in the lawyers. However, even here the distinction between reasons and conclusions applies. The objection to the reasons is consistent, Bentham's attitude about radical conclusions varies. So even the late, much more radical, Bentham is still able to write to the French on the occasion of their 1830 revolution in the following terms: 'Rights are fictitious entities – *the people* real ones. Realities on this occasion, as on all others, realities I prefer to fictions' (XI 57). However good the cause, it is wrong, now just as fifty years before, to use fiction as a reason. As he said then of the original contract, 'the indestructible prerogatives of mankind have no need to be supported upon the sandy foundation of a fiction' (FG 441).

It seems, therefore, that although natural rights were cited on the side of change, and although Bentham was generally on the side of change, his handling of natural rights was exactly the same as those parts of natural law which were cited in defence of established institutions. However good or bad the end, such things could not properly be used as reasons. This would be the straightforward application of the positions described in Chapter II to this new but strictly comparable area of natural rights. However, the discussion in Chapter III of Bentham's new device of paraphrasis has put the whole question back into dispute. For if fictions were found guilty and condemned in Chapter II, they have just been explained and rehabilitated in Chapter III. Bentham has there been shown as inventing a method of analysis by which sense can be given to sentences naming fictitious entities. Furthermore, many of these entities, such as powers, obligations, rights, and duties, form the fundamental material of the law which Bentham wishes to explain. No longer do we have to stop short at the horrid name of fiction. Fictions can be explained. Rights can be explained. They can be clarified, made respectable, and so enter into perfectly legitimate description and justification. The problem is, if this can be done with rights, why cannot it also be done with natural rights. We do not now, after the brilliant invention of the device of paraphrasis, stop short just because natural rights are fictions. So perhaps natural rights and natural law can also be clarified and made legitimate, so that they also could enter into justification. This problem, the problem of the differential treatment of rights and natural rights in Bentham, forms the centre of this chapter. It will demand further discussion of both kinds of rights, in an attempt to discover whether Bentham's distinction between blameless and wicked fictions is viable or justified.

The problem starts with the claim that both rights and natural rights are fictitious entities, and his claim, already several times illustrated, that fictions cannot appear in justification. The heading to one of the sections of preliminary material to the *Traités* concocted by Dumont out of Bentham is simply 'fiction is not a reason' (*Traités* 1 114; LEGIS 71). Yet Bentham is quite clear that rights are fictions, as several quotations given above testify. In one of the 1770s plans to his major work he considers a section on 'what things exist' and notes down 'rights and wrongs do not exist . . . law of nature does not exist' (UC 69.43). So it is the case for both that they are equally fictitious entities, that they do not exist. On the other hand, it is also clear in Bentham that he considers them to be quite different kinds of fictions, different in status. Rights, legal rights, are called 'real' rights; natural rights are called 'imaginary rights'. As he puts it in the *Pannomial Fragments*: 'those who govern allege legal rights – the rights of the citizen – real rights; those who wish to govern allege natural rights – the rights of man – counterfeit rights' (*III 220). It looks here as if we have a distinction between fictions which are real and fictions which are not real; or perhaps it is between things which look like fictions, but are not really so, and things which really are fictions. This sets the problem.

Bentham is quite clear that this distinction goes with a distinction in appropriate attitude; whereas the lawyers' lies were wicked, the fictions involved in rights, obligations and so on are blameless falsehoods. He also thinks that he can provide a clear explanation of the difference. It lies in the source of the fiction, which differs significantly in the two cases. As he puts it against the French

Declaration, 'from *real* laws come *real* rights; . . . from *imaginary* laws come imaginary ones' (ANARCH, Parekh 288). This refers to Bentham's analysis of a right, a triumph of his new method of paraphrasis. This relates sentences about rights to sentences about obligations, and sentences about obligations to sentences about laws or commands. As commands and laws are real, this analysis provides justification for the analysed fictitious entities. The relation is summed up pithily as follows: 'rights cannot exist without obligations. Obligation — a fictitious entity, is the produce of law — a real entity' (*PANN III 217); or slightly more fully as:

> an act is a real entity: a law is another. A duty or obligation
> is a fictitious entity conceived as resulting from the union of
> the two former. A law commanding or forbidding an act there-
> by creates a duty or obligation. A right is another fictitious
> entity, a kind of secondary fictitious entity, resulting out of a
> duty. (OLG 293-4)

The structure in each case is the same, with the same two step analysis of rights. The important point is that the termination of the analysis is with real entities, that is with real people and their real acts; for Bentham's analysis of a law is a command of a sovereign, where he understands by a sovereign that person or persons to whom a body of people are in the habit of obeying. So, assuming for the moment that the analysis is correct, Bentham can give a source for rights in real actions of real people; and this provides the required basis for clarification as discussed in the last chapter. By contrast, although natural rights could be analysed back in terms of natural obligations in an analogous way, and these natural obligations analysed in terms of natural laws, the end point of this analysis is quite different. For we still have something fictional, and furthermore, something fictional which cannot be related to the real. Hence the analysis cannot provide the required kind of justification; hence it is appropriate to distinguish between real and imaginary fictions, and presumably between blameless and wicked fictions, according to the availability or otherwise of a paraphrastic analysis relating them to real entities.

The supposition, then, is that the attack on fictions in Chapter II is quite compatible with the explanation and justification of fictions in Chapter III; and Bentham's treatment of natural rights is quite compatible with his treatment of legal rights. The difference depends upon whether or not a paraphrastic analysis is available; which in turn, if the account given in the last chapter is correct, depends upon whether or not some verification procedure is available with respect to the concept in question. Statements about legal rights can be verified; statements about natural rights cannot. So what has now to be seen is whether the existence or non-existence of an analysis is indeed what carries the evaluative weight in Bentham, enabling him to distinguish between good and wicked fictions. For this we need a further account of fictions in Bentham, preferably in an area outside politics, and so one in which the evaluative effect of something being classified as a fiction, and of how it is classified as a fiction, can be tested quite independently of any political valuation. We want to see whether Bentham elsewhere distinguishes between good and bad fictions, and says that the good ones are in some sense real. The best place to look is at his chief account of fictitious entities, which is in a block of manuscripts written at about the same time as the *Logic*, and which was posthumously published under the title *Fragment on Ontology*. In this work Bentham describes and classifies a multitude of fictitious entities, and makes some general points about them. The first is that the distinction between real and fictitious is not that between perceptible and inferential, as will be remembered from the last chapter from Bentham's classification of normal material objects as real, inferential entities. This means that we must be careful about thinking that the real-fictional distinction just consists in inferential distance from the perceptible, taken as the paradigm of reality. The next important general point that Bentham makes is that the distinction between real and fictitious entities is made inside language: 'the division of entities into real and fictitious, is more properly the division of names into *names* of real and *names* of fictitious entities (VIII 198n). So it is not as if Bentham were engaged in the self-defeating project of first getting hold of all the entities, that is all that exists, and then dividing them into those entities that really exist and those that do not really exist. He needs no Meinongian space in which to park golden mountains. Instead the claim is that we work from language to reality, and concentrate on the grammatical forms of the language. Substantives are the names of entities, so 'every noun-substantive which is not the name of a real entity, perceptible or inferential, is the name of a fictitious entity' (VIII 197); and this means that 'a fictitious entity is an entity to which, though by the grammatical form of discourse employed in speaking of it, existence be ascribed, yet in truth and reality existence is not meant to be ascribed' (VIII 197). Something which normally, or primarily, is used to refer to real existents is used without any intention of doing so and (presumably) can easily be recognised as such; a normal language speaker would know that this was the standard intention involved in the use of such a substantive on such an occasion. In any case, whatever the correct way of understanding Bentham's introduction of intention here, it is clearly the substantive form that is crucial in his account of fictitious entities; fictions come with the use of substantives.

The next important point Bentham wishes to establish is that 'every fictitious entity bears some relation to some real entity' (VIII 197). On a natural interpretation, this remark would seem to be fatal for the account of the distinction between good and bad fictions being proposed here, since this account depends upon some fictions (the bad ones) not being related to any reality at all. Natural rights are only related to imaginary laws. However, this remark should not be interpreted with full generality; it refers to the kind of fictitious entities that Bentham is talking about in the *Ontology*, and in this context it enables him to classify these entities into different orders according to the relation which they bear to real entities. Fictitious entities of the first order are those that only need real entities to be understood; fictitious entities of the second order need also fictitious entities of the first order; and so on. Examples of the first order are *matter, form, quantity, space*; and of the second order, *quality, modification.* There is some uncertainty in the account, and variation between different accounts, and Bentham further complicates the matter by introducing an account of 'semi-real' entities (for example, *space* (VIII 202)). However, the important thing for present purposes is that although these fictitious entities vary in degree of distance from the real, and although this can lead Bentham to talk of one being 'so to speak, a still more fictitious fiction' than another (VIII 200), his general attitude to the whole lot is that of acceptance or approval. This is shown by his distinction in these papers 'between a *fictitious entity* and a *non-entity*' (VIII 198), which he holds to be completely disjoint classes. Non-entities, such as the devil, are 'fabulous'; they are completely different from the fictions which are 'indispensable'. Of fictitious entities he says that they are those 'objects, which in every language must, for the purpose of discourse, be spoken of as existing' (VIII 198); the object of them is 'neither more or less than the carrying on of human converse' (VIII 199). Since this is clearly a good object, then if fictions are necessary for it, they must also be good; calling them fictions indicates nothing pejorative. This applies to the whole lot described in these manuscripts, and so validity or worth has nothing directly to do with distance from the real. Instead, it must depend upon some other way of establishing it such as (as is argued here) the availability or otherwise of an analysis of the concept in question.

This is to claim that when Bentham says that 'every fictitious entity bears some relation to some real entity', he is referring to the 'fictions with which the Logician is conversant', that is the fictions necessary for any discourse. This means that the word 'fiction' is potentially ambiguous in his hands. He starts with a normal language word with mild pejorative overtones used to refer to non-existent objects invented for various purposes. These objects are as nothing; their effect is the effect of nothing. He then realises that there are no independent objects corresponding to many nouns which are properly, indeed indispensably, used in the language. So, using the analogy of non-existence, he also calls them names of fictitious entities. 'Fictitious entity' has now, however, become a technical term; the pejorative implication has disappeared, and the names have the force and use in the language that the names of real entities have. Bentham therefore distinguishes between these fictions and non-entities, also called fabulous entities. However, he still wants to continue to use 'fiction' in its old way in which it comes to the same thing as a non-entity, and in which the pejorative overtones are still present. So we have seen that the fictional law of nature is described as a 'formidable non-entity'. When he is discussing natural rights, Bentham is sometimes at pains to stress that the effect of the supposed existence of a natural right is the same as nothing. For example, he says that natural rights can never form a rampart against tyranny since 'the shadow of a rampart is not a rampart' (*PANN III 219); or that 'a man is never the better for having such natural right: admit that he has it, his condition is not in any respect different from what it would be if he had it not' (*PANN III 218). It is this double use of 'fiction' that leads to the central problem of this chapter, how rights and natural rights, both fictions, could be treated so differently by Bentham.

What we now need is a distinction in Bentham's ontological work which corresponds to the problematic distinction he makes between the 'real' fictional rights and the 'imaginary' fictional natural rights. Something very similar comes right at the end of the *Ontology*, when Bentham is talking about *necessity, impossibility, certainty, uncertainty*, and so on. He comments that 'throughout the whole expanse of time, past, present, and future, put together, where will room be found for anything real to answer to any of these names?' (VIII 211); his point being that we only find the existent and the non-existent. Either things happened or they did not happen; there is nothing else involved in the claim that they necessarily happened. Bentham is here clearly influenced by Hume; and if the problem is thought of in terms of verification, it becomes the (now) familiar problem of the verification of counterfactual statements. Verifying that something is necessary, as opposed to being simply true, involves verifying that it would have happened even if other things had been different; and this involves verifying facts about situations which never have or never will exist. Bentham, like Hume, solves the difficulty by making these properties properties of the perceiving mind rather than of the facts themselves ('what there is of reality in the ideas expressed by such words as *impossibility, necessity, certainty*, is ... not any property ... in the facts themselves, but only the degree of persuasion by which the opinions we entertain in relation to those facts is accompanied' (RJE iii 271n)); and backs up this account by a prophetic account of how those propositions which really do seem to be necessary are, in fact, merely verbal. Taking the proposition 'it is impossible for the same thing to be, and not to be' as an example, he declares that 'examined closely, it will be found to be no more than a proposition concerning the signification of words' (RJE iii 272); and claims the same for 'two and two make four' (274). Necessity is obviously a highly interesting and important philosophical topic, and Bentham's claims are also obviously highly interesting and contentious. However, for present purposes it is enough to recognise that here we have an area where, for a purely logical or ontological category, Bentham holds that there really is nothing at all that exists which corresponds to the terms in the facts themselves (although, of course, the use of the terms can be explained). The interesting thing for present purposes is what this leads Bentham to say about the supposed qualities of necessity and certainty in the *Ontology*. He says 'quality itself is but a fictitious entity, but these are all of them so many fictitious qualities. They do not, as real qualities, — they do not, like gravity, solidity, roundness, hardness, belong to the objects themselves to which they are ascribed, — in the character of attributes of objects to which they are ascribed, they are mere chimeras, mere creatures of the imagination — nonentities' (VIII 211). Here we have an exact parallel to the treatment of legal and natural rights. Again the fictitious entities are divided into those that are 'real' and those that are imaginary; to the 'chimeras dire' (ANARCH, Parekh 288) of the rights of man correspond the chimeras of necessity and certainty. So the corresponding problem to the original one is how Bentham can be justified, if he calls all qualities 'fictitious entities' in holding some of them to be real and some not.

Quality is, as Bentham notices, closely related to *mode* or *modification*, and Bentham started on his analyses uncertain whether modes were or were not real. For example, in his early account for d'Alembert, he starts with the claim that what is real is substances and modes (UC 169.55), but then later holds that this is a mere distinction of reason (55). He is firm throughout that 'a quality is something which properly speaking does not exist' (54). Yet, as the passage just quoted shows, Bentham held that objects really were round or hard. So when Bentham claims that qualities are not real, he does not mean that a ball is not really round, but that a ball does not really contain an object known as roundness. Substantives are the clue, the key to what makes fictions. Once the quality is nominalised, and treated as an object referred to by a noun, trouble begins. For since we have no object corresponding to the noun, we have a fictitious entity. The ball cannot be cut up into smaller objects, such as its redness, roundness, or solidity, which can be thought of as the entities which make it up. In a passage in the *Chrestomathia* Bentham carefully distinguishes between the 'physical analysis' involved in separating an individual plant from its roots and the 'logical analysis' involved in concentrating on one or other of its qualities such as beauty or agreeable odour. The 'parts' are 'real entities', the 'qualities' 'fictitious entities' (VIII 122). However, as the passage above shows, this is not to say that a ball is not really round or red, or a flower sweet smelling. Although qualities are fictitious, objects can still be talked of as if they possessed them, and this is to say something real about the objects. Hence Bentham can distinguish between such qualities and imaginary qualities such as necessity or certainty which, in his view, say nothing about the object at all. There is a difference between a red ball and a blue one, even if quality is a fictitious entity; but there is not (for him) any difference in the object between something being true and something being necessary. Similarly, there is a difference between someone having one legal right and his having another, but no difference between having natural rights and having none at all. If I lose a legal right, this has a real effect, just as a body losing heaviness does; but if I lose a natural right, this makes no difference at all.

On the assumption that sentences like 'the ball is solid' or 'the ball is red' describe reality, it can be seen how sentences about some fictitious entities such as solidity and redness can be translated into, or replaced by, such sentences. Instead of saying that the ball has solidity or redness, we can say that it is solid or that it is red. That is, instead of sentences explicitly about the qualities, using substantives to refer to them, we can use sentences with predicates. Hence an analysis is possible for sentences containing names for such fictitious entities as roundness and redness; and this fits in with the claim that the acceptable (or logical or necessary) fictions are those for which analysis is possible. Similarly, in the closely analogous case of a *class* or *species*, although Bentham again regarded such entities as fictitious ever since his letter to d'Alembert (UC 169.56), he notes that the same word is used to talk about both individual members and also a species (*Chrest.*, VIII 123n). So 'the cow has two horns' might on one occasion be a remark about a particular cow; on another occasion about cows in general (about the species *cow*). This again suggests how easily an analysis could be produced of the fictitious entity, the species, in terms referring only to real entities, to individual members of it. Again we have a logical, useful, fiction; which again can be analysed. (Although, again, Bentham does not himself produce the analysis). So as well as finding an analogy to the distinction between real and imaginary fictions in the rights case, Bentham's treatment of logical fictions seems to support the general thesis that fictions are acceptable or otherwise according to whether or not analysis is possible. Good fictions can be analysed, and here 'fiction' becomes a technical term; bad fictions cannot.

Talking in *Of Laws in General* of the fictitious entities used in law, such as *power, right*, and so on, Bentham comments that, with the availability of the analysis that he can provide, 'these phantastic denominations are a sort of paper currency: if we know how at any time to change them and get sterling in their room, it is well: if not, we are deceived, and ... we possess nothing but sophistry and nonsense' (251). This nice metaphor carries the idea that as long as the terms can be backed by an analysis, their use is quite acceptable. It is not necessary always to change paper money for gold; it is just necessary to know that the gold is available if required. The analogy is used to give a different result for rights of man in the *Pannomial Fragments*: 'rights of man, when placed by the side of legal rights, resemble assignats, whether false or genuine, placed by the side of guineas or Louis d'or' (*III 220); that is, the false rights spawned by the French Revolution are compared to their new issues of paper which could not be converted into gold (the *assignats*). So the idea is not to get rid of fictitious entities, just to show that they can be explained and supported if necessary. Once this has been shown to be possible then the legal fictitious terminology is quite acceptable. Changing the metaphor: 'I would not, therefore, employ the word *title* as a fundamental term, but once translated from the language of fiction into the language of reality, I hesitate not to employ it. It is not luminous in itself, but when it has received light, if it be properly placed, it may serve either to reflect or to transmit it' (*General View*, III 189). Once clarified, illuminated, by relation to realities, this fictitious vocabulary is perfectly perspicuous. Hence Bentham is at pains to emphasise that for these legal fictitious entities, just as in the more purely logical fictions, they are blameless; 'in no instance can the idea of *fiction* be freer from all tincture of blame' (*Chrest.*, VIII 119). This is mainly because, 'though fictitious, the language cannot be termed *deceptious* in intention at least' (*PANN III 218n) when legal rights are considered.

So Bentham holds that these legal fictitious entities are acceptable, and there is nothing blameworthy about an analysis of the law (such as his own) which makes use of such terms as *power, right, obligation*, and so on. However, he goes further than this. It is not just that such terms are not bad, when properly explained. It is the case that they are positively a good thing. He calls rights 'fictitious, but none the less valuable objects' (*Procedure*, II 98). This refers to the value of the object rather than the value of the way of referring to it; but if the object is of value, then there is naturally value in the most convenient form of reference. Convenience is in fact the key; 'fictions are feigned for the convenience of discourse' (IMPL 125; the example is *disposition*). It will be remembered that Bentham held that the logical fictions were not only convenient but necessary if there was to be discourse at all; and this is a claim he makes about other acceptable fictions. One such fiction is that of talking of psychological entities as if they were physical ones. Discussing this case in the *Essay on Language*, Bentham notes that 'no deception is intended' (VIII 327), and then says that 'from what there is of falsehood not only is pure good the result, but it is the work of invincible necessity, − on no other terms can discourse be carried on' (327). Here we have exactly that transition traced above from fictions being not bad ('blameless') to their being positively good (productive of pure good) to their being necessary. This particular example, of psychological terms, is repeated elsewhere and again held to be a 'necessary fiction' (*Chrest.*, VIII 73n), or '*fictitious* framed by necessity for the purpose of discourse' (SPRINGS I 205). So it is perhaps not surprising that he makes this strong claim also for the legal fictitious entities such as rights. These are also, on occasion, declared to be 'those fictitious indeed, but indispensably employed, creatures of imagination and language, viz. *rights* and *obligations* (*Introductory View of the Rationale of Evidence*, VI 7) or 'feigned for the purpose of discourse, by a fiction so necessary, that without it human discourse could not be carried on' (*PANN III 218; example, *right*). It has been seen above that Bentham himself had a subjective view of necessity as representing an attitude of mind rather than a feature in the object. So too much should not perhaps be made of a distinction between calling fictions convenient and calling them necessary. They are always declared to be necessary means for an end, namely discourse; and the main point is that they are highly convenient, indeed as far as we can see unavoidable, means towards talking sense about a particular subject matter. As he expresses his view, somewhat more fully and carefully, in *Of Laws in General*, (here considering the example *property*): 'It is not necessary on the present occasion to enter into the examination of the necessity there may be for setting up this fiction: it is sufficient that it be actually and universally set up, and that it is so firmly engrafted into every language that it is now impossible to carry on discourse without it' (284-5).

If these defences of fiction as not just not harmful but as positively beneficial or unavoidable merely involve the claim that the language we actually have cannot be used to say what it actually says without these terms, then it is not a very powerful defence. It could be used for any other term regularly used in the language, such as natural rights. Users of natural right vocabulary could also claim that these terms were necessary for discourse, that is necessary for saying just what they were trying to say, and that they were now engrafted into common language. Bentham's claim, however, is never for the acceptance of the language as it stands but for its criticism, just like any other institution. He ends his chief attack on the French Declaration of rights with the claim that 'the language of plain and strong sense is difficult to learn; the language of smooth nonsense easy and familiar. The one requires a force of attention capable of stemming the tide of usage and example; the other requires nothing but to swim with it' (ANARCH, Parekh 289). He recommends 'education' as a way of showing the nothingness of the laws of nature. So the emphasis is still upon analysis rather than use. It is analysis which makes the fictions respectable, it is use which makes them convenient and desirable. Without respectability, convenience would not be enough. However, the necessity of certain terms for language, or for particular areas of language, does highlight the problem that even though these respectable fictions may be explicable in terms of realities, it still might not be the case that they were eliminable, even in principle. Continuing the paper money metaphor, it would only be possible to change some of the money at any one time; eliminating all the paper would be impossible, even in principle. There is a pessimistic reflection in *Of Laws in General* that 'the tyranny of language makes its sport of scientific industry' because, in any attempt to explain some fictions, other fictions enter into the analysis making an 'illogical and vicious circle in which it seems probable that we shall for ever be condemned to run' (279). Here any one fiction could only be explained against the background of others; there is no fiction that could not be explained, but it would not be possible to explain them all at once. This would still be acceptable for the project of clarification, if it is allowed that it is perfectly permissible to use the fictions once they could be analysed; for no fiction appears for which an analysis cannot be provided. It is the next step which would be fatal; the step of having a circle of fictitious terms where no analysis was possible at all into any terms referring to real entities. Then, in the analogy of paper money, we would have a situation (like the present-day position, rather than the position in Bentham's day) where it was not possible to change any bit of paper for gold, let alone the whole lot at once. Once such self-sustaining circles of fictions, such self-verifying portions of language, are allowed, then it becomes impossible to rule out any fictions, or language, as unacceptable.

So, with this last caution in mind, it seems that Bentham can make the distinction between good and bad uses of fictions in terms of the possibility of analysis, and that this would be a permissible method of distinguishing between legal rights and natural rights, and of justifying the fictitious entities which Bentham himself uses in his positive analyses. Granted that this apparatus might be sufficient for the job, however, it still remains to be shown that legal rights can indeed be analysed successfully and natural rights cannot. To this we must now turn; although since the analysis of rights is a contentious topic in the more sophisticated regions of jurisprudence, our treatment here will inevitably have to be shorter and cruder than the topic warrants. It will be remembered that Bentham's analysis of rights involves two steps: first rights are analysed in terms of duties, and then duties are analysed in terms of commands, backed by a threat of sanctions. This means that there are two claims to be evaluated in the analysis, the analysis of rights in terms of duties (which applies as much, as far as it goes, to natural rights) and the analysis of duties in terms of commands. With regard to the first it is a frequently made (and frequently contested) claim that rights and duties are correlative. This is not Bentham's own position, as he believes that there can be duties without rights. Such is the case, for example, where there are 'self-regarding' duties; duties owed by someone to himself (IPML 206n; OLG 58). In the normal case of duties, however, when the duty is 'extra-regarding', that is directed towards others, then, if there is a duty, then there is also a right. This is because Bentham regards a right as something which the law creates by imposing duties on others. It is a kind of protection. My own natural powers are in these specified cases shielded, and so increased, by the power of law. So, if I have the right to walk unimpeded along a public highway (a 'right of way'), for Bentham this consists in my ability to walk down the street being protected by law in that it lays duties on all other persons not to prevent me. Such duties may, of course, be defeasible, as when, for example, I am escaping from justice, but this in turn just shows the limits of the right. As Bentham puts it: 'to know then how to expound a right, carry your eye to that act which, in the circumstances in question, would be a violation of that right: the law creates the right by prohibiting that act' (IPML 206n). This is sometimes called, for example by H.L.A. Hart (Hart 1973 p. 178), the benefit, or beneficiary, theory of rights: for someone to have rights is for him to be the beneficiary of duties laid on other people. As Bentham puts it in the *Traités*: 'rights are in themselves advantages, benefits, for him who enjoys them' ('bénéfices'; **Traités* ii 1; LEGIS 98); or, as he says in the case of property in the *Manual of Political Economy*: 'the end in view . . . is the securing to a certain individual the enjoyment of a benefit. This benefit he can not enjoy except in the first instance all persons are debarred from acting in certain ways upon a particular thing' (Stark i 265n).

Whether ultimately correct or incorrect as an account of rights, Bentham's treatment of them in terms of duties is an undeniably sophisticated instrument in his hands. This is because he is not only aware of the different kinds of ways in which right and duty can be related, but also aware of the different kinds of commands and so of the different kinds of duties to which they give rise. Aware that this involved 'entering . . . a particular branch of logic, untouched by Aristotle . . . the several forms of *imperation*: or . . . of sentences expressive of volition' (IPML 299n), he had to invent a deontic logic, in which he distinguished between commands, prohibitions, permissions, and non-commands and worked out their logical relations with great detail and sophistication (OLG 95f). For our purposes here, the distinction between command and permission will serve, since the others can be formed by negation of them (and they can be formed by negation from each other; a permission means that 'it is not the case that you must not . . .'). Awareness of these distinctions and logical relations means that Bentham can distinguish between three kinds of

91

rights, according to the different ways in which they relate to commands (and so to duties). In the first case we have simple permission to perform an act. Here no duty is laid on someone either to perform or not to perform, and no duty is laid on anyone else either to assist or not to prevent the act in question. The law, as it were, declares a gap in itself, so that the legal situation with respect to the acts in question is just as if there was no law. Such a right is very like, or is an example of, a natural right. Bentham says that one 'efficient cause' of a right is 'absence of correspondent obligation. You have a *right* to perform whatever you are not under an obligation to abstain from the performance of. Such is the right which every human being has in a state of nature' (*PANN III 218). This is therefore to be distinguished from a second kind of right when 'the efficient cause of right is, presence of correspondent obligation' (*PANN III 218), as in the case of normal legal rights discussed above. When he makes the distinction at this point, he calls the former 'naked' rights and the latter 'established' rights. However Bentham realises that the latter class of established rights can in turn be divided into two subdivisions, by again considering the different relations which they bear to duties. For the obligations imposed on others from which I benefit may be obligations not to interfere with me, or they may be obligations to render me positive assistance. In the first case my right is secured by their being commanded not to do something. In the second case it is secured by their being commanded to do something, such as being compelled to afford assistance (*Manual of Political Economy*, Stark i 232), or 'such acts as are judged to be necessary for the removal of . . . obstacles' (IPML 206n).

Bentham was therefore aware of the distinction which is more familiar to students of jurisprudence from Hohfeld between what Hohfeld calls a liberty and what he calls a claim right, between the case in which I am said to have a right to do something because I am not under an obligation not to, and the case in which I am said to have a right to something because someone else is under an obligation to me about it. In both authors the distinction is constituted in the same way by obligations placed on the rightholder and on other people. Bentham also uses the same special terms as Hohfeld on occasion, such as 'liberty', 'privilege', 'immunity' (IPML 241), although not always in the same way (for example, in the *Manual of Political Economy* he distinguishes the first two kinds of rights mentioned above as 'liberties' in distinction to the third (Stark i 232). Furthermore, he says quite a lot about another way in which Hohfeld says that rights can be understood, when my right consists in my ability to change the legal status of people or objects. Bentham also calls these a kind of right and like Hohfeld he calls them a power, more specifically an 'investitive power' (OLG 84). So, given that Hohfeld has been generally regarded this century as providing a sophisticated analysis, which has been copied in several books on jurisprudence, Bentham can also be taken to have provided a sophisticated treatment which, if it is wrong, is not obviously wrong. Furthermore, the distinction between the second and third kind of right, as described above and which was not brought out by Hohfeld, is as important as the distinction between both of these and the first. This is the distinction between those rights in which my benefit consists in the law making others leave me alone, and those in which it consists in the law making others help me. Examples of the former are such as the rights to property, liberty, and (in its normal use) life; examples of the latter are a child's right to care and protection, or people's rights to social services. Satisfying these latter rights involves people positively doing something, which brings in its turn other differences, such as the problem of identifying who it is that is under the obligation to do this thing. In the ceaseless chatter about rights, which is as conspicuous a feature of contemporary political argument as it was of the argument of Bentham's day, confusion results from failure to distinguish these two kinds of rights.

Bentham's treatment of rights can, therefore, provide illuminating and important distinctions. However, it might be thought that the very last problem mentioned, the problem of identifying who it is in some cases that is under an obligation when someone has a right, shows that Bentham is mistaken. It can be thought that he mistakes the order of production and importance of rights and duties. So, it might be thought, duties are imposed to protect rights, rather than rights arising out of imposed duties. It is the rights, either natural or legal, with which we start. These rights then form the ground for the imposition of duties to protect them. So, for example, I start with a right to work and then, if I am lucky, duties are imposed on the administration or on employers which allows me to exercise my right. I start with a legal right to the free exercise of my trade or profession, and the courts struggle along, deciding by their treatment of particular cases what duties such a right does or does not impose on others. In a country with a written constitution, it might declare that I have a right to the due process of law; again it is only discovered subsequently what duties this imposes on officials, or what duties it prevents a legislature imposing on people. Some of these examples have a natural right, some a legal; but in all cases it seems that we start with the right rather than the duty. Examination of particular legal systems can also reveal that the relevant statute law sometimes explicitly creates rights rather than imposing duties, and that these duties may exist in some cases in which there is no person subject to a duty (so MacCormick 1977, pp. 190, 200 respectively).

Examples like the last are not really threatening to Bentham's account once it is remembered the looseness of fit between his analysis and what it analyses. The analysis gives the meaning, rather than restating the already existing meaning. It does not have to be thought to be in an entailment relation, but, rather, gives the procedure of verification. So finding some rights without duties is not threatening to Bentham, providing that the normal way we understand a right is by a duty. Once we can talk of some rights, then others may be introduced for systematic purposes, to simplify; or as place-holders for a complex of duties which still needs fully to be worked out. So the imposition of the right by a statute could be taken as the declaration that there should be a duty, together with a method (either specific or understood) to discover who is under the duty. Although the right may be cited first, it actually comes to depend upon what the duty is. The precise nature of the right can only be learned by discovering the precise nature of the obligation. This is Bentham's analytical point: not that we cannot use a language of rights, or even that it is simply translatable into a language of duties, but rather that it must ultimately be understood in terms of duties. The central point is that if you really want to see what you have got when you are told that you have a right, see what duties are laid on other people.

Even so, such concessionary remarks do not seem sufficient to meet the force of the other examples, which seem to show that rights have an essential and ineliminable explanatory function, so that what duties there are are explained by what rights there are, rather than vice versa. However, to put the objectio: in this way is to confuse two kinds of explanation which Benthan clearly distinguished. There is the explanation of why the law is as it is, which is intended to justify or criticise it (what Bentham called 'censorial jurisprudence'), and there is the explanation of what the law actually is ('expository jurisprudence'). Both can properly be called explanation, but they are quite different from each other. Bentham had himself, of course, a system of evaluation which he used to criticise the law, and which he proposed as the basis for making law as it ought to be. This was utilitarianism, that is, taking the greatest happiness as the proper end of the legislator. According to this system of evaluation, law is only a good thing in so far as it has good consequences. It is a means to an end. The means used, which are the imposition of obligations, are in themselves bad, involving as they do threats, or impositions, of pain. They are, therefore, only justified if this badness is outweighed by the goodness of the end, that is by the benefits which the law secures. On Bentham's analytical, expository, treatment it has been seen that these benefits are rights. So for Bentham also rights are what the law is all about. According to his censorial jurisprudence, rights are the point of the law, the reason for having it. The duties are only a means to an end, to be explained in terms of that end, that is in terms of the rights to which they give rise. It is because security of my person and property are good things that duties are laid on others to leave me alone. So it does not form a problem for Bentham if rights form the starting point of explanation. It is just important that the two kinds of explanation are separated. The rights there ought to be gives the reason for the duties there ought to be; but what rights there actually are are discovered by seeing what duties there actually are. It is this which shows how far what ought to be established really is established; which shows what it really is that my rights come to, as things are at present.

Bentham can, therefore, be given some support for his project of understanding what rights there are ultimately in terms of duties, even if the language of rights may have a useful (essential for discourse) simplifying function, tying whole bundles of disparate duties together. It is a particularly suitable example for his kind of account of fictitious entities, given (as has been seen) that the way that these entities arise is from the use of substantives in language. For, as has often been observed, the modern treatment of rights in which they are spoken of as if they were independent entities is a comparatively recent innovation. For a thousand years Roman Law carried on quite happily without any such things. It was, of course, right to do certain things; but people did not have rights. Things had the property of being right, but there was no substantial or fictitious entity, talked of as existing, or as possessed by people. This historical background lends some support for Bentham's analysis. The fact that people managed to get on without them so long gives some, weak, reason for thinking that they are not needed; a suggestion entertained, but not really endorsed, by John Finnis (Finnis 1980 p. 209). More importantly, the transition from the use of the predicate 'is right' to the noun 'a right' seems exactly in line with the account of logical fictitious entities discussed above;

and just as the fictitious qualities such as roundness could be eliminated by taking the nouns back to predicates, so here rights can be eliminated by taking them back to right action (duties, obligation). At one stage, indeed, in the *Anarchical Fallacies*, Bentham considers such a grammatical transformation. Talking of the word 'right' he says: 'in its adjective shape, it is as innocent as a dove; it breathes nothing but morality and peace. It is the shape that, passing in at the heart, it gets possession of the under-standing; it then assumes its substantive shape, and joining itself to a band of suitable associates, plants the banner of insurrection, anarchy, and lawless violence' (Parekh p. 287). This is strongly addressed against the French use of natural rights, and here it looks as if the whole trouble comes from using a substantive instead of an adjective. This would be too simple an overall account, because the perfectly respectable legal rights are also substantives; however, the situation here is like that of *necessity* and the real and imaginary fictitious qualities discussed above. The substantive shape is tolerable in the legal case, where the conversion to adjective form is clear; however, it is important to realise that natural rights are different.

Once the fictitious entities of legal rights were invented, they inevitably were not just regarded as mere reflections of duty, but took on free standing significance. They came to be thought of like items of property, areas of petty control or dominion. Hence the perhaps surprising connection traced by Richard Tuck between the rise of the conception of rights as things which people possessed and justifications of slavery and absolute govern-ment; for as long as rights are a mere reflection of duties, then everyone's duty not to infringe the liberty of others means that everyone has a right not to be enslaved, whether he likes it or not; while once his right is thought of like a piece of property over which he has the power of disposal, then it is open to him to dispose of his right to liberty, for example, by entering into a contract with an absolute government or by selling himself into slavery (Tuck 1979, e.g. p. 54). These unsavoury consequences apart, it does not seem necessary that a right has to be thought of in this way as an area of active control or power rather than as an area of passive receipt of benefits (as Hart, for example, proposes against Bentham (Hart 1973)). I can, of course, choose to exercise my legal powers (of which Bentham has a separate account), and the benefit I receive on Bentham's view of rights is the opportunity to exercise my natural powers in whatever way I wish (with my land, person, and so on) providing I don't infringe duties to others. However, in positive law my rights are not identified with legal opportunities to promote actions, that is, to exercise my will in bringing a case against someone (for example, Lord Diplock: 'it is elementary law that diplomatic immunity is not immunity from legal liability but immunity from suit' *Empson v Smith* (1966) 1 QB at 438). It is also the case that the property analogy on which this view of rights rests is fragile. It applies much more naturally to the second rather than the third kind of right identified above. Life and liberty might possibly be thought to be things I possess, over which I exercise control. If, however, there are also rights constituted by other people's obligation to assist, then the point about them is that they refer to things that I do not possess. They are things which I need (health, work, care, and so on), and which must be provided by others. Having a need (that is a lack of something) is even less like possessing an object than having life or liberty is. Here clearly to talk about rights is not to talk about an entity, but rather to talk about the way I ought (morally or legally) to be treated by others. The fictitious entity is the shadow of an obligation, in just the way Bentham wants. The child with the right of care and protection cannot choose to dispense parents from their duty. From a Benthamite point of view the whole basis of the analogy in property itself is not a help, since on a Benthamite view, property is merely a creation of law, made by duties imposed on others (e.g. OLG 255). So it cannot help in the explanation of other rights, life, liberty, and so on, as not being reducible to duties.

Given the importance of natural rights, and of the contrast Bentham wants between legal rights and natural rights, rights have been discussed at some length. We can afford to be much briefer with duties, not because Bentham's account is any less contentious, but because (as well as their having been discussed in the last chapter) it is plausible to suppose that there must be some method for the verification or recognition of the existence of legal duties, for example in terms of court procedure. In Bentham's own account it has been seen that liability to punishment forms a central element ('without the notion of punishment . . . no notion can we have of either *right* or *duty*' (FG 495n)). Again this relation allows Bentham to make distinctions, and he distinguishes between kinds of duty according to the kind of sanction to which a transgressor is liable: political, religious, 'moral' (which is what Bentham calls the force of public opinion; the sanction is social mortification), and even physical. It has also been seen that Bentham regards law as the command of a sovereign, and his overall account varies a bit according to whether he is concentrating on the source of the obligation (command) or on its sanction (punishment).

Essentially he wants both: 'political duty is created by punishment: or at least by the will of persons who have punishment in their hands; persons stated and *certain*, — political superiors' (FG 496n). The adequacy of the account also depends upon having both, for as long as law is just taken as command, it is hard to give an account of customary law, either of common law or of customs which are recognised by the courts; while as long as the concentration is just on sanctions, it is hard to give an account of general commands issued by a sovereign which specify no punishment for non-performance. For example, to take the case of common law, if punishment is central, then it can obviously be reduced, in view of the sanctions threatened by the courts. If, however, command is central, then Bentham is reduced to saying that it becomes law by the 'acquisience' of the supreme body, which gives it 'tacit' adoption (COMM 162). Reduction to pains would make common law a justifiable fiction, but tacit adoption can no more make common law a justified fiction than tacit consent can make the original contract a justified fiction. So, to save the analysis, both elements have to be thought of as working together and, just as with rights, we must think of it as giving the normal criteria or verification for the use of the concept in question, rather than as providing propositions invariably entailed by propositions containing the term in question. We then get that legal duties are the result of commands of that body to which the people in question have a habit of obedience, and which give as a reason for obedience the threat of future punishment. This covers the normal case, and the others can be handled by analogy or extension. Explicit commands without sanctions, for example, are on this account parasitic oddities which necessarily could not become the normal case; otherwise the habit of obedience would break down, and whatever body issued them would therefore no longer be issuing commands, but instead merely wishes about what they would like people to do.

Bentham's analysis is an attempt to produce a completely neutral, descriptive, account of legal obligation, shorn of any normative elements. It is expository rather than censorial jurisprudence, treating of the law as it is, not of the law as it ought to be. In this treatment law is not only demythologised but also demoralised. This produces some strange consequences. It results, for example, in treating every law as if it were the command of a disjunction: either do this, or else take the consequences. Either action would, on the face of it, be an equally legitimate way of obeying the law (of discharging one's legal duty). The obligation implied by punishment in the political case is just as amoral for

Bentham as is the obligation he says is imposed by a purely physical sanction, such as the pain that would result from the removal of the tooth. In one case the relation of painful consequences to possible actions is artificially produced, in the other case it is natural, but in both cases it provides reasons for action. The pain specified by the legislator is a reason for not doing some actions, just as the pain of a tooth coming out is a reason for keeping out of the way of someone swinging a heavy weight round his head. In both cases, however, someone can reasonably choose on occasion to undergo the pain, that is when he thinks that the pain is outweighed by the advantages. He can choose the present pain of the removal of a tooth in order to prevent future toothache, and he can choose to undergo the specified punishment rather than undertake the commanded action. The fine for parking on the yellow lines is exactly like payment for the dog licence; in both cases the legislator commands that people engaging in that kind of thing must pay up. Interestingly enough, Bentham himself on other occasions criticises the tradition of passive obedience which held that the good citizen commanded to do something against his religious conscience should choose to take the punishment rather than to obey (*Swear*, V 211; COMM 81; FG 440n). On his general acccount, however, he must think that reasons for following the command rather than taking the punishment involve extra-legal moral or social considerations; as far as expository jurisprudence is concerned the law must be analysed by him as a completely amoral choice of conforming to the command or taking the punishment.

It is at least *prima facie* plausible, therefore, that an analysis can be given of legal rights and duties which shows that they belong to the class of acceptable fictions; although this does involve drawing a sharp line between censorial and expository jurisprudence, and taking a completely demoralised view of the law. This, therefore, means that he can talk of them (as was seen in the last chapter) as having some sort of reality. As he puts it in *Chrestomathia*:

> from the observation, by which, for example, the words *duties* and *rights* are here spoken of as names of fictitious entities, let it not for a moment so much as be supposed, that, in either instance, the reality of the object is meant to be denied, in any sense in which in ordinary language the reality of it is assumed. (VIII 126n)

This sort of 'verbal reality', as it will be remembered he assigns to such fictions, fits in with calling them 'real rights' in the *Pannomial Fragments* and *Anarchical Fallacies*. It now has to be seen why the same treatment is not also available for natural rights; that is, why they also cannot be rendered respectable and given a kind of reality by relation to real entities. Bentham, it will be remembered, thought that they were merely imaginary rights; that they were nothing at all, mere nonentities, fabulous entities, chimeras. His explanation of this was that the law of nature was really imaginary, and therefore the same sort of reduction of rights to duties and duties to commands would not in this case relate them to anything real. As far as this goes, however, it just shows that natural rights are not like legal rights; which is something no user or defender of natural rights need deny. It does not show that there might not be some quite different way of relating them to real entities; they are, after all, accepted and used parts of the language of many people, as Bentham was only too well aware, and this must mean that the claim that they cannot be analysed needs considerable support.

The key to the central point of Bentham's attack on natural rights lies in the same distinction as has been seen to be important in his account of legal rights, that between censorial and expository jurisprudence, between how things are and how they ought to be. In one of his draft manuscript prefaces for his great work which he wrote in the 1770s, Bentham quoted extensively from the passage in which Bacon distinguishes between 'what is received law' and 'what ought to be law' (UC 27.12; Bacon, *Advancement of Learning* II xxiii). However, not surprisingly, he normally attributes his appreciation of this distinction to Hume; he notes in *Chrestomathia* that, when he read Hume's *Treatise* the observation presented itself to him 'as one of cardinal importance' (VIII 128n), and says that for anyone not completely separating what *has been done* from what *ought to be done* 'the whole field of Ethics ... must ever have been, — yea, and ever will be, — a labyrinth without a clue'. He then immediately goes on to say that this is the situation with writers on international law like Grotius and Puffendorf. These are leading natural lawyers, and so the point Bentham wants to make against users of natural law is that they confuse what ought to be with what is. Similarly, in his article on Humphrey's real property code, originally published in the *Westminster Review* for 1826, Bentham attributes to Hume the distinction between is and ought and criticises the lawyers for lack of appreciation of it (V 389). It will be remembered, also, that part of his attack on 'everything as it should be' Blackstone depended upon attributing to Blackstone this confusion. So, as indeed he graphically displays himself as being in the *Auto-Icon* when giving reasons for preservation of his body (14), we have Bentham on one side against a tribe of natural lawyers on the other, his objection to them being their confusion of what is with what ought to be. As he writes in a footnote to the *Introduction*:

> Of what stamp are the works of Grotius, Puffendorf, and Burlamaqui? are they political or ethical, historical or juridical, expository or censorial? Sometimes one thing, sometimes another. . . . A defect this to which all books must almost unavoidably be liable, which take for their subject the pretended *law of nature*; an obscure phantom, which, in the imaginations of those who go in chase of it, points sometimes to *manners*, sometimes to *laws*; sometimes to what law *is*, sometimes to what it *ought* to be. (IPML 298n)

Whatever he had thought before of Grotius and Puffendorf, by the time the French Revolution had got properly into its stride, he declared that what in them 'were little more than improprieties in language' had become a '*moral* crime' (ANARCH, Parekh p. 290). The central point is, however, the same; it is just that the consequences have become more serious. This is that in their confusion of how the law is with how the law ought to be, the users of natural law and natural rights, while thinking they are merely describing how things are, are really engaged in changing it. They are 'making laws on pretence of declaring them' (ANARCH, Parekh p. 271). They are not describing, but really legislating; hence Bentham talks of 'the legislating Grotii' and declares that 'the jurisconsult in his arm-chair is an individual sufficiently peaceable: he lies, — he fabricates false laws in the simplicity of his heart' (*PANN III 220). For, of course, as well as the confusion involved in really legislating while pretending to be describing, there is also the problem that someone in his armchair, to whom people have no habit of obedience, cannot legislate at all. So Bentham's real point is that what look like descriptions of how the law is are really expressed wishes, desires, ideas, about how the law ought to be: 'if I say a man has a natural right . . . all that it can mean, if it mean anything and mean true, is, that I am of the opinion that he ought to have a political right' (*PANN III 218). They are not descriptions of how things are in any sense, and so there is no way that they can be reduced to, or replaced by, other descriptions of how things are which would provide a clarificatory or paraphrastic analysis of them.

While this may serve very well as criticism of items like the French *Declaration of the rights of man*, which are thus not declarations at all, it merely opens up another problem, or another direction in which the main question can be attacked. For once it is seen that such statements are normative, that they are about reasons for having rights rather than descriptions of established rights, then this might be thought to provide the required clarification which makes natural rights respectable. Bentham, after all, in the last quotation, talks of what someone using such a term means 'if it mean anything and mean true', and this seems analogous to the kind of provision of meaning which was seen in the last chapter to be the function of paraphrastic analysis. Bentham's immediate reply to this would no doubt be that 'reasons for wishing there were such things as rights are not rights; a reason for wishing that a certain right were established, is not that right; want is not supply; hunger is not bread' (ANARCH, Parekh p. 269). However, once it is allowed that natural rights can be distinguished from legal rights, this objection falls away. Natural rights are reasons for having legal rights; but the natural right, the hunger, can exist without the legal right, the bread. Indeed, at one point in the *Comment*, while discussing the law of nature, Bentham proposes a reformulation of what Blackstone says putting an *ought* for an *is*, and saying that this '*would* have been intelligible' (294). So, once its normative force is explicitly recognised, it seems that Bentham should allow that natural law, and so natural rights, can be made intelligible; it is not, after all, 'nonsense'.

This picks up again the problem, mentioned in passing in Chapter II, of Bentham's own critical standpoint. It was mentioned there that Bentham needs a standpoint very like natural law from which he can criticise established law. Bentham's critical basis, the foundation for his censorial jurisprudence, is the principle of utility; so the point could be made by saying that the principle of utility is very like a principle in natural law. Indeed the bit of natural law in Blackstone which it has just been mentioned that Bentham thinks can be made intelligible is the claim that performance of actions tending to man's real happiness are part of the law of nature. In any case, whatever is thought about the assimilation of the utility principle to natural law, many of the claims which Bentham makes for the utility principle, which is an explicitly normative principle, are like the claims he makes for his approved analyses of such descriptive items as legal rights and duties. For example, he says that 'when thus interpreted, the words *ought*, and *right* and *wrong*, and others of that stamp, have a meaning: when otherwise, they have none' (IPML 13). This is exactly like the claim made with respect to (legal) duty that the analysis gives the meaning; and it is for the same reasons in that in both cases the proffered analysis relates the term being discussed to pains, which are real entities. In the one case the maximisation of pleasure and the minimisation of pain are taken to provide an analysis of, give meaning to, *right* and *wrong*; in the other case pain is taken to provide (part of) the analysis of, or give meaning to, legal *duties* and *rights*. Furthermore, Bentham not only provides a similar kind of analysis, or account, of his normative principle, but also talks about how it 'may be convenient, for the purposes of discourse, to imagine a kind of law or dictate, called a law or dictate of utility' (IPML 13). This is but only one example of a more general claim that when a man is prompted by any motive to engage in an action, 'it may be of use, for the convenience of discourse, to speak of such motive giving birth to an imaginary kind of *law* or *dictate*, injoining him to engage, or not to engage, in it' (IPML 117n). So Bentham not only thinks that the utility principle gives meanings to evaluative language, he also thinks that it can properly be looked at as some kind of imaginary law. So not much more would be required to make the law of nature a perfectly respectable imaginary law, used for the convenience of discourse, and justified (as in the utility principle) by the possibility of analysing it as a normative principle which recommends certain courses of action, perhaps, indeed, courses which have reference to human happiness or utility (reference to pleasures and pains).

How Bentham regards such normative requirements, and what justifies his particular candidate, the principle of utility, are topics to be dealt with later in this book. For the moment it is enough to say that Bentham himself, who uses such principles in his censorial jurisprudence, cannot regard the very idea of a normative principle as disreputable; it therefore cannot follow just from the observation that the law of nature is normative rather than descriptive, that it is worthless, that it is a mere nothing, that it is nonsense, or any of the other derogatory things which Bentham says of it. So if Bentham's point is to be viable at all, it has to be more limited. It has, in fact, to retreat to the original claim that the proponents of the law of nature (or of natural rights) confuse questions of fact with questions of value, and that if the law is taken in a purely descriptive way, no analysis is possible. Hence, taken in this way, it cannot be given a meaning; and so does not describe anything which is in any sense real. This depends very much upon thinking of natural rights as strictly analogous to legal rights. Starting with the idea of right as given, say, by property rights, we find in Bentham's analysis that 'right is . . . the child of law', hence that 'a natural right is a son that never had a father'

103

(*Escheat*, Stark i 334). Accordingly, a natural right 'is a contradiction in terms' like 'round square' or 'incorporeal body' (ibid.); more accurately, the only way of giving 'right' meaning is incompatible with giving 'natural' meaning in the same expression. So the general, if limited, point here is the original one that since Nature is a purely fictitious personage, there is no legislator which can produce natural law, and so natural rights. Given this, and Bentham's general claims about analysis conferring meaning, he can indeed claim that the French *Declaration* contains 'words without meaning'; that 'look to the letter, you find nonsense; look beyond the letter, you find nothing'; that 'natural rights is simple nonsense' (ANARCH, Parekh pp. 261; 261; 269). If, however, natural rights are considered as a contribution not to the question of what rights there are but of what rights there ought to be, then, at least as far as we have seen up to now, Bentham goes too far in saying that 'to talk of a *Law of Nature*, giving ... or not giving ... a *natural right*, is so much sheer nonsense, answering neither the one question nor the other' (*Escheat*, Stark i 310).

If natural rights were for Bentham simple nonsense, it was natural and imprescriptible rights that were nonsense upon stilts. This brings out why Bentham was so concerned to separate questions of fact from questions of value and why he said 'that this distinction should, on every occasion, be clearly perceived, is ... the interest of the great bulk of mankind' (*Chrest.*, VIII 128n). For if the distinction is made, then what *is* can be found to be not what it *ought to be*; the laws can be criticised and proposals made for reform. Part of Bentham's objection to the idea of natural property rights is that this would prevent the operation of his proposals for reform of administration or taxation since any such change involves alteration or removal of property. More generally, the idea of imprescriptible rights, that is of entrenched, unalterable rights, Bentham thinks of as a potential block to the path of reform. It would place limits on a sovereign legislature; it would be a part of how the law is that prevented that legislature making the law be as it ought to be. So the point of Bentham's distinction between fact and value, and of his attack on natural rights, is, at least in his eyes, a progressive one: it allows criticism and change of the laws. It enables rights, that is benefits, to be created. For, as Bentham puts it: 'it is not the rights of man which causes government to be established: – on the contrary, it is the non-existence of those rights' (*PANN III 219). It is this creative, legislative, programme which will be looked at in the following chapter.

Notes

(a) Considerable use has been made in this chapter of the *Pannomial Fragments*. Although asterisked, like the same editor's *Nomography* in the last chapter, they read very like Bentham and are, again, probably reliable enough.

(b) The other possible source of natural law, not discussed in the chapter, is divine law. In this case there is an identifiable law-giver; here the problems relate to knowledge of this law-giver's intentions. In respect of normative principles (which in his eyes is what natural law comes to) Bentham held that the principle of utility was epistemologically superior to knowledge of God's desires or commands; hence God's commands could not be the foundation of the right normative principle. See, for example, IPML chapter X 40 (119ff). In the *Comment*, Bentham treats Divine Law separately from Natural law.

(c) For Hohfeld, with whom Bentham's views are here compared, see Hohfeld (1919).

(d) For criticism and discussion of Bentham's legal theory, see not only the Hart article mentioned, but a whole series of Hart articles now most conveniently collected in Hart (1982). The Benthamite doctrine of law as emanating from a law-giver is criticised in Raz (1970) and Hart (1961). The Benthamite sanction theory of duties, as discussed in both this chapter and the last is criticised in Hacker (1973).

(e) It was, I think, Schumpeter who first claimed that utilitarianism is just a variety of natural law: 'utilitarianism was nothing but another natural law system' (Schumpeter 1955 132).

V

The Duty and Interest
Junction Principle

Up until now the emphasis in this book has been upon fiction, clarification, and enlightenment. Various legal practices, various justifications of these and other practices by lawyers, and various accounts of the nature of law itself have been successively clarified by proposals involving replacement, elimination, analysis, or redescription. Bentham's purpose, however, was not just to reach or promote greater understanding by means of clarification. He was a practical as well as a theoretical thinker. Indeed, it follows from his master principle, the principle of utility, that practical consequences are the only justification for theoretical activities. What he intended to do with the law was not just to show how its nature could be better understood but also to show how it could be used as an instrument in a particular practical project. For this project more than clarification is required. Other principles and assumptions are involved, and it is the task of this chapter to draw them out and to distinguish them one from another.

It was seen briefly at the end of the last chapter that something analogous to the grand project of clarification of the nature of the law, which was discussed at length in it and the previous chapter, could also be applied to the normative principles which were concerned not just with what the law was but with what the law ought to be. Bentham's own master practical or normative principle, the principle of utility, was also explained or justified as being a clarification of the ideas of good or right, as a method of giving meaning to these terms. Just as the law itself, moral principles were clarified by relating them to such real entities as pleasures and pains. It was also seen, however, that an additional clarificatory point which he wished to make was that these two clarificatory projects were quite different from each other and should

106

not be confused. For it was seen how Bentham, after Hume, stressed the distinction between *is* and *ought*, between how things are and how they ought to be, between expository and censorial jurisprudence. He said, it will be remembered, that this distinction was one of 'cardinal importance' without which the whole of ethics would remain 'a labyrinth without a clue' (*Chrest.*, VIII 128n). Failure to make the distinction was the basis of his objection to the natural lawyers and to 'everything as it should be' Blackstone. The distinction was claimed by him to be not only of great theoretical but also of great practical importance: without it not only would the labyrinth remain unthreaded but there would also be significant damage to the interest of the people. It is this practical importance, and the practical project which is founded on the distinction between *is* and *ought*, which is the concern of the present chapter.

Bentham's grand project was a project for legislation. Legislation was the master science. In discussing the principles upon which this project was based it is natural to turn to Bentham's own work entitled *An Introduction to the Principles of Morals and Legislation*. This not only has the advantage of being the most significant work published by Bentham himself, under his own personal superintendence, but also of being, as the title suggests, an introduction to the principles involved in his central project. As it is set up in the original, 1789, edition, it looks genuinely like an introduction, with the pages paginated in small roman numbers in the normal way for introductory material which precedes the main body of a work paginated in arabic numerals. Turning to the rousing first paragraph of the first chapter we read the ringing declaration that 'Nature has placed mankind under the governance of two sovereign masters, *pain* and *pleasure*. It is for them alone to point out what we ought to do, as well as to determine what we shall do. On the one hand the standard of right and wrong, on the other the chain of causes and effects, are fastened to their throne.' (11) Various modifying remarks have been made about this famous opening: its source in Helvetius has been stressed by Halévy, followed by Baumgardt (1952 p. 167); and Baumgardt also urges that we should take seriously the decidedly drier start to the next paragraph, 'but enough of metaphor and declamation' (11; Baumgardt p. 170). However, even if Bentham might have thought them slightly overwritten, and even if he got the ideas from elsewhere, Bentham certainly endorsed the main point of the sentences with which he starts his main treatise. The important thing to notice about them is not the introduction of Nature, which was indeed unnecessary or even unfortunate but that

Nature (or whatever) had given a double task to pleasure and pain. Pleasure and pain not only determine what it is that we ought to do (as in the principle of utility) but also determine what it is that we shall do. This is something quite separate from the *oughts*, a quite separate *is*, whose domain is descriptive psychology. As Bentham puts it in the next quoted sentence, it is a concern with the chain of causes and effects rather than with the standard of right and wrong. The repetition of the distinction in this following sentence, together with its phraseology which makes clear that it is a distinction ('on the one hand . . . on the other hand') shows that there should be no temptation to assume that Bentham is really asserting an identity in its predecessor, making what we ought to do and what we shall do the same thing. The *is* and *ought* are clearly kept separate, and so this famous opening clearly promises a double enquiry. There will be enquiry both into what we ought to do and also into what we will do. Principles will be proposed with respect to each; but these are separate enquiries, and the principles proposed will be separate principles.

The principles are proposed to guide a project, and the project is also stated in this opening paragraph. The paragraph ends with the claim that 'the *principle of utility* recognises this subjection, and assumes it for the foundation of that system, the object of which is to rear the fabric of felicity by the hands of reason and of law. Systems which attempt to question it, deal in sounds instead of sense, in caprice instead of reason, in darkness instead of light.' The point of the last sentence quoted here will already be familiar from previous chapters, with their stress on (to reverse the order of Bentham's remarks) enlightenment, reason, and the particular analyses which are necessary in order to endow phrases with meaning (give sense to sounds). The project is stated in the preceding sentence: given a particular end, a particular means is to be used. The end is set by the principle of utility, the clarified principle about what ought to happen as expressed in terms of pleasures and pains. It shows what ought to happen: the fabric of felicity ought to be constructed. The means, however, are reason and law. Law is the instrument which will be used, by the help of theoretical and practical reason, in order to promote the given end. Part of the use of reason is in understanding the nature of the instrument, so that what law is is clarified, as in the paraphrastic analyses discussed in the last two chapters. More, however, is required; reason needs more on which to work. It is not enough just to know the nature of the end and the nature of the means. It must also be known how this means can be used to promote that end. For this a psychology is required; that is, a factual or descriptive study of the nature of human beings which would enable a reasoner to predict how they will behave in specified particular circumstances. The laws have to be chosen rationally as a means of promoting the happiness of the people. It is only possible to choose them with this end in view if it is known what the effects of choosing any particular law will be; otherwise there is no reason to choose one law rather than another. Yet knowledge of the effects of laws upon people, just like knowledge of the effects of anything else on people, is a part of psychology. Therefore something else needs to be known for the project to work, some other deliverance of nature, namely the nature of human nature. This knowledge, however, is available. For as well as the principles guiding the end, which makes it comprehensible in terms of pleasures and pains, there are principles describing the means, which found a descriptive psychology also in terms of pleasures and pains. In the first case the principle is that pleasure ought to be maximised and pain minimised. In the second case the principle is that people act with the motive of maximising their own pleasure and minimising their own pain. These, however, are quite separate principles, the former being the standard of right and wrong, the latter the ground principle of the chain of causes and effects. For the project to work, both are needed and both must continue not to be confused.

Both these principles are highly contentious, and they will be examined separately in the two following chapters. In the next chapter, the psychological principle with the associated possibilities assumed by Bentham of calculation of the amounts of pleasures and pains will all be examined. Then in the following chapter, the grand normative principle, the principle of utility itself, will be subjected to scrutiny. However, before looking separately at the two principles it is important to realise that there are two, and how the essential nature of Bentham's project depended both upon their separation and upon their co-operation. It is important for understanding Bentham, but it is also important in placing some long-running criticisms of Bentham's kind of thought. It has been persistently claimed that utilitarianism rests on a confusion of *ought* with *is*; that is that it commits what G.E. Moore called the naturalistic fallacy (e.g. Sidgwick 1907 p. 412; Moore 1903 pp. 64-73). Yet if Bentham himself not only strongly emphasised this distinction, as has been shown, but also made it the fundamental basis of his system or grand project, as will be shown, then this is not an objection that can be easily levelled against him.

It was seen that at the end of the *Anarchical Fallacies*, Bentham declared that the practical importance of the separation of *is* and *ought* was that it permitted reform of established institutions. Whatever things were, it could be considered whether they were as they ought to be, and that this gave reason for changing them if they were not. It avoids the trap in which to say that something is established is taken to serve not only as a description but a recommendation. As Bentham asks rhetorically in another place, when considering opposition to the principle of utility, 'does it follow that it must be *good*, because it is *established*?' (*Codification Proposal*, IV 542). He answers the question by mentioning how we can say that gout is established in the body. If the established gout is clearly not good, then why should the established government be? The normative, critical principle must always be kept independent of what actually happens, so giving an independent position from which criticism and proposal for reform is possible. This is why Bentham made a minor mistake in the exposition of his own principles in making the goddess Nature the provider of the *oughts* as well as the *is*'s. For, just as in his objection to natural law, this is liable to make the two seem closer than they are. As he puts it in *Defence of a Maximum:* 'between what does naturally take place, and what ought to take place, there is indeed some difference: but it is a difference which moralists are apt to overlook, [and] which they constantly overlook as often as they talk of the law of nature' (Stark iii 257). Nature is better left just with the *is*'s, as the provider of that psychology which must be used by the legislator or the reformer as a means of making law what it ought to be, and so serving the interest of the people by rearing the fabric of felicity.

It has also been seen that Bentham attributes discovery of the *is-ought* distinction to Hume. However, when it comes to the principle of utility, Bentham thinks that Hume has forgotten his own precepts. In a late letter to Dumont Bentham explained why he had called his main principle the 'principle of utility'. He says that he chose this phrase because 'Hume was in all his glory. The phrase was consequently familiar to everybody' (UC 10.129). He then adds: 'The difference between Hume and me is this, the use he made of it, was to account for that which *is*, I to show what *ought to be*' (UC 10.129). This seems an accurate enough statement about Hume. It is certainly possible to use something like the principle of utility as a basic descriptive law of the behaviour of people in communities. The point then is that whatever they think they are doing; whatever the ideology of rights, justice, or whatever in terms of which they think that they are operating; what they are really doing can be exposed by seeing that whatever principles they adopt have the effect of promoting the utility of the members of that society. Here the principle is used as a piece of descriptive politics, sociology, or anthropology: people as a matter of fact (normally) do what promotes the greatest happiness of the greatest number. The ideology which has this effect can indeed be claimed, or explained, as having evolved just because it does have this effect, much as in Leslie Stephen's *Science of Ethics*. However, Bentham is clear, and right to be clear, that this is not the way that he himself is using the principle. The principle is unashamedly normative. It is not like a general scientific principle providing a deep understanding into what actually happens in societies. It is not part of an explanation of people's ethical beliefs, part of a science of ethics. It is, instead, a straightforwardly critical principle, an independent standpoint from which what actually does happen can be assessed and, if necessary, changed. Ideology, the beliefs with which the people operate, is not only to be explained but also, if necessary, discarded.

The claim being made about Bentham is, then, that pleasures and pains as guides to action enter in two quite different and separable ways into his system. As the guide to the action of the reformer or legislator, they lay down what ought to happen, and here it is the greatest happiness of the greatest number which ought to be promoted. As the guide, or motive, of the actual actions of actual people, they lay down what will happen, and here it is the greatest happiness of the individual which any individual will attempt to promote. This joint claim poses obvious problems, perhaps most succinctly expressed in the thought that legislators or reformers are people as well. However, both parts are needed for Bentham's system, because the legislator operates by acting on the motives of the people. It is because they seek their own happiness that he is able to design the laws so that they lead to the greatest happiness of the greatest number. So far, apart from the general statements in favour of the *is-ought* distinction, the claim that pleasures and pains as motives or guides enter in in two quite distinct ways has rested upon a rather close reading of the first paragraph of the first chapter of the *Introduction*. It does not have to be limited to this textual base, however, and it is probably important for its plausibility that it need not. Going on to the next, second, chapter of the *Introduction*, we find Bentham considering and dismissing principles opposed to the principle of utility. He comments that 'other principles in abundance, that is, other motives, may be the reasons why such and such an act *has* been done: that is, the reasons or causes of its being done: but it is this alone that can be the reason why it

111

might or ought to have been done' (IPML 32-3). Here we again clearly get the principle of utility, as Bentham uses it, taken as a normative principle, and distinguished from any explanation of people's actual motives in their actual actions. Hence any explanation of those motives involves a separate principle.

In a proposed introduction to his Civil Code, laying out its general principles and written after the *Introduction* was printed but before it was published, Bentham declares that we should follow intrepidly the guidance of the principle of utility in legislation and says again that following it involves attempting by means of the laws to provide the greatest happiness for society. He then adds that 'le bien' and 'le mal' (which he goes on to explain in terms of pleasures and pains) have a double title to the regard of the legislator, as means and as ends (UC 32.134). Here again we have a quite explicit statement of the double use of pleasures and pains, but the best piece of textual evidence of the lot to this proposed double use is probably some manuscript remarks which Bentham wrote thirty years later while composing the *Springs of Action*. This time he does it by giving a double sense to the principle of utility, saying that 'in its *censorial* sense it holds up the greatest happiness of the greatest number as the only universally desirable end. In its *enunciative* sense, each man's own happiness his only *actual* end' (UC 158.61). It is dangerous for Bentham to put the point in terms of a double sense of the principle of utility, given that this principle is so explicitly given only a normative, or censorial, sense in his earlier writings. However, in spite of this, the central point is absolutely clear, which is that happiness (or pains and pleasures) enter as guides to action ('ends') in two quite separate and clearly distinguishable ways.

Given that the case for separation of these two principles in Bentham has now been made, the next thing to be seen is how they are combined in the legislator's project. This is the project created by taking the normative principle as specifying the end and then using the descriptive principle to provide the basis for reasoning about how to provide this end. Man is to be taken as he is and with him society made as it ought to be. Discussing the ends of law, Bentham says in *Of Laws in General* that

> as to the sovereign, the end or external motive he can have had in view in adopting the law, can upon the principle of utility, have been no other than the greatest good of the community: which end we suppose his measures to be directed to of course: since it is only so far as that is the case that these enquiries are calculated or designed to be of any use to him. (31)

The utility principle, setting the end, is presupposed. The point of the enquiry, which in the overall project, is to issue in a practical handbook, is to show how a legislator ought to act if he wishes to promote that end. The end being given, the problem to be solved is the right means of achieving it. Bentham's overall project, and many of his particular more limited projects, consist essentially in solving various versions of this problem. So far as he can properly claim to have solved them, he can properly claim to be an inventor or discoverer, able to provide needed practical information (that is, information about how a given end is to be achieved) just the same as any other provider of practical information, whether it be about the construction of gardens or the maintenance of cars.

The project of taking man as he is and making society as it ought to be by the use of legislation did not arise with Bentham. He made few claims for originality and was over-conscientious in ascribing the source of the ideas he made use of to others. Indeed, it was so familiar from the writers he respected that it seemed obvious to him. His work consisted largely in taking the principles which created the project as given and applying his mind to the solution of the particular problems which arose. This is why, in the production of proposals for legislation he can be taken to be as practical a thinker as someone who takes the point of cars and the physical properties of materials for granted and designs practical proposals for car maintenance. With these ends, with these materials, this is what ought to be done. The problem of how to build a constitution, or how to build the right set of laws, was as much a standard problem as the problem of how to build a watch. In both cases the end to be achieved (greatest happiness, accurate time-keeping) could be taken almost for granted. In both cases there was also supposed to be knowledge of the materials to be used (men as maximisers of their own interest, metals obeying various natural laws). The problem was set by the use of these known materials to achieve the given end. Anyone who solved the provision of the right set of laws would be as much an inventor, would be as entitled to esteem, would be as worthy of prizes and rewards for their services to humanity as Harrison who solved the problem of making an accurate watch. Just as a good watch might be designed, so might a good prison: and just as a good prison, so might a complete code of laws.

'From Locke [the law] must receive the ruling principles of its form — from Helvetius of its matter.' So Bentham noted in his Commonplace book kept in the 1770s (X 71), and there are frequent references to Helvetius in the manuscript material at this stage. On first reading Helvetius' *De l'Ésprit* — a work which

Bentham would ostentatiously read while walking along some distance behind the rest of his family — Bentham asked himself 'Have I a *genius* for anything?', and seeing that Helvetius said that of all earthly pursuits, legislation was the most important, the question he put himself was 'And have I indeed a genius for legislation? I gave myself the answer, fearfully and tremblingly — Yes?!' (X 27). This is not as pretentious as it might sound. Any reader of Helvetius's book would be led naturally to consideration of the question of genius since the first chapter of the third of the four essays which compose it is entitled and is all about 'genius'. Furthermore, Helvetius traces the etymology of genius from *gignere*, to bring forth or produce; and so it involves in him the idea of discovery or invention. Bentham was perfectly aware of this etymology as given by Helvetius, and it appears in the above quoted recollections. So when he asked himself for what he had a genius, the question which he was asking himself was what he could bring forth or produce. The question was which area was the one in which he could engage in practical construction. The answer, as in Helvetius, was legislation, and so Bentham set himself as a young man the task of engaging in this practical project.

It is not just the idea of legislation or of genius that Bentham would have found in Helvetius' *De l'Esprit*, but also the particular principles which have been identified as framing the project, and the way that the project was formed by their combination. For example, Helvetius says of 'public utility' that it is 'the principle on which all human virtues are founded, and is the basis of all legislations', adding that 'it ought to inspire the legislator with the resolution to force the people to submit to his laws' (1759 translation, p. 41). Earlier Helvetius had declared that 'if the physical universe be subject to the laws of motion, the moral universe is equally so to those of interest' (27). That is, interest, or a man's regard for his own happiness, was the great causal principle which explained human behaviour just as gravitation was the great causal principle which explained the behaviour of the heavenly bodies. So we can see how Bentham as an ardent student of Helvetius found the principles determining the ends and the principles describing the means both ready and waiting for him. So also was the project formed by their combination. Helvetius claims 'that all men tend only towards their happiness, that it is a tendency from which they cannot be diverted; that the attempt would be fruitless, and even the success dangerous; consequently, it is only by incorporating personal and general interest, that they can be rendered virtuous' (81). That is, virtue, the *oughts*, can only be achieved by so designing a system so that each person following his own self-interest will in fact do what will result in general utility. Hence 'morality is evidently no more than a frivolous science, unless blended with policy and legislation . . . if philosophers would be of use to the world, they should survey objects from the same point of view as the legislator' (81). This is, as seen, exactly how Bentham hoped to be of use, taking in the same way as fixed the principles of motion in the moral world. The legislator by his artifice or construction makes self-interest coincide with the general interest. As Helvetius puts it, rewards and punishments are to be used

> to connect the personal with the general interest. This union
> is the master principle which moralists ought to propose to
> themselves. If citizens could not procure their own private
> happiness without promoting that of the public, there would
> be none vicious but fools (111); all the art therefore of the legis-
> lator consists in forcing [men] by self-love to be always just to
> each other (120-1).

The legislator, like the watch-maker, takes his materials, each following their own natural courses, and puts them in such a system that by following those natural courses they produce the result which he desires for the system as a whole, whether it be accurate time-keeping or general utility. None will be vicious but fools. Any rational being able to engage in calculation of self-interest will by following it alone be virtuous. When the legislator has done his work duty and interest will coincide.

The above remarks were quoted from Helvetius since Helvetius played such a large role in the origination of Bentham's own think-ing, and because he puts the nature of the general project which they share particularly clearly. However, if one were interested in origins, all the bits could be traced back before Helvetius. Taking utility as the end is endemic in numerous eighteenth-century thinkers (there is a full account in Baumgardt 1952 pp. 33-59), and before Helvetius Hume had declared that 'it is . . . a just *political* maxim, *that every man must be supposed a knave*' (*Essays* 42), that is, solely concerned with maximising his self-interest. After Helvetius, we have the independent influence of Beccaria, also quite frequently acknowledged by Bentham. Bec-caria, in the English translation uses exactly the same formula as Bentham for the end, '*the greatest happiness of the greatest num-ber*' (*On Crimes and Punishments*; 1767 translation, p. 2; in the original, '*la massina felicita divisa nel maggior numero*', Venturi ed. p. 9). He also makes the comparison between interest and gravity: 'that force, which continually impels us to our own private interests, like gravity, acts incessantly unless it meets with an obstacle to oppose it' (22); such obstacles will be punishments provided by the legislator: 'punishments, which I would call political obstacles, prevent the fatal effects of private interest, without destroying the impelling cause' (22). This is clearly again the same project as in Helvetius: the laws are to be used so that men following their natural course will in fact create the greatest happiness of the greatest number. What Beccaria adds to Helvetius, and what Bentham takes over, is a much greater interest in calculation, for 'if mathematical calculation could be applied to the obscure and infinite combinations of human actions, there might be a corresponding scale of punishments' (23). With this calculation, with measurement of utility, with 'geometrical precision' (41), an exact account of appropriate punishments can be constructed, based on the supposition that the point of punishment is to deter. Once people, acting on their own self-interest, are deterred from crimes, then the system of laws and punishments will have been so constructed that self-love is in harmony with social. So again we get the same project of practical construction, rearing the fabric of felicity by solution of a particular kind of problem; as Beccaria puts it 'the legislator . . . is a wise architect, who erects his edifice on the foundation of self-love, and contrives, that the interest of the public shall be the interest of each individual' (176).

The need for such contrivance and construction, for the creation of an artificial identification of interests, did not only occur in the grand overall project of the construction of a complete code of laws. It was also a way of solving much more particular problems concerned with the construction of particular, more small-scale, institutions. As well as the general theory of law and punishment, and the problem of discovering the best code of laws and the right kinds and amounts of punishment, Bentham was also concerned with its practical implementation by penal institutions. The influence of Howard made the question of penal reform a topic of current interest in late eighteenth-century Britain. The draft for a Bill designed to promote the construction of a penal institution was sent to Bentham in 1778 for comment. It was just at the time that he had taken up again his work on punishment and the general theory of legislation after the interval spent in criticising Blackstone and composing the *Fragment*. Bentham published a series of detailed comments on the proposals as *A View of the Hard Labour Bill* (1778). The Bill, which became

116

the Penitentiary Act of 1779, in fact had quite an influence on Bentham's subsequent life, for his proposal for a model prison, the panopticon, which he struggled for twenty years to get accepted by the British Government, was made under this act and its later renewals. When Bentham wrote, however, this was all many years in the unforeseeable future. He was commenting, without any particular personal interest, on the proposals and the theoretical basis on which they rested. Among the elements he selected for approval were the principles behind the payment of the manager of the proposed institution. Section 24 of the Bill, repeated as section 18 of the act, made the salary of governors and task-masters to be in proportion to labour performed 'that it may become the *interest* as well as the *duty*' of them to see that tasks were performed. Bentham commented on this that 'the principle here laid down . . . is an excellent lesson to legislators' (26). This was the stuff of practical proposals based on 'genius and penetration' (27). 'The utopian speculator unwarrantably presumes, that a man's conduct . . . *will* quadrate with his duty, or vainly regrets that it will *not* do so' (27). Always a magpie, content to pick up other people's bright things and make use of them, Bentham seems to have gained from this ephemeral source the idea of a junction of duty and interest as the leading principle which should guide the construction of institutions, particularly with regard to their administration. It led him into continual promotion of contract management, rather than salaried managers, so that the manager would have a stake in the financial efficiency of the institution. As he put it in the detailed panopticon proposals of 1791, manage-ment of the panopticon was to be by contract rather than trust so as 'to join interest with duty, and that by the strongest cement that can be found' (*Panopticon Postscript II*, IV 125). The wise constructor, who joins duty and self-interest, can not only frame complete codes of laws but also design the administration of particular institutions, such as prisons.

Once this principle of management was established, Bentham continued to make use of it in his later proposals such as (in the 1790s) his proposals for a new poor law and for a kind of death duty which would take up much of the tax burden. For example, in the latter, the *Escheat vice Taxation* proposal, Bentham held that the actual operation of the proposal should be by an Eschea-tor or Administrator General in each county, who would take a percentage of the proceeds, for 'his interest will thus be con-nected with his duty' (Stark i 71). The poor law reform proposals were a much more elaborate plan in which workhouses were to be built all over the country at a regular distance from each other and all on the same architectural lines as the panopticon. Once he had the general idea, Bentham's fertile imagination, propensity for detailed planning, and belief in the possibility of solving all sorts of problems led him into making his proposed new workhouses the means of promoting a great variety of useful ends. They would not only put the out of work or destitute to work and provide food but would also be schools, savings banks, 'crucibles' for psychological experimentation, and so on. The principles of management, however, just as the principles of architecture, were taken over straight from the earlier *Panopticon* proposals. As he wrote:

> *Duty and Interest* junction principle — No means to be omitted that can contribute to strengthen the junction between *interest* and *duty*, in the instance of the person entrusted with the management: — i.e. to make it each man's *interest* to observe on every occasion that conduct which it is his *duty* to observe. (PAUPER, VIII 380).

Following from the same principle, management, just as in the Panopticon prison, was to be by contract, with the contractor taking the profits of the venture, rather than by a salaried, state, official.

These were all specific projects, which Bentham urged upon the existing government. However, once Bentham realised that the principle of joining duty and interest was not just a working principle for legislation, ordaining rewards and punishments for the citizen, but also a principle which could be used in constructing systems of management, ordaining rewards and punishments for managers or officials, it was natural that he would develop such proposals in areas other than the construction of highly specific institutions. The state as a whole had to be administered, not just prisons and workhouses. To echo Bentham's sentiment when reflecting on the first prison proposals, it was utopian to expect an official's conduct to quadrate with his duty just because it was his duty. The system had to be made to work. Officials, just like citizens, had to be placed in such a structure that following their natural courses would in fact lead them to doing what they ought to do. The problem could be put like this. We can start with the device, actual or fictional, of someone called a legislator, who is constructing a system of rewards and punishments for his citizens so that they will fulfil a given end. The citizens are assumed to be self-interested, but the officials who are to operate the system are supposed to operate it just because that is what the system is. They are in positions of trust and they will do what they are entrusted to do. They can be thought of as part of the legislator, aiming at the good and manipulating the motives of the citizens to that end. However, once some particular institutions are designed, like prisons, for more specific ends, it can be seen that it is not enough to construct a prison so that the inmates are motivated to do what they ought in the most efficient manner, but there is also a problem as to why the managers should be motivated to run the prison in the way that it is designed to work, that is, in the way that it ought to work. The managers, that is, have as it were come out of being part of the 'legislator' and are further, self-interested, human beings whom the legislator has to allow for. They cannot just be entrusted to do what they ought, but their interest must be quadrated with their duty. However, the process need not stop here. Even if a system is designed to guard the prison guards, this system like all the others must be operated by someone. All the officials in the state have therefore to be recognised as self-interested human beings, and the system designed so that they will nevertheless in spite of this (or, rather, because of this) do their duty; that is, fulfil their allotted roles and positions of trust in running the system. The whole state has to be designed, just as a prison is designed, not just so that the average citizen or inmate will do what he ought, but that so also will all the officials or guards who are concerned with its management. Hence Bentham's increasing interest in the administration of the state, which culminated in the massive *Constitutional Code* on which he was working at the time of his death.

As the title of this Code indicates, this increase of interest can be mapped by following Bentham's awareness of, and interest in, constitutional law. In the 1770s, when he was engaged in the basic Helvetian or Beccarian project of framing the right system of criminal law (classification of offences and specification of punishments), Bentham seems not to have worried about constitutional law. He recognises this in a later footnote added to the *Introduction* where he says that at that time (that is, before 1780, when this part of the *Introduction* was printed) 'that branch, notwithstanding its importance ... had ... scarcely presented itself to my view in the character of a distinct one' (IPML 281n). Part of the difference seems to have been made by Bentham's introduction to the leading Whig politician, Lord Shelburne who, besides being interested in Bentham, was also naturally interested in power and corruption (see Bentham's letter to Shelburne, CORR III 28). In any case, by the time that the *Introduction* was published in 1789, the new preface of that year has 'public distributive' or 'constitutional' law as one of the parts of the whole body of law for which this book was meant to be an introduction (IPML 6). He had, furthermore, in the meantime written an extensive series of manuscripts on reward, in which he had dealt at length with 'Rewards applied to offices' (this is the title of Book II of the *Rationale of Reward*, (*REWARD 144sq.)). This proposed general principles in the design of a structure of rewards for offices, such as (unsurprisingly in view of the above treatment) that which he calls 'rule 1', namely 'emoluments ought in such manner attached to offices, as to produce the most intimate connection between the duty and the interest of the person employed' (*REWARD 150). By the end of Bentham's life he declared that, of all the codes of law, 'the constitutional code is the first in importance' (CODE IX 3). The code that was ignored has become the head of the corner; or rather, the foundation, for Bentham had come to recognise that without an appropriate constitutional code, no other would be of any use. This is because, without a code which guided the actions of officials, no others had any chance of being implemented. In the trailer which Bentham issued in the *Pamphleteer* of 1823 to promote the great work of his last years, and called *Leading Principles of a Constitutional Code for any state*, Bentham explained the importance of such a code by saying that people were under threat from two sorts of adversaries, internal and external, against which they needed security. The external were normal enemies, but the internal divided into two kinds, against both of which protection needed to be provided by law. There were the unofficial ones, normal criminals. Then there were also official ones, 'those evil-doers, whose means of evil-doing are derived from the share they respectively possess, in the aggregate of the powers of government' (II 270). He says that 'to provide, in favour of the rest of the community, security against evil in all its shapes, at the hand of the abovementioned and — so long as they continue in such their situation — irresistible adversaries, is the appropriate business of the constitutional branch of law, and accordingly of this code' (II 270). Since unless checked they are irresistible, it naturally follows that 'as in difficulty so in importance, this part of the business of law far surpasses every other' (II 270). Bentham has moved from a position in which the chief problem to be solved by combining duty and interest is the protection of normal people against the depredation of criminals to a position in which the chief problem to be solved by the same means is the protection of normal people against the depredation of officials. First, the code must guard against the guards.

Just as the chief principle produced contract instead of salaried management for prisons or workhouses, so in the more general administrative proposals, Bentham promotes the idea of bidding for offices. Rather than high salaries being attached to them, it is preferable that people pay to do them. Another of the rules of the *Rationale of Reward* (rule 3) is that 'the amount of salary, or other emoluments, attached to every office, ought to be the least that the individuals, qualified to execute its duties, are willing to accept for their performance' (*163). As he put it, after enunciating the same principle twenty-five years later when writing *Defence of the Economy against Burke*, 'this is the measure of all prices ... this is the measure of the value of all labour' (V 294). So comes the 'Office competition process' of the *Constitutional Code* (IX 283), designed to maximise aptitude and minimise expense in the filling of offices. Offices were to be put up to auction between those on a list of suitably qualified people, and assigned to the lowest bidder; that is, the person who would do it for least, or even in some cases pay to have it. So would the expense to the public be minimised; so, thought Bentham, would the unimportance of the financial rewards maximise 'the degree of *relish* which the candidate is likely to have for the functions which he is desirous of having the exercise of' (CODE IX 290). Whatever else he did it for, he would not be doing it for the money.

This interest in the economics of management and the use of financial incentives reflects Bentham's wider economic interests. At the time that he was writing *Reward* in the 1780s, with the rules just quoted, he was deeply absorbed in study of Adam Smith. Competition for official posts was only one example of a general, Smithian, belief in the beneficial effects of competition. As Bentham put it in *Reward*: 'in all trades, and in all arts, competition secures to the public not only the lowest price but the best work' (*118). So, in setting up and solving the problems involved in his major project, Bentham was relying not just on the latest legislative but also on the latest economic theory; 'studying the lessons ... furnished ... by Beccaria and Adam Smith' (*REWARD 191). Smith, to whom Bentham wrote in the open letter published with the *Defence of Usury* that 'I owed you everything' (Stark i 167), is not only cited by him as a forerunner in promoting the principle of utility (*Escheat*, Stark i 336), but also specifically talked in *The Wealth of Nations* of duty and interest. In universities in which the professor is salaried, Smith writes, 'his interest is ... in this case, set as directly in opposition to his duty as it is possible to set it' (ii 284). It is no doubt with

Smith in mind that Bentham draws out one of the consequences of the principle of payment enunciated in his first rule in *Reward* that if the salaries of professors had 'been interwoven with their services, it might have been the custom for some of these pretended labourers to have laboured for their hire' (154).

It has been thought that inconsistency, or at least a severe sense of strain, comes from combining the latest economic and legislative theory in this way. For the basis of the project of Helvetius and Beccaria, as has been seen, was to create an artificial identity of interests between the individual actor and the people as a whole by the creation of a system of rewards and punishments. Artifice would result in the self-interested actor acting in the general interest. Yet the economic theory, resting on the belief that increase in competition and freeing of markets maximised general utility, seems to rest on the idea of a natural identity of interests. No watchmaker, designer, or architect is required. Left to themselves, each person pursuing his own individual interest, the general interest will be served. As Smith put it in a famous phrase, 'he intends only his own gain, and he is in this, as in many other cases, led by an invisible hand to promote an end which was no part of his intention . . . by pursuing his own interest he frequently promotes that of the society more effectually than when he really intends to promote it' (*Wealth of Nations*, i 477-8). Of course this kind of unintended consequence is also part of the legislator's design; but the point of the hidden hand is that it is not only hidden from the self-interested actor but also from everyone else. Instead of the legislator artificially making the sums come out right, they come out right on their own. The hand is not only hidden but does not exist; at most, it is as if there is a hand. So, it might be supposed, and was famously supposed by Elie Halévy, whose thesis this is (Halévy 1928 pp. 17; 33), the legislative theory and the economics are in conflict; the legislator is supposed to be both essential and also redundant.

In fact there is no such problem or conflict in Bentham's thought (or, come to that, in Adam Smith's who says only in the remark just quoted that the beneficial results of the pursuit of individual interests is 'frequent'). In both Bentham and Smith the area in which it is held that there should be unimpeded pursual of private interest is bounded by a context of law and government, which places limits on such pursual. Both held that the state interfered too much in purely economic matters, but this did not prevent them thinking that there was an appropriate role for the state (the active legislator). The free market only works in a context of law which supports the institution of possession (or private property) and can be used to enforce agreements (contracts). The game might be free, but the state looks after the rules, and acts as umpire in their enforcement. As can be seen from the stance of current political parties, there is no obvious conflict in combining a belief in free market solutions with a belief in the support of law and order. Even in more purely economic questions Smith, and even more Bentham, both believed that there was room for positive action by the state. Settling the question of when this was appropriate was indeed the central question of economic theory for Bentham. He writes in his *Manual of Political Economy* that 'the great object, the great *desideratum*, is to know what ought and what ought not to be done by government. It is in this view, and in this view only that the knowledge of what is done and takes place without the interference of government can be of any practical use' (Stark i 224). In other words, Bentham writes wholly as a legislator. The natural laws of economics, just like natural psychology, are only useful as a means to this end, as a means to the decision of when and how the legislator should act. The result, given the sort of results achieved by Smith, is that he should not act so much as had been thought on purely economic questions. When trying to augment national wealth, Bentham writes in his much later *Institute of Political Economy*, the general motto should be 'Be quiet'. All interference needs special reasons. However, having made his general rule, Bentham then set up special cases where interference was justified. These areas he entitled '*agenda*', that is, things to be done by the government (Stark iii 333). Even here the legislator is active; there is no question of a conflict between the legislative and economic theory.

One occasion on which Bentham felt that the market mechanism was not working properly was with respect to the price of corn at the beginning of the new century. He wrote a pamphlet which he did not publish, proposing an upper limit to corn prices, the *Defence of a Maximum*. Perhaps he suppressed it because he, as the man who had made his economic reputation by proposing the freeing of interest rates (the *Defence of Usury*), might give too big a target to opponents by now proposing controls. However, some of the particular opinions he express in it seem accurate enough expressions of his standing convictions. He writes that

> I have not, I never had, nor ever shall have, any horror, sentimental or anarchical, of the hand of government. I leave it to Adam Smith, and the champions of the rights of men . . . to talk of invasions of natural liberty, and to give as a special argument against this or that law, an argument the effect of

which would be to put a negative upon all laws. (Stark iii 258)

Bentham is presumably thinking of the famous peroration which closes Book IV of the *Wealth of Nations* where Smith writes that

all systems of preference or of restraint, therefore, being thus completely taken away, the obvious and simple system of natural liberty establishes itself of its own accord. Every man, as long as he does not violate the laws of justice, is left perfectly free to pursue his own interest his own way . . . (ii 208)

Given Bentham's view of natural rights, it is unsurprising that natural liberty moves him no more than natural equality. As was seen in the last chapter, the point of government is to provide rights for its subjects; that is, provide benefits for them. Instead of natural rights, real rights; instead of natural liberty, real liberty; instead of anarchy, security in the defence and use of one's property. There must be law. The legislator must act. As Bentham writes in *Anarchical Fallacies*, 'the great enemies of public peace are the selfish and dissocial passions'. Hence self-interest (or 'natural liberty') can not be allowed complete scope. 'Society is held together only by the sacrifices that men can be induced to make of the gratifications they demand: to obtain these sacrifices is the great difficulty, the great task of government' (Parekh 260). Even in the remark quoted from Smith, the individual is only to be left alone as long as he does not violate the laws of justice. Hence for Bentham, if not perhaps for Smith, 'the interference of government, as often in my humble view of the matter any the smallest ballance [?] on the side of advantage is the result, is an event I witness with altogether as much satisfaction as I should its forbearance, and with much more than I should its negligence' (*Defence of a Maximum*, Stark iii 258).

Not only is there therefore no deep tension or contradiction at the heart of Bentham's theory, but he is also prepared to support interference by the government or legislator in purely economic matters, such as fixing prices. It is worth looking a bit more at why this is so, both in Bentham and in terms of abstract theory. With the same psychological postulates as Bentham and Smith, of men as self-interested maximisers of their welfare, modern economics can demonstrate with the help of a set of unrealistic subsidiary assumptions (perfect information, perfect competition, costless transactions) that the market (that is, leaving people to strike their own bargains) will result in the most efficient distribution of productive capacity, use of raw materials and distribution of final products. This is all also on the assumption that each person or firm has the private control or exclusive use of what it possesses; that its benefits or costs accrue only to the owner. However, some goods are such that, if they exist at all, it cannot be controlled whom they benefit; hence they cannot be sold to such individuals (or self-interested individuals, saving their money, would have no interest in buying them). Examples of such so-called 'public goods' are defence or a clean atmosphere; everyone benefits, it is supposed, from the defence of a nation or a healthy environment whether or not he pays. Somewhat similar are so-called 'externalities' where even though we have a product or item which is privately used or controlled, benefits or costs accrue to others. Examples are pollution, or the benefit which an apple farmer provides for the bee keeper next door. In such cases, in modern welfare economics, we need some form of tax, so that the use or production of the product is regulated in a way that takes account of external effects as well as the benefits or harms to the user. Tax is like law here: the legislator has had to step in, artificially adjusting the situation, so that the general interest is served by everyone following their own interest (a tax on pollution makes the self-interested factory owner reduce it unless he is producing goods of more worth, of more benefit, than the tax). The natural harmony of interests has broken down. So much, in a very condensed form, for modern theory. Returning to Smith, immediately after the declaration of a return to natural liberty quoted above, he reserves for the 'sovereign' the areas of defence of the country, administration of justice, and 'certain public works and certain public institutions, which it can never be for the interest of any individual, or small number of individuals, to erect and maintain' (ii 209). Believer in free trade, he still believed that the state might restrict trade in items important for defence (i 484); believer in the state leaving people alone, he still believed that it should build public works. He recognised, that is, the nature of public goods; and that their provision was not necessarily best left to the market.

Bentham took this further. The basis of the general rule of non-interference was the supposition that each person knew his interests best and was sufficiently motivated to pursue them. The tax the government needed to raise for its projects was a burden, and hence the criterion for state intervention was that it produced more good than the mischief of the most burthensome form of tax extant (*Institute of Pol. Econ.*, Stark iii 334). However, sometimes this criterion would be met. For people to act successfully in their own interest demanded 'power, knowledge or intelligence, and inclination' (335), and although it could do little about inclination (thought Bentham) it might act successfully in someone's interest when he lacked interest or power. Hence Bentham thought that it was appropriate for the government to establish institutes for the propagation of knowledge such as the Board of Agriculture or the Royal Institution (338n), which (in the same spirit as Smith) would not be practical if set up by a limited number of individuals as a source of profit. That is, he recognised them as public goods; and he obviously also supported various forms of security provided by the state, such as by justice or national defence. He is less sure about public communications (Smith had thought that they could be provided and paid for privately) although he recognises that part of the profit of a new canal is distributed 'in portions altogether unassignable, among individuals more clearly unassignable, viz. among the community at large' (338n). He recognises, that is, that there are external effects, which may sometimes make it appropriate for a state to engage as a partner in the promotion of such projects.

This is a sample of the general kind of prescriptions flowing from Bentham's combined legislative and economic theories: as much information as possible should be provided; certain things, price of corn, the money supply (*The True Alarm*, Stark iii 189) should be controlled; security and subsistence guaranteed. Bentham also engaged in trying to get the government to accept particular economic projects, just as he tried with workhouses and prisons. The most elaborate of these, which seems to have occupied him fairly fully for about a year at the turn of the century was his proposal for a new form of paper currency which would not only circulate but also bear interest. It has all the marks of a Bentham practical proposal: eccentric or devastatingly logical, according to one's point of view (and so on neither count having the slightest chance of success); based on immense research, both empirical and theoretical; worked out in devastating detail, so that even the exact design of the notes was lovingly engraved; urged upon treasury ministers by private approach; put out by them for external assessment by an interested party; an immense subsequent correspondence in which all particular criticisms are buried by Bentham in such a mass of detailed refutation that no one was likely to try and read it all; and the whole project being a total failure, in that the administration did not adopt any fragment of it, let alone issue copies of the specimen note thrust upon them. However, as well as being another failed practical project, it showed how even in the economic sphere the government could interfere to keep duty and interest in line. The working classes, without access to ways of realising interest on their savings, had no motive to save. They were, that is, not acting in terms of their true, long-term, interest (or duty). Hence the provision of a form of readily available currency which would encourage savings; that is make savings in their immediate, apparent, short-term interest. By artifice, this short-term interest would be made to coincide with their long-term interest.

The most famous of all of Bentham's particular projects is, of course, his prison, the panopticon, in which, as he enthused in the original preface, there would be 'morals reformed — health preserved — industry invigorated — instruction diffused — public burthens lightened — economy seated as it were on a rock — the Gordian knot of the poor-laws not cut but untied — all by a simple idea in Architecture' (PANO iii; IV 39). The simple idea in architecture was to build the prison in a circular form so that one warder in the middle could see all of the prisoners (although even this turned out not to be so simple, as Bentham tried to devise a way in which he could see without being seen). As such, it was the one part of the package that was accepted, having an influence on subsequent prison design. However, as has been seen, the prison was also meant to incorporate a system of management; hence lightening public burthens and seating economy on a rock. More than this, it was not just a particular project which Bentham tried to force on a reluctant government in the corridors of the treasury or by having the prime minister to his house to see the model he'd had constructed of it; it was also a project in which Bentham was personally financially interested. It was a speculative venture in just the way that a new blast furnace would be. Bentham intended not only to promote, within limits, the freeing of the market, but make use of his own individual enterprise in order to make money. Reforming morals, preserving health and so on may well have been his duty, but Bentham wished also to make it in his interest.

In 1785 Bentham travelled to Russia, where his brother Samuel Bentham was helping Prince Potemkin in the enormous development of his estates. As was described in Chapter I, the purpose of his visit was meant to be connected with his plan of getting Catherine the Great to accept his new criminal code; but in fact it enabled him to do a lot of his own work, including writing the material on reward which has just been discussed. He was clearly thinking more deeply about economics at the time, and his *Defence of Usury* was written and published while he was in Russia; it takes the form of a series of letters, each headed 'Crichoff, in

White Russia'. He added at the end an open letter to Adam Smith in which he disagreed with the great man's criticism of 'projectors'; the spirit is in favour of projects and projectors, of innovation, of the manufacturing interest; the golden age is yet to come (Stark i 180). This is what the panopticon became: Bentham's own project, a use of capital with risk and enterprise, on which he also hoped to win rewards. The idea was also hatched in Russia, based on a factory observed by Samuel, and the original *Panopticon* was also written as a series of letters headed 'Crichoff, in White Russia'. As was also described in the first chapter, when both the brothers returned to England they set up in a sort of partnership in which Jeremy's social inventions were to be married to Samuel's mechanical inventions in a project designed to profit them both. Bentham was to be the contract manager of the new prison, building and running it for his own profit. The prisoners were to provide the motive power for Samuel's newly invented machinery, so that the building was to be not only a prison but also a factory. As Bentham reported to a later committee of investigations (in 1798): 'we were upon the look-out for a steam-engine. Human labour was substituted to the steam-engine' (XI 167). It might have been a slightly unusual source of power for a factory in the industrial revolution; but the central idea, the projecting use of risk capital, was there. The panopticon was a machine, 'a mill for grinding rogues honest, and idle men industrous' (X 226); and for making profits for its builder and minder. However, rather than making profits, the risk capital which Bentham had come into on the death of his father was soon swallowed up. He was soon badly in debt, begging meals, laying off his cook, and depending on the generosity of the corner butcher. He eventually managed to find a site, on Millbank, where a prison was indeed later built, and later still the Tate Gallery (so the Tate is the only surviving monument of the project, which put the land into the hands of the government). However, having only verbal agreement with the treasury, but lacking any proper written agreement with the government, or Acts of Parliament which gave him sufficient enabling power, Bentham's own prison was never built, let alone run for a profit. Of course, as was also described in the first chapter, Bentham himself did not in the long run suffer too badly financially from it. After the Committee of the House of Commons had finally killed off the project in 1811, Bentham was fairly handsomely compensated by special Act of Parliament. The profits enabled him to rent the palatial country house, Ford Abbey in Devonshire, where he retired to cultivate his garden, literally and metaphorically, and

write his most searching papers on logic, psychology, and ontology; that is on the abstract foundations of the whole system. The
profits which enabled him to do this, however, were not the
rewards which his enterprise or ideas had extracted from his own
risk capital, but money paid to him by parliament out of an old-
fashioned idea of breach of trust. The profits were not from pro-
jection, but were another burthen on the tax-payer; a burthen in
this case in return for which the tax-payer had received nothing at
all.

The panopticon story has other ironies. The chief reason which
the parliamentary committee seized on when recommending its
rejection was that, although its system of management might be
appropriate to 'the personal character of the party, in whose
custody the prisoners were on the first instance to be placed', it
might fall into other hands with unfortunate results (XI 149-50).
In other words, a system which Bentham had designed for any
arbitrarily chosen individual, on the assumption that that individual would attempt to maximise his own interest, was rejected
because it was felt to need the guarantee that it was operated by
a high-minded individual such as Bentham, who would put duty
before interest. Otherwise, the prisoners would be insufficiently
protected. Bentham protested that the Committee were incorrect
(he had built in protection in the shape of insurance, making the
governor pay for loss of, or damage to, prisoners); but they were
correct in that Bentham was highminded. Unlike his view of
others, his interest seemed to quadrate with his duty just because
it was his duty. The panopticon was unusual among his proposals
in this respect. Most of his life he was urging proposals on people
without hope of personal gain; offering to write constitutions for
all and sundry at the mere hint of a request; drafting bills, pub-
lishing political pamphlets and a review at his own expense. Even
with the panopticon at first he did not want any financial reward.
There are puzzles here about the status of Bentham's principle
of universal self-preference, and of the utility principle which
seems, for some people for some of the time, to motivate them
to prefer the general interest. These will be unpicked in the next
chapters. However, even if untypical, the panopticon cannot be
ignored. Quite apart from the psychological effect of the twenty
years' struggle on Bentham himself, and its place in turning him
from appeals to an external legislator, such as Catherine the
Great, to institute reforms based on the duty and interest junction
principle to a position in which the external legislator disappears
and the duty and interest junction principle works at every position, there is the question of whether the fact that Bentham

attempted to make profits out of his venture in itself condemns him. This seems to be the implication of Gertrude Himmelfarb's paper on the subject (Himmelfarb 1968), in which mere revelation of this fact is meant to make us think less well of Bentham. But if it does, the duty and interest junction principle is impossible. We have a Kantian idea that duty is only duty if it is done for the sake of duty; so if it happens to coincide with interest, or if something is done because of interest, it cannot be duty. This is quite contrary to Bentham's own point of view. If someone does something of general use and happens to get something out of it himself, so much the better. Utility is simply additative: to the general utility is added the utility of the individual. Bentham notes, obviously from personal experience, that this does not work where there is 'envy and jealousy' (*Defence of a Maximum*, Stark iii 297); and 'envy and jealousy' would no doubt be his reply to a contemporary Professor Himmelfarb. That is, if he had in fact succeeded in making the money.

Not only was it unusual for Bentham to seek personal reward but, in his general principles, economy of management was only one of several ends. The duty and interest junction principle was, even in the design of the particular institutions, intended to promote more than purely economic ends. Minimisation of expense, and the resulting contract management, was only part of the complete proposal for the prison or the workhouses. Otherwise the prisoners would indeed have been ground down by the manager, whether Bentham or someone else. It would be unlikely that there was a natural harmony of interests between the prisoners and the manager, so that the manager's relentless pursual of his own profit would result in greater benefits to the prisoners. In any case, Bentham did not rely on it. Immediately after introducing the duty and interest junction principle in *Pauper Management Improved*, Bentham notes that the manager of a workhouse has two duties, humanity and economy (PAUPER 51; VIII 380). Economy has been dealt with, but humanity also involves building something into the design of the institution to make the manager be humane. It was noted above that Bentham sometimes did this by insurance on the inmates, with profits to the manager (working rather like a tax on externalities; if making too many window frames had the external effect of the death of convicts, the profits of the company would suffer). However, in *Pauper Management* and *Panopticon*, the chief sanction designed to get the manager's interest in line with his duty to be humane was publicity: '*publicity*, the most effectual means of applying the force of moral motives, in a direction tending to strengthen the union between his interest and the *humane* branch of his duty' (PAUPER 52; VIII 380). The same control as was applied to the prisoners in the panopticon — continuous observation — was also to be applied to the under-keepers and the head keeper. Being under the 'same irresistible controul', this would be an answer 'to one of the most puzzling of political questions, *'quis costodiet ipsos costodes?'* (who would guard the guards?) (PANO 26; IV 45). The doors of the panopticon were always to be open to the passing public 'the great *open committee* of the tribunal of the world' (30; IV 46); and Bentham thought that they would be sufficiently curious to keep a close eye on what was happening. Nor was reliance just to be placed on casual observation. Bentham made plans, particularly for the workhouses, for regular reports; for publication of all sorts of statistics; and for the account books to be published. (Typically, he found the current system of book-keeping full of 'fictions' and took time off to invent a new system to be used; it was Leigh Hunt who observed, after experiencing it, that Bentham could not even play badminton without stopping to design a new shuttlecock.)

Publicity is a device which re-occurs through the particular projects in just the same way as the more economic principles; and is also similarly given a place in the final master plan for the complete administrative state. So, for example, it was part of the control on the Escheator (*Escheat*, Stark i 304). It was also part of the control of correct judicial procedure and of parliamentary practice; indeed of the whole of political life ('the eye of the public makes the statesman virtuous' (X 145). In his *Draught of a new Plan for the Organisation of Judicial Establishment in France* Bentham wrote that 'publicity is the very soul of justice. It is the keenest spur to exertion, and the surest of all guards against improbity. It keeps the judge himself, while trying, under trial' (IV 316). So the management of the judiciary, just like the management of other institutions, has to solve the problem of the threat posed by internal, official, adversaries; the problem of who was to guard the guards. Here also it was to be solved by making it in the officials' interest to do their duty; and the method used was publicity. In his own *Procedure* papers, this led him to invent the special device of a 'quasi-jury' as a check on the judge (*II 145); the first of the 'fundamental principles of natural procedure' he lists is 'publicity maximised' (*II 178). Similarly, in the *Constitutional Code*, Bentham speaks of the 'public opinion tribunal' and lists ways in which the force of public opinion can be brought to bear (IX 41sq).

This constant reference to publicity illustrates two things about

Bentham's thought. It shows that in the design of specific institutions, just as in the design of a legal code for the anonymous citizen, all forces which act on a man's interest can be considered and manipulated to make that interest coincide with duty. As well as the natural, or self-executing, rewards of economic gains on the free market, there are factitious rewards provided by government; and as well as rewards, there is the use of sanctions. Bentham had a well developed account of the various sanctions, physical, political, moral, religious; and the operative sanction here is the so-called moral or social sanction. It is because someone is interested in not doing something which is thought immoral by the general public, and so being condemned by public opinion, that he refrains from certain actions. His interest in avoiding the social sanction leads him to do his duty. The first thing this illustrates is that there is a variety of methods of control available to the legislator, which may well pose problems of choice and also knowledge, since he will want to know what their combined effects are. This is one problem for the next chapter: as long as people are not just looked at as interest maximisers, but as people with several interests, it is not so clear what is the content of the basic psychological law that everyone pursues their own interest. The other thing which publicity illustrates, and the other problem which it poses, is more specific. Publicity only provides a sanction, forcing people to do their duty, as long as it can be relied on that most people think that people ought to do just those things which actually are their duty, and will make it unpleasant for them if they do not. When everyone commits parking offences, no one is deterred by the thought of an offence being reported in the papers. This poses the problem of the knowledge of duty, and of why people should have an interest in doing their duty, and trying to make others do so, a problem which has already risen in the particular case of Bentham himself, and will be looked at in the chapter after next.

So the project of combining duty and interest, which has been described in this chapter, leaves problems both about duty and also about interest still to be resolved. The project, as stated clearly at the start of the *Constitutional Code* arises from two 'first principles', 'the greatest happiness-principle and the self-preference principle' (IX 6). The first of these lays down what ought to happen, the second lays down what actually does happen. The first guides the legislator as to the ends he ought to aim at, the second gives him the means of attaining them. Hence they can be combined in the grand project, or practical science, of legislation guided by the leading '*ruler's* rule', namely 'what you would have done make it a man's *interest* to do it' (UC 158.70). This depends upon a knowledge of interest, that is, a psychology of motives. This, however, can be established on good empirical principles, and so make 'the science of jurisprudence as strictly and properly a science of experiment as any branch of Natural philosophy' (UC 70A.22). Or so thought Bentham; whether this is true or not is the next thing to be considered. Once this knowledge of motives, or interests, was available the legislator could then construct society, particular institutions, and legal systems like a series of machines in which people mechanically following their natural courses would lead to the desired final result. In the *Introduction*, while discussing punishment, Bentham uses specifically mechanical analogies: 'to say ... that the punishment ought not to increase with the strength of the temptation, is as much as to say in mechanics, that the moving force or *momentum* of the *power* need not increase in proportion to the momentum of the *burthen*' (IPML 166n). The legislator uses these natural forces in his artificial constructions designed to make self-interested men do their duty; he adds the 'artificial tutelary motives' of 'the law' (IPML 137), for '*punishment* ... is an *artificial* consequence, annexed by political authority to an offensive act' (IPML 157). So much for the project; so much for the distinction between *ought* and *is* which is required to set it up. The next question is whether, if indeed 'the business of the government is to promote the happiness of the country, by punishing and rewarding' (IPML 74), the knowledge is available which would be needed for carrying out the task. All the projects, large and small, depend crucially upon knowledge of natural psychology; upon an empirically based knowledge of man's interests. It must now be seen whether this knowledge in Bentham was adequate to take the load which his projects demand.

Notes

(a) For the general idea of the legislator, see Burns (1967). For Bentham's own more particular development of the idea, see Chapter VIII.

(b) For the history of the panopticon, see Bentham's own, unreliable, *History of the War between Jeremy Bentham and George III, by one of the Belligerents*, substantial extracts of which are reprinted in Bowring XI (the original manuscript is now in the British Library). One unreliable aspect of it is Bentham's belief that it was the king who personally frustrated his panopticon project: 'But for George the Third, all the prisoners in England would, years ago, have been under my management' (XI 96). For a contrasting, reliable, modern account, see the double article by L.J. Hume (Hume 1973; Hume 1974).

(c) For Bentham's administrative projects more generally, see Hume (1981).

(d) The classic study of externalities such as pollution and the recommendation of compensating payments in Pigou (1932). The example of bees and apples (where the externality is a benefit) is in Meade (1952). How the tax can be assessed can be seen in any modern textbook of welfare economics, for example Ng (1979), where there is a relatively simple graphical treatment (169f). That there should be taxation is not unquestioned othodoxy, as an argument can be based on the controversial 'Coase theorem' (Coase 1960) to the effect that externalities are best handled by the market; a recent simple statement from this point of view is Cheung (1978).

(e) That, with certain assumptions, the market most efficiently realises production and distribution is elegantly demonstrated in Bator (1957).

(f) Bentham's more theoretical economic writings are discussed in Hutchison (1956); an extended critical study of the papers edited by W. Stark.

(g) Bentham's poor law proposals are discussed in Poynter (1969), which makes considerable use of unpublished material.

VI

A Clear View of Interest

'The business of government is to promote the happiness of the society, by punishing and rewarding.' So starts the seventh chapter of the *Introduction* (IPML 74); and it has been seen in the last chapter how the legislator with the given end of promoting happiness acts upon people's interests so that he artificially brings their interests in line with their duty. He does this by offering threats of punishment or offers of reward. Punishment, or the threat of pain, is the primary instrument used by the legislator in carrying out his task with respect to the people at large, although it has been seen how reward plays an important part in the administration of institutions designed to promote that task, from prisons to the state itself. Pain is, accordingly 'that instrument to which the law itself owes all its powers' (UC 69.47). Although evil, the idea is that its use forms an example of homeopathy: pain is used to fight against pain, evil is applied to prevent greater evil; the method is 'the method of combating one evil by another' (LEGIS 54). A tincture of evil results in the greater good of the organism as a whole. However, as was also observed in the last chapter, it is not possible to use this method unless it can be known, for particular people and particular occasions, what the results of a particular appeal to their interests would be. The legislative project demands and depends upon a knowledge of human psychology, a grasp of the facts of human nature. Unless it can be predicted how people at large will act when subjected to the threats of particular punishments or the hope of particular rewards, it cannot be told which threats ought to be applied in order to bring about the desired result. To bring duty and interest into conjunction demands a clear view of the nature of interest. The legislator requires it so that he knows how to appeal to the interests of particular people;

and these particular people also require it if any such appeals are to be successful. Even if people wish to follow their own interest, and the legislator successfully constructs a system in which the desired end is also in the several interests of the particular individuals concerned, the whole system would be worthless unless it is also the case that these particular individuals know what their several particular interests are. Otherwise, however much they may wish to, they will not succeed in fact in promoting their own interests; and by failing to promote their own interests, they will stultify the legislator's plan which depends upon their doing so. So the project of legislation, as sketched in the last chapter, depends upon the presupposition of the possibility of a knowledge of human psychology, available to both the legislator and his subjects. It assumes that people act in their own interests; that it can be known what these interests are; that the precise force of the different motives resulting from these different interests can be known and compared with each other; that it can therefore be told not just what kind but also precisely how much punishment should be employed as a motive to a particular action; that, in other words, human nature should not only be known but also be calculable. It is these assumptions, which are the essential presupposition of Bentham's varying applications of his central project, which will be examined in the present chapter.

That success in government depends upon success in knowledge of human nature is not, of course, a tenet particular to utilitarian political theory. Any manual of instruction to a statesman, or to someone with political power, only succeeds if it explains what he has to do in order to carry out his desired projects; and since these will depend upon getting people to act in particular ways, this explanation must depend upon knowledge of what the varying actions of people depend upon. The end, the desired projects, might be quite other than utilitarian ones; successful realisation will still depend upon knowledge about how to make people behave in particular ways. So a book of advice to a prince, such as Machiavelli's, might take as the desired end that the prince wished to maintain his 'state', that is, his position or power. To be successful, the advice will have still to be based on an accurate understanding of people; that is, of what the prince should or should not do to those people who are his subjects if he wishes to stay in his job. Unlike earlier books of advice to princes, Machiavelli thinks that he has such understanding: it is important to realise that 'so many [people] are not virtuous' (*Prince*, 91). Given the actual nature of people, the prince is advised to depart from standard virtues like promise-keeping or generosity. Of course, he does even better if he succeeds in looking as if he is upholding standard virtues even on the occasions he is departing from them. There is here the same sort of distinction between what should appear to happen and what should really happen as is often thought typical of utilitarianism, and (related to this) a distinction between those courses of action which should be promoted as a general rule and those courses of action which should be promoted in every particular case. The reason for these distinctions is the same: the introduction of the possibility of calculation based upon a (real or supposed) knowledge of the nature of human beings; hence a knowledge of how they can be manipulated to promote a given end. Yet the ends are sharply different. The Machiavellian prince has the selfish end of holding on to his position. The Benthamite legislator has the altruistic end of promoting general happiness. Nevertheless in both cases we get similar manipulation of human beings; in both cases pain is threatened in order to achieve desired results in a precisely calculated manner; and in both cases such economy, such efficiency in the use of threats, depends upon the possibility of accurate knowledge of human nature.

Bentham's own awareness of the importance of psychology can be seen from the structure of the *Introduction* itself. After the first two chapters in which the proper end of legislation is displayed and defended, there follow nine chapters which are basically about psychology (consciousness, intentionality, motives, actions, and so on). As he says at the beginning of this sequence of chapters,

> it has been shown that the happiness of individuals . . . is the sole end which the legislator ought to have in view . . . but whether it be this or any thing else that is to be *done*, there is nothing by which a man can ultimately be *made* to do it, but either pain or pleasure. Having taken a general view of these two grand objects . . . in the character of *final* causes; it will be necessary to take a view of pleasure and pain itself in the character of *efficient* causes or means. (IPML 34)

In other words, as was seen in the last chapter, there is a double appearance of pleasure and pain, both as specifying the end to be aimed at (final cause) and also the means of achieving it (efficient cause). Before it is known how pleasure and pain can be used as the means of achieving the desired end, considerable study both of them and also of human nature more generally is necessary. Hence the nine psychological chapters; and it is only after these

137

chapters that Bentham proceeds to the examination of the application of this study in legislation, that is in the consideration of the
appropriate kinds and quantities of punishment or the correct
classification of offences. Furthermore, because this study has to
result in the general principles for considering not only kinds but
also amounts of punishment, these psychological chapters have
to deal not only with quality but also with quantity. They have to
deal not only with the kinds of motives but also with their force;
not only with the kinds of pleasures and pains but also with their
value. Therefore Bentham has a separate chapter, Chapter Four,
on 'value of a lot of pleasure or pain, how to be measured'. From
the title of this chapter, it might be thought that it dealt only with
the subject matter of ends, that is, with what ought to happen;
and it is true that it provides the general principles by which the
legislator can assess the value of a particular portion of pleasure
or pain before he sums various possibilities in order to discover
which leads to the greatest happiness. However, this calculation
or assessment of value is also important in assessing how pleasure
and pain are to be used as a means. For if it is true, as Bentham
has just asserted in the remark quoted above, that the only way in
which someone can be made to do something is by pleasures and
pains, and if the way to make them do what leads to the desired
end is to threaten just sufficient punishment to deter them doing
anything else, then the values of specific threatened pains will
need to be known if it is to be known just how much punishment
to threaten to achieve this. So just as pleasures and pains play a
double role in Bentham's thought, so also do the values of pleasures and pains. They form the basis for the calculation the legislator makes about ends and also the calculation which every
individual makes about his own interests. The legislator uses
these calculations about interests as means to achieve his ends;
but it is important to realise that calculation, or evaluation, comes
into Bentham's thought in these two separate positions. If the
economy of violence is to be successful, if punishment is to succeed in its object of preventing mischief 'at as cheap a rate as
possible' (IPML 165), then there has to be calculation of means
as well as ends.

The idea of utilitarianism as involving calculation is part of the
standard, traditionally received, idea of Bentham, and like much
of that idea it comes via Dumont in the *Traités*. While condensing
the *Introduction* chapter on value, Dumont talks of 'moral calculation' ('calcul moral', *Traités* i 53; LEGIS 32), an expression
which does not translate any phrase in the original text. Nor, so
far as I know, does Bentham ever use any such expression as

'felicific calculus'; certainly it is not prominent. So the stress on calculation could be thought to be due solely to Dumont. It is true that Bentham later talks quite happily of 'political arithmetic' or 'applying arithmetical calculation to the elements of happiness' (*Codification Proposal*, IV 540); but this could be due to the influence of the *Traités* back on Bentham's own later thought. Yet, here as elsewhere, Dumont has only sharpened and over-simplified what is latent in Bentham's thought. Bentham engaged in calculation, and there is an important early block of manuscript in which the use of money in order to evaluate pleasures and pains is discussed. More importantly in the present context, where Dumont uses this phrase he is introducing an example of evaluation, which, unlike the phrase itself, is taken from the Value chapter of the *Introduction*. It is the example of the factors which enter into evaluation (in financial terms) of a piece of property. That is, in spite of the talk about 'moral calculation', it is nothing to do with 'morals' in any narrow sense; that is, with 'oughts' or 'ends'. It is intended to be a piece of pure descriptive psychology showing how people as a matter of fact actually do evaluate things. As such it forms part of the essential psychological material which the legislator needs in order to calculate the strength of human motives. Bentham himself is in no doubt that humans do calculate their interests in this way. 'Who is there that does not calculate?', he asks rhetorically towards the end of the *Introduction* (IPML 173), answering his own question: 'men calculate, some with less exactness, indeed, some with more: but all men calculate' (IPML 173-4). Calculation of interest is a fact of psychology; and it is also a fact how the calculation actually proceeds. Such are the facts which the successful legislator must know.

The texts, therefore, to consider in consideration of Bentham's psychology are the main central block of the *Introduction*, together with earlier work in the manuscripts and later developments. The earlier manuscripts chiefly about value are UC 27.32-40, and are easily accessible since reprinted in full in both Baumgardt (1952) and Parekh (1973). Later development of the work on motives in the *Introduction* is best studied in *A Table of the Springs of Action*. However, after Bentham wrote the main text of the *Introduction*, which was printed in 1780, he branched out into civil law. Instead of just considering criminal law, as in the 1770s, that is the right system of offences and punishments, he now considered the correct allocation of rights and duties across the whole field of human activity. The question became not just how the law should impose punishment in order to deter clearly wrong behaviour, but, rather, how the law should impose duties and create rights in order to achieve the end of the greatest happiness. However, this more general project again depends, and was specifically seen by Bentham to depend, upon a knowledge of human nature. It must be known what the natural laws of human happiness are, before the appropriate action (if any) to be taken by a legislator can be known. Bentham talks in these 1780s manuscripts, which became the *Civil Code* of 'axioms of mental pathology'. When he eventually published the *Introduction* in 1789, he notes in the appended Preface that these axioms had occurred to him since the printing of the main text, and that they ought to be placed in priority to the more specific material on punishment (IPML 3). They are used, both in manuscripts not used by Dumont and also in the work which he did incorporate into the Civil Code part of the *Traités*, as the basis of quite sophisticated calculations about happiness. So here there seems to be the makings of a demonstrative science of human nature, which allows those calculations to be made which will form the basis both of an accurate assessment of the right quantity of punishment and also of the appropriate 'creation and distribution of propriety and other civil rights' (IPML 3). Such is the material; such is the interest of Bentham in psychology; such is the need which an adequate psychology must fill if his system is to be operable. It must now be seen whether the need is satisfied; the interest justified; the material adequate to bear the load.

Bentham's use of the term 'axioms' and his apparent unwavering confidence in the principle that all men pursue their own interests might lead one to think that his psychology must be purely *a priori*; that is, that it is a deductive or demonstrative science similar to geometry based on unquestionable first assumptions about how people are or behave, similar to classical economic theory. With the hindsight of J.S. Mill this would be natural, since the 'geometric' method was exactly how he described the method of his father's work in political theory, and James Mill's *Essay on Government* looks to be a highly Benthamite production, starting with a factual principle about what people do do (pursue their own interest) and with an evaluative principle about what they ought to do (act in a way which results in the greatest happiness) and showing deductively that the only form of government which jointly satisfies these two principles is democracy. The conclusion is the same as Bentham's; so also are the principles. Yet Mill seems just to assume the vital psychological principle as an *a priori* axiom. Furthermore, Bentham himself, presenting the same two principles at the start of the *Constitutional Code*, says that the principle that 'self-preference has place everywhere' 'may be termed an axiom' (IX 5). However, the assumption that Bentham's psychology is purely *a priori* is not correct. Just like Hume before him, Bentham aspired to be the Newton of parts of the science of man, and the model of science was in each case the same: a model of Newton's procedure, which, based on the *Optics* more than *Principia*, thought of scientific method as based on experiment and observation. He describes his attempt to provide a new basis in psychology for civil law as 'an attempt to extend the experimental method of reasoning from the physical branch to the moral' (UC 32.158). Although he does compare the axiom of self-preference with Euclid's in the *Constitutional Code*, he not only makes it clear that to take something as an axiom is to suppose that it is not possible to disprove it, but actually adds on purely empirical considerations which he thinks demonstrates its truth to those that might doubt it. These depend upon the fact of the survival of the human species. More importantly, with respect to the axioms of mental pathology which form the foundation of the civil code, he introduces them in the original 1780s manuscripts with the claim that 'the science of legislation . . . ought to be built on the immovable basis of sensations and experience' (UC 32.6; *Traités* ii 18; LEGIS 102). When he himself much later came to rewrite this material in what now forms the *Pannomial Fragments*, the principles are still referred to as 'axioms' but the same analogy to the apparently observational science of medicine is preserved, and the claim is still that the basis is observation. In his 1780s manuscripts, Bentham writes:

> medicine, commonly so-called, the medicine of the body . . . has for its basis the observations of the axioms of pathology, commonly so-called. Morals is the medicine of the soul. The science of legislation is the practical part of this medicine. The science of legislation ought to have for its basis the axioms of pathology which could be called the axioms of mental pathology. (UC 32.6; compare *Traités* ii 19; LEGIS 103)

In the manuscripts making the later *Fragments* of perhaps thirty or forty years later, he writes: 'experience, observation and experiment − these are the foundations of all well-grounded medical practice: experience, observation, and experiment − such are the foundations of all well-grounded legislative practice' (*III 224). There is no doubt, therefore, that in spite of his use of the term 'axiom', Bentham intended his psychology to be an observational science, based upon the facts of human nature as learned by experience rather than as assumed *a priori*.

However well-intentioned he might be, there are formidable problems of performance blocking the way for someone attempting to found psychology on general observation. Bentham's claims to be interested in discovering the facts by experiment were not just claims: while working on poverty he tried to use Young's *Annals of Agriculture* as a way of distributing a questionnaire to be filled in and returned to him to find what the facts of poverty were. (It had 3,000 spaces of entry and, in spite of Young's promotion — he wrote a note urging co-operation — it is unlikely that many were returned.) He approached the Foundling Hospital in order to get a series of statistics with respect to the cost of living while working on economics, and he approached bankers in order to try and derive accurate figures with respect to the quantity of paper money in circulation while writing on this. So his actual method was not *a priori*, not only in intention but also in practice, even though it was not a propitious time for the collection of statistics. Bentham, of course, hoped to change that; as part of his particular proposals, for example for workhouses, it was important that 'everything is to be registered' (PAUPER 103); and part of his admiration for Young was based on the fact that Young had turned himself into a one-man accumulator of facts about agriculture. Yet when we reach the very general observations on human nature which Bentham calls 'axioms', such as the principle of self-preference, it is difficult to see how large-scale questionnaires or observations could help in establishing their truth or otherwise. It seems here that Bentham had no alternative to treat them otherwise than as mere assumptions, even if he did not think of them as being *a priori*.

Indeed, taking the principle of self-preference, the situation seems even worse than this. For if observation enters in, it seems that the principle could not hold to be other than disproved. It takes little research or experiment to show that altruism is a fact of human life. So if the principle is to be protected, it has to be taken to be an *a priori* claim, which is then used to define what counts as being in someone's interest. It is then recognised that people help each other in a way which damages themselves, but this is then explained by saying that they have an interest in helping other people. The claim that everyone acts in his own interest can then be taken to be either trivial or false: either it is a mere definitional device which identifies 'interest' or else it is a substantial claim which is disproved by experience. Yet, it could be urged, Bentham wants it both ways and takes the wrong

142

option on each. He wants it to be observational, but in fact introduces it as an *a priori* principle; he then uses it as if it were a substantive truth, unaware that it is not substantial and that, if it were substantial, it would be false. This would be highly destructive of Bentham's use of 'interest' but, like several such claims, it is too simple for the original Bentham. For Bentham himself recognised the possibility of altruistic behaviour, and was also aware of the crucial ambiguity of status in the principle that everyone prefers their own interest. Very late in his life he heads off a possible objection to a piece of constitution-building based on the principle of self-preference that he is an 'old and gloomy-minded man' unable to recognise 'philanthropy' or 'self-sacrifice' with the claim 'Yes: I admit the existence of *disinterestedness* in the sense in which you mean it. I admit the existence of philanthropy . . . I have not far to look for it' (*Peers and Senates*, IV 430-1). In the less occasional *Table of the Springs of Action*, a whole section is devoted to the pleasures and pains of 'sympathy', that is, to establishing a list of motives placed upon the desire for the welfare of other persons (sympathy, mercy, patriotism, pity, kindness, good-nature, and so on). Sympathy always features strongly in Bentham. Unlike antipathy it is held to have a 'primeval and constant source' in 'human nature' in the *Introduction* (IPML 61), and in the later thought, sympathy is erected into a fifth sanction alongside the more obvious self-regarding ones of the earlier work (for example, *Logical Arrangements*, III 290; RJE v 704). He says in *Evidence* that the judge should work on a 'general presumption of mutual sympathy' (RJE v 665). So it is clear that Bentham recognised and allowed so-called disinterested behaviour, and this recognition was based upon observation.

Once this recognition is made, what then remains of the principle of self-preference, particularly as a tool for constructing institutions in the spirit of the project outlined in the last chapter? It is helpful to divide this question into two parts, the use of the principle in general psychology and its application in particular projects. As a piece of general psychology, Bentham himself recognised its ambiguous nature. In a note to *Of Laws in General* he observes that the observation that no man acts without a motive is

of a piece with another observation equally trite concerning man in general, that he is never governed by any thing but his own interest. This observation in a large and extensive sense of the word interest (as comprehending all sorts of motives) is indubitably true: but as indubitably false in any of the

confined senses in which upon such an occasion the word
interest is wont to be made use of. (OLG 70n)

In other words, Bentham himself recognised that the principle
was either trivial or false. As well as recognising sympathy, he
includes it on occasion under 'interest' (as when he notes in
Evidence that 'interest' should be taken as including 'not only
self-regarding interest' (RJE i 65n)), however it is clear here
that the principle is just being used to specify someone's actual
motives. Taken in a substantial way, as he says clearly enough,
the principle is false.

This may be enough to exculpate Bentham from the charge of
equivocation over the status of the principle, but seems to make
it even worse for the prospects of its use in the construction of
constitutions and lesser institutions. For this planning depends
upon not merely knowing that men act from motives (the trivial
sense) but that they actually prefer themselves to other people
(the substantial sense). Otherwise the legislator has no guide at
all about what he should do in order to bring duty and interest
into line. However, here Bentham has another answer, and one
that would quite naturally occur to him given the previous history
of the subject. It is not that it is true that everyone always acts
in his own interest (in a substantial sense); it is just that it is safer
to assume that they might and so design institutions that, even
if they were to, they would still in fact act so as to bring about
the desired consequences. Just after the passage quoted above in
which Bentham rebuts the suggestion that he is an old and gloomy-
minded man, he remarks that 'all men are not *Frenchmen*. Frenchmen have not been at all times what they are at the present times.
. . . all French kings have not been Louis Philippes' (IV 431). In
other words, even if there is altruism and philanthropy, it is best
not to depend upon it; 'it is upon *this* that all practice, if it has
any pretensions to the praise of prudence, must be built' (ibid.).
This would be quite a natural thought for Bentham as a careful
reader of Hume, for not only did Hume hold (as noted above)
that the construction of political institutions ought to proceed
on the basis of the assumption of universal self-interest, but he
also held quite explicitly that the assumption was false. It was not
that it was true that there was no altruism, it is just that it was the
safest thing to believe. This stress on safety and prudence makes
the legislator like the games player who believes in a maximum
strategy: he is not concerned with the fact that he may not be up
against the worst, or even with what normally happens; his concern is solely to protect himself against the worst. Even if most

office-holders are perfectly disinterested, the offices must be so constructed so that we are protected against the ravages that might be wreaked by a self-interested incumbent.

In Bentham, the reason that the legislator should assume self-interest, even if not universally true (in the substantial sense), goes beyond the mere possibility of there being self-interested persons and the need to protect the rest of society against the damage which such a person would cause. He thinks that it is the normal state for man. Acts without the least tincture of self-interest are 'heroic', that is, rare (IPML 155n); 'heroes form the exception' (*Draught Judicial Establishment*, IV 375); self-interest will prevail 'here and there an extraordinary case excepted' (**Introductory Rationale Evidence*, VI 11), these are examples of a self-denying ordinance 'out of the ordinary course of human nature' (*Scotch Reform*, V 15). So since it is the normal course of events, it is quite reasonable for the legislator to assume it in the design of institutions, quite apart from his desire to protect himself against the worst that could possibly happen. As he puts it in the introductory matter to the *Constitutional Code*, even if the truth of the self-preference principle 'held good in no more than a bare majority, of the whole number of instances, it would suffice for every practical purpose, in the character of a ground for all political arrangements' (IX 6). Institutions are not homes for heroes; they are constructed for normal people.

Bentham can survive, therefore, the falsity of his principle of self-preference once it is taken as a substantial, empirical, principle and tested by observation. He holds it to be no more than a generalisation, and this he does think has good observational support in that it is the only possible explanation for the survival of the species. This idea appears all over Bentham's later writings, in the *Book of Fallacies* (*134; *364), the *Procedure* papers (*II 120), *Peers and Senates* (IV 431), and the *Rationale of Judicial Evidence* (RJE iv 457-8). Normally he seems to think that the mere mention of the idea is sufficient to demonstrate it. His fullest account of why the very existence of the species depends upon a general habit of self-preference probably occurs in the Introductory material to the *Constitutional Code* where he uses a *reductio ad absurdum* argument. He imagines the alternative situation to self-interest in which 'the whole care for the happiness of A [is] confined to the breast of B . . . and the whole care of the happiness of B [is] confined to the breast of A' and concludes that, 'in this state of things, the species could not continue in existence' (IX 6). It is not quite clear why; and the clue must be provided by his claim that in a more complex case, in which the happiness of A is put in the care of both B and C, the destruction would be even speedier. This seems to make the vital point one of co-ordination. With the best will in the world, the individuals concerned would not be able to do those things which led to the happiness of the individual with whom they were concerned. Bentham compares it to the blind leading the blind. So the crucial point seems to be that no one knows the interest of an individual so well as he does himself. Hence the most efficient way of caring for someone's interests is to let him care for them himself. Bentham certainly does believe this but, as will be seen, he does not believe that it is universally true. In any case, even if it is the most efficient way of promoting interests, it is not clear that a less efficient way might still not be sufficient to ensure survival. If knowledge is the key to the problem, this depends upon the possibility of knowing about the interests of others. It would be implausible for Bentham to assume that individuals cannot know, and hence cannot care successfully for, the interests of others. Apart from the minor problem of its being false, it would not allow him to make sense of the project of the legislator, based as it is upon the supposition of the possibility of knowledge of interests. Also, if it is really survival of the species that has to be explained, it is not obvious that knowledge needs to come in at all. All that is required is that some co-ordination procedure has evolved which prevents action against the general interests of the species. Any device will do. If it is built into the individuals by nature (genetically) that they are reluctant to kill each other until they have bred successfully, this would do; it is not necessary that they have knowledge of the interests of other individuals in any more than a metaphorical sense. So even though the argument about survival is supposed by Bentham to furnish a conclusive proof, the possibility of various forms of explanation of the undoubted fact of survival casts doubt on the necessity of the self-preference principle in order to explain it.

On the other hand, empirical evidence for departures from the self-preference principle lay readily to hand. For Bentham was himself, and thought himself to be, one of those heroic exceptions who was not guided (in any substantial sense) by self-interest. Again and again in pressing his particular projects upon reluctant officials, he stresses his disinterestedness. In pressing his annuity proposals on the Treasury officials, Bentham writes that not only will there be no trouble that he will not take, but that he seeks no 'pecuniary indemnification' (Stark ii 76). 'No share in the profit' is aimed at in the *Procedure* proposals (*II 6). Seeking for work as a parliamentary draughtsman, he wants the 'labour' without the

146

'emolument' (X 293); and when pressing a plan to codify the English law he stresses that 'what is NOT necessary is reward' (X 470). The irony here is that it was Bentham's friend Romilly who urged on Bentham that he must not make proposals like this to the House of Commons since it would just expose him to ridicule. They would find it 'absolutely incredible' (X 432). This illustrates that Bentham had in himself a counter-example to universal self-interest, but also that the common prevailing view was so strongly that people acted from self-interest that they would find it difficult to believe in exceptions. This provides empirical support for both the denial of the universal claim and the acceptance of the claim that the principle is, on the whole, true.

Whether true or otherwise, or whether it was needed in the strong form for successful legislation or otherwise, all the above discussion has proceeded upon the supposition that it is possible to identify and compare interests. It has been assumed that it makes determinate sense to hold that someone is self-interested, the only question was whether or not it was true (universally, generally, or as a useful assumption). This assumption must now itself be questioned, and the meaning of 'interest' examined, particularly since not only the kinds but also the force or value of interests have to be known for the legislative project to succeed. In accordance with the general principles of meaningfulness laid down in Chapter IV, this will require giving an account of interests in terms of real entities. Statements about interests will be explained or given meaning by means of statements which refer to nothing but real entities, that is, to directly perceptible entities or entities which can be immediately inferred from directly perceptible entities. Or, to put it another way, statements about interest will be rendered meaningful by an account of how verification is possible of such statements. 'Interest is one of those words, which not having any superior *genus* cannot in the ordinary way be defined' (IPML 12n); so, like other fictions, only paraphrasis analysis is available by which statements about interest are explained ultimately in terms of statements about such real entities as pain and pleasure. 'To understand what *interest* means, we must look to motives: to understand what motive means, we must look to pain and pleasure, to fear and hope: fear the expectation of pain or loss of pleasure; hope the expectation of pleasure or exemption from pain' (RJE v 35); 'a man is said *to have an interest in any subject*, in so far as that *subject* is considered as more or less likely to be to him a source of pleasure or exemption [from pain]' (SPRINGS I 207). The key concept here is *motive* rather than *interest*. The legislator has to understand motives; to know what they are and calculate their force. He can do this by seeing that they can be made meaningful (like anything else) in terms of real entities, in this case pleasures and pains. Furthermore, since this analysis reduces diverse motives to a single basis, it looks as if it should be possible to compare motives with one another. If the value of a portion of a pleasure or pain can be determined, then the force of the different motives can be compared with one another by reduction to this common basis and evaluation in terms of it.

Bentham hence wants to produce a reductive analysis of human psychology in which all motives, all 'springs of action', are made sense of in terms of seeking pleasure and avoiding pain. Fear, for example, is 'the prospect of pain' (IPML 18), and, more generally, the principal motive, from which all other motives flow, 'is always some pleasure, or some pain' (IPML 100). After he had finished writing the chapter on motives in the *Introduction* (from which the last quotation comes) Bentham wrote to his brother in a letter that 'people's intentions, motives and dispositions will now be as clear as the Sun at noon-day' (CORR II 287). This would be the result expected on the official doctrine on which relation to real entities like pleasure and pain gives meaning and so provides clarification. It will, however, only be the case if pleasures and pain are clear in themselves prior to the analysis; that is, if they are unproblematic real entities about which there are no problems of identification. However, notoriously, this is an over-confident assumption. It would only be the case if both pleasures and pains were particular types of sensations, directly comparable with each other. Intentions, motives, dispositions, emotions would then be clarified by reduction to actual and possible sensations, sensations being clear in that there would be no problem about whether or not they were occurring and about what was their nature. On this account, hope is not just taken as the expectation of pleasure in some abstract sense, but as the expectation of a quite specific kind of sensation. Similarly fear, the expectation of pain, is the expectation of another quite specific kind of sensation. The motive of sympathy, which is the expectation of the pleasure of sympathy, must be taken to be the expectation of another way of achieving the first specific kind of sensation. Yet, when subject to the briefest amount of elementary, do-it-yourself, introspective psychology, this does not seem to be an accurate account. Pains are more like particular sensations than pleasures are; and, whether or not pleasures are sensations, they do not seem to have a single, directly perceptible, element in common. The different pleasures which Bentham lists in the *Springs of Action* such as the pleasures of sympathy, sex, power, religion, intoxication, and so on, seem to have no more in common than that they are different motives to action. Rather than the motive being explained by the sensation, it seems that it is used to identify it, and so account for it. Otherwise there would be a single, directly perceived thing (a 'real entity') called pleasure, which single thing could be achieved in many different ways, and would explain these various actions. On that account, sympathy, sex, or religion would all be various ways which one could choose of achieving exactly the same thing; and how one would feel after a spot of successful indulgence in drunkenness, sex, wrath, piety, or sympathy would be exactly the same. This just does not seem to be true; and, in so far as it is not true, it means that the supposed sensation should be analysed in terms of the motive rather than the motive in terms of sensation. What makes all pleasures pleasures is that they are reasons for engaging in action, rather than what makes motives motives is that they are expectations of pleasure.

In so far as what we have are different kinds of pleasure rather than different ways of achieving a single kind of sensation, there is going to be a problem of comparing these different kinds. For the knowledge needed by a legislator depends upon being able to compare the force of different motives and so knowing, for example, just which prospective pain will deter someone from attempting to realise a pleasure of which the legislator disapproves. Lack of reduction to a single basis means that the relative force of say, drunkenness and piety, cannot be compared by measuring the strength of the single sensation of pleasure to which they both lead. So it does not look as if the psychology provides an adequate basis for the calculations in which the Benthamite legislator needs to engage. On the other hand, Bentham himself was clearly always more interested in quality than quantity. It has been seen how he believed in experimental science; but the sciences which he knew about, and in which he engaged, were such classificatory sciences as chemistry or botany rather than such quantitative sciences as astronomy. Bentham admired and corresponded with Priestley; his brother married the daughter of the leading chemist with whom Bentham was friendly, Fordyce; he was pleased to report that he had been distilling urine when the Archbishop of York called on him in his chambers to solicit his vote. He had a life-long interest in botany. Yet these (at this time) were classificatory sciences. Moving nearer the science of legislation itself, Bentham's interest in pleasures and pains was also much more in their classification than in their measurement. After the short chapter on value laying down general principles of measurement, there follows in the

Introduction much longer chapters classifying the various kinds of pleasures and pains and of 'circumstances influencing sensibility'. There is little attempt here to compare the different kinds of pleasures or the different motivational forces which they assert. The final, long, part of the *Introduction*, which, at least in Bentham's eyes forms a keystone to the work, is the chapter on the classification of offences. When concerned with punishment he is also more interested in classifying than comparing in a quantitative manner. He thinks that it is a special case if two punishments can be made 'perfectly commensurable' (IPML 177). Even the two basic elements themselves, pleasure and pain, were not always thought by Bentham to be commensurable. In considering the inappropriateness of pecuniary penalities for assault, for example, he asks, in a case where a man falls upon you and beats you, 'what pecuniary loss is there that you could be sure would give him so much pain as the satisfaction of giving vent to his ill-will promised to afford him pleasure?'; and concludes: 'it is plain that between quantities so incommensurate there is no striking a sure balance' (OLG 213). So even Bentham himself seems on occasion to have expressed scepticism about the required measurement and calculation.

The method of giving an account of interests or motives in terms of pleasures and pains, therefore, even though it was supposed both to give clarification and make them amenable to quantitative analysis, seems to run into problems on both accounts. There is also an additional problem with any such method of giving determinate meaning to terms referring to psychological entities, which has been much more discussed recently than in Bentham's day. This is that, even if it is supposed that the kinds of verification available should be considered in determining or clarifying the meaning of a term, it is no longer obvious that the basis of verification should be in terms of sensations directly available only to those whose sensations they are. A public language of psychological states, it is thought, should rest upon a publicly available verification. Pleasures and pains, that is, are not thought to be so secure a verificationist base; so obviously paradigmatic real entities as Bentham thought. If it is thought, therefore, (to put it in Bentham's own words) that 'a common measure [is] necessary to enable men to annex the same ideas in point of quantity to the same words' (UC 27.36), then the right place to start is not with individual sensations available only to their possessors and not available to others to serve as a common measure. Rather, it should be done, by attribution of psychological states in a way which makes sense (public sense; sense for anyone) of an individual's actions in a certain context. Beliefs and desires are attributed to the individual so that the resulting action is explained (that is, justified; is shown to be the rational thing to do with those beliefs and desires). This is to divide up the mental faculties in a way that was absolutely standard for Bentham, between will and understanding (for example, IPML 145; OLG 105, 134, 226; RJE iii 356). His standard preconditions of action are inclination, knowledge, power (for example IPML 244; OLG 280; RJE iv 279; *LEGIS 362). Inclination picks up the will; knowledge the understanding; power both of them and also the context. So, in that context as perceived, belief and desire issue in action. This means that, given certain beliefs and context, we can compare the varying force of particular desires. If a person is subject to two conflicting desires and acts in accordance with the one rather than the other, this forms a basis for saying that that desire is stronger. So some of the problems described above resulting from taking pleasures and pains as a basis can be avoided. Instead of measuring one pleasure against another and so explaining one desire or motive as being stronger than another, it is seen what people actually do. The objection made above, that the motives seemed to be explaining the pleasures rather than the other way round, now becomes a virtue. Motives are attributed, or clarified, on the basis of action, and are then used for an account of which things someone finds pleasure in. On such an account 'pleasure' no longer names a single, particular, kind of sensation but, rather, is a generic term referring to all those states towards which someone is positively motivated. It means no more than 'satisfaction', and 'satisfaction' no more than successful fulfilment of desire. So, using Bentham's own faculty account of the human mind, and of the antecedents to action, together with his own general classificatory practice, many of the problems of his official accounts of motives can be avoided.

In such an account, in which beliefs and desires are primarily attributed on the basis of the explanation of observed behaviour, and in which pleasure and pain are identified in terms of the satisfaction of frustration of desire, it is still possible to understand beliefs, desires, pleasure, and pain, in a realistic way, that is as descriptions of really occurring states of mind rather than as merely instrumental descriptions which are only sophisticated ways of describing behaviour. They can be taken, in Benthamic language, as being inferential real entities rather than as fictional entities. So, in that they are still real entities, even if not basic ones, pleasures and pains can still in this account feature in a similar way to Bentham's; and it is possible to consider that they

151

are the objects of introspective awareness, so that people's reports of their desires or states of satisfaction can be taken seriously. Even if preferences revealed in behaviour are taken as fundamental, this does not mean that a state of pleasure or satisfaction need be attributed to someone just because they succeed in achieving something which they previously desired (worked for). There are perfectly obvious and identifiable behavioural signs of people not being satisfied with what they get in such circumstances, signs which reveal the desire for something else incompatible with the achieved object (such as for more or less of the thing in question, if it is something susceptible of degrees). These, in turn, can be correlated with introspective reports, with how it seems to the person in question. Working in terms of explanation of behaviour, or of motives to behaviour, also solves the problem of lack of comparability between the basic entities of pleasure and pain. These now automatically become dual ways of explaining any action; someone says, or acts as if, he wants X instead of Y. To that extent X is perceived as pleasurable by him, Y as painful. Of course, he could be wrong. In that case, on actually achieving X, he will discover that what he (really) wants is Z, or whatever. The more experienced or informed someone is, the less likely this is to happen; but mistakes about interest (pleasure), which are clearly possible, can be accommodated on this model, as well as in Bentham's more primitive one. It is in any event relatively unusual. Normally, to find what people want, what gives them pleasure, we see what they do. It is sometimes thought that something like slavery forms an objection to Bentham's ethics, since there would be nothing wrong with slavery on his account if only the slaves were happy. However Bentham, who was a life-long opponent of slavery, has no difficulty with this sort of objection. Saying that it is 'necessary to show the evil inherent in the very nature of the thing' he does this by observing that it is certain that the condition is disagreeable to slaves 'since they are never kept in that condition but by constraint. No man who is free wishes to become a slave, and there is no slave who does not wish to become free' (*Civil Code*, *Traités* ii 181; LEGIS 202; I 344). We find out whether someone is happy by what he does. If no one voluntarily enters into slavery, then people do not desire to be slaves, and it is not the case that slaves are happy.

Attributing desires and pleasures and pains on the basis of behaviour, therefore, allows some possibility of comparison between various desires, or various kinds of pleasures and pains, and so restores some possibility of calculation to the legislator. The strongest desire is the one which actually leads to action;

152

the greater pleasures or pains are those which normally have the strongest influence on action. This will allow some comparison between different objects in the case of one person, and in so far (as in the case of slavery) such comparisons are general, it will allow the legislator to rely on general knowledge of the greater pleasure (in this sense) produced by the one object than by the other. Of course, people differ, and are motivated in different ways and to different extents by the same objects. Bentham is only too aware of this and spends a long cataloging chapter in the *Introduction*, 'on circumstances influencing sensibility', listing and bringing out such differences. Some of his labels are mere place holders, saying little more than that there is difference ('bent of inclination', 'frame of mind'), but some are genuinely explanatory ('pecuniary circumstances', 'bodily imperfections') and open the possibility of a genuinely causal account which would explain and, in principle, predict such differences. In any case, given that what Bentham says in this chapter seems more banal than absurd, it is reasonable to suppose that there are differences between people of the kinds that he describes, and that it might be possible to make knowledge of such differences more precise and systematic. It is not actually crazy to suppose that a sighted man might take more pleasure in painting than a blind one; that is, was more likely to prefer being in the presence of paintings to doing other things than a blind one would. If knowledge of desires of others is possible, as explained above, then so is knowledge of differences. What is much more important to Bentham, however, than these differences are similarities. Differences are only important when people are being treated individually, as by the judge, or where there is an identifiable class of people who will need special treatment. Similarities, by contrast, are essential for the general project of legislation. It would be impossible unless it were generally the case that men did not desire those things proposed as punishments and did desire those things proposed as rewards. The legislator must have access to knowledge about the behaviour of at least the average man, or average citizen. Yet this does not seem to be an insuperable objection. If, as above, there can be knowledge of differences, then there can be knowledge of similarities. Men are sufficiently predictable to make it a well-based generalisation that they no more desire to go to prison than they desire to be slaves; or that they prefer social esteem to obloquy. It is true that Bentham, at least as he is phrased by Dumont, wishes more than 'vague approximation', which he regards as 'the language of indifference or incapacity' (*Civil Code*, *Traités* ii 18; LEGIS 102). On the other hand it is clear that he neither wants nor needs universal truths. Generalisations are sufficient, providing that 'they approach nearer the truth than any others which can be substituted for them' (UC 32.5; *Traités* ii 19; LEGIS 103). The fit of the best generalisation to how things really are, even though not perfect, is enough for the practical business of legislation. There is no reason to suppose that such generalisations are not available; at least unless one is completely sceptical about the possibility of attributing desires to other people at all.

In so far as Bentham wishes to calculate the value of pleasures and pains or the resulting force of motives (and he does talk in this *Civil Code* body of manuscript of the principle of utility making 'legislation a matter of observation and calculation' (UC 32.136)), he needs a single measure of comparison by which desires can not only be compared ordinally in terms of some being stronger than others but also quantitatively (or cardinally) so that he can say how much stronger one desire is than another. Calculation demands a way of attaching numbers to the various desires or objects of desire. In the chief body of prefatory manuscript in which he considers calculation, that is the 1770s manuscript in UC 27.32f, Bentham is quite clear both about the need and the distinction. He makes a comparison with physical size:

> You tell me St Paul's is bigger than the Pantheon: I agree with you that it is so. This agreement does not hinder our ideas of the proportion of those two bodies from being very different. You may think St Paul's ten times as big as the other building: I may think it not more than half as big again.

This defect is remedied when we can talk in terms of cubic feet: 'We have found a common measure for them viz: a foot ruler an instrument the use of which is familiar to both of us' (UC 27.36). So what is needed for such quantitative comparisons is a 'common measure' (or, more precisely, a ratio scale with unit comparability capable of being used indifferently by several people). In the manuscript Bentham then goes on to claim that 'the only common measure the nature of things affords is money'; so that 'money is the instrument for measuring the quantity of pain or pleasure' (UC 27.36; 37). Here then is a proposed method in which the legislator can both assess the amount of punishment or reward he needs to specify in order to promote the courses of action he desires; and also a means of finding which elements to add up to find which course of action does promote the most pleasure and least pain. With money as a measure the legislator's task becomes a sort of cost-benefit analysis, in which it can be calculated that one course of action is, say, twice as good as another. Bentham also specifies the means of conversion. Two pleasures or pains are held to be equal in value if someone is indifferent between them; hence the value of a particular pleasure can be calculated by specifying that sum of money between which and that pleasure a person is indifferent:

> if I having a crown in my pocket and not being thirsty, hesitate whether I shall buy a bottle of claret with it for my own drinking or lay it out in providing sustenance for a family . . . it is plain that so long as I continued hesitating the two pleasures of sensuality in the one case, of sympathy in the other, were exactly worth to me five shillings: to me they were exactly equal. (UC 27.36-7)

Here we have a way of comparing two quite dissimilar pleasures and evaluating them in quantitative terms; it is interesting to notice that he moves from observation of behaviour, even his own, rather than introspective examination of the sensations themselves, which is exactly in accord with the approach thought above to be most feasible. The use of money also allows a zero point to be fixed, corresponding to the transition from pleasure to pain, and so allows the numerical scale used to be a ratio scale allowing calculation of relative proportions.

In these early manuscripts, which Bentham drafted as proposed prefatory matter to his major treatise, he wrote that no one should 'be either surprised or scandalized' at finding him 'in the course of this work valuing everything in money' (UC 27.37). Yet, in the *Introduction* itself, in the final text as written shortly after these manuscripts, there is very little mention of money and (as has been noticed) not a great deal about evaluation. This raises the question of how seriously Bentham took these early remarks, even if he is right that only with money 'we get aliquot parts to measure by' (ibid.). What he did hold to steadily throughout his work was that money was the chief means of bestowing pleasure; it was an instrument which someone could convert into pleasure. As he puts it here, 'money is the only current and universal means in the hands of the Legislator of producing pleasure' (UC 27.36). Or elsewhere: money is 'the instrument' of pleasure (OLG 135n); 'the only efficient cause of interest' (RJE v 634). So at least for pleasure, if not for pain (which can be created by the legislator in many different ways other than deprivation of money), the universal nature of money as a means gives it some standing as a measure of the pleasures which it is a means to; and at least allows Bentham to use evaluation in terms of money as a means of illustrating the aspects of something which bestow value on that thing.

These aspects are carefully spelt out in the Value chapter of the *Introduction* and adhered to by Bentham through the rest of his life. The value of a pleasure or pain is held to be in proportion to its intensity and its duration; the multiplication of these gives what Bentham consistently calls the 'magnitude' of that pleasure or pain. Yet value is taken to be value for a person at a position (in space and time), so in addition to the magnitude, which could be taken to be the quantity in itself of the pleasure or pain, we have to consider how this quantity is modified as apprehended from that particular position. Here Bentham adds two further elements, propinquity and certainty, by which the magnitude must also be multiplied. For Bentham, distance diminishes the value of something as, independently, does certainty. In a numerical calculation, these will be represented by fractions, showing how much the magnitude is to be reduced when calculating the value of the pleasure or pain from that position. All these elements of value are discussed in the manuscript just mentioned; Bentham repeats them in the *Introduction*, together with the less important properties which Bentham dubs fecundity and purity, by which he means the number of other sensations which a particular one gives rise to, and whether these are of the same or different types. A pleasure which gives rise to more pleasures is obviously better than one that does not. Or this is how Bentham puts it; but from the point of view of decision, the value of all these pleasures can be calculated separately and added together; it is not necessary that they be thought part of the value of the first pleasure. In any case, Bentham needs a means of adding different pleasures when he considers the calculation which the legislator should undertake to find the total effects of a particular proposed action. This he calls *extent*. So he could have dispensed with fecundity and purity (as he himself notes in the manuscripts (UC 27.34)).

The crucial problem with these aspects of pain and pleasure if they are to be assessed in a quantitative way is, of course, how to evaluate each one, and it is here that money might be supposed to serve. For although some of these aspects, such as duration, propinquity, and certainty have relatively clear ways of measuring (and on scales allowing zeros), it is not so clear how these different measures should be translated into measures of value. Halving the certainty should, perhaps, halve its value, but should halving its distance or its duration? Is a pain for ten minutes twice as bad as a pain for five minutes? Perhaps it is not as bad (the bad thing is to have the pain at all, not how long it lasts; going to prison for two weeks is not twice as bad as going to prison for one week). Perhaps it is worse (there are limits to what people can stand: any one can take five minutes, but ten is intolerable). Other aspects such as intensity do not even start with a natural measure of their own, let alone a way of converting it into value. So it is noticeable, even if it is only illustrative rather than supposed to be the standard or universal procedure, that on those occasions on which Bentham introduces such discussion of value (such as in these early UC 27 manuscripts or the much later *Codification Proposal*), he uses money in order to make the calculations. So, for example, to take the *Codification Proposal*, he says, when discussing propinquity, 'pleasure itself not being ponderable or measurable, to form an estimate of this diminution, take the general source, and thence representative, of pleasure, viz. *money*' (IV 540). He then proceeds to cite the current rate of interest, which makes £20 ten years away half as valuable as £20 today. Similarly, although money does not appear conspicuously in the *Introduction*, at the end of the chapter on Value he tests out the proposed aspects by the particular example of the valuation of an estate. This describes how people actually do value a piece of property in financial terms and claims that 'the value of such an article of property is universally understood to rise or fall according to . . . the nearness or remoteness of the time at which, if at all, it is to come into possession' (IPML 40-1). Similarly, although more cautiously, he says in the UC 27 manuscript that it is 'difficult to ascertain' the proportion by which the value of pleasure is diminished by remoteness but notes that 'the proportion in which the value of a sum of money that is a fund of pleasures is diminished by this circumstance is different in different countries, according to the rate of interest' (UC 27.39). It is doubtful whether Bentham should have taken propinquity as a separate aspect of the value of a pleasure or pain; but he obviously thinks himself justified because it is possible to value pleasures in terms of the means of producing them, money, and it is universally the case for money (although varying in amount) that people exhibit time preference, preferring a smaller sum of money today to a larger sum tomorrow. So Bentham, just as in standard modern cost-benefit analysis, uses the current rate of interest as a measure of the rate at which to discount items of future value.

However seriously or otherwise Bentham took the possibility of evaluating pleasures or pains in terms of money, there was a fundamental problem in doing so, of which he was well aware and which indeed he may have been an influence in introducing into general intellectual circulation. This is the phenomenon of the diminishing marginal utility of money (or of other goods productive of pleasure). It is not just a historical problem; for if it is not permitted to assume a constant marginal utility of money, then the evaluation of projects in terms of money in modern cost-benefit analysis, as a way of evaluating their utility, is also called into question. Bentham took this as one of the general truths about human beings which he incorporated into his 'axioms of mental pathology'. For, he held, although we may assume that 'of two individuals with unequal fortunes, he who has the most wealth has the most happiness', 'the excess in happiness of the richer will not be so great as the excess of his wealth' (*Civil Code*, UC 32.5; *Traités* ii 20; LEGIS 103). In other words, although adding an increment to someone's wealth will (normally) make them happier, and so as increments are added continuously, the happiness will also increase continuously, nevertheless the amount of increase in happiness will not be as great as the amount of increase in wealth. Each equal new increment of wealth brings successively less of an increase in happiness. So, if there is a choice between giving an additional increment to a rich man and to a poor man, more happiness would be provided by giving it to the poor man. Or, to put it the other way round, money cannot be a direct measure of utility because the utility which a particular sum of money represents varies according to the wealth of the person being considered. All changes considered by the legislator which give his subjects £10 worth of reward are not equal in the production of happiness or equal in the motivation they create for those subjects. It all depends upon who it is that would get the reward; that is, on how rich they are already.

Although presented as an axiom (that is as a general, and generally agreed, observation about human nature) in both the *Traités* and also the manuscripts from which the *Traités* derive, Bentham does provide some justification of it. There is a rather hard to follow numerically worked example in the *Civil Code* manuscripts, probably wisely ignored by Dumont, in which the central point is the proportion of addition or reduction an extra element makes to what is possessed already. Bentham imagines two people, Peter and Paul, of equal fortunes of 120 pounds and considers whether it is better to allow a loss of 60 pounds to fall on one alone or to divide it equally between them. He tries to demonstrate that it is better that it should fall equally by imagining the deduction divided into two parts. Once £30 has been deducted from Peter the question is whether the other £30 should also be deducted from Peter or whether it should be deducted from Paul. Bentham's answer, Paul, which achieves equality in deduction, is in accord with the principle of diminishing marginal utility, and Bentham claims that the deduction would hurt Paul less than Peter because his 'fortune is still of 120 pounds, while that of Peter is not more than 90, but 30 which is only the quarter of 120 is the third of 90' (UC 32.9). In other words, Bentham is depending on the proportion of the reduction to the amount possessed already to decide upon its importance; and, if viable, this is a principle which would support and explain diminishing marginal utility. However, in spite of the neatly chosen numbers, I think that this example does not do what Bentham needs it to do, since it relies on the supposition that Paul with 120 is comparable with Peter with 90 when it decides that a reduction of a quarter for Paul is better than a reduction of a third for Peter. Yet it is just such a comparison of different levels of wealth which the principle is designed to provide; it cannot be presupposed in an argument for the principle. The idea of the importance of proportion is on stronger ground when starting from the same base point; and here it does serve as the basis for Bentham's frequent observation that a gain of a particular amount is not as important as the loss of the same amount. For example, to quote from a footnote in the *Traités*, talking of the evils of heavy gambling, if I have a thousand pounds and the stake is five hundred then, even 'though the chances, so far as relates to money, are equal, in regard to pleasure, they are always unfavourable'; for 'if I lose, my fortune is diminished one-half; if I gain, it is increased only by a third' (*Traités* ii 24; *LEGIS 106). 'Sums and circumstances equal, the enjoyment produced by gain is never equal to the suffering produced by loss', as Bentham announces in *Circulating Annuities* (Stark ii 286).

These considerations with respect to proportion may well seem suspicious, even in the case of gain or loss from a single base. Luckily, however, Bentham has other, more certain, considerations to support his principle of diminishing marginal utility, and hence such results as the difference between gaining and losing. He held that the ratio of increase in wealth to increase in happiness only stayed constant with small sums and similar amounts; 'in large sums the ratio of pleasure to pleasure is ... less than the ratio of money to money' (UC 27.35). Doubling the money will no longer double the pleasure. This is for the good reason that 'there is no limit beyond which the quantity of money cannot go: but there are limits, and these comparatively narrow beyond which pleasure can not go' (ibid.). In other words, there is the possibility of saturation of happiness, a bliss point beyond which it is impossible to go. Given, as Bentham says, there is no similar phenomenon for money, it follows necessarily that at some stage equal increments will not bring equal increments of happiness; that is, that diminishing marginal utility will set in. However, this is not the only consideration which Bentham adduces in support of his principle. It is also the case that the first parts of my wealth are needed for physical support while the later parts are only needed for relative luxuries. Bentham comments that a reduction in my wealth which takes away 'what is necessary for my physical support' means a reduction which would be 'four times, ten times, indefinitely greater' than one which does not. Hence 'there are cases in which the proportion would not be the same' between reduction in wealth and reduction in happiness (*Traités ii 24; LEGIS 106; nearly as UC 32.5). If the first part of wealth is spent on relative necessities and the next part on relative luxuries, then this provides good grounds for a principle of diminishing marginal utility. As someone's wealth increases, he can spend it on, to him, successively less important things; equal increments of wealth will not bring equal increments of utility.

Bentham therefore constantly held the view that the ratio of increase in pleasure is not as the ratio of increase in wealth, usually choosing the case in which someone's wealth is increased by a thousand. In the Civil Code he compares a prince with a thousand farmers each having enough to live on (that is, not short of necessities) and holds that the prince, although probably greater in happiness than the average level of happiness of the farmers, is not probably 'equal to the sum total of happiness composed of all these little bits of happiness taken together' (UC 32.5; nearly as *Traités ii 22; LEGIS 105). If the prince were a thousand times as rich, he is less than a thousand times as happy. Earlier, in the 1770s, Bentham thought perhaps not more than fifty times (UC 27.35); later, in the next century, it is a matter of doubt whether, if someone's property is multiplied by a thousand, 'you add as much to his happiness, as you take away from it by dividing his property by 2' (RJE v 656). So far all these reasons (to quote now from a tract of the 1790s) 'fifty pounds is . . . a sum of less importance to a Duke of Marlborough or Bedford, than a single shilling . . . to many a man, in truth to probably the majority of men in the kingdom' (Law Taxes II 578). It therefore follows that it is not possible to use money on its own as a measure of utility.

These are problems about why money cannot be used as a measure of the value of pleasure and pain even if it is possible to evaluate pleasures and pains in terms of money. This was meant to have been possible, it will be remembered, by finding the least amount which would be spent by someone in purchasing the pleasure or avoiding the pain. However, if as is notoriously and obviously the case, not all pleasures can be purchased nor all pains avoided, there are problems about the evaluation of pleasures and pains in terms of money quite apart from the problem that the same sum of money means different things to different people or in different circumstances. Such pleasures and pains, which could not be directly evaluated in terms of money, could only be evaluated if they could be compared with pleasures and pains which can be so directly evaluated. It is not obvious that such comparisons can be made. It would involve finding situations in which someone had to choose between the pleasures in question. In any case, whether or not it is possible to devise a procedure by which all pleasures and pains could be measured in terms of money, Bentham himself clearly held that not all pleasures and pains can be measured in terms of money. It has already been noticed that he objects to pecuniary punishments for assault because of the difficulties of such comparisons. He also holds that it is not always possible to provide financial compensation for damage or injury; that is, that the damage cannot properly be measured in financial terms, and so no specific sum could be a proper restitution. In the chapter on 'pecuniary satisfaction' in the *Penal Code*, he lists several cases in which financial compensation is inappropriate, such as injuries to honour. In such cases 'it is not possible to value in money either the evil of the party injured, or the advantage of the offender' (*Traités* ii 319; LEGIS 286); or, as he puts it in an earlier chapter, 'to offer a man, whose honour has been outraged, a compensation in money for the insult is a new affront' (*Traités* ii 312; LEGIS 282). Similarly, as he notes on several occasions, 'pecuniary rewards paid to informers have failed of their object' (*Traités* iii 132; LEGIS 434) because the shame has outbalanced the reward; that is, the financial reward is no substitute for loss of honour.

Bentham is able to make all these, perfectly sound, points because he holds that it is a 'vulgar error' to suppose that only money has value (*Draught for a Judicial Establishment in France*, IV 375). Similarly, in the *Defence of the Economy against Burke*, he criticises Burke for forgetting that other things than money, such as power and reputation, have value (V 290). Power and reputation are cited in numerous other places as motives as well

161

as money (*Fallacies 146; 239; *Introductory View of the Rationale of Evidence*, VI 10; *Defence of the Economy against Rose*, V
322). Here again the cataloguing trait of Bentham's nature makes
more difficult his desire for quantification. As long as there are
several different ends, and as long as one of these, such as honour
(or 'reputation'), is not commensurable with, or exchangeable for,
one of the others, such as money, then there will be inevitable
difficulties in quantifying the different ends. The motives can be
listed in a catalogue; but no infallible method can be laid down
of determining their value to an agent. We may have achieved a
clear view of interests, but not a clear view of a single scale of
interest: the analysis is qualitative rather than quantitative. On
the other hand, as has just been seen, Bentham himself does not
suggest that such a single scale can be constructed. In fact he
neither claims, nor needs to claim, that a single, universal, measure of value is infallibly attainable. Lists of the few different
fundamental, and the many different derivative, motives are
sufficient to bring them to the legislator's attention. Some generalisations are possible about the normal comparative force of different features such as imprisonment or slavery. The possibility of
worked numerical examples shows that there is some possibility
of refining and improving such generalisations. This should be sufficient for the practical business of legislation.

If the legislator could attain perfect knowledge of interests and
motives, however, even this perfected part of the science of human
nature would not clear up all the problems about value. As seen at
the start of the chapter, the grand project of legislation consists
in taking a psychological principle, namely that people do follow
what they take to be their interests, and a normative principle,
namely that they ought to promote the greatest happiness of the
greatest number, and constructing a system in which people
following their interests would lead to them doing their duty. For
this project psychological knowledge is required by the legislator,
so that he knows what people's interests are, and so how to mani-
pulate their actions by manipulation of their interests. However,
the people also have to know what their interests are, if they are
going to be successfully manipulated. Otherwise, however much
the legislator makes what is someone's duty also in his interest,
the person will still fail to do it through ignorance of what his
interest is. So the knowledge needed by the legislator if he is to
predict their actions is of their apparent interests, that is, what
they think their interests are. Yet the knowledge needed by the
legislator in deciding the specific aims towards which he should
direct their actions is of their real interests. So if people make

mistakes, then the legislator will need to be able to calculate separately the strengths of both people's apparent and also their real interests.

This introduces another problem about the evaluation of happiness. There is an ambiguity deep in Bentham's account of the evaluation of pleasures and pains, as given for example in the chapter on Value in the *Introduction*. The valuation is needed for both the psychological part of the overall project, in which the point of the evaluation is the prediction of actions, and for the normative part of the project, in which the point of the evaluation is the assessment of the appropriate overall ends. Yet the factors involved in the two evaluations may not be the same. It seems at first sight that they are, because what motivates an individual is taken to be what is in his interests, that is what gives him most happiness (greatest pleasure and least pain); and what someone has to do to find out the appropriate end is just to find the greatest total quantity of such individual portions of happiness. This is not to say that the greatest happiness for all is necessarily the sum of the greatest individual happinesses for each, because some individual sacrifice may be necessary. However, at first sight the way of calculating such sums is the same for both projects; the greatest happiness as calculated for the study of motivation is *ceteris paribus* the greatest happiness as incorporated in the grand utilitarian calculation of the best end. If, however, people can make mistakes about their interests, that is, make mistakes about what will lead to their happiness, then the kind of calculation involved in the two projects comes apart. Either the legislator continues to calculate the real interests of people, in which case he will fail to predict their actions correctly and fail to motivate them in performance of their duty, or else he calculates their apparent interests and uses his exact psychological knowledge in manipulating their motivations, in which case he needs a wholly separate study to tell him the ends, the real interests, to which this manipulation should be directed. So when a chapter, like the Value chapter of the *Introduction*, looks as if it is indifferent about both the valuation involved in assessment of motives and also the evaluation involved in decisions about ends, then it may rest upon a crucial, unresolved, ambiguity.

One good place to test for this is with one element in evaluation which Bentham lists in that chapter, propinquity. It will be remembered that Bentham holds that distance in time reduces the value of something, and that this could be shown by the way people value property so, for cases of future possession, the value of property is discounted by the distance in time until the possession, normally at the current rate of interest. This may be taken as a given psychological fact, as a true report about how people are actually motivated. Hence it is something which the legislator needs to take into account when considering the effects of rewards and punishments. Distant objects exert less motivation, hence remote punishments are less effective. So far, so good; this is in accordance both with what Bentham says about punishment (IPML 170) and also with actual observation, where the prospect of remote damage to health does not stop people smoking. However, the next question is whether this is the right way to evaluate benefits when we are not just concerned with what people actually do but concerned with examining what ought to happen if we are to promote the greatest happiness of the greatest number. Here the answer that future benefits should be discounted is much less obvious, and it is quite plausible to suppose that someone charged like the legislator is with maximising happiness should take the happiness at any one time as of equal value to the happiness of any other time, just as he takes the happiness of any one person as of equal value to the happiness of any other person. Of course, the legislator works at a particular position in time. This gives him some reason for disregarding the future and the past, since the future is to some extent outside his control and the past totally so. However, if it is in his control, it is not obvious that mere remoteness should influence him, so that he should arrange a lesser benefit to happen sooner in preference to a greater benefit to happen later. The future is, of course, less certain, and the further off it is (in general) the less certain it is; however, it will be remembered that Bentham distinguished certainty as a quite separate factor from propinquity in evaluation. The present question is whether distance in time alone ought to lead to a reduction of value, quite apart from any reduction brought about by uncertainty.

This example of propinquity is not picked at random but has been selected because Bentham himself thinks elsewhere that it is precisely with respect to the future that people make mistakes about their interests. In both his annuities scheme and also his poor law proposals he wished to encourage savings. Yet he did not feel that all that was lacking was opportunities so that, given the chance, people, knowing their interest, would save. On the contrary, he held that people did not save as much as they ought; that is, that they were mistaken about their own interests. He writes that *the sacrifice of the present to the future* is the common basis of all the virtues ... important in all classes, it is most particularly so in those which most abound in uncultivated minds.

In these to promote frugality is to promote sobriety' (*Annuities*, Stark ii 195n). Although he is talking about virtue, or real value, what this refers to here is people's real interests. People don't know their real interests, and won't do so until they can be got out of the alehouses (Bentham thought that his savings bank scheme in his poor law proposals was superior to his rivals' because they tried to promote savings in public houses, and 'choosing a tippling house for a school of frugality would be like choosing a brothel for a school of continence' (PAUPER, VIII 193)). Hence, although 'generally speaking, [there is] no one who knows what it is for your interest to do, as you yourself' (*Institute of Political Economy*, Stark iii 333), there are cases where enlightenment of the people is required. Hence, as seen, in Bentham's belief that the state should be involved in the dissemination of knowledge. When, later on in the *Introduction* Bentham applies his elements of the measure of value to consideration of the appropriate quantities of punishment, he notices that there are 'prejudices' which are 'properly therefore a property not so much of the punishment as of the people'. These prejudices, 'it is the business of the legislator to endeavour to correct' (IPML 183). Otherwise, having correctly calculated the quantities of punishment to make it in people's interest to desist from undesired actions will not serve; prejudice will lead to mistakes in interest. The apparent value of punishment, its motivational effect, will no longer coincide with its real value. In his more extended writing on punishment Bentham thinks that capital punishment is only an effective deterrent because people have 'a confused and exaggerated notion of the intensity of the pain of death' (*Punishment* 179). So, for Bentham, a legislator who does not correct prejudice is weak 'in suffering the people, for the want of some instruction, which ought to be and might be given them, to quarrel with their own interest' (IPML 183-4). However, this does reveal that mistakes about interest are possible, and in so far as these 'prejudices' are not cured, that the calculation of value which, based on apparent value, produces an account of motives, may diverge from the calculation of value, based on real value, produces an account of what it is that the legislator should be aiming at. By making people's interests in accord with their duty, he may not motivate them; or, alternatively, by finding out their motives by what they do, he may not find out what is really in their interests. However, this brings us to the subject of real interest, of value, and this is the topic of the next chapter.

Notes

(a) The intelligibility, truth, or importance of claiming, for example as a

165

fundamental postulate of economics, that people are motivated by self-interest has come under considerable criticism recently, for example by Martin Hollis in Hollis (1979) and elsewhere and by Amartya Sen in Sen (1976-7).

(b) The claim that it is not rational to discount future value was held by other utilitarians, for example Sidgwick (1907 381). I have given a much longer criticism of the idea in Harrison (1981-2).

(c) A classic treatment of the problem of the measurement of welfare is Sen (1970).

(d) There is a full exposition of Bentham's psychology in McReynolds (1968).

VII

The Greatest Happiness Principle

For the past two chapters the problems and the prospects of success of the Benthamite legislator have been considered. The legislator has a given end, that of promoting the general happiness, and has the task of so arranging law and other social institutions that each man following his own interest (or, more accurately, what seems to be his own interest) will be led to do those things which result in the greatest happiness for the people as a whole. The legislator has knowledge of the given end and knowledge of the human nature on which he has to work so that he can artificially create a system or an organisation in which pursuit of self-interest leads to promotion of the general interest; in which there is a junction between interest and duty. In the last chapter the assumed knowledge about human nature was questioned, and it was considered whether the legislator could have the knowledge about individual self-interest which the general project requires. What interest was, and that people pursue their own interest, could not just be taken in the axiomatic way that Bentham himself sometimes did. However, as well as these problems about interest, there are also problems about duty. If the axiomatic psychology which Bentham uses demands study and defence, then so also does the axiomatic morality. It was suggested at the start of Chapter V that Bentham's reason for assuming each of his two ground principles, the one which founds the psychological description of the means and the one which founds the normative recommendation of the ends, was that they were around in the intellectual air of the time. The same project as Bentham's, with the use of the same founding principles, was traced in predecessors whom he admired such as Helvetius and Beccaria. So Bentham's assumption of these two principles as axioms was not unnatural: it might have seemed plausible at that time that they were something adopted by any right-thinking man which could be adopted without further question as the foundation of a new enterprise. The problems would then be all problems of construction; of the practical application of the unquestioned principles. This was indeed part of the spirit of Chapter V. However, the intellectual air which Bentham breathed is not the air which we breathe, and even at Bentham's time not all men, or even all learned, writing, men, were right-thinking men. These principles were held by a sect, a party, the *philosophes*, to whom it was seen in the first chapter that Bentham attached himself. As a party they had opposition. So the principles were neither then nor now uncontentious. They need explanation and defence. Bentham himself knew this and at times provided defence for both of them. In the last chapter the defence of the psychological principle was examined. In this chapter the fundamental evaluative principle, the grand master principle of utility, will in its turn be examined together with Bentham's actual and possible defences. Rather than just presupposing that the legislator may adopt it as an unquestioned end, it must now be seen whether such an adoption can be defended.

On the first page of the first work which Bentham published, the *Fragment on Government*, the 'fundamental axiom' is confidently proclaimed that '*it is the greatest happiness of the greatest number that is the measure of right and wrong*' (FG 393). Similarly, the major work which Bentham himself published, the *Introduction*, starts off with a chapter entitled 'Of the Principle of Utility' in which Bentham declares that 'the principle of utility is the foundation of the present work' and goes on to state that 'by the principle of utility is meant that principle which approves or disapproves of every action whatsoever, according to the tendency which it appears to have to augment or diminish the happiness of the party whose interest is in question' (IPML 11-12). Or, to take a later unpublished work, the *Institute of Political Economy*, Bentham starts in the first paragraph by saying that the object of the work is to see what is the suitable course for 'the sovereign' with respect to economics given 'what in every government ought to be, and is to a certain degree, the end or object aimed at — viz. the maximum of happiness with reference to the several members of the community taken together, and with reference to the whole expanse of time' (Stark iii 307). In all three works the leading principle is conspicuously placed in a commanding position, and in all three there is reference to happiness. However, in the second, it is called the 'principle of utility' and, earlier, in the *Fragment*, Bentham several times referred to utility. He says that it was from

Hume that he learnt 'that the foundations of all *virtue* are laid in *utility*' and that it was when he had seen through the original contract that he 'learnt to see that *utility* was the test and measure of all virtue' (FG 440n; 441n). Earlier in the *Fragment*, Bentham had connected the two qualities of happiness and utility together, saying that the tendency in any act to promote happiness 'is what we style its utility' (FG 415). This links them both exactly as in the later *Introduction*, so it is not necessary either to think that there is any change of doctrine between the different works or that it matters much whether Bentham talks in terms of happiness or in terms of utility.

With his penchant for worrying away at details, and in particular for fretting about the exact details of something that happened forty years before, Bentham himself thought that it did matter, and several times recommended in the 1820s that the leading principle should be called the 'greatest happiness principle' rather than the 'principle of utility'. He added new footnotes to the new editions of the *Fragment* and the *Introduction* which were published in that decade pointing this out, and saying that 'the word *utility* does not so clearly point to the ideas of *pleasure* and *pain* as the words *happiness* and *felicity* do' (FG 446n; IPML 11n). At this time he felt that 'utility' was 'an unfortunately chosen word' (X 582), the choice of which he blamed on Hume (UC 10.129). The result is that in all his later writings, he used the expression 'the greatest happiness principle', and the last statement of the principle in a foundational position, that is in the introductory material to the great work of the last years, the *Constitutional Code*, the formulation has reverted back to the place at which he had begun in the *Fragment*. He says there: 'the right and proper end of government in every political community, is the greatest happiness of all the individuals of which it is composed, say, in other words, the greatest happiness of the greatest number' (CODE, IX 5). Here we have the last phrase exactly as in the *Fragment* over fifty years before; and exactly as in the English translation of Beccaria.

Given that Bentham is consistent in the way that he relates 'happiness' and 'utility', the change of emphasis is not important, nor in itself is the variety of terminology. Bentham himself, at all periods, was prepared to run several different terms together and explain them in terms of each other. Just after the formulation of the principle of utility in the *Introduction* he goes on to explain the term as follows: 'by utility is meant that property in any object, whereby it tends to produce benefit, advantage, pleasure, good, or happiness (all this in the present case comes to the same thing)' (IPML 12). Here, just as earlier in the *Fragment*, 'utility' is introduced as something of a technical term, with a special meaning, explained in terms of consequences, which consequences are happiness, benefit, pleasure, and so on. The only difference in later thought is that Bentham thought that the departure from the ordinary usage of the term could cause confusion and so was best avoided. The only thing to remember, therefore, if the term is still being used, is that it has a special sense. In particular, anything which gives pleasure or amusement has utility in Bentham's sense; it is not necessary that it has to be useful in the normal sense of that word. Climbing mountains or sailing boats are not in the normal sense of the word useful activities if they are done for no further purpose; however for Bentham they are. They provide amusement, and 'what is *useful*, is what promises an advantage: amusement is an advantage' (*Tactics*, II 312).

What Bentham is proposing here is a programme of continuous explanation or clarification, just as was described before in respect of such legal terms as *obligation* or *right*. Starting with the most abstract evaluative terms, *good* and *ought*, these are explained in terms of the semi-technical term, *utility*. *Utility* in turn is then explained in such terms as *benefit, happiness, pleasure* and so on. This later straggle of terms is again reducible. Bentham, it will have been noticed, says that they come to the same thing. More specifically, *benefit* or *advantage* can be reduced to the others. In the manuscript *Comment on the Commentaries* Bentham considers how the words *right* and *wrong* could be made intelligible and suggests substituting 'the words beneficial and mischievous which are intelligible'; for 'by a beneficial, and by a mischievous sort of action, I know perfectly well what I mean: and I am inclined to think that others do so too. By a beneficial sort of action I mean a sort of action that is more apt to produce pleasure than it is pain: by a mischievous, more apt to produce pain than it is pleasure' (COMM 67). Here the analysis has gone by way of *benefit* rather than *utility*, but it ends up at the same point with pleasure and pain. Pleasure and pain will in fact be the final end point of all these analyses, because *happiness* is in Bentham a generic notion which merely refers to pleasure and pain. To talk, therefore, of the greatest happiness principle is to talk of the principle which proposes the maximisation of pleasure and the minimisation of pain. In Bentham these come to the same thing as happiness, because the one is to be explained in terms of the other. It is convenient for him to express the principle in terms of happiness because it seems to give a single, simple, end and distracts attention from the problem mentioned in the last chapter of the possible non-commensurability of pleasures and pains. However, he is clear throughout that 'happiness is a vain word — a word void of meaning — to him to whose mind it does not explain itself with reference to human feelings: feelings painful and pleasurable — pains and pleasures' (*Institute of Political Economy*, Stark iii 308); '*happiness* is a word employed to denote the sum of the pleasures experienced during that quantity of time which is under consideration' (*Pannomial Fragments*, III 214). We have here, therefore, an analysis which reduces, or gives meaning, to the abstract terms of evaluation by giving an account of them in terms of the two basic terms of *pleasure* and *pain*. As he puts it in the *Introduction*, 'when thus interpreted, the words *ought*, and *right* and *wrong*, and others of that stamp, have a meaning: when otherwise, they have none' (IPML 13).

Just as before, therefore, it was seen how an analysis in terms of real entities such as pleasure and pain could give meaning to the fictitious entities of the law, so here a meaning is given to the fundamental terms of evaluation. The two basic principles, the normative and the psychological one, both possess precise meaning because both can be expressed in terms of the precise, determinate, notions of pleasure and pain. It would seem, therefore, given the similarity of the language of 'giving meaning' and the similarity of the end point with the real entities of pleasure and pain, that the justification of this way of understanding 'ought' should be similar to the earlier justification of this way of understanding 'obligation'. That is, the method of verifying whole sentences containing the phrase or word for which an analysis is desired should be taken as what gives that phrase or word its meaning. In Chapter IV, however, it was seen that a procedure which worked for legal rights did not work for natural rights, and that, although there were clear similarities between the greatest happiness principle and natural law, the problem with natural law as Bentham saw it was that it confused fact and value, *is* and *ought*. Given the clear separation of fact and value, on which it has been seen that Bentham always insisted, and which is the foundation of his general project, it is not obvious that a technique which can be used to give meaning to terms in factual contexts (that is, a method of finding out how sentences containing the term express truths) can also be used to give meaning to terms in evaluative contexts (where there is no obvious analogy to the verification which establishes the truth of a sentence). So the procedures examined in Chapter III and applied in Chapter IV cannot just be carried over automatically to this new area. The question of the justification of Bentham's analysis of basic evaluative terms, and, hence or otherwise, the question of the justification of his basic evaluative principle need separate and close attention.

In fact, some of Bentham's earlier polemical claims were seen to provide particular difficulties for his support of the principle of utility. This was particularly the case when he was attacking natural law. The problem first came up in Chapter II when the question was raised of what justificatory space Bentham had left himself given that he attacked both the justification of institutions by history, or custom, and also by the use of an independent right reason, or natural law. Both Coke's artificial reason of the law and Bacon's (or Locke's) natural reason of the law were condemned; and the question was what space Bentham could occupy outside these two on which he could rest his criticism of institutions. When Bentham's account of giving clarification, meaning, and understanding, was then examined in the following chapter, exactly the distinction between how meaning could be given to the (descriptive) legal rights but not to the (evaluative) natural rights which has just been referred to was also seen to create a difficulty for Bentham's own master principle. The polemical vigour addressed to the rights with which the French Revolution was underpinned could, it seemed, also be turned against the base principle with which Bentham's rival practical projects were underpinned. If one were not allowed to use the imaginary law of nature as justification then why should one, as recommended in this first chapter of the *Introduction*, 'imagine a kind of law or dictate, called a law or dictate of utility' (IPML 13). If this latter imaginary law is to be obeyed while the former is condemned as a mere shadow or chimera, then further justification must now be provided sufficient to distinguish one from the other.

In Chapter I Bentham's constant invocation of 'reason' was noticed. The greatest happiness principle was taken to be justified because it accorded with reason. In this spirit, Bentham could write in the *Principles of International Law* that 'vulgar prejudice, fostered by passion, assigns the heart as the seat of all the moral diseases it complains of, but the principal and more frequent seat is really the head' (*II 553). Against the forces of prejudice and passion stands the force of reason; moral mistakes arise from mistakes in thinking, from mistakes in calculation. However, once it was moved from the realm of rhetorical invocation, 'reason' by itself was too weak to carry the justification of the greatest happiness principle, as Bentham himself well knew. It could signal a side in an argument, but it could not enforce conviction on those who disagreed with the master principle. After all, the rival natural law, explicitly picked out as a source of principles opposed to the principle of utility in the second chapter of the *Introduction*, is there described as 'instead of the phrase, Law of Nature, you have sometimes, Law of Reason, Right Reason . . . Any of them will do equally well' (IPML 27n). In other words, the opposition can also cite reason to its own purpose; reason alone is not going to be sufficient to distinguish the principle of utility from the natural reason used in natural law. Furthermore, when Bentham is attacking someone who relied at times on natural law, that is Blackstone, he does so at times by explicitly attacking Blackstone's invocation of 'reason'. The fallacy in one of Blackstone's paragraphs, for example, 'lurks in the words "reason" and "unreasonable": and consists in supposing them to stand for something fixed and certain, and that all men are agreed about'. On the contrary, 'reasonableness or unreasonableness is nothing but conformity or nonconformity to, at least can be decided by nothing but, opinion' (COMM 159). So here there is recognition that 'reason' by itself cannot supply an independent justification. Indeed, as he says later about Blackstone, 'had our Author . . . instead of reason said utility, he would have said something. He would have referred us for a foundation for our judgement, to something distinct from that judgement itself' (COMM 199). So, if anything, it is the use of utility which justifies the use of 'reason' rather than the other way round. Therefore 'reason' by itself is too vague, too open to rival interpretations, too subject to collapse into mere opinion, to be used to provide the ultimate justification which it has been seen that the principle of utility requires. Fine for waving a polemical flag, it cannot give a precise, convincing, conclusive, justification.

The collapse of 'reason' into mere opinion shows that no more can be hoped for from intuition, or moral sentiment, or any other use of individual perception or feeling. Bentham both consciously wants and also needs the principle of utility to have an objective quality, so that its correctness does not depend upon the way that it is perceived or felt by particular people, and which can therefore be used as an absolute and unchallengeable foundation for the particular legislative proposals which he recommends. So it is perfectly correct of him to single out what he calls 'the principle of sympathy and antipathy' as one of the two principles chiefly opposed to the principle of utility in the second chapter of the *Introduction*. This principle, which he footnotes in the Second Edition would be better called 'the principle of *caprice*', serves as a generic phrase encompassing all those methods of decision about what is right which depend in the end upon mere opinion, and including, as has just been seen, the various invocations of natural law. Only the caprice, the mere opinion of an individual, supports the position being proposed. This cannot provide sufficient justification for Bentham's purposes. He often calls this in his later thought, *ipse-dixitism*, the idea that the mere saying-so by someone is sufficient to make it so. Without considering in detail the various other proposed justifications or foundations which Bentham lumps under the principle of sympathy and antipathy besides natural law, such as moral sense or common sense, we can accept for the moment his own judgement that none of these are sufficient to be able to provide the kind of justification which he requires. The invocation of a perceptive, or quasi-perceptive, faculty, such as moral sense or intuition, looks at first sight as if it should provide, like other perceptive faculties, a means of discovering how things really are. Yet, notoriously, it runs into the problem that different people who seem to be equally well endowed with the faculty in question disagree about the content which the faculty is supposed to reveal. There is not usually sufficient agreement or convergence to pick out the people with defective faculties merely by the lack of agreement of a small minority. The problem of agreement, or lack of it, is a problem for all supposed justifications of evaluative principles; and it must be met later on in terms of Bentham's own preferred justification. Even so, as will be seen in the next chapter, it provides problems for Bentham's recommendations about the political realisation of his proposals. However, even though it is a problem for all accounts, it is sufficient to mean that it would be unsatisfactory to rest justification upon the mere unsupported perception (or feeling or intuition) of an individual. For however confident it makes that individual, it can give no justification to anyone not sharing the feeling or intuition. Furthermore, lacking massive and obvious agreement, there is bound to be doubt about the objective status of the principles so supported. It would be pleasant to be able to support the principle of utility by saying that it was intuitively obvious. This might seem the right basis for its axiomatic status, just as with Euclid's axioms. However, if, unlike with Euclid, many people hold quite different things to be intuitively obvious, this would not work as justification for them. The supposed axiom needs further support; and it was seen in the last chapter that Bentham was not averse to providing support, empirical or otherwise, for principles which he called 'axioms'. At least for the moment, he seems right in holding that such support is not provided by anything like moral sense or moral intuition.

Although Bentham wants and needs the principle to have authority, he does not wish this to be achieved by citing authority. Similarly, although he does not want it to rest on the mere opinion of an individual, he wants it to be, in principle, accessible to any individual, so that any individual can use it for himself as the foundations of a moral system and as a basis for criticism of the political arrangements to which he is subject. Under a government of laws, he says in the Preface to the *Fragment*, the 'motto of a good citizen' is *'to obey punctually; to censure freely'* (FG 399). The individual has to be in a position in which he can censure on the basis of his own resources; hence if he uses authorities, he has to be able to tell that they are authorities. The mere say-so of an authority cannot by itself provide justification for him, for he has also to be justified in treating the say-so (rather than another one) as authoritative. The use of authoritative pronouncements (pronouncements by authoritative people; authoritative texts), that is, merely defers the question of justification. And in any case, it has been seen continually how Bentham is hostile to the use of history or historical texts as the basis for support or criticism of political institutions. This is the basis of his objection to common law. Several times in early manuscript work he compares 'utility' and 'texts'. One head of a proposed draft is 'Pr[inciple] of Utility a clearer standard than texts' (UC 96.73). Another comment is that 'utility [is] sooner found out per se than truth from Texts' (UC 70A.28). Bentham is constantly aware that texts need to be interpreted; hence it is more direct and clearer to work with utility. Texts, or more generally authority, can provide no justification; hence the justification of the principle has yet to be found. A text citing the principle of utility cannot be used in its support since another text can be found which opposes it. If we interpret the texts with the principle of utility in mind, then we shall accept the former texts rather than the latter, and so (at Bentham's time) support Helvetius and Beccaria rather than Blackstone or Beattie. However, this just means that we have to look elsewhere for support. Bentham's critical method, in which particular texts are subject to continuous and ruthless criticism, demands another support for criticism than texts. Similarly, someone who takes the present state of the historically acquired institutions of the law to be an 'Augean stable' only to be cleaned by a 'body of severe and steady criticism', as it was seen in Chapter II that Bentham did, cannot rely upon mere history as providing a basis for such criticism. To find something to be good, more is needed than the fact that it has sometimes, or even always, happened in that way.

A variant of this problem about the use of authority in providing justification is the suggestion that God, the ultimate authority, might provide the justification. Again, in Bentham's eyes, this is to get things the wrong way round. 'We may be perfectly sure', he notes, 'that whatever is right is conformable to the will of God: but so far is that from answering the purpose of showing us what is right, that it is necessary to know first whether a thing is right, in order to know from thence whether it be conformable to the will of God' (IPML 31). Knowing that God is good, we can tell what God wants by knowing what is good; but we can't tell what is good by finding out what God wants. The latter would raise all the problems of justification all over again. Bentham, as admirer of Voltaire, would scarcely tolerate priests playing the role; texts again need interpretation; and the individual natural light which gives each man direct access to his God is again a fickle faculty. Of course, particularly in the natural law tradition, there have been several attempts to use God to give exactly the kind of independent justification of evaluative principles which is being sought; and (as Bentham says) there is no reason why this justification, if it existed, might not support the principle of utility. However, quite apart from any epistemological difficulties he might have felt about the very existence of God, this is clearly a method of justification which Bentham feels that he cannot use. If it could be found out that God did not support utility, in his eyes this would show not that utility was not good but, rather, that God was not good. As he notes in a manuscript: 'God is not good, if he prohibits our possessing the least atom of clear happiness which he has given us the physical capacity of attaining' (UC 70A.25). Given his understanding of 'benevolent' (based on his understanding of 'good'), God is not benevolent unless he aims at increasing happiness; 'in the only sense in which benevolence has a meaning', he says 'the dictates of religion [can] be neither more nor less than the dictates of utility' (IPML 120). Whatever founds the utility principle is more certain and more direct than anything which comes by way of God, and any understanding of God's goodness has to be understood in terms of it. Again, this is not the direction in which any justification of the first principle of utility can be found.

It was noted above that Bentham held that axioms could be provided with empirical support, and so it might be thought that the evaluative axiom about utility could be supported in the same way as it was seen in the last chapter that Bentham attempted support of his descriptive psychological axiom about every man pursuing his own happiness. It might be supposed, that is, that mere observation of human behaviour would establish it, or that it could be invoked as the only fact which could explain another undoubted fact, such as the survival of the human species. Then, instead of the Law of Nature, we would have a natural law; natural psychology would underpin the evaluations. This would not be an absurd way in which to attempt to read Bentham, given the stress in earlier chapters on the observational, empirical, verificationist, basis for Bentham's thought. If observation confers meaning on factual claims, including the leading psychological principle, then it seems that observation should confer meaning on evaluative claims, including the leading evaluative principle. It is because pleasure and pain are directly observable entities that they can be used in both cases to confer meaning. Furthermore, J.S. Mill wrote his much later work, *Utilitarianism*, in defence of some of the views which Bentham also defended. Both philosophers use and defend a similar principle of utility, even if they interpret it somewhat differently. Yet Mill, infamously, provides some sort of proof for the principle in which, at least on a natural reading of the text, the principle depends upon psychological facts about what actually is desired by people. It is because, as a natural fact, people actually do desire happiness that Mill holds that happiness can be shown to be desirable, that is good; and it is because all people desire it that Mill seems to hold (again on a natural reading of the text) that they desire the happiness of all. Hence the evaluative principle about the greatest happiness of the greatest number follows directly from natural, psychological, facts. Mill was Bentham's secular godson, well used to him and his thought. So the fact that this argument occurs (or, at least, seems to occur) in Mill gives some reason for thinking that it might also be present in Bentham. Certainly the psychological basis is the same: it has been seen in the last chapter how Bentham held that all people desire their own happiness. The question is whether Bentham thought that this alone supported his leading evaluative principle.

It is very difficult, however, to think that there could be any such attempt at proof from psychological premises in Bentham. The two leading principles are always expressed as two. If one of them could be directly derived from the other, it would be redundant; and if Bentham thought that it could be so derived, it would have been natural for him to have pointed this out in his discussion of the two principles particularly on those occasions when he discusses them together. In fact the separability of the two principles is essential for his overall project to make sense, as was proposed at length in Chapter V. There would be no need for artificial interference with men's motives, or elaborate constructions to bring duty and interest into line, if in fact following their interests, which men naturally do, led to them doing their duty.

The split, as noticed for example in *Of Laws in General*, between the assumed motive of the legislator as the 'greatest good of the community' and the actual motive of the person to whom the law applies which 'in many instances ... is no other than his own particular benefit' (OLG 31) would make no sense if all men's actual motives were the good of all. So Bentham could not endorse a version of Mill's proof in which the moral end comes from a psychological axiom that every man desires his own happiness; and it is indeed notorious that Mill's proof, if given the natural reading suggested above, commits a fallacy equivocating between the happiness of all understood distributively and collectively. The happiness of all, in the only sense in which it can follow in the proof, which is merely the total sum of the separate happinesses separately aimed at by each man, is not the happiness of all in the sense in which it is needed for the evaluative principle. The legislator must not just aim at his own happiness but at the happiness of other people. Given that the psychological principle describes him, like anyone else, as aiming at his own happiness, a separate, evaluative principle is needed in order to say that he should aim at the happiness of all. The continued and clear support in Bentham of the distinction between *is* and *ought* is again relevant here, for as long as he holds on to this, there is no way in which an evaluative *ought* can be derived as the consequence of an immediately observed *is*. So there is no way that Bentham can be represented as supporting his leading evaluative principle by straight descriptive observation. Even if there is concern for observation and verification, and a consequential interest in reduction to the observable, there is no reduction in Bentham of the evaluative to the descriptive. Ethics is propounded, not eliminated; the leading principles of morals and legislation are expounded and defended, not found to be merely fictional. Holder as he was of the belief of extending the methods of the natural sciences into the moral sciences, Bentham did not wish to make morality itself a natural science; if there is a naturalistic fallacy, then it was not committed by Bentham. It is true, of course, that Bentham repeatedly said such things as that on his principles morals became a matter of observations and calculation. This, however, was just because, once the first principle was accepted, calculation became possible and observation relevant to the settling of moral disputes. The first principle itself was not based upon any such observation or calculation; and was, indeed, required before any such observation or calculation could make sense as relevant to the solution of moral disputes. The principle of utility does not make moral questions into purely factual ones but, rather, so rearranges the continuing moral content of a question that the problems to be solved and the decisions to be made are concerned solely with the factual part.

As part of his descriptive study of human motivation, Bentham lists the forces, or 'sanctions', which can be applied to someone in order to get him to do something. This is part of the essential psychological knowledge needed by the legislator. As well as the political, religious, and physical sanctions, Bentham talks of a 'moral sanction'. That is, it is held to be a descriptive, psychological fact that people desire things in what they conceive of in a specifically moral way, and that they apply specifically moral pressure to each other. This raises another way in which it might be thought that the ground master principle of utility could be founded upon a descriptive, psychological, base. For it might be held to be a matter of observation that what people hold to be moral, and the way that they in fact apply the moral sanction, was such as would be recommended by the principle of utility. This, in effect, would be to return the question to the question of whether or not there was agreement about fundamental moral principles. If it was found that there was indeed such agreement, then the agreement could be used as a base for the principles. This could happen in two ways, either anthropologically, as a cited fact about the nature of the society which was taken to justify its morality, or else internally, as an agreed consideration which could be presupposed in any discussion or argument occurring within the society. However, the former runs again into the problem about the is-ought distinction; just because members of a society are found to agree that they ought to do something does not mean that they really ought to. So only the latter is left as a method of justification, and this is not now to justify the moral principle by the facts but, rather, to point out that since the facts about moral belief are as they are, there will be no need to justify this moral principle in actual conversations with other members of the society. In fact, even this latter consideration is merely hypothetical for, as was noticed above when considering intuition, there is not sufficient appearance of agreement about moral principles for someone either to reach sound anthropological generalisations about them or for us to be able happily to presuppose that everyone agrees on the basis of moral discussion and so no more needs to be said (to these people, here, now) about it.

Of course Bentham himself was happy to claim considerable agreement about the principle of utility, and it no doubt gave him confidence to feel that support for the principle of utility was increasing, so that he felt that he was on the winning side. 'The dictates of the moral sanction', he wrote 'approach nearer and nearer to a coincidence with those of utility every day' (IPML 121). On the other hand, he was clear that agreement was neither necessary nor sufficient for the truth of the ultimate moral principle. Although it suited him to cite agreement when he found it, he was also equally suspicious of agreement when it converged on something other than the principle of utility. He holds that it is wrong, for example, over capital punishment (*Death Punishment*, I 530), and there is a perfectly good explanation of this, namely that 'public opinion *has* a sinister interest . . . public opinion is . . . the child and disciple of aristocracy' (530-1). Elsewhere he notes that the present system (which he is trying to overturn) is popular just because it is depraved, the depravity is the cause of the popularity (*Packing*, IV 97). So, as was seen when examining his attack on the French Revolution, Bentham knows that he is often working against public opinion in his criticism. Hence he cannot rely upon agreement. Of course, he has an explanation, in terms of corruption, sinister interests, and depravity, about how public opinion can be misled. This, however, just shows that even if public opinion did converge on the principle of utility, this would not be sufficient to support it. Agreement is not a basis on which Bentham can rest the principle of utility. In the *Evidence* papers, in which the prime aim is to object to the exclusion of evidence, he considers the objection that exclusion has the 'universal voice of all mankind'. He agrees with this and then notes that 'its reasonableness is proved by that medium of proof, by which, till within this century or two, supernatural evidence of various kinds . . . was pronounced superior in trustworthyness to all human or other natural evidence' (RJE iv 483-4).

Bentham's own view about the accord between the moral sanction and the principle of utility was that this varied according to nation, class, and time. Noting in the *Rationale of Punishment* that 'to prove an institution is agreeable to the principle of utility is to prove . . . that the people *ought* to like it: but whether they *will* like it or no after all, is another question', he goes on to suggest that people will govern themselves by the principle 'in proportion as they are humanised and enlightened; accordingly, the deference they pay to its dictates is more uniform in this intelligent and favoured country than perhaps in any other' (*69). Later in the same work he notes that 'the middle ranks of society are the most virtuous, it is among them that in the greatest number of points the principles of honour coincide with the principles of utility' (*218). Coincidence, as noted, was held to be increasing; it was what was to be expected of a 'late and polished age'

(RJE v 344). That middle-class Englishmen at the end of the eighteenth century were more likely to believe in the principle than other people of other countries, at other times or other places, perhaps helps to explain why Bentham himself (a middle-class Englishman of that time) believed in the principle. However, it does nothing to support his belief. For the whole point of the principle, as the basis of the criticism or censure of established institutions, is that it can be applied at all times and at all places. 'The *Censor* is, or ought to be the citizen of the world' (FG 398). Bentham writes of his rules about punishment that 'all these, if they are just and proper now, would at any time have been so, and will be so every where, and to the end of time. They will hold good as long as pleasure is pleasure and pain is pain' (*Time and Place*, I 193). This was the point of deriving them from reason rather than custom, even if reason seemed insufficient to bear the load: reason remains the same although custom varies with place and time. The gradual coincidence of the moral sanction with the principle of utility which Bentham thought that he observed turns out to be a double-edged weapon. Although it gave him a feeling of correctness, it also revealed that men had not everywhere at all times believed in the principle of utility. Since this was so, the principle needed support. Furthermore, given the possibility of corruption or manipulation of public opinion, even if there were agreement about utility, the most this would show was that support was unlikely to be requested, not that it was not needed.

Having now unsuccessfully considered various ways in which it seemed that the principle of utility might be given a justification, the next possibility to consider is that there can be no such justification. The assumption at the beginning of the chapter was that the principle needed justification so, if none can be found, this would seem to undercut the base of Bentham's project. There is no reason why the legislator should aim at promoting the greatest happiness if this is neither something which he naturally believes or does, nor something which can be given any other justification. On the other hand, it may be that the initial assumption was mistaken and the fact (if it is a fact) that no justification can be provided does not after all tell against the viability of the utility principle. There are two reasons why this could be so. The first is that no justification is required because there is always something for which no further justification can be required, and this just happens to be that thing. The second is that no justification is required because it is a moral principle, and the nature of moral principles is such that since they possess no truth value but are mere expressions of emotion, the whole topic of justification in this area is irrelevant nonsense. Bentham himself at times promoted, or could be taken to promote, both of these reasons why lack of justification would not be damaging to use of the utility principle. The former will now be considered, but the latter left until the end of the chapter. The former is the application of a familiar point in epistemology to the particular case of morals. If we are interested in justification or support for our beliefs, it is supposed, then it must be recognised that justification comes to an end. Unless some beliefs are either accepted without justification or held to be self-justifying, then there would be an endless regress of justification. Nothing could be justified at all, since the justification could never get started. Hence the need for supposed foundations of knowledge or belief, which are not supposed to rest on anything else, and which play the role of axioms in the deduction of other elements of knowledge. Bentham, it will have been noted, held that the greatest happiness principle had the status of an axiom and, more specifically, in the chapter about the utility principle in the *Introduction* he asks about the principle: 'Is it susceptible of any direct proof? it should seem not: for that which is used to prove everything else, cannot itself be proved: a chain of proofs must have their commencement somewhere. To give such a proof is as impossible as it is needless' (IPML 13).

The general epistemological principle which is applied to the special case of moral beliefs here is contentious. It is possible to provide justification without the assumption of things which can be given no further support. The beliefs, for example, might be mutually justifying, so that every belief was justified and there was no belief for which support could not be given. Nor need the potential infinite regress of justification in such a situation be vicious. It only becomes that if it is thought that all the justification has to be gone through (like a mathematical proof from axioms) before anything is believed; it ceases to be vicious if it only expresses the thought that further justification is always available, if desired. However, in the particular case of the utility principle, Bentham does look at its relation to the other principles as being hierarchic, so that the utility principle supports the others but they do not support it. There is not here what John Rawls calls a 'reflective equilibrium' between the more abstract and the more particular principles, so that they are mutually supporting or mutually corrective. So, if the utility principle is to be given support, it will not be by other, particular, moral principles. So it might seem that Bentham was right: at least in the particular case of the utility principle, in the particular way in which he uses it, it has to be taken as a first principle for which support is both impossible and needless. However, this would be the wrong conclusion because of at least two considerations, namely that it would take away the point of Bentham's enterprise and is in fact belied by his own practice. The points about intuition and agreement still remain relevant. If the principle of utility appeals to an objective standard of justification, such that it can properly be used in an argument designed to appeal to the unconvinced, and which can form the solid foundation of a criticism of actually established institutions, then the mere claim that something does not need further support, and that this happens to be it, is not strong enough. Every man may indeed have his own first principles, but the fact that a particular principle is the first principle of one man neither gives a reason nor need motivate any other man to accept it. Here we would have shades of *ipse-dixitism* all over again. Furthermore, just after this claim by Bentham that there can be no 'direct' proof, he does in fact provide some sort of proof of the principle. This combination is followed later by J.S. Mill who similarly declares that 'questions of ultimate ends are not amenable to direct proof' (*Works*, X 207) and then, as has been seen, later provides some sort of proof. So the emphasis in these remarks is on 'directness'; if proof is on the analogy of the axiomatic method, then there can be no further axiom from which the axiomatic principle of utility is deduced in the same way that more specific moral principles are deduced from it. However, this does not mean that what Mill calls 'considerations . . . capable of determining the intellect' (208) cannot be provided. Since Bentham does provide such considerations, and since these form his positive attempt to support the principle of utility, the adequacy of the justification which he actually provides must next be considered.

This justification, which also is in the first chapter of the *Introduction*, reintroduces some of the themes already touched on, such as the use of reason and the possibility of agreement. Bentham's aim is to show that the principle of utility is not just a first principle which cannot be given any further direct support but is the only such principle. If it has no possible rivals and if a first principle is needed, this provides sufficient justification for adopting it even if it cannot be proved directly from further uncontestable assumptions. This kind of indirect proof is quite common in philosophy: something is shown to be the case because it is the necessary presupposition for something else we believe or do. Here, if we are to make moral judgements at all, then we must accept the principle of utility because it is the only possible foundation or ultimate principle of morality. The uniqueness, if it can be demonstrated, is what then gives the principle special status and justification. Of course such a proof is not absolute: showing that this is the unique first principle will not convince someone who thinks that there should be no moral principles, and hence no moral first principles, at all. An amoralist, who disbelieves in the very existence of moral or evaluative judgements, is not going to be argued into morality by such a uniqueness argument. The argument would place no constraint on the amoral legislator. However a legislator, commentator, or censor, who is prepared to believe that there might be something which ought to be done but is not sure what it is would be constrained by such an argument. Such is by far the most common case, so this kind of argument, if only it can be made, is of undoubted power.

Bentham's first step is to claim that it is impossible to disprove the principle of utility by argument ('to disprove the propriety of it by arguments is impossible' (15)), for someone can only 'move the earth' by finding 'out another earth to stand on'. So far this is only an invocation of its status as a first principle; it does not show that it is a unique first principle. If another earth could be found, then the two first principles would just be in conflict, each being primary from its own point of view and the other derivative (whichever earth one occupied while looking would seem to be the one carrying the load; just as people sometimes feel that whichever position they occupy in a particular organisation seems to be the one carrying the load). However, just before this, Bentham claims, more specifically, that 'when a man attempts to combat the principle of utility, it is with reasons drawn, without his being aware of it, from that very principle itself' (14), and he cites a particular example of this in a footnote he added to the second edition. If Bentham can show this generally, then it would indeed establish his claim to uniqueness; if all apparent rivals in fact presuppose it, then it is a necessary presupposition of all principles, and so of all moral thought. However, to show that any rival, any attempt to combat it, in fact presupposes it takes more than the mere claim that this is so or the citing of one or a few examples. To establish his position, Bentham would have to show that it was necessarily the case that any possible rival presupposed the principle of utility. This is far more than he can show by citing examples. The examples he chooses or has come across may just happen to be ones in which this is the case; they do not show that it has to be the case in the examples he has not chosen or come across. Yet if the principle is to be shown to be unique, then it has to apply in all the examples.

Bentham, therefore, needs further argument if he is to get anywhere in establishing the principle's uniqueness, and this he provides in a fairly conversational manner in the next section by listing considerations which, rather than being taken to provide an absolute proof, may lead someone to accept the principle who is 'disposed not to relish it' (15). They are, that is, as in Mill 'considerations determining the intellect' in the absence of a direct proof. However, they amount to a fairly powerful argument in which Bentham attempts to establish the uniqueness by exclusion. He asks someone who wishes to discard the principle to 'consider what it is that all his reasonings (in matters of politics especially) can amount to?', and provides the only two alternatives: either he 'judge[s] and act[s] without any principle' or there is another principle. In fact, Bentham suggests, these two alternatives come to much the same thing for he asks someone who thinks that he has found a separate principle

> to satisfy himself whether the principle he thinks he has found
> is really any separate intelligible principle; or whether it is not
> a mere principle in words, a kind of phrase, which at bottom
> expresses neither more nor less than the mere averment of his
> own unfounded sentiments; that is, in another person he might
> be apt to call *caprice*.

It will be remembered that caprice, Bentham's alternative name for the rival principle of sympathy and antipathy, was something which was regarded above as not providing adequate justification for any moral principle (including the principle of utility itself). Bentham introduces this second chapter of the *Introduction* in which the principle of sympathy and antipathy is discussed by saying that since it is opposed to the principle of utility, it must be wrong. However, the argument here in the first chapter shows that really the order of demonstration is the other way about: it is because the principle of caprice is an inadequate principle that enables the principle of utility to be defended as the unique acceptable principle. Exclusion of caprice excludes the chief rival to the principle of utility and so leaves it in unique possession of the field.

That such exclusion is justified Bentham does not leave to the next chapter but neatly demonstrates in the next considerations he mentions in his informal demonstration. He asks of someone who 'is inclined to think that his own approbation or disapprobation, annexed to the idea of an act, without any regard to its consequences, is a sufficient foundation for him to judge and act upon' to 'ask himself whether his statement is to be a standard of right and wrong, with respect to every other man, or whether each man's sentiment has the same privilege of being a standard to itself'. Either way he has his opponent, for on the first option his principle is 'despotical', whereas on the second there would be 'as many different standards of right and wrong as there are men', and even to the same man the same thing would be right today and wrong tomorrow. In this case then the same thing would be 'right and wrong in the same place at the same time', all 'argument' would be 'at an end', and when two men have said, 'I like this', and 'I don't like it' they can have nothing more to say. This, at least in Bentham's eyes, forms a convincing *reductio ad absurdum* of the rival suggestion of using 'sentiment' or 'caprice' as a standard; once this is rejected then the only alternative left is the use of 'reflection', and the 'particulars' on which reflection can turn can, thinks Bentham, only be utility. Hence utility gets established as the unique principle by elimination through *reductio ad absurdum* of rivals.

The first part of this *reductio* argument is certainly powerful. The claim is that if there is to be argument about principles in morality, if there are to be objective standards laying down what should happen in matters of politics, then every individual's unfounded sentiment is not good enough. This would (if not hopelessly despotical) make the same thing both right and wrong; which would mean that rightness and wrongness would cease to be properties of things at all, hence there would be no more objective standards. Argument would then clearly be impossible. Bentham's claim is that if the judgements made in this area are real judgements, then it must be possible to provide for them reasons; judgements demand justification, and justification is something independent of the making of the judgement itself. He is really proposing a moral private language argument similar to the private language argument of the later Wittgenstein. Wittgenstein claimed in the *Philosophical Investigations* that if the mere appearance to someone of how his sensations were would be sufficient to found a proper, objective, descriptive language of them, then 'whatever is going to seem right to me is right. And that only means that we can't talk about "right"' ($258); in other words it can't be done as the same thing would be both right and wrong, the sense of 'right' would have disappeared. Similarly, Bentham shows that if we attempt to found the moral language on people's mere say-so, on how things just appear to people, then again we can't talk about 'right'. A public, moral, language, a language of argument and discussion of the standards to be applied in politics and in the criticism of institutions, would be impossible. Yet (just as with sensations), it seems that there is such a language. Hence its basis has to rest elsewhere than in mere caprice.

This part of the argument brings back into play the use of reason and the use of agreement, both of which were seen earlier to be too weak on their own to found the principle of utility. It is not that utility follows directly from reason. It is that, if there is to be a public language of evaluation, then there have to be publicly accessible reasons which are independent of the judgements for which they act as reasons, and utility can provide such reasons in a way that caprice cannot. Nor is it that there is public agreement about utility. It is just that agreement has to be possible, because discussion and argument have to be possible, and utility is a way in which such agreement can be reached. This is a point which will be more fully discussed shortly.

Utility is therefore given some sort of support or indirect proof by showing that it is a way in which certain necessary conditions of having a moral or evaluative language at all can be met. This, however, is not enough to establish its uniqueness or necessity. All that is shown is that any principle which is to be adopted as a fundamental principle has to be such that it is capable of providing reasons and so allowing there to be argument and discussion which might in principle result in agreement about the actual moral qualities of particular acts, properties, or institutions. The argument shows (or strongly suggests) that these are necessary conditions, and utility triumphs over caprice in being able to meet them. This, however, merely shows that it is a possible first principle (on these standards), not a necessary one. To show its uniqueness, it would have to be shown not just that utility meets the standards, but that no other principle does. This is not demonstrated merely by the defeat and rejection of caprice, since it would have to be shown that this was the only alternative principle. Bentham has not done this. His argument is powerful in getting rid of sentiment as a foundation, but when he goes on to the basis of moral reasoning, he can do no more than assert or suggest that nothing else than utility could provide reasons. He asks, rhetorically, 'if not on those particulars, on what other particulars?' (16). Yet there are obviously many other *prima facie* candidates for reasons independent of a moral judgement which do not relate to utility, some of which have already been mentioned: justice, order, the Will of God, natural law. Bentham could only prove the uniqueness by rejecting all such alternatives.

This he has clearly not done and, even if he did, it would be insufficient. For there is a problem in establishing uniqueness common to all arguments of this kind: merely to exclude all alternatives which are thought of is not sufficient to demonstrate something's necessity or uniqueness, because there may always be another alternative which has been overlooked. A uniqueness proof is only possible if there is a way of establishing independently just how many alternatives there are. Given the variegated bases for moral thought that have been considered throughout history, it does not seem that there could be a way of establishing this in this particular area.

The proof, therefore, is not conclusive. On the other hand, it was always meant to be informal, and it could be said that it put utility in a position ahead of its rivals by showing how this principle, unlike others, could meet the general, structural, demands of an adequate fundamental moral principle. Nor is this all that can be said. The informal proof which has just been discussed at length can be supported by claims about understanding, clarity, and agreement made elsewhere in Bentham's work. At the start of this chapter it was noticed that Bentham claimed that it was only if words like 'ought' were interpreted in terms of pains and pleasures that they had a meaning. This claim seemed to be analogous to claims made by Bentham in other areas, such as that of legal rights and duties, and to rest on the same basis, namely that relation to the observational conferred meaning. Behind both seems to lie Bentham's technique of paraphrasis, by which a word is given meaning not in isolation but in the context of a whole sentence, and the way that the sentence is given meaning is by considering how it can be verified. However, at the beginning of this chapter, the claim or purported analogy was not considered further because it seemed to run into the problem that there was an obvious and important disanalogy between factual and evaluative statements which meant that verification of the latter, if it existed at all, would be quite different in kind. The time has now come, however, in which to retrieve and reestablish Bentham's idea. Verification only works if it is appropriate to ascribe truth values. However, once it is recognised that a condition on moral terms is that they should be capable of featuring in an objectively directed public language, then it becomes appropriate to talk of verification of sentences containing moral terms. For the upshot of the above argument was that reasons, or verification, was required for moral judgements; and that such verification had to be publicly accessible and such that (in principle) public agreement was possible about it. There has to be a publicly accessible and acceptable way of establishing moral standards. Now, if these reasons are given in terms of utility (that is happiness, that is pleasure and pain) then this can be achieved. For the analysis that is possible of utility in terms of directly observable entities means that statements made in terms of utility can be verified. Hence such statements have meaning, that is, are in terms of something which may be publicly observed, discussed, and measured. So if utility is to be contrasted with other purported ways of giving reason for moral judgements, such as appeal to Natural Justice or Natural Equity, then 'on most occasions ... it will be better to say *utility*: *utility* is clearer, as referring more explicitly to pain and pleasure' (IPML 27n). The method of giving clarification and meaning, considered at length in Chapter III, can now after all be used to bestow clarity on moral terms.

Another way of putting this point is that it is just because so much is transferred from the evaluative area to the factual area on the principle of utility that moral discussion and disagreement can proceed or be resolved in much the same way as factual discussion and disagreement can. This is not to say, as was noticed above, that moral judgements are eliminated in some form of naturalistic reduction. It is, rather, that this ultimate moral principle (unlike others) allows subsequent discussion and argument to proceed in the same way as (because it is indeed an example of) discussion and argument about natural facts. The principle of utility sets a context, sets a language, in which there can be public moral discussion. 'The footing on which this principle rests every dispute, is that of matter of fact; that is future fact — the probability of certain future contingencies' (FG 491). It is not that people are necessarily going to agree about what will in fact lead to the greatest happiness, but this is a discussion about a fact, in principle resolvable. If not agreement on the fact, at least there is agreement about the language, about what is at stake. 'They would at any rate see clearly and explicitly, the point on which the *dis*agreement turned' (ibid.); there is 'a visible and explicit issue' (492). 'All else', as he also says at this point, 'is but womanish scolding and childish altercation, which is sure to irritate, and which never can persuade' (491). If there is to be agreement, even an agreed public language of moral discussion, then the principle of utility has to be adopted. What Bentham says here is directly in line with his early proposals to establish a dictionary of terms, including moral terms. The aim of this was to 'give the death stroke to that legion of disputes, which otherwise the abuse of words would make immortal', so if 'propositions moral, political, metaphysical [can be] rendered equally demonstrable with any in mathematics, the ideas relative to those sciences will be the same in all men' (UC 27.5). By finding a public method of verification, of reaching agreement in judgements, a public method of reaching agreement in meaning, that is of having a public meaning at all, will also have been found.

If, therefore, agreement is desired, if 'nothing will serve you, but that you and he must needs be of the same mind', then immediate moral sentiments or immediate moral impressions must be overcome, 'it is for you to get the better of your antipathy' (IPML 29n). By thought, by discussion, by consideration of how ideally agreement might be reached, first impressions can be corrected. Another feature of the principle of utility mentioned by Bentham becomes relevant here when considering how such agreement might be reached. Bentham, as was pointed out in Chapter VI, knew well that people act altruistically and are motivated by benevolence; hence the convergence in fact, as noted above, between what people motivated by the moral sanction desire to do and what is prescribed by the principle of utility. However, this coincidence varies according to how 'enlightened' the benevolence is. Enlightenment, reason, thought, clarification, are needed to correct the first moral impressions, even if they are benevolently inclined. Once this is done then 'the dictates of utility are neither more nor less than the dictates of the most extensive and enlightened (that is well-*advised*) benevolence' (IPML 117). Enlightenment can, of course, be cited by every man to his own purposes, so that someone else is not considered to be enlightened unless he agrees with that man or does what he wants. However, the idea of extent is much more specific. Utility coincides with benevolence when benevolence considers not just one or two people but, rather, all points of view; when, that is, it is applied in the most extensive possible manner. This idea gives another lead in to the possibility of agreement which can arise when first impressions are put aside and thought is applied. For if the content of this thought is to consider not just how the thing appears from the point of view which the person considering happens to occupy but instead from all possible points of view, then this more extensive treatment can result in enlightenment which changes the initial view. If, that is, considering something from other points of view is to consider what other people want, or think important, or what is in their interests, then to consider it from all points of view is to consider all interests. So an extensive treatment consists in consideration of the interests, or happiness, of all; extensive benevolence results in adoption of the greatest happiness principle. One's own point of view no longer looks special. This means that utilitarian morality is the kind of morality which would be prescribed from no particular position. It is an absolute morality, prescribed from an absolute, or external, point of view. It does not represent morality as it appears to a particular individual caring just for his family or his honour or whatever it is that is exclusively his and matters more to him than others. This property of the morality prescribed by the principle of utility has often been thought to leave it cold, that is, motivationally inert. However, in the present context, it is an important key to how agreement in principle could be possible about the greatest happiness principle in a way that it could not for other principles. For if no particular point of view is special in it, then it is a position on which people starting from different, incompatible, particular points of view can converge. Just as the idea of an absolute scientific language which describes things from no particular point of view offers the possibility of convergence or agreement for people starting with different, and possibly incompatible, sense impressions, so also does the idea of an absolute moral language offer the similar possibility of agreement to people starting with different moral impressions.

Extensive benevolence is impartial benevolence. No position is special. Starting from anywhere the final position reached would be the same. Hence Bentham declares at the start of the *Constitutional Code* that 'in the eyes of every impartial arbiter, writing in the character of a legislator, and having exactly the same regard for the happiness of every member of the community in question, as for that of every other, the greatest happiness of the greatest number of the members of that same community, cannot but be recognised in the character of the right and proper and sole right and proper end of government' (CODE IX 6). The point made here in terms of impartiality could be made in terms of the possibility of agreement by asking what would be necessary if a legislator, a sovereign, and his people were to agree on the standards of legislation that ought to be adopted. If the legislator merely proposed his own interests as setting the standard and each of the groups of the subject people similarly proposed theirs, then clearly there could be nothing but 'childish altercation', or when any two groups 'have said "I like this", and "I don't like it"' there is nothing more to say. If, however, each of the several parties involved approach the question not just in terms of their immediate, directly apparent, desires but instead consider the interests of the other parties, then in principle there is the possibility of reaching agreement by converging on the answer that would be reached by anyone, starting from any position, who considered all the initial views as of equal importance. The impartial legislator would then reach the same answer as the impartial subject, and in each case it would be the Principle of Utility.

Given this extensive repertoire of interconnected arguments in support of the principle of utility, which were not only available to Bentham but also, on occasion, actually used by him, it is surprising that Bentham also sometimes seems to write as if no such justification is available. It will be remembered that two reasons were given above why it might be thought to be inappropriate to defend the principle; firstly that it was an ultimate principle, secondly that it was a moral principle. The first has been dealt with, but Bentham also shows signs at times of supporting the second. This is, perhaps, not so surprising after all once the later tradition of using verification as a way of determining meaning is remembered. For Bentham's successors in the earlier part of the present century who like him related meaning and verification held (to put it crudely) that because moral or evaluative judgements were incapable of verification they were mere expressions of emotion. So perhaps it is only to be expected that Bentham who also held to this connection and who also (as has been seen) held firmly to a distinction between factual and evaluative judgements, should have justified this distinction by making moral judgements mere expressions of emotion. And this, indeed, does seem at times to be his view. In the *Pannomial Fragments*, for example, which was one of the texts discussed in Chapter IV in which legal and natural rights were distinguished and which in the process relied on a strong distinction between *is* and *ought*, Bentham writes: 'he ought to be so —that is to say, the idea of his being so is pleasing to me' (*III 218). Here 'ought' seems to mean no more than that one particular person has a particular emotion; *ought* becomes completely subjective and emotive in import. Nor is this an isolated example. In the prefatory material to the *Constitutional Code*, where Bentham explicitly claims the foundational status of the Greatest Happiness Principle, he says: 'when I say the greatest happiness of the whole community, ought to be the end or object of pursuit . . . what is it that I express? — this and no more, namely that it is my wish, my desire, to see it taken for such' (IX 4). Here we have expression of desire rather than emotion, a description of 'the state of that faculty in me which is termed the will' (ibid.). However, it is again wholly personal and expressive.

192

These remarks are both from late work of Bentham, although earlier remarks can be found which, while being less explicit, would seem to point in the same direction. Thus, in the early *Comment on the Commentaries* manuscripts, he says that 'were I to be asked what it is I mean when I call an action a *right* one. I should answer very readily: neither more nor less than, an action I *approve* of ' (53), and in the same spirit notes in the *Introduction* that the Principle of Utility is a 'sentiment of approbation; a sentiment which, when applied to an action, approves of its utility' (IPML 12n). Approval is a much more complex matter than the mere expression of a desire or an emotion; yet, in calling it a sentiment of the speaker, the same personal, individual, basis of the moral judgement seems to be proposed. After all, the indirect proof which was discussed at such length above was designed to make someone who disagreed with the principle 'relish' it, that is, feel a particular emotion towards it, rather than merely to agree with it. However, whatever textual support there may or may not be for this view in Bentham, it is quite fatal for his own view, and for the arguments examined above. Conversely, in so far as these were good arguments, then there is no need for Bentham to indulge in what might appear at first sight to be an attractive way of getting out of problems of justification. If judgements about *ought* are mere expressions of individual sentiment, then they are exactly the position they would be in according to the principle of caprice which Bentham derides so strongly and attacks so successfully. It would make the legislative project hopeless. It is all right for Bentham to remark at the start of an enormous work on the *Constitutional Code* that he just happens to desire the greatest happiness of the greatest number, and then say, if he is asked why he does that the establishment of it 'would in the highest degree be contributory to my own greatest happiness' (IX 7), and, on being asked what proof he can give of this, point to the enormous labour he has engaged in in writing the book (which is actually what he says). The most this shows is what Bentham thinks and feels. It gives no reason at all why anyone else should attempt to feel likewise or why they should bother to read the book; a natural reaction to Bentham might be to tell him to stuff the whole thing, asking why on earth anyone else should struggle through mounds of badly written pages just because of something he happens to feel. As shown extensively above, not least by Bentham himself, a successful project in legislation must depend upon more solid reasons than caprice or individual sentiment. Since he can, and did, show this, he should not also have indulged in the emotivist retreat from the common pursuit of true judgement.

In this chapter it has been outlined how the principle of utility can be justified by, and play a role in, a procedure which leads to an agreed public language of discussion. It is a language in which the legislator and the citizens, the amateurs and the experts, can talk to each other. Utility makes things clear. Once the consequences of the law and other political institutions are expressed in terms of utility, then since '*pain* and *pleasure* at least, are words which a man has no need, we may hope, to go to a Lawyer to know the meaning of' (FG 418), there can be a common discussion and the possibility of agreement. In the next chapter this relation between the sovereign legislator and the people at large will be discussed, and it will be seen whether or not the theoretical possibility of discussion, dialogue, and agreement, which has been discussed in this chapter can in fact be realised in actual political practice, given the nature of people as they really are. After having discussed the two leading principles separately, it is again time to put them together.

Notes

(a) I have taken the comparison between Bentham and Wittgenstein further, and discussed the general structure of this kind of argument in Harrison (1976).

(b) The idea that utilitarianism is the doctrine on which people would converge when starting to discuss from different points of view is implicit in much recent work of R.M. Hare, for example Hare (1973) and Hare (1976).

(c) The occasions on which Bentham seems to give an emotivist meaning to 'ought' cited in the text (and to which could be added *Deontology* I.5 (149) and II.1 (ii) (253)), can, perhaps, be taken to support the view that this is part of the meaning of 'ought' for Bentham. This still leaves the central point, which is that since this is part of the meaning of ought as used by both Bentham and his opponents, it cannot be all there is to 'ought' as used specifically by him. As Bentham puts it in the *Deontology* 'to say it *ought* to be done is easy in the extreme . . . to say *why* it ought will in every case be matter of comparative difficulty' (II.1 (ii); p. 253). In this chapter an attempt is made to answer the difficult question; and it is to this question that emotivism cannot provide an answer. For the *Deontology* see Chapter X.

VIII

The People is my Caesar

In the last three chapters it has been seen how Bentham's thought is based on the presupposition of an *is-ought* distinction. In Chapter V his general project was described as an attempt to solve the problem bequeathed to him by his predecessors of how a legislator, given certain assumptions about the way in which people actually do behave, can so construct the laws and institutions of society that, while still continuing to follow their natural tendencies of action, the people in that society will in fact do just those things which they ought to do, as prescribed by a quite separate evaluative assumption, the principle of utility. In the two chapters which followed the descriptive and evaluative assumptions which together form this general project were separately examined and, to some extent, defended. It might now seem, therefore, that there were not any further problems about the overall project and that the legislator should just get on with solving the more specific problems about the ways in which the two sets of assumptions could be combined. However, this would be to ignore the problem of the legislator himself, the problem of who he is, of what he is doing, and why. So far he has remained an unquestioned, but wholly mysterious and shadowy, figure. As soon as the question is raised of who he is and why he does what he does, then it seems that it can no longer be presupposed that the legislator occupies a unique position in which the only relevant considerations are what he ought to be doing. If for no one else is consideration of what they ought to do supposed to be directly relevant, and if for no one else is direct appeal to their recognition of moral duty thought to be appropriate, then it is anomalous that both of these are supposed to have a proper place just when dealing with the legislator. Who, it can be asked, is the legislator supposed to be? If it is

195

supposed that he is mortal, a human being or a collection of human beings, then he is also a subject for natural psychology and is subject to the laws of natural psychology. However, in that case, just like anyone else, given the facts are as they are, the legislator will be naturally inclined to do certain things. There would then seem to be no more point in making moral recommendations to the legislator than there is to anyone else. If, on the other hand, it is supposed that the legislator does not correspond with any real person or set of people but is just regarded as a merely fictional device designed to give expression of what ought to be done, then this obviously, automatically, solves the problem of why moral recommendation to the legislator is appropriate, but leaves it completely problematic both how and why any of the particular proposals for reform which Bentham worked out should be adopted. To ensure adoption the legislator would need to be a real, flesh and blood, sovereign.

The central problem here can be put in terms of a problem about communication. It is the problem of to whom Bentham was appealing in his writing, and of how and why he thought that the appeal was likely to have any affect. Of course, if he is not making an appeal, then there is no such problem. If he were writing external descriptions of particular societies, their psychology, sociology, or politics, then he would merely be setting out the facts as he saw them; and he might or might not be right, and what he said might or might not be recognised. However, as well as doing this, Bentham was an extremely practically minded thinker. All description was for a purpose, and the purpose was to change society. By writing, he was trying to make things happen. He was formulating and urging on people particular proposals for particular projects which would replace the present way in which things were done. Description was in the service of criticism, and criticism was in the service of improvement. So his writing was an appeal: because he wrote people were meant to act differently and change how things were. So, as an appeal, the question is indeed relevant to whom Bentham was appealing to do these things and why this person or persons should pay any regard to what Bentham said. The answer to the first question is probably not the same throughout Bentham's life. When he inherited the eighteenth-century project couched in terms of a 'legislator', he certainly at times thought in terms of an appeal to particular, individual, powerful monarchs, to the enlightened despots who were, or appeared to be, in power in several European countries. At the end of his life he wrote tracts for the people at large. Yet even though the person or persons appealed to may vary, the problems involved in any appeal are similar. Whether it is enlightened despots or the people at large, there seems no reason why they, if indeed they were only motivated by their apparent self-interest, should listen to him. If the psychology is correct, then neither need respond to mere appeals to duty; nor is it obvious why appeal to reason should fare any better. Whoever the legislator is, the problem remains of why he should take any note of what Bentham says; and the problem for Bentham is that, if there is no reason why the legislator should take any note of what he says, why and how he is appealing to him.

It might be thought that this problem was solved in the last chapter in which it was seen that the principle of utility, in its appeal to reason, and hence to the possibility of a certain kind of agreement, was distinguishable from mere caprice. This would seem to solve the problem of appeal or persuasion, because the possibility of appeal to reason means that here is a principle on the basis of which one person can address an argument to another. However, although this is important, it is only part of the story. Using the principle of utility means that, indeed, argument can be mounted instead of mere assertion. This, however, will not solve the problem of appeal, the problem of producing particular writings as part of an attempt to get particular proposals put into effect, unless the people to whom the appeal is made are susceptible to argument and take notice of reason. Even if the psychological and evaluative principles on which the general project is founded are both perfectly true and both perfectly justifiable on the basis of reason and experience, this will not serve at all in getting any particular person to adopt either the general project or any of its more specific consequences unless that person happens to be motivated by appeals to reason and experience. Although true, they will not be recognised as such, and so will not be acted on. Although demonstrable, no one will bother with the demonstration, and so discover the truth. More specifically, if the Benthamite psychology itself says that people act only (or normally) on the basis of self-interest, then appeals to reason or experience will not motivate a particular person to action unless it happens to be in his interest to recognise such appeals. So, although the argument of the last chapter might be sufficient for an external or dispassionate observer or commentator, interested only in discovering the truth, it is not obviously sufficient for Bentham's purposes. However many arguments he can advance in support of the principle of utility, and however good these arguments are, they are not going by themselves to get either

197

enlightened despots or the people at large to take on particular proposals for reform of penal codes, prisons, or complete states unless these people either happen, or can be made, to be motivated by good arguments. Who the legislator is, and why he acts, are still questions which have to be considered, however well founded the principle of utility may be.

Bentham himself was constantly aware of the problems of persuasion. In much of his early manuscript writing, he writes like a man in search of an audience. In this material of the 1770s and 1780s, designed for an uncertain audience, and hence often uncertainly designed, there are draft addresses both to specific individuals, in the shape of letters, and also to the public at large, in the shape of draft prefaces to work intended for publication. In both cases the tone is sometimes despondent. In a draft letter written for George III, intended to cover a presentation copy of the *Introduction*, he is not hopeful: 'if it were pardonable to suppose your majesty might have prejudices I should fear they would not be in favour of this book. Accordingly though I have the boldness to offer it to your majesty, I must confess it is not with any very sanguine expectations of its being acceptable . . .' (UC 169.119). George III, of course, was neither enlightened nor a despot, but even with the highly regarded Catherine of Russia, there was the problem about how she could be got to take notice of the great work, diverting Bentham into considering such problems as the right sort of bindings which any book presented to her should possess. Bentham, in these early manuscripts, is also worried about persuading the people at large. He writes in a draft preface to a proposed book that 'many positions in it will be found obnoxious to prejudices that are popular' (UC 27.8). Again the keynote is prejudice; prejudice will prevent his voice of reason being heard. So although Bentham declared grandly in his Commonplace book of 1774-5 that 'the people is my Caesar', he promptly added 'I appeal from the present Caesar to Caesar better informed' (X 73). In the preface which actually was published in the *Fragment* in the following year he noted again that some of his positions 'promise to be far from popular' and commented that 'he that is resolved to persevere without deviation in the line of truth and utility, must have learnt to prefer the still whisper of enduring approbation, to the short lived bustle of tumultuous applause' (FG 421). Yet once the interest is just in truth, the problem of persuasion has been given up. Truth is fine for an external, dispassionate observer, or for the whisper of Bentham's intellectual reputation in the twentieth century, but it does not solve the problem of how particular people are to be persuaded to do particular things. Even if he thinks that the principles with which he starts are self-evident, this will not help him in the task of persuasion if 'self-evident propositions must not expect to be easily admitted, if at all, if the consequences of them clash with prevalent passions and confirmed prejudices' (*Colonies and Navy*, Stark i 212). People must be persuaded if things are to be done, yet prejudice blocks the way. The problem is a problem about power. For Bentham to give effect to his plans he needs power. Yet he does not possess political power and, at least according to his view in the *Book of Fallacies*, 'on no occasion, in no place, at no time, by no person possessing any adequate power, has any such end in view as the greatest happiness of the greatest number been hitherto entertained' (*239). So the power on which he has to rely is the power of persuasion, changing the ideas of those who do possess political power. Bentham's faithful disciple, Dumont, in his last note about Bentham, written after three decades of faithful work in the cause, wrote that 'Mr Bentham's ensign leads neither to riches nor to power' (XI 24). The question is whether, if prejudice blocks the way, Dumont's last judgement is inevitably correct.

Bentham's thought in this area shows continuous development and change, so the exact date of material being studied is more important here than it is elsewhere (even though the seeds of later thought can nearly always be found in the earlier thought). Some of these changes, such as the fuller account of the mechanisms of persuasion and of the non-rational sources of belief, made his problem more difficult. Others, such as his idea of the legislator, made it easier; so to some extent the developments in his thought cancel out. Let us start with the developments which tended to make the problem more difficult, that is, with the fuller account of the mechanics of belief. Fifty years after he wrote the Preface just quoted Bentham wrote a new preface for the second edition of the *Fragment*. In it he remarked that what at the time of the first edition he had thought not to be 'the effect of any worse cause than inattention and prejudice' he now realised was 'the elaborately organised and anxiously cherished and guarded products of sinister interest and artifice' (FG 508). So, although there were problems earlier on, he thought that they just came from prejudging the issues. If only people could be brought to attend then they would realise the answers. Later on he realises that this is not mere carelessness but has an explanation. Because it is in the interest of particular people to have particular views, these views are very hard to change; there are sinister interests at work. The substitution of 'sinister interest' for mere 'prejudice' means that he has a much more formidable obstacle to overcome in the change of thought. Mistake or blindness is not accidental; the sinister interests of the statesmen means that they add to their 'power, by means of *corruption* and *delusion*' (FG 513). There are echoes of such a view in earlier work, but it is only after *Scotch Reform* that Bentham set out to show systematically how certain groups maintained their power by the means of delusion. The lawyers were an obvious and long-lasting target. The abuses and absurdities which, as was seen in Chapter II, Bentham pointed out early in his life remained unreformed because they were in the interests of lawyers. Lawyers gained financially from a monopoly of the legal process so that no one could understand their work but themselves. So, from this time onwards, Bentham refers to them as 'Judge and co' (as, extensively, in the *Rationale of Judicial Evidence*), as if they were a company attempting to make profit. So also, here in the quoted Preface and in the *Book of Fallacies*, also finally published in English in the 1820s, we have an examination of how 'ruling statesman's interest' leads to the use of fallacy; that is, to attempts to mislead and delude the people. Bentham's attempt to set up educational institutions also led him to realise the entrenched power of the church. So in *Church of Englandism* (1817), he talks of a single 'Establishment', religious and secular (127). As he puts it in the Second Edition Preface to the *Fragment*, 'the consequence is a confederacy ... among the ruling few of all classes, to defend themselves and one another, against all endeavours, as, by service rendered to the universal interest, act thereby in necessary opposition to that particular and sinister interest' (539). In other words, they defend themselves against all of Bentham's efforts. They have a sinister interest, distinct from the universal interest, which will lead them to mistake in belief and to the attempt to defraud other's belief, and so will block any attempt at achieving change by means of rational persuasion.

This is (to use more modern terminology) the theory of ideology and its associated sociology on which Bentham relies. Beliefs can be explained in terms of the interest of groups, of classes. Some of this, as when the content of the law is not just identified as being in the class interests of the lawyers as a group but as being in the interests of the lawyers as part of what is now more normally called a class, has a modern ring. Part of the argument on *Death Punishment* is that it is applied to crimes of the 'lower orders' as opposed to the crimes of office (I 531). As he commented in the *Evidence* papers: 'if by the poor you mean the great majority of the people, there is no regular justice for them

at all, unless it be for hanging them, or something in that style'
(RJE iv 372). Like many of the later thoughts, such considerations
of Bentham go back at least to the early French Revolution period
of the early 1790s; to the time at which, in writing against *Ashurst*
he claimed that '99 men out of a hundred' are outside the law's
protection (V 231), so that, as he put it in *Law Taxes*, justice is
denied to people in contravention of Magna Carta; justice is not
for 'the working classes ... the great majority of the people'
(II 578). However, the concern of the present work is with Bentham's philosophy rather than his sociology; so the interesting
question here is not the accuracy or otherwise of Bentham's
description of how law serves the interests of particular groups
or classes, but, rather, with what his account of mind, belief,
and interest is that makes it possible for interest to mould belief.
The problem is that, if belief were an action, then it would be
easy to see how it could be explained as being in someone's
interest. As was seen in Chapter V, a natural explanation of any
activity is that it is in the interest of its perpetrator. Since this is
an acceptable reason for action, it justifies action, and can explain
why action has occurred. Yet it does not seem that belief is like
action, so it does not seem that an acceptable reason for belief is
that it is in someone's interest, or that belief can be so explained.
However much it might be to someone's advantage to believe in
something (such as what the church or the party says), realisation
of this advantage does not normally lead someone to adopt the
belief (as opposed to acting as if the belief were true). Beliefs are
not normally thought of as subject to choice; hence not thought
of as chosen because of the pay-offs which they provide. To
believe something is to believe it to be true, and it does not seem
that truth can be chosen, other than by choosing to alter the
world, or object of belief, in a way that makes it true. I cannot
just decide to believe that a certain drug is safe, but I can decide
to make it safe. So Bentham's sketchy sociology would seem to
run into the problem of both needing and also not being able to
provide an account of how interest influences belief.

The way in which this problem has just been set up is certainly
in accord with Bentham's thought. It is a psychological question,
and Bentham's psychology is a faculty psychology, in which the
events and activities of the mind are portioned between such
faculties as the will, the understanding, 'sense', 'judgement', and
so on. 'These faculties, these fictitious psychological entities', as
Bentham calls them at one point (*Introduction to the Rationale
of Evidence*, VI 18), form the basis of his descriptive psychology
just as other fictitious entities form the basis of his descriptive

jurisprudence. The chief division is that between the understanding and the will, which occurs throughout Bentham's work (for example, IPML 145; OLG 105; RJE iii 356). When considering interest, the relevant faculty is the will. So, for example, at the start of *Scotch Reform*, Bentham notes for the first time in public his change of mind about the obstacles to reform. He says that consideration of the lawyer's rules of evidence had given him reason to suspect 'that what at first view had presented itself as the result of primeval blindness and imbecility, was referable, perhaps, in a certain degree, to those causes, but probably in a much higher degree to sharp-sighted artifice' (V 4). He then comments that, for the lawyers, '*power* found itself in company with the *interest*, and consequently the *will*' (ibid.). So the question is how the faculty associated with choice and decision could influence belief in the same way as it influenced action. In terms of an account of corruption, of how the 'sinister interest' of a few rulers could influence and so corrupt the beliefs of the many, it is the problem of how the will of the few could change the understandings of those few, and could change the wills and understandings of the many. As Bentham puts it in *Fallacies*, 'the influence of understanding on understanding is, in a word, no other than the influence of the human reason' whereas the 'sinister' influence of will on will is called 'corruption' (*225; *229).

This taxonomy of influences which can be expressed by different combinations of the two faculties of understanding and will again goes back to, or to just before, the French Revolutionary period. Bentham, replying to Necker on representation in 1788, promoted the secret ballot as a way of avoiding the influence of 'will on will' (UC 170.77). This influence is, as he says in *Packing*, 'power' (V 96) and is obviously important in the overall problem of how Bentham can appeal to the legislator given that the (corrupted) legislator or people may not listen. However, for the present problem of how interest can influence belief, the important relationships are those between the will and the understanding. A standard account of this relationship, available to Bentham from Hume, is that the understanding, or 'reason', is 'cool' and can only motivate actions in conjunction with desire. What it then does is refine or alter the primitive ends originally desired. Bentham expresses this standard account in the *Fallacies*: 'the understanding is not the source, reason is of itself no spring of action, the understanding is but an instrument in the hand of the will: it is by hopes and fears that the *end* of action is determined; all that reason does is to find and determine upon the *means*' (*326). In other words, hopes and fears, namely interest, influence the will, and this sets the ends of action which reason then works out the most efficient means of achieving. Although Bentham says that the 'understanding is but an instrument in the hands of the will', he does not mean here that the will influences how the understanding is, but, rather, that the understanding works in the service of the will, doing what it does because the will is as it is. If there is any influence, it is the understanding which is influencing the will, because use of the understanding changes the objects desired by the will. However, sometimes Bentham has the influence working in the other direction, so that the will straightforwardly influences the understanding, and this is the problematic case. The 'intellectual faculty', he says 'is on every occasion, exposed to the action and influence of the *sensitive* and *volitional*: judgement – opinion – is liable to be acted upon, influenced, and perverted, by interest' (SPRINGS, I 217); 'judgement, opinion, persuasion, is in a very considerable degree under the dominion of the will' (RJE iii 360). So, in terms of this faculty psychology, we have Bentham claiming that interest alters belief, and it does so by means of its effect on the will, and the will's effect on the understanding. This route via the will shows that, for Bentham, the account of how interest alters belief should be like an account of how interest leads to action (as being chosen because in the agent's interest). Yet it is exactly this that was seen to be problematic.

However, although the faculty psychology sets the problem, and although Bentham, particularly in late, incidental, despairing, remarks, can claim that 'when interest closes the eyes, the whole force of reason cannot open them' (XI 73) or that 'interest appeals to the *will*, argument to the understanding. What can argument do against interest? The understanding is but the servant – the very slave to the will' (X 511), he did not, in fact, hold that it was just possible to choose to have particular beliefs if it was in one's interest to do so. He is quite explicit and clear about this in several places. For example, he says in *Fallacies* that 'it is impossible by reward or punishment to produce real and immediate belief' (*65) (even though the whole point of punishment in Benthamite thought is that, by adjusting interest, it can create desired action). The particular case which occurs several times is that of religious belief: 'when a man has formed his opinion, can punishments make him change it? The very question is an insult to common sense' (*Traités* iii 135; LEGIS 435). Nor is it just that Bentham at various times gives varying and inconsistent remarks. He has, in fact, quite a sophisticated account both of how interest can influence, and of how this does not happen by direct choice of belief, even though it does operate *via* the will. This is given in the

Book of Fallacies, though the main points are in the *Evidence* and elsewhere, if *Fallacies* is considered to be too unreliable a text. The key notion is that the acquisition or maintenance of belief depends upon the acquisition or availability of evidence; and the acquisition of evidence is an action which, like other actions, is unproblematically under the control of the will, and may be undertaken or otherwise according to the interest someone has in acquiring the evidence. Bentham notes that the probability of correctness of an opinion will be in the 'joint ratio of the sufficiency of the *means* of collecting such information and the strength of the *motives* by which [someone] was urged to employment of those means' (*FALL 34). Removing ignorance demands labour and the 'quantity of mental labour' will be 'as the aggregate strength of the motives by which a man is excited to labour' (*56). So interest influences belief by making people reluctant to attempt to refute beliefs in which they want to believe, if they have them, or eager to establish them, if they don't have them. As Bentham noted much earlier about witchcraft in the time of Hale: 'being satisfied of there being such a thing [because of the Bible] it was an easy matter to find instances of it' (COMM 200n). Not only is evidence only sought when it is wanted but, when it is wanted, things look like evidence which would not do so if they were not wanted. There is nothing particularly late in Bentham's thought in this account of the relation of will and belief. In his 1780s Commonplace book he had noted:

to say, believe this proposition rather than its contrary, is to say do all that is in your power to believe it. Now, what is in a man's power to do, in order to believe a proposition, and *all* that is so, is to keep back and stifle the evidences that are opposed to it. For, when all the evidences are equally present to his observation, and equally attended to, to believe or disbelieve is no longer in his power. It is the necessary result of the preponderance of the evidence on one side over that on the other. (X 146)

This succinctly expresses his continuing account, and one of the key words is 'attended'. For, as well as the labour of gathering evidence, something which is also under a person's control is attention ('attention is in great measure at the command of the will' (RJE v 642)). So interest can also influence the attention which someone gives to a particular question, and hence also the beliefs which he reaches on that subject.

The 'interest-begotten prejudice' which features largely in

Bentham's later works, *Scotch Reform, Fallacies, Springs*, and so on, can therefore be given a psychological context in his thought taken as a whole which makes it possible for prejudice (mistaken belief) to arise because of interest. There is only development, not fundamental change, in the thought. What before was thought to be the effect of 'inattention and prejudice' and is now thought to be the product of 'sinister interest' is indeed, throughout, inattention and prejudice; it is just that the lack of attention is seen not to be accidental but, rather, the result of interest. Hence the prejudice is 'interest-begotten'. On the other hand, as noted in Chapter II, Bentham cited 'interest' as an 'obstacle' to reform in his early manuscripts, singling out exactly the same classes as in the *Fallacies*, lawyers and divines, as those where it was most prevalent. He had always realised that 'interest smooths the road to Faith' (FG 442). Part of the change in his thought Bentham describes as seeing that the things that he was trying to reform were not just accidents but, rather, the result of 'artifice'. However, this should not be understood as saying that Bentham came to see them as being consciously created. He came to realise (or to realise more fully) how it was in the interest of the lawyers to have particular procedures, and how it was in the interests of lawyers not to attend to the exact nature of these procedures too closely or to bother about criticism. In this sense he saw that the procedures were not accidental: they survived because they fulfilled a purpose; because they fulfilled a purpose, the resulting inattention enabled them to survive. However, it was inattention more than conscious artifice; the procedures were not consciously planned in order to extract profit. So, in his psychology Bentham also has an account of self-deception. A man is not necessarily the best authority on the state of his own mind. As he puts it at the end of the *Fallacies*, influence on the intellectual faculty is 'secret' even to the man himself; the rare case is where a man knows his motives. In this area people have an interest in not knowing their own motives. For Bentham 'not infrequently, as between two persons living together in a state of intimacy, either or each may possess a more correct and complete view of the motives by which the mind of the other, than those by which his own mind is governed' (*372-3). The causes, the motives, operating on the lawyers and other promoters of interest-begotten prejudices are unknown even to the perpetrators; Bentham's sociological analysis exposes the artifice to the artificers; the unconscious origins of the ideology, repressed by the believers, are extracted.

Bentham's account, then, is one in which it still remains possible to use reason in persuasion, although it is also an account in which it can be shown how people may not give attention to the attempt to persuade. It is a world in which 'the thicker the ignorance, the more completely is the furniture of men's minds made up of those interest-begotten prejudices, which render them blindly obsequious to all those who with power in their hands stand up to take the lead' (*FALL 54), yet mere provision of information will not by itself serve to remedy the ignorance, given that interest may divert a man's attention, and that 'be the absurdity ever so gross, — make it a man's interest not to see it, — as often as it presents itself he will shut his eyes' (RJE iv 464). So persuasion is possible, but difficult; mere mention is certainly insufficient to overcome inattention, and even shouting may be insufficient. In considering whether persuasion is possible at all, the next question is whom Bentham wished to persuade. This returns the question to that of who the legislator is in Bentham's thought, and it must now be seen who he was and how he was, or at least might be, motivated. For what the interest of the legislator is, and how he might be motivated by interest, are questions which need to be settled before it can be considered how he can, or might, be persuaded. Here, also, unlike the relation of understanding and will, we do get substantial changes in Bentham's thought.

In his early work, where he just took over the problem of his predecessors, Bentham's legislator remains just an expository device by means of which an account can be given of what ought to happen when things are organised so as to promote the greatest happiness of the greatest number. So, as noted, he can remark in *Of Laws in General* that he only writes for legislators for which that is the end, or expect in the *Defence of Usury* that, unlike the 'bulk of mankind', the legislator will not be frightened by the sound of the word 'usury', that 'a little more inquisitiveness may be required of legislators' (Stark i 130). Here the legislator is automatically expected to do his duty and have an unusual, or unnatural, ability to attend to reason and ignore prejudice; the legislator is all attention, and cares as much as Bentham himself that the right answer be reached. So, to move on a decade to a time when the development of the French Revolution made Bentham suspicious of popular reaction and belief, the fact that 'the dictates of reason and utility are the result of circumstances which require genius to discover, strength of mind to weigh, and patience to investigate' (*Escheat*, Stark i 335) is not a problem; the legislator is just such a patient, attentive genius, who will suppress none of the evidence, and show the same genius in legislation as Bentham had for legislation. However, as was seen in

Chapter V, when Bentham turned his attention from how the legislator could get interest in line with duty for the normal citizen in the criminal law to how he could create institutions such as prisons and workhouses where interest was in line with duty for the officials, then new problems arose. In the same decade of the 1790s, it was realised that institutions had to be planned so that they ran as they were meant to as well as looking at the effects of the institutions, if they ran correctly, on their recipients. As was seen there, once this idea was generalised, then the whole state itself could only be constructed so that each official of the state found that his duty coincided with his interest. None was supposed to be sufficiently heroic that he could be entrusted with the unadorned performance of his duty. However, once this has been seen, then the same considerations must apply to the legislator himself. No more can he be taken to be the disinterested, heroic, genius, creating the law as his duty. He also will be seen as possibly interested, and so he also will be seen as subject to prejudice and inattention. By the time of the *Fallacies*, 'if there be any one maxim in politics more certain than another, it is, that no possible degree of virtue in the governor can render it expedient for the governed to dispense with good laws and good institutions' (*120). On the contrary, since power corrupts, since 'power, in whatever hands lodged, is almost sure to be more or less abused' (*188), the governor needs to be watched more carefully than anyone else. Hence it is not surprising that although Bentham said that his great work on *Evidence* was designed for a legislator, it was designed for a legislator yet to be formed, namely one who 'neither is under the dominion of an interest hostile to that of the public, nor is in league with those who are' (RJE i 23). No actual legislator would serve; nobody actual was sufficiently heroic.

If not even for the legislator, if at no position, can people be supposed to be motivated by mere perception of their duty, then the whole state, legislator included, must be subject to the same design problem as particular institutions are. The problem is to find the form of state in which it is in the interest of the creators of law, or legislators, that they will do their duty, that is create law which promotes the greatest happiness of the greatest number. The answer is that the greatest number of the people itself should be the legislator; there will then be a junction of interest with duty, since in caring for their own interests, which is what they are naturally led to do, the greatest number of the people will also be caring for what they ought to be caring for, namely the greatest happiness of the greatest number. So the form of state in which the psychological principles are allowed to apply at every position, and in which even the legislator is not allowed to escape their effect, and yet in which nevertheless the legislator cares for what the Benthamite legislator ought to care for, is a democracy. The caesar, the sovereign, is the people. Ever since Bentham first recognised that the 'foundations of all *virtue* are laid in *utility*' and hence 'learnt to call the cause of the people the cause of Virtue' (FG 440n), it was perhaps inevitable that he would also come to realise that this cause would involve not only working for the people but also working by the people. For only with a democracy, if man is self-interested, will people having power be motivated in the cause of virtue. With the eighteenth-century despots, the problem was why a particular despot should be motivated to pursue the greatest happiness of his people, however good the arguments in its favour. With the move to democracy in the following century, this problem is solved. However bad the arguments in favour of utility, there is no problem about why the greatest number of the people should be motivated to pursue the greatest happiness of the greatest number.

The later thought, or jargon, of Bentham is full of references to the 'subject many' and the 'ruling few'. Where 'sinister interest' was concern for the interest of the 'few' at the expense of the general interest, or the interest of the 'many', then clearly the chief problem of politics, the 'only regular and constant means of security' is to find a way in which the 'will of the people' can influence the 'ruling few' (*FALL 240). This could be achieved by democracy, more precisely by representative democracy, 'the only practicable democracy' (*Parliamentary Reform*, III 451). Hence, starting in 1817, Bentham became a public propagandist on behalf of a very considerable extension to the suffrage, linked with the introduction of secret ballot in parliamentary elections. He promoted 'virtual universality of suffrage' (ibid., 452). The plan he published that year had, he says, been worked out as a draft bill in 1809. Even before then, at the start of the French Revolution, Bentham wrote in favour of a greatly extended franchise and of the ballot. The, as he saw it, unfortunate turn of events which followed in France led him for a time to change his mind. However, as so often in Bentham, the published ideas of 1817 and after are very much as worked out long before, between 1788 and 1792. It was then that he thought of the arguments, and followed those arguments to their natural conclusions. If there was an important change of mind in Bentham's thought, it was then that it took place. As he confesses in his *Draught of a new plan for the organisation of a judicial establishment in France*, written for the new revolutionary government and concerned to help them with organisation of the judiciary, he had thought that the people.

> might choose for chief-justice an Hottentot, or an orang-
> outang . . . my thoughts were divided betwixt the King and
> the representative assemblies. I could scarce think of look-
> ing so far down the pyramid, as to the body of the people.
> But now the committee has given me courage to look the
> idea in the face, I have little fear of the success. (IV 309)

This is frank and sounds correct. Bentham had to adjust his thoughts; he also had to put aside prejudices. However, once he had thought; once he had realised what the arguments were and had followed them through, then his new beliefs were both genuine and deep-seated. As he puts it at the start of *Political Tactics*, an earlier work designed to help the new government, the composition of assemblies is better 'in proportion as its interest is similar to that of the community' and that the first condition for this is direct election (II 301). As for the general idea, so for the more specific proposals. It was seen above that the first mention of the influence of will on will came with promotion of the ballot to Necker in 1788; the same argument in the same shape comes with the proposals at all periods.

'Were every man his own legislator laws would be made as badly as cloaths would be, if every man were his own taylor', Bentham wrote in a manuscript of this earlier time and continued: 'it is not every man that can make a shoe; but when a shoe is made every man may tell whether it fits him without much difficulty. Every man can not be a shoemaker but any man may choose his own shoemaker' (UC 127.2). In other words, Bentham recognises that knowledge and skill are needed for successful legislation; he hasn't changed his mind about the strength of mind, care, and attention that is required. However, as he wants to show with the shoemaker analogy, this does not mean that he thinks that the choice of who should legislate should be restricted to people with such knowledge or abilities. On the contrary, most people can judge whether it has been successfully performed. Indeed, it is necessary that it is the great majority of people who do judge since it is only they who will be sufficiently motivated to see that their interest has been properly protected. Any smaller group are liable to judge legislation only in terms of their partial, private, interest. If, for example, the rich were given greater say, 'it is difficult to say what feature is more conspicuous, absurdity or injustice: as if a poor man's happiness were not as much to him as a rich man's: as if the happiness of the one did not form as large a portion of the happiness of the state as that of the rich' (1789; UC 170.149). For all happiness to be considered equally it was necessary that all equally consider; hence, in his later proposals Bentham glossed his 'virtual universality of suffrage' as being 'practical equality of representation' (*Parliamentary Reform*, III 452). The balance between having legislators with unusual knowledge or skill and everyone equally being able to judge and control their work was to be achieved by representative democracy. The representatives (or, as Bentham often preferred to call them, 'deputies') should be chosen on an annual basis. Various other minor controls were built into the later plans, such as declarations to be made, but the chief control maximising their aptitude was that annually they were to be subject to the scrutiny of virtually all the people. These people, being able to say best if what was being done was really in their greatest interest, just as the client could tell the shoemaker if the shoe fitted, could then continue or remove their deputies according to whether they were performing satisfactorily or otherwise.

It was seen in the last chapter that the general agreement of the people was neither a necessary nor a sufficient condition for achieving the correct moral view. It was seen in this chapter that Bentham, particularly when contemplating some of the more lurid developments of the French Revolution, thought that the dictates of utility (unlike chatter about natural rights), were only known to a few who exercised extra special discrimination or attention. Furthermore, it has been seen how small groups in power can promote ideologies which serve their own interests, corrupting the understandings of the general public. Even though no doubt there should have been widespread objection to the denial of justice to ninety-nine men out of a hundred, there was not; Bentham's later 'petitions for justice' failed to gain any massed signatures. So Bentham, in promoting representative democracy, has a problem about why the expressed will of the people as a whole should really be the best judge of the general interest. He attempts to meet this by isolating two factors which would prevent it being so: by excluding from the suffrage those incapable of making such a judgement, and by protecting those who did vote from the sinister influence of those more powerful than themselves. The latter was the point of the secret ballot, which Bentham recognised right through to be the keystone of his proposals. It has been seen that right back in 1788 he proposed it to Necker as the way of excluding the influence of will on will. In the *Draught* he said that 'secrecy of suffrage kills corruption in all its shapes, by disarming it of its hold' (IV 365); and this is the view in the later tracts for reform. Secrecy, he says, is necessary to secure 'freedom', that is that the vote should be 'the will of that person and that person only', detailing at length the ways in which someone may be subject to someone else's influence, and how this is prevented when it is not known how a particular person votes (*Parliamentary Reform*, III 453). The other factor he employs in trying to ensure that the vote forms a proper judgement of the interests of the people, namely exclusion of the incapable, is not so simple, nor are Bentham's proposals (at any period) so clear cut.

Once the general idea has been launched of the people being the best judges of their own interest, then it is difficult to promote substantial exclusion. 'The people?', Bentham asks rhetorically in the Introductory matter to *Parliamentary Reform*, 'What interest have they in being governed badly?' Obviously none, hence the 'remedy — two words, viz *democratical ascendency*' (III 445-6). Once this is allowed, then it would just be hypocritical to say that the ascendency was in fact to be exercised on behalf of the people at large by some privileged group of people who in fact knew the interests of the people as a whole better than they did themselves (a group like Bentham and his radical friends). Once he is committed to democracy on the basis of the general claim that people are the best judges of their own interest, then he cannot allow many exclusions. Nor does he, using, unusually, an argument based on equity: 'if, in the instance of any *one* individual of the whole body of the people, it be *right* that the faculty of contributing to the choice of a representative ... be possessed and exercised, — how can it be otherwise than right, in the instance of any one other such person?' (452). So the general rule is that everyone should be included unless a specific case is made why they should be excluded; hence the 'virtual' universality of suffrage.

This still leaves Bentham with outlining the particular cases. At the point in the Introduction to the *Plan of Parliamentary Reform* just quoted, Bentham contents himself with mentioning '*idiots*, and *infants* in leading-strings' to show that there must be some examples of people not 'capable of exercising [the suffrage] to the advantage either of others or of themselves' (452). However, the other cases are more difficult. Following his general principle of inclusion if possible, he is quite happy to include aliens (*Catechism of Parliamentary Reform*, III 541), and in his earlier *Radical Reform Bill* he argues against several standard exclusions, being quite happy to grant '*persons insane*, and *crimi-*

nals' (III 559) (on the assumption that if they were under confine-
ment they would not be able to vote anyway). So the chief class
of excluded persons, which he consistently proposes, are those
that are not able to read. As he says in the early manuscripts, 'it
is the only circumstance which can serve to draw a distinct line
between the condition of those who may reasonably be deemed
to have it in their power to exercise the right in question to the
advantage of the community and those who can not' (1789; UC
170.146). This is because Bentham wished to rely on written
reports of parliamentary proceedings, so that only those who
could read would have direct access to what their representative
had been up to while representing them. Accordingly, typically
elaborate Benthamite proposals were incorporated in the *Radical
Reform Bill* drafted in 1809 to test a putative elector's reading
capacity. Just like the exclusion of infants, Bentham held that
such exclusion was much fairer than others because it did not
exclude the individual as such. Just as (nearly) everyone grows
up, so (or at least Bentham supposed) anyone who sufficiently
desires it can teach himself to read. Hence it is 'an exclusion
which every man has it in his power to free himself from whenever he thinks proper' (1789; UC 170.146); it 'involves no exclusion: for every man who chose could give it [the reading quali-
fication] to himself' (*Radical Reform Bill*, III 560).

Although this involves a touch of a fancy franchise, it must be
remembered that Bentham's proposals, early and late, amounted
to proposals for a massive increase in the suffrage, and at a time
when the whole idea of democracy was, as he says, a 'bugbear'.
They have to be judged as being made to a time when the emotive
connotations of the word were quite different, and totally different views were accepted. This causes even more problems
with the category which Bentham also considered in passing at
times as possible subjects for exclusion, that is women. It seems
clear that, as soon as he had considered the matter fully, Bentham
realised that there were no good arguments for the exclusion of
women, yet that any proposal for their inclusion would be howled
down as ridiculous. Bentham's original collaborator as a pamphleteer, John Lind, thought that he could make speedy work of
reducing Price's democratic proposals to absurdity by showing
that the argument that made 'every man his own legislator' would
make 'every woman her own legislatrix' (*Three Letters* (1776)
40). So Bentham knew that any public espousal of the idea
of female suffrage would endanger the rest of his proposals,
and contented himself with questioning why it should be thought
to be absurd. In the Introduction to the *Plan of Parliamentary*

Reform he attacks the way that the question is removed with 'a *horse*-laugh, a sneer, an expression of scorn, or a common-place witticism' (III 463), and shows that arguments normally advanced against it do not work. Yet he does not draw the conclusion in favour of inclusion himself; he leaves it to the reader. Similarly, in the *Catechism*, he says merely '*females* might even be admitted' (III 541), again holding his position open and tentative. In the *Constitutional Code* he is more explicit that he is in favour of exclusion 'because the prepossession against their admission is at present too general, and too intense, to afford any chance in favour of a proposal for their admission' (IX 108). Yet the arguments which he adds to this bleak and negative remark are all arguments in favour of inclusion: women are equal in intellectual aptitude, have been successful monarchs, if physically weaker are all the more in need of representation, and so on. It is true that on other occasions Bentham was in favour of the exclusion of women from somewhat analogous assemblies: from listening to debates (*Tactics*, II 327) or from membership of juries in some circumstances (CODE IX 566-7). However, the place to find Bentham's real views is as they evolved in manuscript; these public pronouncements are liable all to be constrained by consideration of public practicability. Here the most interesting document is Bentham's early 1788 essay on representation for Necker. This is reprinted as an appendix to Halévy (1901), and translated as an appendix to Mack (1962), but they have both left out one of the most interesting features of the original manuscript, which is that Bentham went back, probably shortly after his original draft, and added marginal comments meeting his earlier arguments point by point. In the main text Bentham lists the excluded classes, children, idiots, women as if they were a matter of course, and then adds five particular points against women. To all these he adds a conclusive reply in the margin (UC 170.115) (to three, the ballot provides an answer). So, at this stage Bentham had clearly worked through and realised which way the argument went; and hence it is not surprising that in his essay of the following year on the French Constitution, Bentham comes out extremely strongly on behalf of female suffrage: 'whatever benefit belongs to the right of suffrage there is no reason why it should be refused to one more than another', he starts off (although he does interpolate 'prima facie' before 'reason') and continues, 'the custom which has prevailed so generally in prejudice to the softer sex; it has tyranny for its efficient cause, and prejudice for its sole justification'. Again he lists objections and answers them, but this time straight off in the main text. For example, to the objection that females are 'naturally inferior' he replies that 'the fact is dubious: but, were it ever so certain, it would be nothing to the purpose, unless in the best endowed of the one sex they were inferior to what they are in the worst endowed in the other', and so on (UC 170.44). It is clear which way the argument runs, and the way in which the argument runs shows the way in which Bentham thinks; the conclusions he holds.

Once the appropriate exclusions from suffrage have been fixed, the remaining, 'virtually universal' suffrage should control the elected representatives in the interests of the people as a whole. Yet this will only happen if the basis of the argument is correct, namely that the people know their own interests better than anyone else does. Given the low view which Bentham sometimes expresses of the multitude, of 'the unbridled concourse of rough and uncultivated minds' (PAUPER 206, VIII 416), and his view of the way the 'world judges, one upon examination and nine hundred and ninety-nine upon trust' (*Usury*, Stark i 189), this might seem a somewhat surprising and optimistic assumption on Bentham's part. Even if the ballot excludes the sinister influence of will on will at the point of election, there would seem to be sufficient other occasions for corruption of understanding, or just plain stupidity, for people not to be sufficiently aware of their own interests. As was noticed in Chapter VI, people did not judge their future interests correctly, tending to discount them in favour of the present; hence Bentham held that they, particularly the working classes, did not save sufficiently. So an electorate dominated by the people at large might be thought on his own arguments to be one biased in favour of over-consumption in the present. Yet, once he had decided in favour of democracy, Bentham was committed to the view that the general will of the people, if not automatically and invariably, was at least normally and reliably a correct indicator of what was in the general interest (of what led to the greatest happiness of the greatest number). As he put it, just after the shoemaker analogy: 'the surest visible sign and immediate evidence of general utility is general consent' (UC 127.3). Or, as he replied in his acceptance of an honorary citizenship of the new, revolutionary, French republic: 'the general will is everywhere, and for every one, the sole external index by which the conformity of the means to the end [that is, 'the general good'] can be decided' (X 282). It may not be a perfect index, or decision procedure, but it seems to be the best one we have got; perhaps the only one we have got. Whether, even so, it is good enough will be further considered shortly.

Except for this possible problem about the accuracy of the

general will expressed in secret ballot as an index of the general good, it now seems that Bentham has solved his original problem. He has drawn up a plan of a state in which at every point duty coincides with interest. Even the legislator is bound in by his interest in the same way as everyone else. This has been achieved, in effect, by splitting sovereignty, so that the people as a whole, motivated by their own interest, keep the final sovereignty, but delegate the function of legislation to representatives who are closely controlled by publicity and frequent elections. What has happened is that the legislator has ceased to be an external *deus ex machina* creating institutions in the cause of the general good but has, instead, become part of the machine. There is no longer an external legislator. However, although this solves the problem in one way, it merely reopens it in another. For although it now means that the legislator's motives and interests can be discussed and known, it also means that there is now a serious problem about how this perfect state is to be brought into being. As long as the legislator was external it could be supposed that this deity might create the state, institution, or form of law, which was seen to lead to the greatest happiness, once the problem of which it was had been solved. However, lacking such an external legislator, merely solving the problem of the perfect form of state is not good enough. This will do nothing to put it into effect. It may well be true that in a representative democracy the interests of the greatest number are taken care of even if everyone only acts in self-interested terms. This means, at the most, that, once instituted, such a democracy would be self-sustaining, in that it would be in the interests of those in power (that is, the people at large) to have the system that they in fact had. However, it gives no motive for anyone at all to institute such a system. In particular, if other people are in power, a favoured few, this few will have no motive at all to part with power which they are exercising in their own interests in order to create a system which is much less in their interests. So, even if democracy is a solution to the best form of state, and a state in which persuasion might be expected to achieve the right results, it is no solution at all to the original problem of persuasion, the problem of how Bentham, not being in power, could persuade those who were in power to do what they ought to.

In other words, we are back with the problem discussed abstractly at the beginning of the chapter of the possibility of persuasion. It now is given a more specific and concrete context, but this does not necessarily make it more solvable. As Bentham puts it in the Introduction he wrote in 1816 to his *Defence of the Economy against Burke*, the treatise which followed had its 'principles . . . in a state of irreconcilable hostility to the personal interest of that class of persons which forms the subject of it — to which it cannot but look for the greatest number of its readers — and without whose concurrence . . . it could not at any time be in any degree carried into effect' (V 279). Bentham is, necessarily, appealing to a specific group of people to do something against their interests; whether there is any possibility of success at all therefore depends upon whether interest is totally dominant. If there is some place left for reason or argument, then there may be hope of change. But if the scepticism which Bentham frequently expressed at this period is well-founded, then he has to look for another means of change than persuasion. This would be so if the two rules enunciated at the end of the Introduction to *Parliamentary Reform* hold inexorably: '1.*Positive Rule* — To satisfy yourself before hand, what, on a given occasion, will be the course a man will take, look to the state of *interests* . . . 2.*Negative Rule* — . . . pay no regard whatever to professions or protestations' (III 526). This is a world in which interest rules, in which influence is by will on will rather than understanding on understanding. Here the only advice is that 'before you put yourself to any expense in the article of *argument*, look first to the state of *interests*: — think to overcome the force of interest by the force of argument? think as well to take *Lisle* or *Mantua* by peas blown out of a pea-shooter' (ibid. 507). Here Bentham is stuck, because however much he examines the state of interests, this is not going to change them.

On the other hand, the general rules just proposed are taken to apply more and more accurately, the larger the body. They may delineate accurately enough the beliefs and behaviours of groups, but will not necessarily do so for any one particular individual. It was seen in Chapter VI that the axiom that people pursued their own interest was only held to be true on the whole, so that there were heroic exceptions; it will be remembered that Bentham invoked the 1830 revolutionaries in France to remember that other men were not as they were, or other kings not as Louis Philippe. The design of institutions so that duty coincided with interest was intended for the normal case. So it would be possible, even on Bentham's own principles, for a heroic individual to arise who had power. Such an individual, motivated by pure duty, could put all the Benthamite proposals into effect, including the institution of representative democracy. Arising, for example, in the course of a revolution, or as liberator of a colonial territory, he would be a legislator in the classical mould, the creator of the state itself and of all its central institutions. However, although possible, such a heroic legislator would be rare; and, more importantly, there is nothing that Bentham or anyone else could do to promote his appearance. Faced with practical problems, as Bentham constantly felt himself to be, the prescription of waiting for the hero to turn up is no prescription at all.

The actual situation is one in which the 'ruling few' had power, and yet in which, as Bentham saw in *Burke*, he had to appeal to these few to act against their interests. Given that, if they were only open to reason, this is what they would do, it follows that they avoid or elude the force of reason. The devices by which they do this are mapped in the *Book of Fallacies*, in which the arguments used by the ruling classes are systematically analysed and found to be fallacious. This exposes the interest that is at the basis of belief; apparent argument is stripped away and all that is left is the ideology. However, the problem is why this looking at interests, as recommended at much the same time in the Introduction to *Parliamentary Reform*, should help Bentham's cause. For this there would need to be some mechanism which meant that if the causes of belief are exposed, then this exposure itself will tend to change the beliefs. Such mechanisms have been proposed, for example in Freudian theory, but Bentham gives no sign of what he thinks their nature might be, nor is it easy to reconstruct something which seems to be both correct and to serve his purpose. Exposure of the causes of belief cannot be taken as sufficient in itself to change belief. After all, Bentham himself held, quite reasonably, that all beliefs were caused. Causation, that is, is not just something that only applies to false belief, so, if it is discovered that a belief is caused, this would show that it was false, and hence provide a reason for changing it. Nor does it seem that true beliefs might not sometimes be in the interest of the believer, so, again, showing that a belief was in someone's interest would not show it to be false. As Bentham puts it, *'veracity . . . no less than mendacity is the result of interest'* (**Introduction to the Rationale of Evidence*, VI 19); and what he says here explicitly about the expression of belief can be taken to hold also as his view about belief itself. So there seems to be no automatic mechanism by which the exposure of the causes of the beliefs of the ruling classes, as in the *Book of Fallacies*, should serve to change those beliefs, as by a kind of Freudian therapy; nor does the exposure of the causes show them to be false, that is, provide reasons against them. The most that it does, although this might be important, is to remove reasons in favour of the beliefs. The reasons are all found to be sham, fallacies. Hence, if someone does want to act on the basis of reason, he will not come to these beliefs. The exposure in *Fallacies* leaves the field open for utility, democracy, law reform, and so on once anyone is prepared to listen to argument. However, it does not by itself do anything which would make anyone listen to such argument.

If Bentham is to operate against power or interest, therefore, he needs more than mere exposure; and here the intriguing possibility opens up for using the exposed or tainted material, only now for good rather than bad ends. It has been noticed that one of the apparent paradoxes of the *Book of Fallacies* is that Bentham in it and elsewhere seems to commit some of the fallacies he castigates (Burns 1974; Ball 1980). For example, he holds it to be a fallacy to attack someone's motives rather than what he says; yet the whole business of exposing the fallacies as serving the interests of the 'ruling few' is to attack the motives behind the expressed beliefs of those few. Although this looks self-defeating, or self-convicting, once Bentham is in the mood that pea-shooters do not bring down town walls, that only power can talk to power, that corruptions produced by the will can only be met by influencing the will, then it has a brute, practical, point to it. The idea is to meet tainted material by tainted material, propaganda by propaganda; it is recognised that truth is the first victim in war, but since it is momentarily regarded as more important that the war be won, this is not seen as an objection. Bentham himself was aware of, and addresses, the objection to the *Fallacies* made more recently by Professor Burns. Right at the end he claims that, since the mischievousness of the arguments that he has considered 'is supposed to be sufficiently established on other . . . grounds; the object in view now is, to determine by what means an object so desirable as the general disuse of these poisonous weapons may in the completest and most effectual degree be attained' (407). In other words, since he knows from elsewhere that he has his hands on valid arguments and true conclusions, in the present work he is meeting poison gas by poison gas as the best means of getting rid of poisons altogether. Yet, particularly given Bentham's antipathy to poisons, opiates, this is at best a highly dangerous activity; the gas is liable to blow backwards on the wrong side.

A theoretical problem for many revolutionaries and reformers is how far they themselves feel permitted to make use of the institutions objected to before they are reformed. Practically, people rarely refrain from living on the social security services of states they are planning to overthrow; and certainly Bentham himself, at least in his later thought, seems to have little problem in feeling himself entitled to helping himself to any means that were available. In order to reform parliament and eliminate rotten boroughs in which seats could be purchased, for example, he wished that he had sufficient money to purchase enough seats to force his proposals through: 'had I some ten or twenty millions of money at my disposal . . . I would buy liberty with it for the people' (*Parliamentary Reform*, III 486). Nor is this in opposition to utilitarian principles: since consequences count, the end justifies the means, not in the crude sense that anything at all may be done to produce something good, but that something which is normally bad may be done on those special occasions on which it in fact produces more good. On this occasion something whose 'general tendency' is bad (as Bentham had just identified it as being before the quoted remark) is justified by its good consequences. ('The end justifies the means' is, in fact, one of the fallacies identified in *Fallacies* (*341); Bentham is always hostile to its unrestricted application). However, in the particular case of the promotion of belief, there seems to be something peculiarly inappropriate in using any methods that there happen to be in order to produce good results; fallacies in order to procure true belief. Just after the above remark Bentham continues: 'with that money in hand, I could and would open honourable eyes . . . I would enable them to see . . . that liberty is better than slavery' ('honourable' here just means Members of the House of Commons). However, this is disingenuously put: the perceptual metaphor makes it appear that all that Bentham would be doing would be removing scales from people's eyes and allowing them access to the truth; whereas what he would be doing would be inserting belief, and inserting it by exactly the method elsewhere condemned. Even if true belief is caused just as false belief is, this by itself does not entitle Bentham to purchase opinion just because the opinion, for a change, happens to be true.

The danger and the problem inherent in any attempt of Bentham to use the contaminated material to his own ends is that he is liable to lose his grip on what is in fact true. If there is anything wrong about the use of fallacy, in that it leads to error, then Bentham's use of fallacy might well have the same result. If there is anything wrong in presenting fallacious instead of valid argument to the people, in that it is liable to teach them disrespect for argument, and so the method of reaching true belief, then once Bentham indulges, he is also liable to teach such disrespect. Part of Bentham's continuing objection to the lawyers' use of fictions, to the mire of mendacity in which he thought that they were steeped, is that it created a disrespect for truth in the minds of the people. If disrespect for truth is created, then truth is less likely to be discovered. This is why use of the tainted means is much more serious with belief than with other things. For elsewhere the object aimed at and the method of reaching it can be kept distinct. If, however, Bentham departs from the method of arriving at the truth, the disinterested or dispassionate pursuit of argument, then he is in great danger of departing from the truth itself. Then he will merely be using fallacy to support his own, unargued, opinion; which is exactly the kind of tyrannical or despotical use of caprice which he condemned in the *Introduction*.

Any account of ideology, which shows how belief is corrupted or created by interest, or class position, or whatever, has to avoid the self-reflexive problem of why the account itself is not similarly corrupted or fallacious. A position has to be maintained in terms of the account from which the truth may be observed; and it has to be part of the account that it itself is given from that position. Bentham himself can avoid this familiar trap, or problem. If interest influences, then his account will be uncorrupted if he has no personal interest in one account being correct rather than another. So, as Bentham points out at the beginning of his *Procedure* material, because he does not draw a profit from his work, the errors in it will only have intellectual causes (*II 6). By extension, therefore, the kind of ideal situation of agreement in which argument could be made and people converge on the correct answer, as described at the end of the last chapter, should equally be a situation in which people were all disinterested; or, if this is wholly unrealistic, should be in equal positions of power, so that the discourse is not corrupted by influence of the will. It might seem, therefore, that once answers had been reached in such an ideal situation of argument, as in the last chapter, then these answers could be sold to the people at large by any means available, by will, power, fallacy, or whatever. However, this is to suppose too large a division between the esoteric doctrine worked out by the initiates and the exoteric doctrine sold to the people. Since the split is not perfect, since the two groups of people overlap, any technique of argument or persuasion used in the one is liable to have influence in the other. Hence it is better to use throughout the form of argument which would be used in the ideal, or esoteric, case. By this means, the chances are that respect for argument, and respect for truth, will get diffused throughout the community. Unless this happens, the positions based on argument can never properly get established (what can be achieved by trickery or power can be undone by trickery or power); while if it does happen, fallacies may be forgotten. Before his reference at the end of

Fallacies to the elimination of the poison by any means, Bentham says that the use of the exposure he has created is that, if sincerity is an object of public trust, then the exposure might succeed in making men ashamed to utter and receive such fallacies (406). If it can be supposed that there is some concern for argument and for sincerity (else why would the fallacies be so keen to pass themselves off as genuine argument), then the hope can only be that this is extended so that the use of the understanding, in the Benthamite jargon, triumphs over the force of the will.

Bentham's last views about the possibility of change, as he adds to his petitions for justice and codification, is that relief depends upon the chance of men in the situation of legislators in which either 'a sense of moral duty has place'; or their interest appears to be 'so bound up with the general weal' that they have more to gain than suffer from adopting the proposals; or that they fear that 'the subject-many should, in sufficient number, concur in doing for themselves what ought to have been done for them' (1829, V 543). The first is again the hope for a hero, the second is unlikely if there really is a natural antipathy of interest between the subject many and the ruling few, so the force here is on the third where (just as in the more general criminal theory) the lack of a natural identity of interests is made up by one artifically constructed. Fear of the people will make it in the interests of the rulers to serve the people's interests rather than their own. So, in the parliamentary reform proposals, Bentham presents them as the only alternative to revolution: 'the country is already at the very brink: − reform or convulsion, such is the alternative' (III 435). So the final argument that can be used is appeal to the rulers' self-interest; and whether this has force or not depends upon the contingency of how much pressure there happens to be. Yet this cannot be taken just as a pure contingency. Since Bentham is asking for power to be given 'into the hands of those of whose obedience all power is composed' (ibid. 437), he is, as he reminds his reader, noticing that the master is created by the slave; without obedience there would not be power (sovereignty in Bentham is identified by the 'habit of obedience'). So, if groups in general or in the long run act in their own interests, then, since it is in the interest of the people that they exercise power for themselves, in the long run it can be supposed that they will take it back for themselves. So pressure on a ruling few is not accidental. This means that Bentham can console himself with the fact that, even if persuasion fails, history is on his side; and because history is on his side, he can try persuading people that they should give way in their own interests, so that they can control the change rather than damming it up into a flood that will overwhelm them.

Of course, even if a representative democracy is instituted, whether by hook, crook, fraud, force, threat, reason, or whatever, Bentham is still not clear of the problem of persuasion. For, as seen, the majority might make a mistake about its own true interests. Bentham, the disinterested, might still be faced with the problem of how he could make them change their minds. However, this is just where the idea of a long-run tendency becomes even more important. Although the majority might be wrong, the tendency in the long run is that they will get it right. Since they have an interest in discovering the greatest happiness, they have an interest in discovering mistakes, and so mistakes will tend to be self-corrected; just as the democratic system itself will tend to be stable, as being a position of equilibrium.

> A law conformable to utility may happen to be contrary to public opinion; but this is only an accidental and transitory circumstance. All minds will be reconciled to the law as soon as its utility is made obvious. As soon as the veil which conceals it is raised, expectation will be satisfied, and the public opinion be gained over. (*Civil Code, Traités ii 100; LEGIS 151-2; I 324)

It is true that this is an earlier, more optimistic, statement, but the principle behind it endures. There are also two more specific considerations which can be added as to why there is a natural tendency for error in public opinion to correct itself in a democracy. The first is that since (on the pure Benthamite model) external sources of power which have sinister effects have been removed, there is more chance to reach a conclusion by discussion from equal positions of power. Argument being unconstrained by influence, errors are more likely to be detected. The second is that there is more chance for experience to accumulate. Bentham is concerned to show that the power of the ruling few is based upon a reliance on custom rather than reason; hence several of the fallacies he points out such as 'the wisdom of our ancestors; or Chinese argument' (*69). With this influence removed, experience can be regarded, and so there is more chance of refuting false, customary, views. It will be remembered that the nonsense which Bentham thought to be on stilts was the idea of imprescriptible rights; he was always hostile to the idea of trying to build anything permanent, any constitutional checks, or indefeasible laws into an institutional or constitutional arrangement. The key note is openness to the future. However correct things seem, there must be the continuous possibility of refutation. Hence the importance of allowing argument to proceed continuously and of allowing indefinite accumulation of experience with the possibility of refutation. With both of these, of each of which there is more chance in a democracy, the natural tendency of errors in public opinion about the public interest to be self-correcting can operate. 'In the case of the body *politic*, when motion ceases, the body dies' (*Parliamentary Reform*, III 450).

Notes

(a) The general project of the legislator was described in Chapter V, where reference was also made to the analysis of the idea in Burns 1967.

(b) Bentham was not completely hostile to appeals to the imagination and the use of non-verbal forms of communication. Apart from his own use of metaphors, he actually proposes use of symbols and pictures. The picture over the door of the panopticon is carefully considered and reasons mentioned 'for speaking to the eyes by respectable symbols' (*Penal Code, Traités* ii 306; LEGIS 279). For, as Bentham says, 'Speak to the eyes, if you wish to move the heart. The precept is as old as Horace' (*Penal Code, Traités* iii 71; LEGIS 399); or 'preach to the eye, if you would preach with efficacy. By that organ, through the medium of the imagination the judgement of the bulk of mankind may be led and moulded almost at pleasure' (RJE i 403). Here we get good uses of the tainted materials: however, they are tainted. All appeals to the imagination are suspicious, to be carefully controlled. Above all, Bentham attacks the use of sounds rather than sense, the 'harmony' (IPML 22n) which led lawyers to endorse famous maxims, the 'tyranny of sounds' (*Defence of Usury*, Stark i 169) which leads people not to analyse their ideas and so disagree with him.

(c) The idea that people might be deceived in their own interest on utilitarian principles presupposes the possibility of a paternalism which Bentham strongly resists; 'nor', he says, 'is any man now so far elevated above his fellows, as that he should be indulged in the dangerous licence of cheating them for their own good' (FG 441). Even the society of 1776, let alone the actual or proposed society of the 1820s, did not allow a sufficient separation between the manipulating elite and the manipulated others for this to have good results.

(d) On Bentham's attitude to women's suffrage, see the exchange between Terence Ball and Lea Campos Boralevi in *Bentham News Letter* 4 (Boralevi 1980; Ball 1980).

(e) It might be thought incorrect to take Bentham's democratic remarks in *Judicial Establishment* at face value in that he might be just guilding his thought with a democratic veneer in order to sell his favoured institutions, such as law reform or panopticon, to the new, democratic, French assembly. Bentham himself suggests caution in a letter thirty years later to Senor Mora (19 Sept 1820; Bl Add. Mss. 33,551 fo 3). However I do not think that this detracts from Bentham's own working out of such a position in the manuscripts, a position which in any case inevitably follows from the logic of his central positions, as he came to realise. Even in the letter to Mora, Bentham says that the election of judges (itself much more controversial than other democratic elections) was something that he had to presuppose for his plan to have a hearing; he was not prepared to say that he really disapproved of this rather extreme form of democracy.

IX

The Benthamite State

Whether set up by fraud, force, persuasion, accident, or otherwise, there still remains the question of which particular laws and institutions would be adopted in a Benthamite state. The mark of such a state is that its laws and institutions are determined by the principle of utility, that is by consideration of what would lead to the greatest happiness of the greatest number. However, it has not yet been considered which laws and institutions would do this. Furthermore, although there has been continuous discussion of utilitarianism since the time at which Bentham wrote, there has not been a consensus about what exactly a utilitarian moral or political theory would prescribe; this can be seen from the fact that examples which some people urge as objections are incorporated by others into the theory. So the specific content of Bentham's political thought cannot just be read off the fact that he is a utilitarian. Quite apart from his stand on particular issues, such as liberty, equality, justice, and so on, which will be considered in this chapter, it must also be determined how he lines up in terms of some of the traditional splits, or distinctions inside utilitarian theory, such as the conflict between act and rule utilitarianism.

The first characteristic of utilitarian thought in general, and Bentham's thought in particular, is that it proposes a monistic theory of value. There is only one ultimate end, and anything which is of value must therefore possess its value because of the way that it relates to this ultimate end. As Bentham put it in his early *Comment on the Commentaries*, 'the principle of utility once adopted as the governing principle, admits of no rival, admits not even of an associate' (COMM 27). So anything which is of value in the Benthamite state must acquire its value from the way that it contributes to the single end of happiness, that is increase of pleasure and reduction of pain. Whether this is indeed a single end, particularly since it is immediately explained in terms of both pleasures and also pains, was something considered in Chapter VI; however, whatever else it is, and however it is exactly identified, it can be said that this end is certain real states of mind. Whatever leads to these states of mind is good or bad; nothing else possesses value. So, in particular, something else which has been valued in traditional moral or political theory, such as acts or institutions of a particular kind, or the motivation behind actions, or character, is only really valuable on this theory because of the consequences which it may possess in leading to these particular states of mind. Good actions are those with good consequences, valued intentions are those that make people happy; a good character is one which increases the pleasure and diminishes the pain of the world; and so on. Furthermore, the distinction between positive and negative actions, that is from acting and refraining from action, which has been a central feature of particular moral or legal theories disappears: all that is important is the consequences in terms of happiness; whether the consequences are caused by action or inaction is irrelevant. On the other hand, all pleasure or happiness is good; there is no distinction inside pleasure or happiness between those pleasures which are worthwhile and those pleasures which are better avoided.

These are all general features of utilitarian thought, and they are all also features of Bentham's thought. He does not ignore any of the features just mentioned; on the contrary, the *Introduction* has substantial chapters on motives, intention, and human dispositions. The central point, however, is, as he puts it for motives, that 'with respect to goodness and badness, as it is with every thing else that is not itself either pain or pleasure, so is it with motives. If they are good or bad, it is only on account of their effects: good on account of their tendency to produce pleasure, or avert pain: bad, on account of their tendency to produce pain, or avert pleasure' (IPML 100). So, in both the *Introduction* and in the material incorporated in the *Traités*, he has an account of the same act being undertaken with varying motives to show how morally indifferent the motive is. On the other hand, even if these traditional bearers of value only acquire their value in a secondary way, via the consequences, this does not mean that many of the traditional distinctions cannot be preserved. Motives normally or traditionally shunned, such as vengeance or envy, may indeed be bad because such motives have bad consequences. Similarly, Bentham criticises the distinction between acting and refraining from action as incorporated in the (then and now) current law. Part of his proposed criminal code was that it would be the duty of people to save others if they could do so without serious harm to themselves. He thinks that anyone would agree that punishment would be appropriate for anyone just looking on at a woman with headdress on fire when there was water at hand (IPML 293n); and provisions are made for this in the sample of chapter one of the code on corporeal injuries reprinted as the appendix to the *Promulgation of Laws* (I 164). (In British or American law, unlike several Continental jurisdictions, there would be no such duty.) However, he himself talks quite happily in terms of a distinction between '*positive* and *negative*' acts, or acts of commission and acts of omission (IPML 75) and, more importantly, thinks that there is a 'difference of mischief' between them; this difference, again, can be explained in terms of consequences (*Nomography*, III 295). So, again, although his thought has a different basis than traditional thought, it maintains traditional distinctions, only now explained in a different way. This means that the failure to make a particular distinction can often not be appropriately cited as an objection to Bentham's thought.

The reason that utilitarian thought, at least as expressed by Bentham, can take over and relocate several traditional elements or distinctions depends upon Bentham's view of the nature of consequences. It has already been seen that the consequences important for value are narrowed to a single kind (or to a small set of kinds) which are states of the mind, and that of these, all pleasures are good and all pains bad. 'The pleasure of vengeance, considered abstractly, is, like any other pleasure, only good in itself' (*Penal Code, Traités* ii 359; LEGIS 309; I 383). So it would seem at first sight that Bentham has no room in his account of consequences to take over traditional distinctions; that unlike J.S. Mill who later distinguished between different qualities of pleasure in an evaluative way, Bentham is committed to a single, and rather primitive, kind of pleasure. No room seems to be left, for example, for a distinction between those 'higher' human pleasures and those 'lower' ones which are shared by animals. When considering in *Panopticon* how the arrangements might be applied to schools, Bentham considers the objection that they 'might not be constructing a set of *machines* under the similitude of *men*'. He waves the objection aside: 'call them soldiers, call them monks, call them machines: so they were but happy ones, I should not care' (IV 64). Happiness is all; it matters not whether it is the happiness of 'machines' or men. Similarly the concerns of morality and of the criminal law are explicitly extended to animals. The proposed penal code was to have a section on cruelty to animals, for, as Bentham put it, 'the question is not, Can they *reason*? nor, can they *talk*? but, can they suffer?' (IPML 283n). The rational animal, law-making member of a kingdom of ends, takes his place with the other animals; his godlike reason does not distinguish him. So, at least at first sight, there seems to be a great, or gross, simplification of consequences, which would not allow him to preserve the distinctions of traditional thought.

However, even if there are these kinds of simplification, there are also important distinctions made by Bentham with respect to consequences. To begin with, reduction of the final end to be valued to states of mind does not mean that only the states of mind which are actually felt or possessed by people are to be considered. It was seen in Chapter VI that people could make mistakes in calculation of their own interest, both in fact and also according to Bentham's thought. This means that Bentham draws a distinction between the real and the merely apparent value of a state of affairs. Its value is not just as it is felt to be. This was most conspicuous with respect to future value, where Bentham thought that in many cases people undervalued future states of affairs. This means that the value really possessed (now, at present) by a (now) future state of affairs is not necessarily given by the value it seems (now) to possess. So the present state of mind with respect to this future state of affairs does not give its real value. However, neither is its value necessarily given by future states of mind. For if some allowance for propinquity (some discounting for distance in time) is appropriate, as Bentham wanted, then the value of the state of affairs when future is less than its value will be when present. So its value now will not be correctly given by the value that certain future states of mind will possess. Hence at no stage is its value explicable in terms of the value of states of mind actually possessed by someone. If allowance for propinquity is inappropriate, as was suggested against Bentham in Chapter VI, then the point can be made in a similar way by considering certainty. Bentham thinks that an uncertain future state of affairs is of less value than it would be if certain; its intrinsic magnitude should be discounted by the probability of its occurrence. So, again, its value cannot be given by the value it would possess as a present state of mind, for then it would be certain. Nor can its value be given by the present effects of its anticipation, for there may be a mistake about its probability. Hence, again, its value cannot necessarily be explained

228

in terms of the states of mind actually possessed by anyone at
any time.

The important point here can be easily seen by considering
a distinction which Bentham himself draws, that between danger
and alarm. When considering various kinds of activities to see if
they might be fit subjects for punishment, that is for proscription
by the criminal law, Bentham frequently considers these two
kinds of consequences. They both form part of the 'secondary
mischief' of an action, that is of the consequences other than
the immediate ones. So, to take Bentham's example, if a man
robs someone, the victim himself suffers primary mischief, but
the robbery also affects others who thereby suffer secondary
mischief. Part of this secondary effect is caused by the report
of the robbery circulating in the neighbourhood. This may create
a 'pain of apprehension' in others, and this is what Bentham
calls 'alarm'. However, the fact of the robbery does not only
lead to apprehension but also really increases the chances of
others being robbed. This Bentham calls the 'danger'; 'danger
is nothing but the chance of pain' (IPML 144). Not just in this
example but also quite generally, Bentham holds that the two
secondary mischiefs 'are perfectly distinct' (IPML 147). This
means that part of the badness of an action, as measured by
its consequences, consists in something independent of how
these consequences actually appear to people. The danger is not
the same as the pain of apprehension and, even if there were no
alarm, things would be worse if there was an increase in danger.
That is, if there is an increased chance of future pain, then this is
a bad thing, even if everyone continues happy and unaware of it;
and it would still be a bad thing even if the chance were never
realised and the pain never in fact occurred. So even if people
were happy and unaware throughout, both before, during, and
after when the pain might have occurred, the situation would
have been worse than one in which there was no such chance
(and yet people were similarly happily unaware). So, for Bentham,
even if the final bearers of value are states of mind, the value of
a particular situation cannot be reduced to the feelings that are
actually had by people, to the particular states of mind which
actually occur. This means, at least as an objection to Bentham,
the recurring anti-utilitarian fantasy, by which it is supposed that
the position can be rendered absurd by imaging an 'experience
machine' which gave people the states of mind without anything
actually happening, needs to be handled with care. For at least
it is the case that as well as the experiences people actually do
have there has to be considered also the experiences they could

have; and these possible experiences are important quite independently of whether they know that they could have them, or are aware of the probabilities of doing so. Danger is danger even if people miscalculate the chances.

The other complexity in Bentham's account of consequences illustrated by the examples of danger and alarm is his concern that all the consequences be considered. The way in which some traditional distinctions are restored in a new way, at least for some of the time, depends upon going beyond the immediate consequences of an action to such further consequences. Secondary consequences are extremely important in Bentham's political thought, and he even considers a third order of effects (IPML 152n). This is because, since they include the effects caused by the way a particular action is viewed by other people, and the effects it has on a chance of reoccurrence, it tends to bring out the more general features of the particular action and abstract from its idiosyncratic features. Hence, for example, although the immediate effects of what is normally thought to be a bad motive may be better than the immediate effects of what someone does acting with what is normally thought to be a good motive, this will not necessarily mean that Bentham's account will make the former action better than the latter. For, once the secondary consequences are taken into account, then the alarm caused by someone being perceived to operate with a 'bad' motive will be greater; and the real chance, 'danger', of this person really doing something bad in future will also be greater (if it is a 'bad' motive as measured by its normal consequences, then continuing to act under its influence will have bad consequences in the long run). So, once the secondary mischief is considered, the conclusion which would be reached merely after examination of the primary mischief is overturned; the lucky result was fortuitous, normally a case exhibiting those features would have bad consequences, and this gets picked up, even for this particular case, once secondary consequences are considered. Examples could be given by which all the distinctions given above, and others, are restored by consideration of secondary consequences. Bentham, for example, in the *Introduction* chapter on intentions has a complex and sophisticated account which distinguishes between 'direct' 'indirect' intentions, and so on. This account is not a mere piece of psychology but can legitimately found moral and judicial distinctions. For although the primary consequences of someone's being killed are the same, whether it was done by accident; whether not primarily intended but with awareness of the risk; or whether by direct intention, the secondary consequences in terms of alarm and danger are clearly different.

A one in a million chance will not produce alarm or increase danger; whereas a direct killing may, if known, produce alarm and in any case (as in *Macbeth*) increases the danger of others. It is by means of secondary consequences that Bentham makes the distinction noted above in moral status between acting and refraining from action. 'As to the difference between the mischief of the one and of the other,' he says, 'it consists altogether of the mischief of the second order . . . in the case of the negative offence, the mischief of the second order – the alarm and the danger – is next to nothing' (*Nomography*, III 295). Perhaps these examples are sufficient to show how Bentham can use this more extended account of consequences in order to restore some traditional distinctions (as operative at least some of the time in a morally important way). It means that those counter-examples to utilitarianism which depend upon inventing some unlikely conjunction of circumstances in which following the normal rules of behaviour would have less good consequences than departing from them need to be handled with care. It is not that Bentham would not say that in such a situation that departure was required; it is just that all the consequences have to be considered to see if the invented case really is of this kind. When these consequences include danger and alarm, these features are liable to iron out the eccentricities of the particular invented example and make it no longer an example of achieving better consequences by departing from the normal rules.

The possibility of mistake in considering propinquity and certainty described above means that people cannot even be allowed to be infallible judges of their own interest; even though it can be supposed that they will normally try to maximise their interest, it does not follow that they will necessarily succeed in doing so. This means that even if the only duty placed on the Benthamite legislator was the maximisation of everyone's interest, the best way of doing this would not necessarily be to leave people to get on with it. Taking propinquity, for example, the dispassionate contemplation of states of affairs irrespective of the time at which they occur may give the legislator a reason for promoting savings rather than just leaving everyone to value their own futures for themselves. The legislator, occupying a point of view which is more independent of the particular point of view of the person concerned, may see better what is in the interest of that person across time (from all the points of view which he will occupy, taken together). So, even if maximisation of self-interest were all that was in question, there would be a point in having such an external observer or calculator. However, as was seen in Chapter

VIII, the position adopted by the legislator promoting the greatest happiness of the greatest number is external, dispassionate, or from no point of view, in a more important sense in that he is not just concerned to maximise an individual's interest but, rather, to maximise everyone's interest. This means that he must act independently from any person's particular point of view. As well as the features which make up the value of a particular action or state of affairs for an individual, such as intensity, duration, propinquity, certainty, he also has to consider how it affects all the individuals with whom he is concerned. He has, as Bentham, puts it in the Value chapter of the *Introduction* to consider the 'extent' of the consequences of proposed actions, 'that is, the number of persons to whom it *extends*; or (in other words) who are affected by it' (IPML 39). As well as assessing a situation from a point of view, he has to consider how it appears from all points of view, considering them equally. He corrects the individual's desires to see that they promote the real interests of that individual, and then places the real interests of each individual in the context of all other individuals, considering them all equally or dispassionately, so as to determine what is the course which leads to the greatest happiness of the greatest number.

It might be supposed that once the real interests of individuals had been determined, there would be no further need for consideration of extent, or for the balancing of one interest against another. This, however, would only be the case if there were a natural harmony of interests, so that the greatest interest of all was also in the greatest interest of each. There is no reason, however, why this should be so, and normally it is not so. The point of the Benthamite project, as outlined in Chapter V, is to achieve an artificial identity between the interests of each individual and the interests of all the individuals. Even though it was supposed that the utility principle, in Chapter VII, was something on which separate individuals might converge in a free process of continuous argument, this was not because it was supposed that it was a solution which would satisfy all of their interests (a sort of co-operative game which they would all benefit from playing). On the contrary, the convergence was only achieved by each person departing from his own point of view and treating it as equal to others. So, to put it another way, the greatest happiness of the greatest number is not the sum of a whole set of individual greatest happinesses; what is in the interests of all is not necessarily in the interests of each. What the legislator does cannot be explained, or justified, by saying to each individual that it is in his interest. This, after all, was why the project had to operate with two principles, a normative one saying what ought to happen and a psychological one saying what would happen. If what was in the interests of all, and hence should be promoted according to the normative principle, was also in the interests of each, and hence (given suitable enlightenment and correction) would be promoted according to the psychological principle, then two principles would not be required.

The greatest happiness, or the greatest happiness of the greatest number, therefore (to use two formulations which Bentham constantly uses in his later work) is not the same thing as the greatest happiness of everyone. The happiness of some individuals (except in lucky and special circumstances) has to be sacrificed for the sake of the greater happiness of other individuals. The few, the minority, has to be sacrificed to the many, the majority. Hence the constant use of the formula, the greatest happiness of the greatest number. On the face of it, this seems to require the impossible task of maximising two things without providing any information about the trade off between them. (In fact, John Burton, says it was because Bentham noticed this that he contracted the formula to 'the greatest happiness' (I 18); however, Bentham continues to use the longer formulation fairly extensively throughout the later work.) The point of the formula is that the many have precedence. Best of all would be if it was the happiness of all; if this is impossible then the few should be sacrificed to the many. Hence the efficacy of democracy for its promotion as compared with rule of 'the few'; but it is democracy (rule of the majority) rather than unanimity (rule of all) that is required. The 'rule' in 'case of collision and contest' is to 'prefer the happiness of the greater to that of the lesser number' (PANN, III 211). That utilitarianism demands the sacrifice of some people for the sake of others has been one of the continuing objections to it, but in this respect at least, Bentham is sufficiently clearly a utilitarian for the objection to apply (if it is an objection) to him as well. At the start of the *Constitutional Code* he says that the 'happiness of every individual is liable to come into competition with the happiness of every other ... hence it is, that to serve for all occasions, instead of saying the greatest happiness of all, it becomes necessary to use the expression, the greatest happiness of the greatest number' (IX 6). The inaugural declaration by the legislator proposed in the same code requires that he recognise as the only end of government the greatest happiness 'of all without exception, in so far as possible: of the greatest number on every occasion on which the nature of the case renders it impossible, by rendering it matter of necessity to make sacrifice of a portion of the happiness of a few, to the greater happiness of the rest' (IX 199). Sitting interests, rights, or expectations, are not therefore allowed to stand in the way of a reform which would increase the amount of happiness, even if these interests have to be sacrificed in the process: 'no such detriment to particular interests, — number of persons interested and value of their respective interests taken into account, — can afford a preponderant reason for putting a negative upon the proposed system of reform' (*Equity Dispatch Court Bill*, III 325).

That Bentham quite clearly realised that his leading principle involved the possible sacrifice of some for the sake of others, even if it may leave him open to objections, means that he does not need to get involved in the sort of proof that Mill looked as if he later suggested as saying that because each person sought his own happiness, so everyone sought the happiness of all. For Bentham there will sometimes be conflict between what the individual wants and what he ought to do, as determined by the greatest happiness principle. Hence the need for criminal law, and for punishment, to make it in the individual's interest to do things he would not naturally wish to do. So, for Bentham, punishment is not justified to the individual as being really in his own interest ('we're only doing this for your own good . . .'); rather, it is recognised that the individual has no interest in being punished at all. What justifies punishment is the sacrifice of a few individuals for the greater good of others. Punishment deters others from performing particular kinds of actions, and so promotes the greater happiness. The happiness of the person punished is considered equally with the others, it is just that 'it is necessary to the greatest happiness of the greatest number, that a portion of the happiness of that one be sacrificed' (*Codification Proposal*, IV 540). It does not imply any particular moral condemnation; it is a form of surgery performed, sacrificing a part for the sake of the rest: 'no man *deserves* punishment. When a surgeon cuts into a limb, is it because the patient has *deserved* the smart? No: but that the limb may be healed' (*Parliamentary Reform*, III 533). Because it is against the person punished's interests 'all punishment is mischief: all punishment in itself is evil' (IPML 158). That is, in its immediate effects. However, since (when correctly applied) it leads to the greater good, then, once second order effects are considered, it ceases to be an evil: 'a punishment produces an *evil* of the *first order*, and a *good* of the *second order*' (**Punishment*, 18). Things would be even better if the good could be got without the evil, that is if people thought that others were being punished for performing particular kinds of activities, and so deterred, yet no one was really being punished for them; 'it is the apparent punishment, therefore, that does all the service' (IPML 179); 'it is the real punishment that is the expense – the apparent punishment that gives the profit' (*Punishment*, 28). So it would seem that the best penal institution, on Benthamite principles, was a formidable looking prison from the interior of which horrendous groans emerged from time to time and yet which in fact had no one inside. However, as was seen in the last chapter, such a divergence between what seems to happen and what actually happens is unstable; the use of fallacy or illusion to promote the Benthamite end is counter-productive. So the best, that is the easiest, surest, cheapest, way of achieving the appearance of punishment, is by having the real thing. Instead of the prison with mysterious groans we have the panopticon which was open to the whole public, which Bentham indeed expected to be a spectacle, and in which exactly what was happening to anyone could be closely observed. Not only the device carved above its door but also the real sight of people suffering would deter others from risking a similar fate. Therefore the second order goods should be purchased with first order evil, and the few sacrificed, or punished, for the sake of the many.

Another problem of justification which occurs on some forms of thought similar to utilitarianism and which Bentham himself avoids is that of the free-rider, the person who takes advantage of institutionalised practices but does not contribute, even though he recognises that if everyone behaved like him, the institution he takes advantage of would not exist (as, for example, riding on a train without paying the fare). Just as he does not need to show the person being punished that it is really in his interest to be punished, so he does not need to show the free-rider that it is really in his interest to pay the fare. Hence he again avoids formidable, or impossible, problems of justification. The 'protection granted me against other men for my horses is no motive with me for not meddling with [a] man's horse', he says, 'because whether I steal it or no, another man will be hanged all the same for stealing mine' (COMM 74), or, in other words, I still get the benefits of there being this particular law, whether or not I observe it myself. Of course, Bentham can provide justification for not free-riding. This, however, will be done by the kind of argument advanced in Chapter VII in support of the principle of utility. It will, for example, be provided by asking the free-rider in terms of which principle, or reason, he would justify his actions, and, if there is no principle, or reason, which he holds applies equally to himself and others, whether he is not merely despotical, or acting from caprice. However, this is essentially to appeal, as was seen, to a form of reason which does not start from self-interest, and which asks people to consider their own interests as being no different from others. With such a form of reasoning, or justification, a person might indeed see that it was right to sacrifice his own immediate interest for the greater interest of people taken as a whole, and so give up free-riding. This, however, would be exactly what he would be doing: making a sacrifice. Hence Bentham can avoid those forms of justification which attempt to show that no sacrifice is involved.

Two cases have just been examined in which Bentham's preparedness to sacrifice the interests of some for the sake of others means that he has less problems of justification than some rival theories. The fact remains, however, that the sacrifice of anyone for the sake of others is strongly held by many to be the mark of an improper moral or political theory. On the contrary, it is supposed, every individual must be held to be sacred, as a lawmaker, as an end in himself, and it is not permitted to do things to him merely for the sake of others. Or alternatively, an appropriate way of deciding on the basic political structure or institutions of a country might be thought to be by finding which ones self-interested people would choose if they were ignorant about which positions they would be occupying in the society so chosen, the method adopted in John Rawls's *Theory of Justice*. If, furthermore, it is assumed (as Rawls does) that they are cautious, self-protective, people, people who desire to minimise the worst that could happen to them, then they would choose a system in which a certain minimum standard of rights or public goods would be possessed at every position, and which could not be sacrificed for the sake of any amount of greater good to the majority. Against the maximising and sacrificing tendencies of a utilitarian approach stands the bulwark of the rights of individuals, absolute and inalienable. As another leading work of recent political theory starts, 'individuals have rights, and there are things no person or group may do to them (without violating their rights)' (Nozick 1974 ix). Not surprisingly, both these recent leading treatments of the subject argue against utilitarianism; and Bentham has just been seen to be sufficiently clearly in favour of the sacrifice of some for the sake of others for these arguments also to apply against him.

As was seen in Chapter IV, any rights which appear in Benthamite theory will not be natural rights but legal rights. Rights are not prior to the law, framing or constraining it, but are children of the law. As children of the law they are justified, as anything else in the law, in terms of utility. So the Benthamite theory of rights will allow individuals to have rights; but this will be made sense of analytically in terms of the duties which the law imposes on others, and justified because such duties lead to the greatest happiness of the greatest number. The benefits secured by such laws, such as security, control of property, immunity from assault, and so on, will be benefits in the general interest (which lead to the greatest happiness of the greatest number). However, even if rights might have a different source or justification in utilitarian theory, the question arises again whether Bentham might not still be able to make the same distinctions, and defend the same positions as a user of a theory of rights in a more traditional manner can. Might it not, that is, turn out that it promoted the greatest happiness of the greatest number that individuals have rights and that there are things which no other person or group may do to them. It was seen above how consideration of secondary mischief, of danger and alarm, could damp down the idiosyncratic elements of individual cases and lead to their being treated in more general terms, and that this had the effect of preserving more traditional distinctions. It must now be seen whether rights might not similarly be preserved in Benthamite theory and, more generally and abstractly, whether Bentham is not really some kind of rule utilitarian. The distinction between a rule and an act utilitarian is that the former uses the principle of utility in order to justify certain rules of conduct, which are then applied inflexibly without any subsequent calculations, whereas the latter can, at least in principle, calculate the utility of any particular act; all his rules are merely *prima facie* and can be dispensed with in any particular case. The distinction comes from the later development of utilitarian theory, but is useful in asking the question of how Bentham meant his theory to operate. In particular, if he is some kind of rule utilitarian, then it can be seen how he could have an absolute, indefeasible, account of rights. For what rights there should be would be decided by the principle of utility, and then these rights would be inflexibly protected without any consideration of the consequences of so doing in particular cases. Indeed, or so it might be thought, it should follow immediately from the fact that he is trying to decide on the content of the best possible system of laws that he must be a rule utilitarian. For what laws are are rules, and so it would seem that what Bentham must be doing in saying what laws there ought to be is saying what rules there ought to be.

If by rights are meant absolute, indefeasible, rights then it is clear that most, if not all, of the rights produced by Benthamite theory are not like this. For it follows from his view that rights are benefits derived from duties laid on people, that there are very many rights in a complete code of law. Furthermore, as was seen in Chapter IV, many of these rights will be rights to positive assistance from others, not just rights to be left alone by others. For both these reasons, rights are liable to conflict; that is, they must be regarded as being *prima facie* rather than absolute, defeasible rather than indefeasible. For example, the woman with her headdress on fire who has a right to assistance from others means that these others to that extent must forfeit their liberty rights of spending their time, or moving their bodies, as they wish. However, although such conflicts mean that rights cannot be considered to be inalienable, they can still be considered as incorporating some kind of rule which is not to be set aside in particular cases. For rules can be laid down which create a hierarchy of such rights and determine which right has superiority in cases of conflict. Furthermore, many of the rights which arise in a derivative manner in the Benthamite system of law, being created by duties laid on others, are similar to the rights which are adopted by those systems which principally value rights and treat them as primitive. In both cases the protection granted to people by law, allowing them control of their own persons and property, is similar. Indeed it is not clear that some of the standard examples quoted in which utilitarianism would permit invasion of people's basic rights would actually be permitted in Bentham's philosophy. For example, to take two well known cases, both the judicial execution of the innocent, and a transplant hospital which seized passers by on the street outside in order to cut up their bodies and transplant vital organs into its patients, would cause great alarm and increase danger. The alarm would only come about if the practices were known to be what they were; but keeping such practices secret would be almost impossible. As seen above, in such cases secrecy or delusion is unstable. So even if such acts had primary benefits, these would be outweighed by the secondary mischiefs. In the former case, the immediate benefit of the execution might be the mollification of a superior power; in the latter case, perhaps five or six lives are preserved at the cost of one death. However, in both cases it is clear exactly why such practices would cause great alarm when known, namely that there is nothing which any particular citizen can do to ensure that he is not the next victim. The point of a utilitarian society is that people get the chance of ordering their own affairs, and so maximising their utilities, by being able to predict the consequences of actions. This was the reason, as was seen in Chapter II, for the law being knowable by those to whom it applied, and why there should not be *ex post facto* legislation. Yet, if at any stage, whatever he did, any citizen was liable to be tried in a court of law and executed, or liable to be cut up in a hospital, then there is nothing which he could do to prevent such calamity. So such procedures would create alarm, and hence would have no place in a Benthamite society. Here rights form a protection preventing the sacrifice of the individual for the sake of others, just as in rights theories. The basis, however, is importantly different. The decision against sacrifice, arising from considering the secondary mischiefs of such an action, can still be based on calculation of all the consequences of any particular case. Not only does it not start with rights as primitive, it does not even necessarily have to treat them as derived rules, which are inflexibly obeyed.

The benefit, or utility, which comes from such laws comes, however, in part from being able to rely on them. Alarm is diminished because it is predicted that doctors will not rush out of hospitals and seize the first person on the street to cut up, which, in turn, is predictable, because the law declares that it will punish anyone so doing. The reduction in alarm and danger will only occur if such predictions can be relied on; that is if it is the case that the law actually will punish. So the benefits will only be derived from punishment if it is applied fairly inflexibly. Similarly, the benefits gained from promises of reward will only occur if the rewards are made when the time comes. (In both cases, of course, in exceptional cases it would be possible to get the desired effect without performing the threatened punishment or reward, but this would necessarily only be possible in special cases, and could not work in the long run.) Furthermore, the benefit gained from particular institutions created by the law, such as contracts or wills, only arises if the law is fairly inflexible in its operation. The whole point of using the legally created device of a contract or a will is as an instrument in executing a particular desire, and it will not be possible to execute the desire if the instrument breaks or bends; it is only if it is thought to be a reliable instrument that it will be used at all. 'It is for the advantage of all', says Bentham, as edited by Dumont, 'that the promises of every individual should be faithfully observed. There would no longer be any security among men, no commerce, no confidence; — it would be necessary to go back to the woods, if engagements did not possess an obligatory force' (*Traités*, i 131; LEGIS 82). The context of this remark is to promote utility as against original contract, by showing that contracts depend upon utility. However, given (in Bentham's thought) that they do depend upon utility, what does so depend is a legal artifact or institution which gets its point from the fact that it operates in an inexorable and binding manner. Only knowing that engagements can be relied on, thinks Bentham, has man been able to get out of the primeval forest into the clearings of civilisation; certainly only knowing that contracts are enforceable at law has enabled the growth of an individualistic, capitalistic, society. The justification here does seem to be in two steps similar to rule utilitarianism: I am bound by my contracts just because I made them; it is a good thing to have such an institution as (binding) contract because, by safe-guarding expectations, it maximises utility.

These examples, and Bentham's treatment of more traditional rights such as liberty and property considered later in this chapter, give a rather mixed result to the question of whether Bentham was a rule utilitarian. However, the inflexibility with which some-thing should be applied can itself be taken as a question of utility, calculable if necessary in particular cases. And, in general, although expectations, just like alarm, will tend to lead to actions being considered in general categories, it is always possible to go behind the rules to their rationale. Where the generalisation comes in is with knowledge. The knowledge, the calculation, which Bentham requires is 'calculation founded upon matter of fact: future con-tingent utility founded upon past utility experienced' (COMM 199). Such knowledge is, in its nature, general. It depends upon classifying past experience as being experience of certain general kinds of event, action, or state of affairs, and then using this knowledge and its general correlations with pleasure and pain as a means of predicting the likely pleasure or pain arising from possible future events, actions, or states of affairs. Without the classification, or generalisation, the knowledge would be impos-sible. Hence the calculation of utilities in Bentham's thought, however much he is thought of as an act utilitarian, assessing the consequences of every particular event, depends upon generalisa-tion. Individuals are treated as members of types, and hence the results achieved are similar to how they would be by way of rules. Even if the rules are not treated as inflexible standards operating as intermediaries between the principle of utility and particular actions, there will still be generalisations of knowledge, formulable as rules, which are needed to derive the results in particular cases. Furthermore, calculation in every case would clearly be impossible, and Bentham never supposed otherwise ('it is not to be expected that this process should be strictly pursued previously to every moral judgement, or to every legis-lative or judicial operation' (IPML 40)). So, in many cases these derived generalisations are all that there will be. Hence in many, or most cases, it will be desirable to have a rule, a 'mark to steer by' (*Defence of a Maximum*, Stark iii 260). However, the rules are not an essential or ineliminable part of the moral or political theory itself; they are merely involved in its practical application. The principle of utility must conform to itself, must be a usable principle arriving at its results (as Bentham wished the law to) with the minimum of 'vexation, expence, and delay'. So time should not be wasted on calculation or observation; already arrived at knowledge should be pressed into service. On the other hand, this knowledge is always open to refutation or amendment on the basis of further experience; just like the Benthamite state itself, the knowledge on which it is based is open to the future. So the spirit of Bentham's thought is the spirit of act utilitarianism, even if many of the procedures and results involved in it are the same as those which would be adopted, or be produced, if it were rule utilitarian.

This act utilitarian spirit is, perhaps surprisingly, also true of Bentham's work specifically on law. It is true that law incorporates rules and true, furthermore, that Bentham wished to take legislation out of the hands of the judges and make all law statute law in properly codified and comprehensible acts of parliament. These codified laws would indeed lay down rules of behaviour to be enforced by the judges. Rules are such that they apply to everyone fulfilling a particular description: 'it is in the power of making men act by *class*, that the strength of government consists' (**General View*, III 197); 'the mode in which the will of a legislator is expressed is by *rules*' (RJE iv 5). However, even in the properly codified and statutorily imposed system of rules, the actual application of them to individuals is still by means of judges exercising judicial discretion. Nor is this just something inevitable in any system of law. On the contrary, Bentham thought that the judge should sometimes exercise his own judgement in calculating the particular merits of the instant case. He should, that is, apply directly to the principle of utility, rather than applying rules which someone else has worked out on the basis of the principle of utility. Bentham wanted a 'mental' rather than a 'mechanical' procedure; that is that 'of each individual case, of each individual person concerned, the circumstances would be looked to' (*Justice and Codification Petitions*, V 525). The individual discretion left to the judge is clearest in what Bentham called adjective law, that is with the forms of procedure and the use of evidence. The rules of procedure are 'practical general rules' which should never be 'inflexible' (*Procedure*, II 28; 31). In evidence, where the chief question which Bentham considers in his enormous work is the exclusion of evidence, then, as he says on the topic of the calling of witnesses: 'in each individual instance, to weigh mischief on one side against mischief on the other . . . will be a task suitable for a judge' (RJE iv 480). However, even in the more substantial business of the application of the law, or sentencing, Bentham allows individual discretion. Among the cases he lists where punishment is unprofitable, he not only excludes kinds of cases but also individual cases where 'occasional circumstances' mean that in that instance the first order evil of punishment would outweigh the second order good (IPML 163); being consideration of an individual case, such a decision could only be undertaken by a judge. The actual amount of punishment he clearly indicates should be calculated according to the individual circumstances of the person being punished (IPML 169). So, as Bentham says, it is the question of the 'stocks of Pain and Pleasure' which is the 'question . . . which a Judge ought to put to him[self] upon the occasion of every fresh case' (COMM 199). Even in the application of rules of law the spirit is act utilitarian.

This also makes sense of a puzzling feature about Bentham's thought, noted in passing in Chapter VI. This is that, although he officially promotes the idea of a single scale of value, and the idea of calculating where anything falls on that scale, in practice he often draws up lists of the many qualities which are desirable or undesirable without any clear indication of how they should be traded off against each other. Thus, in the *Introduction*, and more extensively in *Punishment*, the qualities of various kinds of punishments and the properties desirable in punishment are listed without much attempt to say how the desirable properties might be compared, or traded off against one another. Similarly, desirable properties with respect to procedure and evidence are listed. If, however, the judge makes the final decision on the instant case, this now becomes a comprehensible procedure. Instead of laying down rules which the judge should mechanically follow, what Bentham is providing is a list of the factors which should be taken into consideration. Past experience has shown that these are the features which are important from the standpoint of utility, but how they should apply in the particular case is left up to individual decision. Again it is the case that what is provided is knowledge, generalisations based on past experience, which can be of great help, but need not be completely conclusive when deciding on particular cases. Many things can be seen clearly to have bad effects, and it can be explained why (in terms of the judges' self-interest) they arose and were preserved. So, as far as things can be handled in general terms, these things should be eliminated. However there is still a considerable budget of features which on the whole are normally bad (have bad consequences) and on the whole are normally good (have good consequences). These can be listed, and their probable effects noted. This draws it to the judges' attention (on the assumption that they all have time for a quick browse through the million words of even J.S. Mill's condensed version of the *Evidence*), but what the judge does after giving it his attention is in the end up to his power of individual calculation, discernment, and discretion. 'Discernment, or the art of judging of individual capacity, is a rare quality, whose use it is impossible to supersede by general rules' (*Reward*, 13).

So although there are features of both rule and act utilitarianism in Bentham, in the end access to individual judgement and decision of individual cases is not prevented by the imposition of rules which have to be followed inexorably or mechanically. Even in a case like contract, where Bentham seems firmest on inflexibility, he is prepared to say (and this is at the same time as the above remark, only now edited by himself):

> that contracts in general ought to be observed, is a rule, the propriety of which, no man was ever yet found wrong-headed enough to deny: if this case [i.e. the example he is discussing] is one of the exceptions (for some doubtless there are) which the safety and welfare of every society require should be taken out of that general rule, in this case, as in all those others, it lies upon him, who alledges the necessity of the exception, to produce a reason for it. (*Defence of Usury*, Stark i 129-30)

In other words, although, as seen, a rule that contracts be observed has a clear utility, it still allows of exceptions. It is not completely inflexible. The question of justification, as was also seen, involves knowledge, which depends upon generalisation. If this knowledge shows a certain kind of thing to be generally good, then not just for this case but also for all others, this means that it is right to depend upon the generalisations, or knowledge, until it is shown that a particular case is special. Hence the onus of proof is correctly put by Bentham on someone wishing to depart from the general rule. However, this is what the study produces: generalisation; and in the consideration of particular rights which follows it should be remembered that Bentham's remarks with respect to such things as security, property, liberty, equality, and so on are generalisations. It would be wrong to treat them as absolute rules. Even if working with rights, such broad descriptions tend to be at too high a level, not even generalisations but more like generalisations of generalisations. 'A right itself must be specifically described, not jumbled with an indistinguishable heap of others under any such vague general terms as property, liberty, and the like' (*Anarchical Fallacies*, Parekh 270).

With this proviso in mind, let us turn now to consideration of such general features, the basic material of political theory and political rhetoric, and see how they would fare in a Benthamite state. For, the odd objection to generalisation aside, Bentham himself was quite prepared to generalise and to use such terms. Indeed, as part of his noted propensity for drawing up lists of desirable features in any area, with respect to the whole of the utilitarian state itself he had a standard list of such desirable features. He drew this up in his 1780s manuscripts and maintained it consistently thereafter. This was a list of what he called 'subordinate ends', that is, of the properties to be aimed at as a means of achieving the single primary end of the utilitarian state, the greatest happiness of the greatest number. As they are listed in the *Civil Code* they are 'subsistence, abundance, equality, security', Bentham adding immediately that 'the more perfect enjoyment is in all these respects, the greater is the sum of social happiness: and especially of that happiness which depends upon the laws' (*Traités* ii 6; LEGIS 96; I 302). The same list appears at the start of the *Pannomial Fragments* (*III 211) and (substantially) in the *Institute of Political Economy* (Stark iii 307). It provides the framework for consideration of the ends separately which follows in the text of the *Civil Code*, summing up the 1780s manuscripts, showing how these subordinate ends promote happiness and how they may be achieved or promoted by means of law (how aiming at these enables the fabric of felicity to be constructed by the hands of reason and of law). With the points made above about generalisation, it is not too important to worry about the objection that the ends might conflict or that pursuing one of these ends might on a particular occasion detract from the over-all end of maximising utility. In any case, unlike with some of his other lists, Bentham on this occasion himself provides material which enables the ends to be ranked (although such ranking is itself, of course, only a further generalisation). Security and subsistence, he says, are clearly prior to abundance and equality: 'without security, equality could not last a day; without subsistence, abundance could not exist at all' (*Traités* ii 9; LEGIS 98; I 303). The relation is then complicated by the fact that the law can do much more for security than it can do for subsistence. This means that, at least from the point of view of the law, security is prior: 'in legislation, the most important object is security' (ibid.). However, clearly, as Bentham's poor law proposals reveal, the law can do something about subsistence; and Bentham is also clear that, in itself, subsistence is 'the first [and] the most important' of the 'four goals' (UC 32.129); the most important of the 'modifications' of 'well-being' (*Institute of Political Economy*, Stark iii 324). Bentham's normal view is that it is just because subsistence is the most important end, it is the one which demands least attention from the legislator (UC 32.129). Everyone so obviously aims at the means of life as a means to happiness, that the end needs no promotion by the legislator; if the legislator helps it is by promoting other ends such as security which, by securing to the labourer the fruits of his labour, helps to ensure his subsistence (*Civil Code, Traités* ii 14; LEGIS 100; I 304).

At first sight it might seem strange that equality appears on this list of subordinate ends at all, equality being exactly the kind of political end proposed by those opposed to maximisation of utility, and which is based upon exactly the kind of justification of which Bentham disapproved, such as a natural sense of fairness or justice. It was, after all, written clearly into the French Declaration of the rights of man, and it has been seen how Bentham disapproved of this Declaration; not just for its mention of rights but also for the actual content of those rights. It is a common assumption that the provision of incentives for the individual accumulation of wealth, and hence the possibility of inequality, leads to a greater total accumulation of wealth and hence (it is supposed) greater total happiness; an assumption, that is, that abundance (which seems to be a natural utilitarian end) is incompatible with equality (which therefore seems not to be so). However, in the actual derivation of equality from utilitarian principles (which was, of course, undertaken before the French Revolution but was repeated happily enough after it) none of these potential difficulties weighed with Bentham. This is because he supposed that he could demonstrate that, people being as they are, equality led to greater happiness. Nor is this just because he invoked some *ad hoc* specific psychological state, such as resentment at, or dislike of, inequality, which would produce this result automatically or trivially. Rather, Bentham thinks that the fact that equality leads to greater happiness can be shown as a necessary and direct consequence of the quite general principles of psychology as they were laid down in Chapter VI. The axioms of mental pathology form an adequate basis for derivation of the theorem, or proposition, that equality leads to greater happiness; that 'the nearer the actual proportion approaches to equality, the greater will be

245

the total mass of happiness' (*Civil Code, Traités* ii 20; LEGIS 104; I 305; after the manuscript which says, 'the nearer the actual distribution approaches equality, the greater will be the total mass of happiness', UC 32.5).

This result follows for Bentham because of his belief in the diminishing marginal utility of wealth or other goods, as was described in Chapter VI. As he observes here just before the above remark (both in manuscript and text), 'the excess in happiness of the richer will not be as great as the excess of his wealth'; an extra pound given to a rich man does not increase his happiness as much as an extra pound given to a poor man. So, if we have an additional sum of money to distribute, more happiness will be added by giving it to the poorer people. Similarly, if we have to take away a specific sum of money, less happiness will be removed if it is taken from the richer people. So, in both cases, happiness will be maximised by a procedure which tends to make people more equal in their wealth. This is all quite specifically and carefully worked out by Bentham and forms a good example of how he can achieve the same result as different theories from a quite different basis. His argument here shows that, *ceteris paribus*, equal distribution of goods or wealth in a society is a good thing. This result would hold on other views as an unargued premise, or as a mere datum of intuition. Here, or at least according to Bentham, it is established on the basis of observation of facts, which show that equality is an appropriate means (or subordinate end) of someone seeking the overall end of maximising utility. Knowledge, psychology, show that, as a matter of fact, equality leads to happiness. Furthermore, because it is a derived result, it can be shown in what ways promoting equality will lead to the overall end and in what ways it will not; that is, when the *ceteris paribus* clause applies and when it does not. Instead of a commitment to equality, liberty, and various other goals as immediate and non-comparable data of intuition, in Bentham's theory it is possible to compare them and decide which to follow in cases of conflict. It is only a generalisation that equality promotes happiness, and attention to particular cases or other factors can tell when it is or isn't so.

The equality considered in this treatment is equality of wealth, but there are many other substantive uses of equality on political theory, such as equality of treatment, respect, or opportunity, which neither imply nor are implied by equality of wealth. Yet the basic idea used to support them, a root idea of fairness, is that which can also be used to support equality of wealth. So it might seem at first sight that Bentham only covers part of the whole topic of equality. However, one basis which can lead to some of these results also does hold in Bentham, and this is the equality which comes from the use of reason itself. The concept of a reason is a general concept, so if something is a reason for something, then anything sufficiently similar to the former thing will also be a reason for something similar to the latter thing; if the situation being of a certain kind gives me a reason to act in a particular way, then any other situation similar in the relevant respects will give me a reason for acting in the same way. So, if someone possessing certain properties is a reason for treating him in a particular way, then there is a reason for treating everyone else with the same properties in the same way. Hence, if I am rational, I should treat these people in the same way, that is, equally. So a particular kind of equality follows purely formally from the concept of acting rationally. Yet, as was seen in Chapter VII, Bentham wants to base his ground principle of utility upon the idea of rational action and of rational morality: it is because reasons are required that utility is superior. So, committed as he is to the production of reasons for action, Bentham is also committed to the kind of equality which follows formally from the use of such reasons, that is to a kind of equality of treatment or respect. Nor is this just a theoretical derivation of what his position commits him to. His actual practice in argument gives several examples of the use of this kind of consideration. As was seen in the last chapter, part of Bentham's argument for the extension of franchise was that if it be right that any one person should have the vote, 'then how can it be otherwise than right, in the instance of any one *other* such person' (*Parliamentary Reform*, III 452). The best way of making sense of this in accord with Bentham's principles is that it follows from consideration of reasons: any reason which makes it right for one person to have the vote will make it right for anyone else (*ceteris paribus*, that is, unless there are stronger reasons against in a particular case). Otherwise it is an unsupported and uncharacteristic brute appeal to equality. However it is for this case, the principle of equal reasons providing equal results must and does come into Bentham's treatment of his basic ingredient, that is, happiness itself. One bit of happiness will form the same reason for action as any other bit of the same size. Hence 'on what ground . . . can any one man's happiness be shown to have any stronger or less strong claim to regard than others?' (*Codification Proposal*, IV 540). If happiness, or interest, forms a reason for action, then calculations must be made 'one man's interest weighing neither more nor less than another's' (**Reward*, 49). So, even in Bentham, equality has to, and does, enter in on other ways than based on the ground principle of utility; however, this is because he conceives of utility itself as being the result of following rational processes, and reason itself provides equality of a kind.

These merely formal stipulations, requiring that the same kind of case be treated in the same kind of way, and which can be eluded by saying that any actually considered case is different, are relatively uncontentious. It is when equality of goods or property is considered, equality of result, that disagreement becomes sharper; and it is in this area that Bentham provides his diminishing marginal utility argument. This does not mean, however, that he thinks that there should be forced appropriation of people's property in order to promote such equality of goods. His resistance to such a conclusion is, not surprisingly, sharper and more firmly expressed when he was writing at a time when (as he saw it) the French Revolutionaries had done exactly this. At this time he wrote the manuscripts reprinted in Bowring as the 'levelling system' and the *Anarchical Fallacies*. Noting, relatively mildly, that there is 'reasonable doubt, whether . . . the smack-smooth equality, which rolls so glibly out of the lips of the rhetorician, be altogether compatible with that undeviating conformity to every bend and turn in the line of utility which ought to be the object of the legislator' (*Anarch. Fall.*, II 508), which in itself is merely making the point about generalisation, Bentham says that the specific French claim that people ought to be equal in property 'would be destructive both of security and wealth' (*Of the levelling system*, I 358). It is 'security' that is here the key word, and the presence of it shows that Bentham's view in this paper, although more harshly put, is of a piece with his thought in general. For, as was seen in the *Civil Code*, security is clearly ranked above equality: if there is a conflict between equality and security, equality should give way. Hence promotion of equality by the expropriation of property (which would be an attack on security) is not to be permitted according to the general theory (rather than just being something thought up when the French were on the loose). The kind of levelling in which Bentham believes is levelling up, the aim is that 'the poorer should be less poor rather than the richer should be less rich' (*Manual of Political Equality*, Stark i 226n). It is also the case that he is interested in showing that increase in equality leads to increase in happiness, and using this to promote some change, rather than arguing that absolute equality gives the greatest possible happiness, and promoting absolute equality. It is the movement rather than the end result which counts. This is because Bentham thinks that other factors come into play at the point of the end result, namely that, as a matter of fact, total equality is impossible, that is sociologically impossible. 'Inequality is the natural condition of mankind ... absolute equality is absolutely impossible' (*Of the levelling system*, I 361). So the final result which would come out of applying the psychological axioms which give diminishing marginal utility as a fact of human nature, namely absolute equality of wealth, is declared impossible by further factual assumptions. This is not inconsistent: the happiness sought for in utilitarian theory is the greatest possible, given how things are. The diminishing marginal utility principles show that, other things being equal, the more equal people are the greater the happiness will be; the other facts show that it is not possible for them to be totally equal.

However, other things are rarely equal, and it has been seen that the chief block to promoting equality in Bentham's theory is what he calls 'security'. Security is 'the principal object of law', the 'inestimable good, the distinctive index of civilisation' (*Civil Code, Traités* ii 29; LEGIS 109; I 307); it is security that is the real mark that we have emerged from the primeval forest. However, security by itself is a rather unspecific idea, and could just be taken to mark all the rights, or benefits secured by law. For, as was seen in Chapter IV, the Benthamite theory of rights is that they are the benefits bestowed on people by imposing duties on others. Every such duty, backed and enforced by sanctions, prevents other people doing things which would affect me adversely, or requires them to do things which affect me favourably. The former class, negative rights, are exactly those which could be picked up as a whole by the single label 'security', because in all of them the law secures a benefit to me by inhibiting the adverse actions of others. Its threats of sanctions creates a wall of protection round me within which I can do what I choose; and so in this metaphorical area I am as secured by law as I would be literally secure inside the literal walls of a fortress. So, incorporating many basic rights, it is not surprising that security is the principal object of the law. On the other hand, since it does incorporate such basic rights, it shows how, on Bentham's theory his quite different basis can, again, provide similar results to traditional theories. I am protected from murder, imprisonment, or dispossession, not because I have a natural right to life, liberty, or property, but because the security which the creation of such rights by law would produce is something which leads to the greater happiness. Back with the savages, when 'like beasts of prey, men pursue men, as a means of subsistence', or in time of war, 'when the laws on which security depends are in part suspended' and 'the cottage is ravaged as well as the palace', then it can be seen how unhappy is the situation without security (*Civil Code, Traités* ii 30; LEGIS 109-10; I 307).

The many headed nature of Bentham's central concept of *security* can be seen in the *Leading Principles of a Constitutional Code, for any State* where Bentham divides security into that for good and that against evil, where the former in turn is divided into security for subsistence and security for abundance and the latter into security against calamity and security against hostility (477-8; II 269-70). Of these only the last has been the subject of traditional theories of negative rights, and even here Bentham is also concerned with security against hostility from officials and enemies of the country as well as security against hostility from fellow citizens. Also he lists the objects to be protected as person, property, power, reputation, and condition in life; which is more embracing than the normal life, person, and property. However, some generalisations can be made. Security is the point at which study of the evils of the second order, in particular danger and alarm, enter political theory in terms of specific political goals. Security is security against danger and alarm; that is, the intro- duction, politically, of duties which protect people against danger and, hence, prevent alarm. Bentham several times brings out the importance of this future dimension for security. It is because future subsistence is secured that alarm is diminished; it is because the future profits of someone's present labour are secured to him that leads him to labour. 'If industry creates, it is law which preserves; if at the first moment we owe all to labour, at the second moment, and at every other, we are indebted for every- thing to law' (*Civil Code, Traités* ii 31; LEGIS 110; I 308). Hence, as Bentham says in the *Civil Code*, the importance of expectation; it is the expectation of reward that leads to labour. So what the law, and in particular those parts of the law identified under the head of security, does is to protect expectations. This is particularly important, as will be seen, with respect to property. However, the security which results from protection of expecta- tions enables people, danger and alarm removed, to plan for the future. It enables people to choose for themselves within the limits laid down how they will attempt to maximise their own, separate, portions of happiness. Within the walls of security, in the little territory secured to them by the fortress of the law, they may play as they please, pleasure themselves as they will. So security, the protection of expectations, is not only important for property but also for liberty.

Bentham's view of liberty has two aspects and the side that gets stressed depends upon the task in hand and on whom he takes his audience or opposition to be. As long as he thinks of liberty as some inalienable natural right permitting anyone to do as they please, then he is hostile. Not only is it a meaningless natural right, but it would be impossible to produce by law an analogous right. For the whole point of law is that it creates rights by imposing duties, and duties are an interference with what people want to do, that is with such total liberty. The acceptance of sacrifice in Benthamite theory means that some are going to have their desires interfered with for the greater benefit of others; the possibility of punishment means that there can't be total liberty (for it will be remembered that in Benthamite theory punishment is not something that can be represented as something the victim really wants, or is really in his interests). However, on the other hand, the only liberty he thinks worth the name, the only liberty whose possession is a real good to someone, is the liberty which can be secured by law. This liberty is the kind of protection just described in which the imposition of duties on others gives people space in which to follow their own desires. As Bentham puts it, 'these two sorts of liberty are directly opposed to one another' (OLG 254); the law can only create the kind of liberty which is worth having by subverting the chimerical original liberty. So it is as a branch of security that liberty fits into Benthamite political theory, which is why it is not listed as a separate subsidiary end (in the way, for example, that equality is). As Bentham puts it: 'personal liberty is security against a certain kind of injuries which affect the person. Political liberty is another branch of security -- security against the injustices of members of government' (UC 32.130; so *Civil Code, Traités* ii 8; LEGIS 97; I 302).

As for liberty, so for property, which is in many ways a special case of liberty, being the liberty to control and dispose of particular physical objects (including immovable objects like land). Again we have a right which in much other political theory is taken as fundamental, and is given the backing of intuition, natural law, or some other form of natural justice (such as the idea that to mix something with one's labour is to create an entitlement to it as one's property). Again in Bentham this natural right, in accord with the general treatment of natural rights discussed in Chapter IV, is taken to be chimerical, a shadow without a substance. So again the only right that there really is, the only right which matters or makes a difference, is the right which is not prior to law but created by law. Hence, as Bentham puts it, 'property and law were born and die together' (UC 32.157);

'the creation of it is the work of law' (OLG 255); 'there is no such thing as natural property, ... it is entirely the work of law' (*Civil Code, Traités* ii 33; LEGIS 111; I 308). The way in which the law creates it, as follows from the above description of security in general, is by placing obligations on other people not to interfere with, 'not to exercise any act upon' (OLG 256), the thing or land in question. In this case, though, unlike certain other cases of security, the law gives me the power to transfer control over the thing in question to others; that is, in Benthamite language, it allows me as an individual to 'issue' 'a countermandate' which overrides the general mandate forbidding interference (OLG 79).

So much for the analytical account, which displays the nature of the right if it is to be anything significant (or meaningful). However, as well as its nature, as given in expository jurisprudence, there is also its justification, as given in censorial jurisprudence. This is the question of whether it is worth having such a thing created by law; that is, whether the undoubted pains of having a law, or imposition of duties, is outweighed in this case by the benefits created. The benefit, as with liberty, is in the satisfaction of desires. By protecting something, in this case land or movable things, from the control, use, or disposition of others, they are reserved to the use of their so-called owner. Hence he is protected in the exercise of his desires with respect to them. Hence he can plan for the future and work to maximise his expected utility; if he uses the land, for example, for sowing crops, he is protected in the expectation that he will be able to reap those crops and so enjoy the benefit of them. As was described for the general case of security, the law adds to his actual walls other invisible ones created by its sanctions which allows him control over what is therefore called his property. 'It is law alone which permits me to forget my natural weakness' (*Civil Code, Traités* ii 34; LEGIS 112). Of course, while the law protects the desires of the owner of the property it frustrates the desires of other people who may also wish to use it, and it is a contentious question whether it is really necessary to the maximisation of utility to have such private, exclusionary, property (the orthodox answer is that otherwise no one would bother sowing the crops). Bentham is in a position to sidestep this problem because he believes that private property is not an option: 'for the carrying on of the several purposes of life, there are trusts, and conditions, and other articles of property, which must be possessed by somebody: and ... it is not every article that can, nor every article that ought, to be possessed by every body' (IPML 216n).

The reason why Bentham holds that property, inevitable or

otherwise, is a benefit is that the law, in creating it and protecting expectations, prevents frustration of desire. It is expectations (or future-directed desires) which are here the key-note: 'the idea of property consists in an established expectation' (*Civil Code, Traités ii 33; LEGIS 112); 'a pleasure of possession ... is a pleasure of expectation' (UC 70A.12). So in deciding whether it is really a benefit, it is necessary to decide whether the satisfaction of these expectations is better than the satisfaction of other desires. However, here there comes a problem, for if it is asked where the expectation comes from, the correct answer seems to be that it is created also by the law. It is because there are laws about, an institution of, private property, that people expect to continue in the enjoyment of their own so-called property. Certainly this is the answer given by Bentham: 'expectation, as far as the law can be kept present to men's minds, follows with undeviating obsequiousness the finger of the law' (*Escheat*, Stark i 290-1). So, once a system of property is established, the benefit of avoiding frustration provides an argument against abolishing it or changing it; it does not, however, provide any reason why it would be a benefit to establish it in the first place, or show that the benefits of change or abolition might not be greater than the benefits of preservation. By the same token, it cannot show that one system of property is more advantageous than another system.

There is a gap here in the Benthamite system of justification which is filled in natural law systems by an account of which particular types of possession legitimate the control of their possessors. Perhaps it could be filled in a Benthamite spirit by using the resources of natural psychology rather than the resources of natural law and finding which system of possession brought most pleasure to the possessors. More precisely, if expectation is the key, then, perhaps, as well as the variable expectations which follow convention or the law, there are natural expectations with respect to the use of lands and goods whose satisfaction would always therefore be a good. If there were such natural expectations, then it could be decided, by use of purely empirical material and without natural law, which system of property, by best satisfying such expectations, was preferable. Bentham mentions this idea in the *Civil Code*. However, he regards the relationship between natural and socially produced expectations to be as the relation between 'an almost invisible thread' and 'a cable' (*Traités ii 35; LEGIS 113); in other words not much can be made of such natural expectations. They extend only to those things which someone has the physical power to protect, and Bentham who thinks that law is the supreme work of civilisation getting us out of the primaeval forests, thinks that such natural power is practically as nothing when compared with the artificial power produced by law. So natural expectation by itself will not help much in deciding between systems of property. In a manuscript of very roughly this time, Bentham says that expectation independent of law is founded on original utility or imagination (UC 70A.19). So, rather than the utility calculations depending on expectations, they would have first to be performed in order to find such expectations (unless there are any universals about imagination). Bentham is careful enough in all his work to distinguish between 'original utility' and 'utility resulting from expectation' (e.g. COMM 242), so room is left for utilitarian calculation which would decide, in general, upon the best forms of property. However, Bentham himself doesn't provide it, and the device of expectation, which he does use, won't provide it. It is no doubt true, as Bentham says in *Humphreys*, that I suffer nothing from my non-possession of watches in others' pockets because I do not expect to possess them (V 414). My expectations are not frustrated by such a system of property. However, this is only because I am used to this system; and forms no grounds for comparison between how I feel about watches now and how I would feel if I had grown up in a different social and legal environment.

The other way Bentham could, and also to some extent does, bring in the newly developed psychology to provide the factual basis on which utilitarian calculations about property may be based is by use of the axioms of mental pathology. Just as for equality, the phenomenon of diminishing marginal utility which these axioms claim enables Bentham to derive significant conclusions with respect to property. For, as was seen in discussion of these axioms in Chapter VI, one result of them is that, *ceteris paribus*, the unhappiness created by the loss of something is greater than the happiness brought about by its gain by someone else. Hence the forced transfer, for example by theft, will, *ceteris paribus*, tend to diminish overall utility. 'Sum for sum, and man for man', as Bentham puts it, 'the suffering of him who incurrs a loss is always greater than the enjoyment of him who makes a gain' (*Manual of Political Economy*, Stark i 239). The claim is frequently made in Bentham. Repeating it ten years later in the *Institute of Political Economy*, he notes that 'in the difference . . . lies the mischief, and the sole mischief, of bankruptcy as of theft' (Stark iii 374); in between he declares that 'the enjoyment produced by gain is never equal to the suffering produced by loss: if it were, the main reason for affording protection to property would cease' (*Circulating Annuities*, Stark ii 286). So, as well as the general principles, the explicit consequences for property and theft are drawn. However, unlike equality, diminishing marginal utility does not help Bentham with his defence of property as much as he thinks it does. For the key point is the *ceteris paribus* condition which is built into Bentham's claims with the phrase 'sum for sum and man for man'. If all else is equal, that is, if we have two people of equal fortune and equal sensibility, then the principles will indeed deliver that the loss in happiness exceeds the gain. The two people have a similar utility function in which successive additions of wealth produce diminishing additions of happiness. So the addition to the thief means less than that amount would mean to the man stolen from, where it occurs at a lesser level of wealth. This, after all, was why the principles delivered equality as the position of maximum utility: reversing this, once people are equal, any departure from this situation diminishes utility. However, it only delivers what Bentham wants when people are equal. In the normal situation; that is, when the *ceteris paribus* clause does not apply, then it does not follow from these principles that the suffering of a loss is greater than the gratification of a gain. If the loser is rich and the gainer is poor, this will not hold. So there is a limit, and a very tight and strict limit, to the extent that Bentham can use this part of his natural psychology to support his belief in property. This is particularly pertinent given that Bentham holds that security (of which property is part) is superior as an end to equality; and, as has been seen, resists political programmes aimed at equalising wealth by the claim that they would upset security.

So the psychology on which property is based has to lie elsewhere, and here it does depend upon maintaining the existing system rather than claiming that it is the best of all possible systems. It was seen that Bentham's stress on expectations provided an argument against change of an established system, and to this can be added the secondary mischiefs of danger and alarm, discussed above. If it is the case, people's psychology being as it is, that they (like Bentham himself contemplating the further developments of the French Revolution) feel alarm when violent hands are laid on private property, this provides good reason for preserving the system once it is successfully established. It may not in itself be better or worse than any other but once it is there, this fact makes it preferable. Bentham himself held that there couldn't be a justification in natural law or natural justice of systems of property because what this would really be about was expectation, and expectation was neutral. So what was established might be quite arbitrary. Once this had happened, though, there is a good, non-arbitrary reason for maintaining it. Just as fear that they will be jumped on when passing transplant hospitals would cause alarm and prevent people planning their lives to maximise their utilities, so would the fear that their crops would be jumped on whenever they had sown them. That is, given the conditioning that people had actually received in the worlds for which Bentham was writing, and have received in our present world; there are, no doubt, quite other forms of social system and expectations.

Although expectation may be imprecise in an *ab initio* choice between systems, it becomes an important and precise means of deciding when considering more particular questions about property within the general context of a system. For since the protection of expectation is the important thing about property no substantial damage will be done by the forced transfer of property when there is no damage to expectations. So instead of property being regarded as a thing over which a person has a unique relation of dominion, and which he has control of in all situations and may alienate at will, it should be regarded as a means to an end (the end of happiness, protected expectations, particular states of mind), which end might be provided in other ways. Hence Bentham's taxation proposal in *Escheat* in which he suggested that the government might revive the ancient practice of escheat by which the crown possessed the estates of those dying without heirs. In this case, since no one could expect to have use of the land at death, no expectation would be thwarted. Hence there would be, as the subtitle of the pamphlet proclaimed, 'supply without burden'; the government would possess money in order to produce happiness elsewhere (for example, by promoting national security) without causing misery in the process. However, the proposal illustrates (just like the original medieval practice) a different conception of property than the contemporary landowners who, assuming it was their land, assumed that they could decide to do what they liked with it when they died. In the original feudal practice, the principal landowners were tenants of the crown; and in his suggestion for its revival Bentham brings out that, on utilitarian theory, landowners are tenants of the principle of utility: if more utility could be provided by other use of the land, then this is a ground for terminating the tenancy. Even if this could never happen — because of people's expectations with respect to the land they hold — it is a ground for replacing a tenant when he dies and has no more expectations with whatever successor tenant would make best use of the land. Similarly, in his later work, when he realised that his reform proposals by abolishing sinecures and cleaning up the administration would be abolishing what people regarded as their property (something of value to them, the expectation of which was secured to them by the current law), Bentham makes use of a 'Disappointment prevention principle' whereby people would be compensated for the damage to their expectations (*Humphreys*, V 413). Again the law, or state, may properly alienate what people regard as their property. But again, care for promotion of utility entails care for what is the really important feature about property, namely care for expectations.

The above account of property has been fairly extensive because of the intrinsic importance to political theory of property rights, and its consequential importance in comparison between Bentham's theories and others. It can be seen that Bentham would emerge from such a comparison with both strengths and weaknesses. Because there are no natural property rights, this means that it is not possible to found or justify government as a means of preserving these rights. Neither property nor contract, since they do not precede government, can be used to justify government. Nor can such rights be used as side-constraints inhibiting certain kinds of state activity: in Benthamite theory the state is unconstrained and may do whatever it wants (lay hands on whatever it wants) in order to promote utility. Nor, as seen, can this be used as a justification of certain kinds of property distribution over others. However, these possible weaknesses have corresponding strengths. As was seen in Chapter IV, one of the particular points to Bentham's attack on natural rights, and in particular natural inalienable rights, was that they would prevent the processes of change by which the sovereign legislature could gradually arrive at the state which promoted maximum utility; this change, this openness to the future, was also seen in Chapter VIII to be an important feature of Benthamite democracy. Experiment, observation, is to replace *a priori* belief or intuition; and the experiments may promote constant change. So the abolition of such side constraints allows scope for experiment. It allows Bentham to propose reform of administration without being constrained by the dead hand of existing property expectations. It also allows Bentham to have a realistic view of taxation. An absolute property right, based on natural law or justice, provides notorious difficulties about taxation (even leading a current thinker in this tradition to declare that taxation is forced labour, i.e. unjustified interference (Nozick 1974 169)). The orthodox solution is supposed to be by representation, so that people, in the person of their representatives, decide to give their property away when deciding on taxes. However, such use of representation was exactly what Bentham (as was seen in Chapter II) regarded as one of the fictions improperly used to justify the present state of the law. Of course, representative democracy is important also for Bentham, but this is because the representative decides in the interests of the person he represents, not because that person is really there in some ghostly way in the shape of their representative. So representation will tend to preserve utility; and as long as it preserves or promotes utility, there is nothing wrong with taxation, or forced seizure of property by the state. Hence Bentham can avoid the problems which rival traditions run into over taxation.

So far it has been seen how traditional, largely negative, rights would fare in a Benthamite state. However, to leave it there would be to present a seriously misleading view of such a state. For, as was seen at the start of this chapter, the point of utilitarian theory is that, with its concentration on consequences, it is relatively insensitive to how these consequences are arrived at. Hence it does not regard the distinction between acting and refraining from acting, or the distinction between negative rights, which guarantee someone's being left alone by others, and positive rights, which guarantee the positive assistance of others, as being of as much importance as they are taken to have in other theories. So far, particularly with security in all its branches, the concentration has been on such negative rights. Someone is secure when the state builds a wall round him protecting him from the desires of others to use him or his property. However, the point of the Benthamite state is to maximise utility, and this requires also the introduction and enforcement of positive rights, by which positive assistance is required from others. It has already been seen that Bentham's model penal code would require people to go to the assistance of others in distress and that in his economic proposals (discussed in Chapter V) various forms of state interference in the working of economic and social institutions are recommended. However, the full flavour of the Benthamite state does not come out unless it is realised that the final blueprint, as given in the *Constitutional Code*, contains such elements as education and health ministers. So, among the twelve ministers proposed who were to give effect to the decisions of the legislature, there were ones specifically to give effect to those decisions having as their object 'education' (IX 441) and 'the preservation of the national health' (443). There was also to be an 'indigence relief minister' (441), a 'preventive service minister' having for his 'object the prevention of calamity' (439), and an 'interior-communication minister' (441) (a minister of transport). Together with ministers of trade and finance who were instructed with some of the more positive management of the economy envisaged by Bentham, such as control of the money supply, and a 'domain' minister entrusted with putting government lands and fixed property to 'the benefit of the community at large' (443), this means that the great majority of the teams of ministers were to be entrusted with various forms of positive interference for the good of the people. That is, as well as government having the function of the protection of people by the enforcement of criminal law, it was envisaged that the government would, in a sufficient manner to justify having specific ministerial executive teams, involve itself in such matters as health, transport, and education; that it would control water supplies (445) and sewage (439; 445); that health in factories (439) or the suppression of harmful drugs was its business. In Benthamite language, ministers were to have a 'melioration-suggestive function' (225).

The idea of ministers of education or health is a commonplace of government, and in that sense Bentham's proposals do not seem exciting. However, when he died (the year before the state granted any money at all of any kind to education), these proposals looked anything but commonplace. The traditional ministries, apart from raising government revenue, were concerned with security, internal and external. The first time that there was a minister of education in Britain was 1902 and a minister of health was 1919. Bentham himself was aware of this kind of historical development, taking it as part of the progress of government from what it was to what it ought to be. Many years before, in a footnote to the *Introduction* (that is, in 1780), he commented in such a historical fashion to the claim he had just made in the main text that the operations of government ought to be averting mischief or making 'an addition to the sum of positive good' (IPML 198). He noted that the latter, which could be called 'a sort of work of superogation . . . in the calendar of political duty, is comparatively but of recent date'. He then gives a thumbnail sketch of development holding that 'it was the dread of evil, not the hope of good, that first cemented societies together' and claiming that the successive stages could be marked by the introduction of new terms into the language. There had always been military and justice departments, they had always 'had a name'. However it was not until 'lately' that 'the power which occupies itself in preventing mischief' had had a name 'and that but a loose one, the police'. 'Police' was indeed used in a looser or wider sense at the end of the eighteenth century, particularly in France and Germany, to mean the more general prevention of mischief. Bentham's chief concern here is that 'for the power which takes for its object the introduction of positive good, no peculiar name, however inadequate, seems yet to have been devised' (IPML 198n). Whether or not such a name has now been devised ('welfare'; 'social services'?), it was such a development which Bentham saw to be completely new and also characteristic of the Benthamite state. Furthermore the historical implications of what he said were accurate: the state did develop into a position in which the great bulk of its revenue was to be expanded on such areas as health, indigence relief (social security), and education (and not just so-called 'welfare states') rather than on the eighteenth- and nineteenth-century staples of security, that is external defence (and repayment of debts incurred in defence) and criminal justice; together (in the nineteenth century) with such preventative measures as police (in the more specific sense). The commonplace nature of some of the structure of the *Constitutional Code* merely reveals the fact that to a large extent the Benthamite state has come to pass: for better or worse, the Benthamite state is our state.

Notes

(a) The idea of using as counter-example to utilitarianism an 'experience machine' which produces pleasant experiences without any real basis is in Nozick (1974 p. 42).

(b) Mill's 'proof' of utilitarianism is in Chapter IV of his *Utilitarianism* (*Works*, X 243ff).

(c) Richard Tuck crisply surveys and refers to utilitarian solutions of the free-rider problem before producing his own solution in his Tuck (1979b).

(d) The claim that Bentham, even in the law cannot be simply regarded as a rule utilitarian is one I owe to the work of Gerald J. Postema, whose forthcoming book on Bentham and ajudication I had the chance to read in draft; but see Postema (1977) and Postema (1980).

(e) Another rule utilitarian element in Bentham, not mentioned in the main text, is his use of the word 'tendency'. His standard utilitarian formula involves approval of acts 'according to the tendency' which they appear to have to lead to happiness (e.g. IPML 12). On a standard reading of 'tendency' this seems to imply that they should be judged by kinds, that is as the basis of rules, rather than as individuals. This standard reading picks up a tendency as what normally happens. However, after looking through many uses of 'tendency' in Bentham and contemporaries, it seems to me that what they mean by 'tendency' is usually the causal effect that something would have, if not prevented by some other superior cause. The standard example is the tendency objects have to move towards the centre of the earth (this would be true even if no object actually fell — even if it was highly abnormal; the meaning is that if nothing else was in the way, this is what would happen). In Adam Smith, for example, the natural price, to which commodities 'gravitate' is what they 'tend' towards (*Wealth of Nations*, i 65). In Bentham 'all bodies on or about the earth tend to the centre of the earth: yet all bodies are not there' (RJE v 40). Bentham can talk of how a 'tendency ... produces a *chance* of punishment' (IPML 149), as if the tendency was not the chance itself, but the cause of it; similarly he can talk of 'real tendency and probable effects' (*Scotch Reform*, V 15) as if they were distinguishable. Of course, in many cases, either way of taking it will in practice come to the same thing, and there are several cases in Bentham which read in the more modern, probabilistic, sense. In so far as the use is causal, the central point again becomes one of knowledge, and the rule utilitarian effect (as in the main text) arises from the conditions for knowledge. For the sort of ideal knowledge of bodies, which finds that they tend to the centre of the world, is knowledge of what will happen, other things being equal. If there is ignorance, therefore, about whether other things are equal or not, then this knowledge is all that can be relied on; and this will have a generalising, rule-like effect. Knowing only some tendencies, abstraction has to be made of all the particular forces which might apply in a particular instance. However, such knowledge is correctable by further research into the instances, or indeed by the knowledge of all the possible tendencies or causal instances. This is how, as in the main text, although the results are as in rule utilitarianism, the spirit which motivates them is more as in act utilitarianism.

(f) The pithy maxim about how people should be considered equally when assessing utilities which J.S. Mill calls 'Bentham dictum', namely 'everybody to count for one, nobody for more than one' (*Utilitarianism*, Chapter Five; *Works*, X 257) seems to have been invented by Mill himself. The closest equivalents seem to be the somewhat more cumberous formulations quoted in the main text. On the topic of equality in general in Bentham, see Parekh (1970).

(g) On Bentham on liberty, see Douglas Long's book on the subject, which pays particular attention to the formation of his ideas and the early manuscripts (Long 1977).

(h) The implication in the text that Bentham's economic doctrines were another area which recommended state interference may seem strange since Bentham's main economic recommendation about the state was that '*Be quiet* ought ... to be the motto, or watchword, of government' (Stark iii 333). However, this was only because of the prevailing economic theories, which he supported, that the best way to achieve the Benthamite end of abundance was by letting people get on and accumulate for themselves. If, in the course of the open, empirically based, testing examination which Bentham always espoused, it should turn out that the doctrine was false or had limits, then Bentham would have recommended more state interference to achieve these ends. He was not opposed to 'the interference of government,

261

as often as in my humble view of the matter any the smallest ballance [?] on the side of advantage is the result' (*Defence of a Maximum,* Stark iii 258). For a more general treatment of Bentham's views of the state's role in the economy, see Chapter V.

(i) Strictly speaking, there was not a minister of education in Britain until the 1944 Act; between 1902 and then, although a cabinet minister, he was known as 'president of the Board of Education'.

(j) In addition to the reason mentioned in the text, Bentham was also worried about the accuracy of the 'greatest happiness of the greatest number' formula towards the end of his life since it looked as if it might permit the exploitation or slavery of a large minority by a small minority. See the long version of his draft article on utilitarianism (UC 14.386), reprinted in the new edition of the *Deontology.* §§ 54; 57.

X

Private Deontology

In Chapter I it was claimed that the disciples who gathered around Bentham's corpse at his death looked up to him as a teacher of public control and organisation (law, institutions, government, education) rather than of purely private morality; and for the twenty years preceding his death Bentham's main effort was devoted to trying to perfect the separate parts of his pannomiom, that is, his complete legal system, rather than working out a system of personal ethics. Day after day he steadily filled up ten to fifteen pages with writing on the civil code, the penal code, the constitutional code, and the procedure code. As described in Chapter I, for a time at least, the work on private ethics, the *Deontology*, was left for after dinner, as a comparative frivolity to be dictated to Bowring along with the *Autobiography*, a work which in many ways it resembles, after the serious business of codification was over. When the *Deontology* was published by Bowring, shortly after Bentham's death, it was disowned as a true expression of Bentham's views by disciples with a good knowledge of his mind, such as Place or the Mills. Since the *Deontology* is the only work in which Bentham concerns himself at any length with questions of morality, the simplest conclusion might be to ignore private morality altogether in an account of Bentham's views. Certainly, one modern commentator, Mary Peter Mack, has held that Bentham does not have any views about private morality (Mack 1962); and another, David Baumgardt, in his massive, six hundred page survey of Bentham's ethics as a whole, refused to subject the *Deontology* to the same detailed commentary as Bentham's other works (Baumgardt 1952).

However, although this would be salutary, in that it makes an important point about the centre of gravity of Bentham's thought

263

as compared with more recent utilitarian thinking, it would be slightly too simple. It may indeed be true, as Professor Burns has recently commented in a lecture, that the *Deontology* is arguably 'the worst book ever written on an important subject' (Burns 1978 24), but the recent work on the new edition by Amnon Goldworth shows that it was at least written by Bentham as opposed to being dreamed up by Bowring, and it is also the case that some of the trivia which Baumgardt found so embarrassing, such as the 'emission of gas from the alimentary canal' (don't do it) appear in the manuscripts. Baumgardt had not the heart to decide whether such detailed instructions are 'the work of Bowring, or concessions which Bentham made to the more "practical" mind of his secretary, or just senile pedantries of the old Bentham himself' (1952 492). However, a considerable quantity of the manuscript was written in 1814, when Bentham was certainly anything but senile, and was writing the important work on logic discussed in Chapter III. With the title 'logic or ethics', written in Bentham's own manuscript hand at Ford Abbey in exactly the same way as the manuscripts on logic and ontology, it must be taken seriously. Also this material, and indeed the great majority of the *Deontology*, as it emerges newly edited from the manuscripts, is concerned with theoretical questions rather than with practical instructions. It is concerned with how there can be private moral instruction at all, and what shape it would take, on Benthamite principles. This question is interesting and important in its own right, and in this short final coda of a chapter, an attempt will be made to answer it. The question is whether it is possible for Bentham, consistently with his principles, to give instructions about private morality and, if it is, whether such instruction would really be moral instruction. The interest of the question is that Bentham is normally taken as a founding father of utilitarianism, and it is just such instruction which utilitarian thought normally takes it upon itself to provide.

As a general political, or administrative, project, it has been seen how the centre of Benthamite thought consisted in attempting a solution in practical terms of a problem posed by adopting two basic principles, a principle about what ought to be done in legislation or government (promote the greatest happiness of the greatest number) and a principle which stated the fundamental nature of the material to be handled (people act in their own interests). Out of this grew the structure of institutions and the content of the legal code. The central idea was to make it in people's interests to do those things which they ought to do if the general end was to be promoted. Government, or legislation, involved interference with individuals, in which motives were artificially produced which would lead them to act in other ways than they would if they were left alone. Sometimes, of course, it could be predicted that the results would be better (the desired end would be more perfectly realised) if there were no interference. Then (as in many economic matters) the best act was for the government to be quiet. However, the central idea here is basically the same. Knowledge of the motivation of human beings would mean that it would be known whether additional artificial motives were required, and the study of which ones to provide is the study of legislation. Obviously for this project a psychology is required and a knowledge of the final end. However, it does not seem to leave any place for private ethics. Either people are made to do what they ought to do by government or else they are just left to get on with it (as in some kinds of economic activity) following their natural drives. In neither case does room seem to be left for private ethics: where there is government interference, it is not private; where they are just left to get on with it, it is not ethics.

This is not to say that Bentham was not aware of the importance of moral feelings. The fully developed psychology, or account of human motivation, brought out the importance of the 'moral sanction', standardly listed as one of four or five central sanctions throughout his thought. People's concern for 'reputation' meant that they were concerned about the opinions of others. Nor was the psychology egoistic, as was seen in Chapter VI, when Bentham's continuing emphasis on the importance of sympathy (elevated in some later work, such as *Nomography*, into a 'sympathetic sanction') was brought out. However, this, as psychology, was just further facts about human nature which should be taken account of by the legislator. It was one more resource on which he could sometimes rely to do his job for him. Just as the acquisitive instinct and the desire for survival could be relied on to further the subsidiary ends of abundance and subsistence without interference from the legislator, so also could the moral sanction make his job easier. Sometimes it meant that things would be prevented without his having to impose the costs of punishment. Sometimes, as with drunkenness or fornication, when prevention by punishment would be inefficient in that the punishments would cause more pain, given the strength and immediacy of the emotions with which they would have to contend, than any possible good, the only course for the legislator was to give them 'a slight shade of artificial disrepute' (IPML 290), leaving it for the moral sanction to complete the job. In this way moral opinions can be considered by the legislator, and this is the main topic of the rather puzzling final chapter of the *Introduction* called the 'Limits of Penal Jurisprudence', from which the above example was taken. Here moral thought enters in in just the same way as economic motives. In both cases the result is an account of cases in which the legislator may achieve his end better sometimes by being silent; but, in both cases, silent is what he is, he does not lay down his artificial motives and start giving moral instruction. Of course, the situation is slightly more complicated than this, because the legislator is not only concerned with an already existing society with its opinions but with moulding it. The advance of the concerns of governments from punishment to prevention, from prevention to welfare, means that the nature of the moral sanction is also properly the concern of the Benthamite legislator. Education is declared in the *Limits* chapter to be part of the 'art of government' (IPML 283); and the papers Bentham wrote on 'Indirect Legislation' shortly after writing the *Introduction* are full of concern for education, for how to mobilise the force of public opinion, and with the 'culture of benevolence' (*Penal Code*, Book IV, Chapters 16, 17, 20; *Traités* iii). Even if the penal code has limits, there are none for the Benthamite legislator. Yet even if he is by every means, directly and indirectly, getting people to act in the way they ought, this still leaves open the question of whether it is possible in Benthamite thought to have genuinely private moral instruction.

The puzzling feature about the *Limits* chapter of the *Introduction* is that Bentham sums up the first section, entitled 'Limits between private ethics and the art of legislation' in a final paragraph in which he declares that 'private ethics teaches how each man may dispose himself to pursue the course most conducive to his own happiness' (298), which not only does not seem to be a summary of the preceding text but also rather different from what most people mean by 'ethics'. If private ethics is the pursuit of the same end by different means, that is by use of the social (or 'moral') sanction rather than the 'political' sanction, then its end should be the general, or the greatest, happiness, not just the happiness of an individual. On the other hand, this brief remark in the *Introduction* is picked up as the centre of the *Deontology*, written between thirty-five and fifty years later, where Bentham declares that 'this work has for its object the pointing out to each man on each occasion what course of conduct promises to be in the highest degree conducive to his happiness: to his own happiness, first and last; to the happiness of others, no farther than in so far as his happiness is promoted by promoting theirs' (I.1; p. 123). In the practical recommendations, such as they are, this is also the course adopted. 'Benevolence' is indeed recommended, and in particular such actions as not responding to outrageous attacks or attempting to persuade people that they hold erroneous opinions when there is little probability of success (II.3 (ii); p. 266; 265). However such benevolence is proposed under the title of 'extra-regarding prudence', and the particular actions are recommended as ways of not making enemies. So the reason given for the actions, even if they are actions which might be done with a purely benevolent motive, is that they are in the self-interest of the agent. Hence, whether or not this was centrally what he had in mind at the time of the *Introduction*, Bentham did think that there was a possible task of private ethics, or (as he later called it) private deontology, which would consist in making recommendations to individuals about how they should act if they were to maximise their own happiness. The question remains of whether such a task can be consistently fitted into Bentham's thought as a whole; whether it does not conflict in its end with the different end of the legislator; whether it is a possible task at all; and, if it is, whether it is in any way an ethical (or deontological) task.

One recent study of Bentham which accommodates such apparent diversity of ends and provides an answer to some of these questions is that of David Lyons. After first proposing the thesis in a short article (Lyons 1972), Lyons then developed it in a book-length study (Lyons 1973) designed to show that Bentham was not in the strict sense a utilitarian at all. This was because the happiness to be considered as a criterion of action in Bentham is held by Lyons to be not universal happiness but rather the happiness of a smaller group of people according to the project in question. The group is decided by who is under the direction of the agent, and this gives two groups and two projects. There is the project of government, or legislation, where the relevant group are all those people under the direction of the agent, or legislator. This is the community for which he is responsible, and so here the end to be aimed at is the greatest happiness of this community (rather than of mankind in general). Then there is the project of private ethics in which man is addressed as an individual agent, and has only himself under his own direction. Here the relevant group is only the individual himself, and so the end to be aimed at is the happiness of the individual himself. In what he calls his 'differential interpretation', Lyons recognises that he provides two independent ends as different understandings of the principle of utility as used by Bentham. However, he holds that this is a tenable interpretation since he argues that Bentham also held that, as a matter of contingent fact, there is not a divergence between the courses of action which would be promoted by the independent ends. As a matter of fact, whichever was in view the course of action suggested would be the same; whether general interest or individual interest was considered, the same action would be recommended. This means that Bentham is, according to Lyons, an upholder of the idea that there is a natural harmony of interests: each person's interest is also part of the general interest, and the general interest is in each person's interest.

If the account of the central part of Bentham's project, as given in Chapters V and VII above, is correct, then Bentham does not espouse the natural harmony of interests. The argument need not be repeated here, but if the whole point of the Benthamite legislator is to introduce motives to get people to do things which they would not naturally do, then it cannot be that these are the things that would be done if only everyone followed their own interests. So, if there really are differential ends proposed in Bentham, with independent public and private ethical thought, then it cannot be held that this would not produce a divergence in practice. On the other hand, Lyons's treatment of private ethics, based on the *Introduction*, seems to coincide with the longer remark just quoted from the *Deontology*; and whether or not Lyons is right about the end of government in Bentham, this is clearly a different end than the end of such a private ethics. So, lacking the comfort of a natural harmony of interests, Bentham's thought threatens to split apart, not just in theory but also in practice. There also still remains the question of how such instruction in people's happiness is possible at all; whether pursuing their own happiness is not just what people will do, according to the psychological theory, without instruction, and whether or not it is in harmony with the happiness of others.

A closer look at the task of the *Deontology*, however, reveals that there is not such a split, either theoretical or practical, in Bentham's thought. As well as the long remark quoted above, in the opening section Bentham also says that 'it never is, to any practical purpose, a man's duty to do that which it is his interest not to do' (p. 121). At first sight, this seems to produce the same problem: either 'duty' in this area of private deontology means something quite different from 'duty' in the area of government, or there is a natural harmony of interests so that someone's interest is always his duty. At first sight the remark seems inconsistent with the large body of Bentham's thought which is devoted to the problem of getting duty and interest in line; if it is in line anyway, such labour would be redundant. However, the crucial mitigating phrase in this remark is the 'to any practical purpose'. It is not that interest and duty might not diverge; it is just that, if they do, then it serves no practical purpose to identify something as being someone's duty. This is because, according to the psychological theory, what the person will aim at is his interest, and so the talk of duty would be redundant. 'The act of sacrifice', comments Bentham in the next paragraph 'is neither possible nor so much as desirable.' That it is not desirable does pose a difficulty or inconsistency in Bentham's overall doctrine, given that, as has been seen in Chapter VII, sacrifice is exactly what on occasion the general theory demands. However, if this is regarded as a bit loose and the emphasis placed on 'possible', again a consistent interpretation can be extracted. Bentham is concerned with the possible, the practicable. It is only practicable to consider duty, that is, the interests and happiness of others as well as one's own, if the result that would be reached is the same as would be reached by considering one's own alone. It is not that there is a natural harmony of interests; it is just that, for the particular project Bentham has in mind in the *Deontology*, it is only practical to consider those cases where there happens to be a coincidence. Luckily, this coincidence is considerable, if not complete. As Bentham puts it, more carefully, towards the end of the same section: 'that regard should any further be had to the happiness of others will be shown to be neither possible nor upon the whole desirable'. This repeats the point about possibility, but notice that this time Bentham more carefully introduces an 'upon the whole' before 'desirable': it is not that there is a complete harmony between what is possible and what is desirable, it is just that it luckily enough happens most of the time.

Private deontology, and the particular task of writing a practical handbook of private ethics, can therefore be made compatible with the overall project because it is also constrained by psychology, by how people actually are. The different end proposed does not amount to a second fundamental end in the overall doctrine but merely an end adopted for a particular practical purpose. This is the purpose of persuasion, of making people do what they ought to do, only now without the sanctions or power of the law. It is another form of manipulation, of operating on people so that they will end up doing what they ought to do, only this time without any use of external power or threats. Given the overall psychology, that people only act for what they perceive to be their interest, the lack of power means that, unlike with government or use of the political sanction, they can't be manipulated by changing their interests (by creating new, artificial, motives). Instead, use has to be made of the interests that already exist. Hence, without power, the only task that private ethics can undertake is persuasion; and the only task of persuasion that is possible is to point out that something is in someone's interests. So this is what private deontology is: a handbook telling people what is in their interests, a handbook explaining how to reach their own happiness. This, however, is not because this is a genuine competing final end, or because, in practice, pointing this out will always have the same result as use of the final end. Rather, it is an auxiliary method of reaching the unique final end, the general happiness. When, as happens in the great majority of cases but not universally, someone's interest coincides with the general interest, this method can be used. Otherwise it is not practical. It fills in the gaps in the legislative programme, and the same procedure could be used to reinforce the effects of the legislative programme, direct and indirect, once it is completed. For since the whole point of this programme, whether by education and change of desire, or by the threat of sanctions introducing new objects of desire (or aversion), is to get duty and interest in line, then, once it is successfully completed, it will always be possible to point out to someone as a means of persuasion, that what happens to be his duty is in his interest. The culture of benevolence will mean that he would now feel miserable if he created harm to others; the development of the popular or moral sanction would mean that his reputation would suffer in an undesirable manner; the imposition of penalties would mean that crime would not pay. However this, like other parts of private ethics, depends upon the contingency of interest being in line with duty. It is at best a contingency and, outside the perfect Benthamite state, it is not even invariably true.

That this is the role of private deontology in Bentham, and not an unnecessarily forced reading of the text, emerges neatly from some manuscript marginal comments designed for the *Springs of Action*. The *Springs of Action* gives Bentham's complete account of human motivation and in these marginals he considers the use to be made of such knowledge. They are developed in a way that brings out a revealing parallel between use to be made by a legislator, or 'ruler' and a private deontologist, or 'moralist'. He constructs two rules, a 'ruler's rule', which is 'what you would have done make it a man's *interest* to do it'; and a 'moralist's rule', which is 'what you would have done, show that it is a man's interest to do it' (UC 158.70). This is the correct consistent account of the psychology as used with people of differing power; of the use of what Bentham calls 'psychological dynamics'. As just mentioned, with the power of political sanctions, it is possible to construct new interests; without it, use has to be made of existing interests. In both cases, we have a project, the use of a given psychology as a means to an end. Given that there is not a natural harmony of interests, the moralist will only be successful in so far as there happens to be a coincidence. So the role of private ethics must be subordinate to that of legislation; rather than setting up an alternative end, it fills in some of the gaps. However, when things are serious, as they inevitably are when there is a conflict of interests, private ethics cannot be relied on. As Bentham puts it in the 'Limits' chapter of the *Introduction*: 'there are few cases in which it *would* be expedient to punish a man for hurting *himself*: but there are few cases, if any, in which it would *not* be expedient to punish a man for injuring his neighbour' (292). In serious cases persuasion by words is insufficient and resource is to be had to a more formidable source of power; to arguments which a man will find it impossible to refuse.

This removes the question of whether Bentham's work on private deontology can be made consistent with the rest of his thought. There still remain the questions of whether such a task of private instruction or persuasion is possible at all on Bentham's psychological principles, and whether it can properly be called a part of ethics, if it is. The problem of whether such instruction is possible is one which Bentham himself tackled when writing the theoretical part of the *Deontology*. His answer, consistent with other parts of his thought and with the description of the psychology and its applications in Chapters VI and IX above, is that such persuasion is indeed possible because people do not have complete knowledge of their own interests. The problem is that, if everyone follows their own interest, any such persuasion would seem to be redundant since it would be merely telling people to do those things which they were going to do anyway; that is, it would not really be persuasion, and there would be no scope for being, or point in being, a 'moralist'. The answer is that, according to the psychology, what people follow is not their interests so much as what they think is in their interests. If mistake is possible, then divergence is possible; but, if mistake is possible, then the task of the moralist is possible, since people can be shown what is really in their interests. Without use of any external political power, or changing people's interests, they can still be persuaded and their minds changed, by showing them the interests which they really have. Yet, as was seen above, although Bentham thinks that in the normal case people are the best judges of their own interests, he does not think that they are universally correct. As Bentham puts it in a piece of manuscript written for the *Deontology*, quoted in the footnotes of the new text, 'Each man best judge of what has been conducive to his own well being. Yes, if accustomed to correct and compleat reflection – and permitted by his passions to employ it' (UC 14.143; *Deontology*, 250n). Given all the scope for error allowed here, it follows that the 'practical moralist' may lay before the eyes of each man 'a sketch of the probable future more correct and compleat' than he can draw for his own use, and show him what is really in his interest (*Deontology*, II.1 (ii), p. 251). The deontologist becomes 'a *scout*; a man ... having put himself upon the hunt for consequences' (ibid.); having found the consequences, he passes on his information for the use of others.

So, in terms of the general psychological theory, such a task as the deontologist's is certainly possible; that is, not redundant. However, there is still the question of whether it is in any sense the task of a genuine moralist. The instructions about how to live in order to avoid aggravation resemble the instructions about how one should fasten up a cylinder head without cracking it; possibly useful, certainly banal and emotionally flat. It might seem excessive to dignify such self-regarding instructions with the title of 'private ethics' or 'deontology'; perhaps they should not be described as moral at all. Interestingly enough, in one way this is a criticism with which Bentham himself would have agreed. Like many of Bentham's works, the critical parts of the *Deontology* are as important as the more purely constructive parts; and making sense of the whole involves recognising what it was that Bentham was against as well as what he was for. With respect to morality, or, more specifically, moral instruction imparted in writing, Bentham was against the whole institution, at least as it was currently practised. He held that the 'office' of the 'deontologist' had hitherto 'with few if any exceptions' adopted the tone of the schoolmaster, and with arrogance dictated what people should do just because something was the deontologist's pleasure. No effort was made to find out the proper basis and so to arrogance was allied 'indolence, and ignorance' (II.1 (ii); p. 252). Just as in his political studies, discussed in Chapter VIII, Bentham did not think that this ignorance was accidental, but the result of interest; the object 'is the deriving from his labours *advantage*' (p. 253). So private moralists were operating to increase their own reputation, and increase their chance of preferment in the institutions of society; the same kind of exposure of the roots of ideology operates here as it does in Bentham's *Fallacies*. That is, the moralists which operate in Bentham's world are moralists inspired by and frequently paid by the church; yet 'religion is misapplied . . . in proportion as it is applied to any part of the field of morals' (*Deontology*, I.10; p. 166). Since these moralists are operating in such a different way from the way in which Bentham thought that the private deontologist ought to practice, in basis, care, attitude, point, he was almost ready to give them the whole title of being a 'moralist' and use something different for himself. At least, at one stage, he is prepared to go so far with the use of 'ought'. With self-conscious paradox, once he has described how contemporary moralists use the words 'ought' and 'ought not', he declares in the *Deontology* that 'these words — if for this one purpose the use of them may be allowed — *ought* to be banished from the vocabulary of Ethics' (II.1 (ii); p. 253). In other words, Bentham is transvaluing values; going beyond good and evil. If good and bad are understood as they are normally used, in terms of the prevailing Christian morality, then Bentham wants to say that this is a bad thing. If to be a moralist is to talk like this, then Bentham would not object to the criticism that his private ethics was not a morality at all. The whole point was to change the content of what was conventionally called morality; if this also involved changing the label, this would be a relatively unimportant further consequence.

In this context the importance of Bentham's criticisms of the idea of sacrifice, which threatened above to create inconsistency in his total project, can now be better understood. What Bentham wants to get across is not that duty would never involve sacrifice (which would only be true if there were a complete harmony of interests) but, rather, that contemporary moralists overdid the idea of sacrifice. They preached sacrifice for its own sake. 'By these physicians of souls, pleasures are ordered off the table' (ibid., p. 255). Yet the whole point about sacrifice is that, as a pain, it was in itself a bad thing. A sacrifice could only be justified, in terms of Bentham's general evaluative theory, if it was outweighed by a correspondingly greater gain in pleasure or happiness. The end of ethics was fulfilment of human need and desire; anything which was not recommended as being done for the benefit of actual people, in the actual secular world, amounted to a perversion of morality. Hence Bentham's criticism of 'asceticism' in the *Introduction*, motivated as he thought it frequently was, by 'fear, the offspring of superstitious fancy: the fear of future punishment at the hands of a splenetic and revengeful Deity' (18). Such belief, false as it might be, at least gave a context of utility in which some sense could be made of the recommendations to asceticism. However, given that 'the strain taken and kept up by books of morality in general is that of one continuous call upon men for the most painful sacrifices' (*Deontology* I.1; p. 121), even this context was frequently lacking. Sacrifice was being prescribed for its own sake, in a world in which 'the bias of public opinion is on the side of severity' (II.1 (ii); p. 254). So Bentham set himself to resist such call for sacrifice. Benefit was to be the test; the criterion of correct action, whether public or private. Unless benefit could be seen to be the result, the action was unjustified. So, in particular in the private deontology, he emphasises that sacrifices are not needed. He may, at times, slightly have over-emphasised the amount of harmony in order to bring this out; but the importance of doing so was to state clearly that sacrifice was not the central feature of morality.

The private deontologist, then, the scout on the lookout for consequences, gives instruction to people about how they should act to make themselves happy. It may still be felt, without any particular religious assumptions, that such self-regarding assumptions could not constitute something properly called a morality. However, this would only be because it was assumed, in an un-Benthamite manner, that the intentions with which something is done are an important part of its moral evaluation. For a consequentialist ethics like utilitarianism, the important thing is that certain things are done, not why they are done. Bentham, in his *Deontology*, gives reasons for performing certain actions which in another context would be called moral actions (being benevolent, caring for others' feelings, and so on). The reason he gives for doing them are purely self-regarding reasons. Yet the motivation is important in Benthamite theory only in so far as it effects consequences. Providing that the private deontologist manages to get the right things done by persuasion, he is contributing to morality (to the production of better consequences) regardless of what sort of persuasion he uses; and, as has been seen, once this form of persuasion is ineffective, then the central Benthamite figure of the legislator has to take over from the relatively unimportant private deontologist, and ensure that the right consequences are produced. It is this common end which is the subject matter of moral assessment, not the manner in which it is produced.

This common end, the greatest happiness of the greatest number, is a genuinely moral end which, as seen in Chapter VII, can be argued for, but by means of a moral argument, not by any kind of reduction of morality to psychology. Although citing a natural and decidable subject matter, human happiness, as the correct topic of moral judgement, it is not a naturalistic ethics. The basis of the ethics is that it is a good thing that human desire be satisfied, but the ethics is not just that which results from the unfettered satisfaction of human desires. Some desires must be frustrated, there must be sacrifice, in order that other desires are satisfied. The satisfaction is not that just of the desires of one individual, but that of the desires of mankind. It is true that, as Lyons brings out, in Bentham's central project of legislation, the desires to be considered are not that of mankind as a whole but, rather, those of that portion of mankind for which the legislator is responsible. As Lyons shows, the formula about utility or the greatest happiness is normally modified by an addition such as 'the community' or 'the community in question' (Lyons cites a list of such passages at Lyons 1973 25n). However this can be explained again in terms of practicalities. The legislator is in a position of trust and has a particular role to perform. It is true that, as time went on, Bentham realised that less and less dependence should be placed on trust and instead the role construed so that self-interest alone would lead to the successful performance of the legislator's duties; but this does not change the basic point that the legislator has a particular duty or responsibility. This responsibility is to the people entrusted to his care, so it is their happiness with which he is concerned. This is the only practical way in which power can be exercised given that he only has power over some of humanity, not the whole. So, given separate nation states and separate legislators, the general principle must be interpreted so that each legislator concerns himself with the greatest happiness of the people under his control.

So far this does not depart too far from Lyons's thesis. However, since it is a point about the practicalities of particular exercises of power, just as in the case of the private deontologist, I do not think that it means that Bentham's final evaluative end should not be considered in a universalistic way (unlike Lyons) as taking the greatest happiness of the whole of humanity as the ultimate criterion. This follows from the argument of Chapter VII, in which it is shown how a suitably enlarged benevolence leads to utility. Such enlargement leads at last to the whole of humanity: 'Men must be persuaded, enlightened, taught little by little, to distinguish the different degrees of utility, and to proportion their benevolence to the extent of its object. The best model is traced by Fénelon in that sentence which paints his heart: "I prefer my family to myself, my country to my family, mankind to my country"' (Penal Code, Traités iii 128; LEGIS 431). If there were a super-national power, such as, for example, the power of God, Bentham seems quite clear what would be its criterion of right action. Both in the *Introduction* and the *Deontology*, he argues that a correct religious ethic must coincide with utilitarianism. In both cases the argument is based on the benevolence of God. As he puts it in the *Deontology*, 'be he God or man, how can any person be benevolent but in proportion to the quantity of happiness which it is his wish to see enjoyed by those who are subject to his power?' (I.10; p. 166). God is not on the side of one nation rather than another. His benevolence is genuinely universal. Since Bentham takes it to coincide with his ultimately evaluative principle, so must that principle also therefore be; just before the quoted remark he identifies it as 'the greatest known happiness of the greatest number of mankind' (ibid.).

Jeremy Bentham declared in the Introduction to his first published work that the 'censor', the critical evaluator such as himself of legal systems, was a 'citizen of the world' (FG 398). He was a genuinely international figure, offering and preparing advice for the people of all nations. Among the proposed codes were to be 'principles of legislation . . . in matters of *international* law' (IPML 6); indeed he was responsible for introducing the new word 'international' into both English and French, as the footnotes of the *Introduction* (296n) and the *Traités* (*i 147) bring out. Among the surviving fragments of this code is the central principle that the end of international law would be 'the greatest happiness of all nations taken together', from which it followed that it would be a positive crime for a nation to 'do more evil to foreign nations taken together, whose interests might be affected, than it should do good to itself' (*Principles of International Law*, II 538). The standard here is genuinely universalistic. So Bentham, in recommending his projects to other countries, such as the panopticon to the French, could write to Brissot 'you love mankind, you love that sort of morality, and that alone, which has their happiness for their object' (CORR IV 342). The love of mankind was the continuing, universalistic, standard. In the 1780s, at a time at which he was writing many of his most substantial productions, Bentham noted in his Commonplace book: 'is there any one of these my pages in which the love of humankind has for a moment been forgotten? Show it me, and this hand shall be the first to tear it out' (X 142). More imperialistically, at the age of 83 he similarly jotted down of himself, only now in the third person, 'his empire — the empire he aspires to — extending to, and comprehending, the whole human race' (XI 72). Just over a year later he was dead, and being transmuted into his own auto-icon in the way described in Chapter I; a transmutation which had as its object, as he wrote in the *Auto-Icon*, to make 'to the fund of human happiness a contribution' (2).

Notes

(a) The new text of the *Deontology*, edited by Amnon Goldworth as part of the new collected edition of Bentham's works, is completely different from Bowring's 1834 work of the same name. In this case, unlike the *Fragment on Goverment* or the *Introduction*, it is important which edition is used.

(b) David Lyons's thesis, briefly summarised in the text, has been extensively commented on and criticised. See Hume (1978) and Dinwiddy (1982), the second of which contains reference to, and comment on, several other criticisms.

(c) In fairness to Lyons, it should be said that he himself considers International law on pp. 102-3 of Lyons (1973). He points out, quite correctly, that in the international case, Bentham thought that general interest is in each nation's interest. In the same context could be quoted Bentham's letter of October 1792 accepting honorary French Citizenship, in which he declares that incompatibility between the 'permanent interests of two nations' is 'purely ideal' (CORR IV 401). On the other hand, in addition to the remarks in the main text, can be cited Bentham's *Anti-Machiavel* pamphlet in which he obviously thought that moral criticism of the actions of his own nation was appropriate, and objected to the idea that strong states could inflict injuries on weak states (X 206).

Bibliography

This bibliography contains all works referred to in the text and the notes together with a few other important or central treatments of Bentham.

Alembert, Jean le Ronde d' (1763), *Mélanges de littérature, d'histoire et de philosophie*, new edn, Amsterdam.

Arnold, Matthew (1865), *Essays in Criticism* (first series), Macmillan, London.

Bacon, Francis (1965), *The Advancement of Learning*, ed. G.W. Kitchen, Dent, London.

Baker, J.H. (1971), *An Introduction to English Legal History*, Butterworth, London.

Ball, Terence (1980), 'Was Bentham a feminist?', *Bentham News Letter* 4.

Bator, F. (1957), 'The simple analytics of welfare maximisation', *American Economic Review*, 47, 22-59.

Baumgardt, David (1952), *Bentham and the Ethics of Today*, Princeton University Press, reprinted Octagon Books, New York, 1966.

Beccaria, Cesare (1965), *Dei delitti e delle pene* ed. F. Venturi, Turin.

Beccaria, Cesare (1767), *An Essay on Crimes and Punishments*, London.

Blackstone, William (1765), *Commentaries on the Laws of England*, 4 vols, Oxford.

Boralevi, Lea Campos (1980), 'In defence of a myth', *Bentham News Letter* 4.

Burns, J.H. (1967), *The fabric of felicity: the legislator and the human condition*, University College, London.

Burns, J.H. (1974), 'Bentham's critique of political fallacies', in Parekh (1974b).

Burton, John, 'Introduction to the study of the work of Bentham', in ed. J. Bowring, *The Works of Jeremy Bentham*, I, 1-83.

Cheung, S.N.S. (1978), *The Myth of Social Cost*, IEA, London.

Coase, R.H. (1960), 'The problem of social cost', *Journal of Law and Economics*, 3, 1-44.

Davidson, Donald (1967), 'Truth and meaning', *Synthese*, 7, 304-23.

Descartes, R. (1911), *The Philosophical Works of Descartes*, trans. E.S. Haldane and G.R.T. Ross, Cambridge University Press, 1967.

Dinwiddy, J.R. (1982), 'Bentham on private ethics and the principle of utility', in *Revue Internationale de Philosophie*, 141, 278-300.

Dummett, Michael (1976), 'What is a theory of meaning?' (II), in ed. G. Evans and J. McDowell, *Truth and Meaning*, Oxford University Press.

Everett, C.W. (1931), *The Education of Jeremy Bentham*, Columbia University Press, New York.

Finnis, John (1980), *Natural Law and Natural Right*, Oxford University Press.

Goldworth, Amnon (1969), 'The meaning of Bentham's greatest happiness principle', *Journal of the History of Philosophy*, 7, 315-21.

Hacker, P.M.S. (1973), 'Sanction theories of duty', in ed. A.W.B. Simpson, *Oxford Essays in Jurisprudence, Second Series*, Oxford University Press.

Halévy, Elie (1901), *La jeunesse de Bentham*, Paris.

Halévy, Elie (1928), *The Growth of Philosophic Radicalism*, trans. Mary Morris, Faber & Faber, London.

Hall, Everett W. (1949), 'The "proof" of utility in Bentham and Mill', *Ethics*, 60, 1-18.

Hare, R.M. (1973), 'Critical study — Rawls' theory of justice', *Philosophical Quarterly*, 23, 144-55, 241-52.

Hare, R.M. (1976), 'Ethical theory and utilitarianism', in ed. H.D. Lewis, *Contemporary British Philosophy, Fourth Series*, Allen & Unwin, London.

Harrison, Ross (1976), 'The only possible morality', *Aristotelian Society Supplementary Volume*, 50, 21-42.

Harrison, Ross, (1981-2), 'Discounting the future', in *Proceedings of the Aristotelian Society*, 82, 45-57.

Hart, H.L.A. (1961), *The Concept of Law*, Oxford University Press.

Hart, H.L.A. (1973), 'Bentham on legal rights', in ed. A.W.B. Simpson, *Oxford Essays in Jurisprudence, Second Series*, Oxford University Press.

Hart, H.L.A. (1982), *Essays on Bentham*, Oxford University Press.

Hartley, (1775), *Hartley's Theory of the Human Mind*, by Joseph Priestley, London.

Hazlitt, William (1825), 'Jeremy Bentham', in William Hazlitt, *The Spirit of the Age*, London.

Helvetius, (1759), *De l'Esprit: or, Essays on the Mind and its Several Faculties*, London.

Himmelfarb, Gertrude (1968), 'The haunted house of Jeremy Bentham', in Gertrude Himmelfarb, *Victorian Minds*, Knopf, New York.

Hollis, Martin (1979), 'Rational man and social science', in ed. Ross Harrison, *Rational Action*, Cambridge University Press.

Hume, David (1888), *A Treatise of Human Nature*, ed. L.A. Selby-Bigge, Oxford.

Hume, David (1962), *Enquiries concerning the Human Understanding and concerning the Principles of Morals*, ed. L.A. Selby-Bigge, Oxford.

Hume, L.J. (1973), 'Bentham's Panopticon: an administrative history I', in *Historical Studies*, 15, Melbourne, 703-21.

Hume, L.J. (1974), 'Bentham's panopticon: an administrative history II', in *Historical Studies*, 16, Melbourne, 36-54.

Hume, L.J. (1978), 'Revisionism in Bentham studies', *The Bentham Newsletter*, 1.

Hume, L.J. (1981), *Bentham and Bureaucracy*, Cambridge University Press.

Hutchison, T.W. (1956), 'Bentham as an economist', *Economic Journal*, 66, 288-306.

Lewes, Gertrude (1898), *Dr Southwood Smith*, Edinburgh.

Lind, John (1776), *An Answer to the Declaration of the American Congress*, London.

Lind, John (1776), *Three Letters to Dr Price*, London.

Locke, John (1975), *An Essay concerning Human Understanding*, ed. P.H. Niddich, Oxford University Press.

Long, Douglas G. (1977), *Bentham on Liberty*, University of Toronto Press.

Lyons, David (1972), 'Was Bentham a utilitarian?', in ed. G.N.A. Vesey, *Reason and Reality*, Macmillan, London.

Lyons, David (1973), *In the Interest of the Goverened*, Oxford University Press.

MacCormick, D.N. (1977), Rights in legislation, in (eds) P.M.S. Hacker and J. Raz, *Law, Morality and Society*, Oxford University Press.

Machiavelli, (1975), *The Prince*, trans. G. Bull, Penguin, Harmondsworth.

Mack, Mary P. (1962), *Jeremy Bentham: An Odyssey of Ideas 1748-92*, Heinemann, London.

McReynolds, Paul (1968), 'The motivational psychology of Jeremy Bentham' in *Journal of the History of the Behavioural Sciences*, 4, 230-44, 349-64.

Maine, Henry Sumner (1861), *Ancient Law*, John Murray, London, 1905.

Marmoy, C.F.A. (1958), 'The auto-icon of Jeremy Bentham at University College London', in *Medical History*, 2, 77-86.

Marx, Karl (1975), *Early Writings*, ed. Lucio Colletti, Penguin, Harmondsworth.

Meade, J.E. (1952), 'External economies and diseconomies in a competitive situation, *Economic Journal*, 62, 54-67.

Mill, J.S. *Collected Works*, University of Toronto Press, Routledge & Kegan Paul, London.

Milo, Ronald D. (1973-4), 'Bentham's principle', *Ethics*, 84, 128-39.

Mitchell, Wesley C. (1918), 'Bentham's felicific calculus', *Political Science Quarterly*, 33, 161-83 (reprinted in Parekh 1974b).

Moore, G.E. (1903), *Principia Ethica*, Cambridge University Press.

Moore, G.E. (1942), 'Reply to critics', in ed. P.A. Schlipp, *The Philosophy of G.E. Moore*, Northwestern University Press, Evanston, I11.

Ng. Yew-Kwang (1979), *Welfare Economics*, Macmillan, London.

Nozick, Robert (1974), *Anarchy, State, and Utopia*, Blackwell, Oxford.

Ogden, C.K. (1931), *The Theory of Legislation by Jeremy Bentham*, ed. with an Introduction and notes by C.K. Ogden, Kegan Paul, London, Harcourt, Brace, New York.

Ogden, C.K. (1932), *Bentham's Theory of Fictions*, Kegan Paul, London.

Parekh, Bhikhu (1970), 'Bentham's theory of equality', *Political Studies*, 18, 478-95.

Parekh, Bhikhu (1973), *Bentham's Political Thought*, Barnes & Noble, New York.

Parekh, Bhikhu (1974a), 'Bentham's justification of the principle of utility', in Parekh (1974b).

Parekh, Bhikhu (1974b), *Jeremy Bentham: Ten Critical Essays*, Frank Cass, London.

Pigou, A.C. (1920), *The Economics of Welfare*, Macmillan, London.

Postema, G. (1977), 'The principle of utility and the law of procedure: Bentham's theory of adjudication', *Georgia Law Review*, 11, 1393-1423.

Postema, Gerald J. (1980), 'Bentham and Dworkin on positivism and adjudication', *Social Theory and Practice*, 5, 347-76.

Poynter, J.R. (1969), *Society and Pauperism: English ideas on poor relief, 1795-1834*, Routledge & Kegan Paul, London.

Quine, W.V.O. (1960), *Word and Object*, MIT Press, Cambridge, Mass.

Quine, W.V.O. (1969), 'Epistemology naturalised', in *Ontological Relativity and Other Essays*, Columbia University Press, New York.

Rawls, John (1971), *A Theory of Justice*, Oxford University Press.

Raz, J. (1970), *The Concept of a Legal System*, Oxford University Press.

Russell, Bertrand (1919), *Introduction to Mathematical Philosophy*, Allen & Unwin, London.

Russell, Bertrand (1956), *Logic and Knowledge*, ed. R.C. Marsh, Allen & Unwin, London, (1918).

Russell, Bertrand (1963), *Mysticism and Logic*, Allen & Unwin, London, (1917).

Schumpeter, J.A. (1955), *History of Economic Analysis*, Allen & Unwin, London.

Sen, Amartya (1970), *Collective Choice and Social Welfare*, Holden-Day, San Francisco, Calif.

Sen, Amartya (1976-7), 'Rational fools: A critique of the behavioural foundations of economic theory', in *Philosophy and Public Affairs*, 6, 317-44.

Sidgwick, Henry (1874), *Methods of Ethics*, Macmillan, London.

Smith, Adam (1976), *An Inquiry into the Nature and Causes of the Wealth of Nations*, ed. Edwin Cannan, University of Chicago Press.

Smith, Thomas Southwood (1824), 'Use of the dead to the living', *Westminster Review*, 2, 59-97.

Smith, Thomas Southwood (1832), *A Lecture delivered over the remains of Jeremy Bentham*, London.

Steintrager, James (1977), *Bentham*, Allen & Unwin, London.

Stephen, Leslie (1900), *The English Utilitarians, Vol. I, Jeremy Bentham*, Duckworth, London.

Tuck, Richard (1979a), *Natural Rights Theories*, Cambridge University Press, Cambridge 1979.

Tuck, Richard (1979b), 'Is there a free-rider problem, and if so, what is it?', in ed. Ross Harrison, *Rational Action*, Cambridge University Press.

Urmson, J.O. (1956), *Philosophical Analysis*, Oxford University Press.

Wisdom, John (1931), *Interpretation and analysis in relation to Bentham's theory of definition*, Routledge & Kegan Paul, London.

Wisdom, John (1955), 'Ostentation', in John Wisdom, *Philosophy and Psychoanalysis*, Blackwell, Oxford (reprinted from *Psyche*, 13, 1933).

Wisdom, John, *Logical Constructions*, Random House, New York.

Wittgenstein, Ludwig (1953), *Philosophical Investigations*, trans. G.E.M. Anscombe, Blackwell, Oxford.

Index

abundance, 244, 250, 265
acting/refraining distinction, 226-7, 231, 238, 258
agreement, public, 174, 179-81, 189-92, 210, 232
alarm, 229-31, 237-40, 255
Alembert, J. le R. d', 7-8, 48-9, 52, 55-6, 58, 75, 86-7
analysis, 51, 54-5, 61, 66-76, 79, 81-105
animals, 228
archetypation, 62, 76
Aristotle, 54, 66, 91
Arnold, Matthew, 22
artificial reason, 12, 172
Atkin, Lord, 32
axioms of mental pathology, 140-2, 158, 245, 254
Ayer, A.J., 54

Bacon, Francis, 12, 100, 172
Baker, J.H., 27
Ball, Terence, 218, 223
ballot, 202, 210-11, 213-15
Bartolus, 30
Bator, F., 134
Baumgardt, David, 107, 115, 139, 263-4
Beattie, James, 175
Beccaria, Cesare, 7, 15, 23, 115-16, 119, 121-2, 167, 175

belief based on interest, 201-6, 217
Bentham, Jeremiah, 1, 12, 14, 15, 17
Bentham, Samuel, 17-18, 127-8
Berkeley, George, 54-5
Blackstone, William, 7, 15-16, 25-45, 47, 52, 65, 100, 102, 107, 116, 173, 175
Boralevi, Lea Campos, 223
Bowring, John, x, 21, 44, 48, 78, 248, 263-4
Brissot, J.P., 276
Brougham, Lord, 2, 11
Burke, Edmund, 161
Burlamaqui, J.J., 101
Burns, J.H., 133, 218, 264
Burton, John, 233

calculation, 116, 126-9, 148-66, 172, 178-9, 228, 231-2, 240-2, 247
capital punishment, 165, 180, 200-1
caprice, 173-4, 185-7, 193, 220
Carnap, R., 64
Catherine the Great, 8, 18, 127, 129, 198
censorial jurisprudence, 94-5, 98-103, 107, 175, 181, 252, 276
Chadwick, Edwin, 2-3, 21
Chastellux, Marquis de, 7
Cheung, S.N.S., 134
circulating annuities, 21, 126-7, 164-5

283

civil code, 139-40, 244-58
clarity, 13-14, 24-5, 48-75, 90, 102, 106-7, 170, 189
Coase, R.H., 134
Coke, Edward, 7, 12, 28-9, 31, 172
common law, 32, 35, 37-8, 44, 98
Condillac, E.B. de, 66
constitutional law, 119, 145, 191-3, 222, 258-60
contract, 40, 43, 63-4, 239-40, 243; see also original contract
custom, 10-11, 98, 181, 222

danger, 229-31, 237-9, 250
Davidson, Donald, 76
definition, 52-8
democracy, 9, 21-2, 208-24, 233
Descartes, R., 49-50, 54
diminishing marginal utility, 158, 246-9, 254
Dinwiddy, J.R., 277
Dummett, Michael, 76
Dumont, E., ix-xiv, 8, 18, 20, 46, 79, 110, 138-40, 153, 158, 199, 239
duty, see obligation
duty and interest junction principle, 117-34, 177, 207, 216, 264, 268-71

economics, 21, 121-7, 130, 134, 258, 265
education, 4, 6, 22, 118, 121-2, 126, 258-60, 266, 272-3
ejectment, 27-32
Eldon, Lord, 12
emotive theory of value, 192-4
equality, 158-9, 210, 243-9, 255
equity, 29-30, 189, 211
escheat, 117, 131, 256
Euclid, 141, 174
Everett, C.W., 23
experience machine, 229
exposition, 53, 94-5
ex post facto legislation, 35, 45, 238

fabulous entities, 83-6, 100
fact-value distinction, 14, 29, 94-5, 98, 100-4, 107-12, 171, 178, 192

fallacies, 204, 217-21, 235
female suffrage, 212-14
fiction, 24-105, 258
fictional entities, 56-62, 72, 75, 77, 79-90, 171, 201
fictions, legal, 26-36, 39, 73, 77
Finnis, John, 95
Fordyce, George, 149
free rider problem, 235-6
Frege, G., 66-7
Freud, S., 217
future, value of, 127, 156-7, 163-6, 214, 228, 231

generalisation, 153-4, 216, 240-4, 246
George III, 133, 198
God, 175-6, 276
Goldworth, Amnon, 264, 277
Grote, George, 2
Grotius, H., 44, 100-1

Hacker, P.M.S., 105
Hale, Matthew, 7, 204
Halévy, Elie, 107, 122, 213
Hare, R.M., 194
Hart, H.L.A., 91, 96, 105
Hartley, David, 66
Hazlitt, William, 1, 3
health, 1-2, 5-6, 258-9
Helvetius, C.A., 7, 9, 13, 15, 23, 49, 52-3, 75, 107, 113-16, 119, 122, 167, 175
Himmelfarb, Gertrude, 130
Hohfeld, W.N., 92-3, 105
Hollis, Martin, 166
Howard, John, 116
Hume, David, 7, 36, 51, 54, 56, 60-2, 85, 100, 107, 110, 115, 141, 144, 169, 202
Hume, L.J., 134, 277
Hunt, Leigh, 131
Hutchinson, T.W., 134

ideology, 33, 111, 200, 217, 220, 273
imagination, 223
imprescriptible rights, 78, 104, 222

induction, 140-1
inferential entity, 67, 82, 151
interest, 33-4, 109, 111, 114-66, 196-224, 231-4, 266-74
interest, ignorance of, 162-5, 205, 210-1, 214, 222-3, 228, 231, 272
international law, 276-7
investive power, 93
ipse-dixitism, 174
is-ought distinction, 100-3, 107-12, 132-3, 171, 178-80, 192

justification, problem of, 14, 25, 34-5, 44-5, 102-3, 171-94, 253

Kant, I., 31, 130

latitat, 27-8, 30-2
law, condition of contemporary, 11-12, 24-8, 47
legislation, 104, 107-8, 112-37, 149, 153-5, 162-5, 166, 172, 191-2, 215, 266, 270-1
legislator, the, 112, 195-8, 206, 215, 231-2, 275
Lewes, Gertrude, 23
liberty, 92-3, 97, 123-4, 238, 243, 246, 249-52
Lind, John, 16, 78, 212
Locke, John, 13, 36, 39, 44, 46, 49-66, 70, 73-4, 113, 172
Long, Douglas, 261
Lyons, David, 267-8, 275, 277

MacCormick, D.N., 94
Machiavelli, N., 136-7
Mack, Mary Peter, 213, 263
Mackintosh, James, 3-4
McReynolds, Paul, 166
Maine, Henry, 29, 45
management, 116-33
Marmoy, C.F.A., 23
Meade, J.E., 134
meaning, theory of, 49-75, 94, 102, 188-9
Meinong, F., 82
metaphysics, 48-75
Mill, James, 2, 21, 140, 263

Mill, John Stuart, 3-5, 8, 140, 177-8, 183, 185, 227, 234, 243, 260-1, 263
Montesquieu, C.L. de S., Baron de, 44
Moore, G.E., 54, 76, 109
Mora, Señor, 224
moral sanction, 179-81, 265-6
motives, 147-66, 226, 230, 270, 274

natural law, 43-4, 77-105, 172-3, 176-7, 187, 189, 251, 253, 255
natural rights, 77-82, 87-90, 96, 100-4, 123-4, 251, 257
nature, 107-8, 110
necessity, 84-5
Necker, J., 202, 209-10, 213
Newton, Isaac, 141
Ng, Yew-Kwang, 134
Nozick, Robert, 236, 257, 260

obligation, 55, 58-9, 62-4, 66, 72-3, 80-1, 88, 90-9, 170-1
original contract, 36-43, 239

pain, 59, 95, 99, 107-9, 135, 137, 148-65, 169, 194, 226
paraphrasis, 53-74, 79-81, 102, 147, 171, 188
Parekh, Bhikhu, 139, 261
pauper management, 6, 20, 117-19, 130-1, 134, 142, 164-5, 245
perception, 51, 54-5, 62, 73-4, 82, 147, 150, 177, 246
persuasion, problem of, 196-9, 215-23, 269
Pigou, A.C., 134
Pitt, William, 17, 19
Place, Francis, 2, 263
poor law, see pauper management
Postema, G., 260
Poynter, J.R., 134
Price, Richard, 17
Priestley, Joseph, 7, 15, 17, 66, 149
private ethics, 263-77
propinquity, 156-7, 163-5
proposition, primacy of the, 64-6
psychology, 108-11, 129, 132-3,

135-66, 176-81, 245-6, 253-7, 265, 268-75
publicity, 130
Puffendorf, S., 44, 100-1
punishment, 59, 72, 97-9, 115, 133, 135-8, 150, 165, 203, 227, 229, 234-5, 239, 251, 265-6
pushpin, 5

Quine, W.V.O., 64, 76

Rawls, John, 39, 41, 182, 236
Raz, J., 105
reason, 9-13, 44-5, 77-9, 108, 172-3, 181, 187-9, 197, 203, 205, 217, 222, 235-6, 247
reward, 120-33, 239
right-duty correlation, 90-7
rights, 38, 58-61, 66, 72-5, 80-104, 170-1, 188, 210, 236, 243-4, 249; see also natural rights
Romilly, Samuel, 147
Rousseau, J.-J., 46
rule utilitarianism, 37, 211, 225, 237-44, 260-1
Russell, Bertrand, 54, 64, 66-8, 76

sacrifice, 233-6, 239, 251, 273-5
sanctions, 97-8
Schumpeter, J.A., 105
second order consequences, 230-1, 234-5, 237-58
security, 45, 58, 126, 237, 243-4, 248-59
self-deception, 205
Sen, Amartya, 166
Shelburne, Earl of (later Marquis of Lansdowne), 17-18, 20, 119
Sidgwick, Henry, 109
simple ideas, 50-1, 53-6, 61-2
sinister interest, 33, 180, 199-208

slavery, 152-3, 262
Smith, Adam, 121-6, 128, 261
Smith, Richard, 8, 75
Smith, Southwood, 1, 5-6, 13, 15, 23, 48
Spencer, Earl, 19
Stephen, Leslie, 111
subsidiary ends, 244-5
subsistence, 126, 244-5, 250, 258, 265
superstition, 9-10, 273
survival of species, 141, 145-6, 176
sympathy, 143-4, 173, 265

taxation, 104, 117, 125, 256-8
transport, 126, 258
transvaluation of value, 273
truth, 14, 25, 69-70, 217, 219-21
Tuck, Richard, 96, 260

understanding, the, 151, 201-5, 216
Urmson, J.O., 76
utility, principle of, 25, 102-3, 106, 108-12, 132, 167-94, 197, 225-62, 268-75

value of pleasure and pain, 154-66, 242
verbal reality, 60-1, 80-7, 99
verification, 74-5, 81-2, 85, 90, 94, 98, 140-3, 147, 150, 171, 177, 188-90, 192
Voltaire, F.M.A. de, 7-10, 24, 33, 176

will, the, 151, 201-5, 216
Widsom, John, 68-9, 76
Wittgenstein, Ludwig, 186, 194

Young, Arthur, 142